A Leonard E. Boyle Book

Father Leonard E. Boyle, OP, Dominican friar, quondam Senior Fellow at the Pontifical Institute of Mediaeval Studies, and Prefect of the Biblioteca Apostolica Vaticana under Pope John Paul II, touched a generation of scholars through his life and work. Following his death, the Pontifical Institute endowed a chair in Father Boyle's name, to ensure that his legacy lived on: the Leonard E. Boyle Book imprint has been developed as part of that mission. It represents an undertaking to provide financial support for books published through the Institute press reflecting disciplines, themes, and methodologies that resonate with Father Boyle's own interests, stretching as they did from Latin palaeography and the technical fields that comprise manuscript studies, to the history of his own order, medieval education, and pastoral care, to canon law, the theology of Thomas Aquinas and beyond. *Omnia disce. Videbis postea nihil esse superfluum.*

M. MICHÈLE MULCHAHEY
Leonard E. Boyle Professor of Manuscript Studies

MEDIAEVAL LAW AND THEOLOGY 7

General Editors

Alexander Andrée
University of Toronto

John F. Boyle
University of St Thomas

Joseph Goering
University of Toronto

Giulio Silano
University of Toronto

STUDIES AND TEXTS 198

The Making of the *Historia scholastica*, 1150–1200

MARK J. CLARK

PONTIFICAL INSTITUTE OF MEDIAEVAL STUDIES

Acknowledgement

The publication of this volume was made possible by funds generously provided by the Basilian Fathers of the University of St Michael's College.

Library and Archives Canada Cataloguing in Publication

Clark, Mark J., 1957–, author
  The making of the Historia scholastica, 1150–1200 / Mark J. Clark.

(Studies and texts ; 198)
(Mediaeval law and theology ; 7)
Includes Latin texts of selected chapters from Peter Comestor's Historia Genesis and from his
  Historia evangelica, together with three versions of Stephen Langton's course on each of
  these texts.
Includes bibliographical references and index.
Issued in print and electronic formats.
ISBN 978-0-88844-198-0 (bound). – ISBN 978-1-77110-370-1 (pdf)

  1. Petrus, Comestor, active 12th century. Historia scholastica. 2. Petrus, Comestor, active
12th century – Manuscripts. 3. Petrus, Comestor, active 12th century – Influence. 4. Bible –
Criticism, interpretation, etc. – History – Middle Ages, 600–1500. 5. Theology – History –
Middle Ages, 600–1500. 6. Scholasticism. 7. Glossa ordinaria. 8. Langton, Stephen, –1228 –
Influence. 9. Langton, Stephen, –1228 – Manuscripts. I. Pontifical Institute of Mediaeval
Studies, issuing body II. Title. III. Series: Studies and texts (Pontifical Institute of Mediae-
val Studies) ; 198 IV. Series: Mediaeval law and theology ; 7

B734.C63 2015   189'.4   C2015-905542-3   C2015-905543-1

MANUFACTURED IN CANADA

Praestantissimo magistro, philosopho, theologoque Stephano F. Brown, qui olim me gratuito docens quomodo huiusmodi labor esset faciendus, fuit mihi auxilio maximo. Qui autem mihi meisque semper amicissimus remanet.

Contents

Abbreviations

Series

CCCM   Corpus Christianorum: Continuatio Mediaevalis. Turnhout: Brepols, 1971– .

CCSL   Corpus Christianorum: Series Latina. Turnhout: Brepols, 1953– .

PL   Patrologiae cursus completus: Series Latina, ed. J.P. Migne. 221 vols. Paris, 1844–1864.

Other sigla

G   Biblical *Gloss*

GI   *Glossa* interlinearis

GM   *Glossa* marginalis

P   Paris, Bibliothèque nationale de France, MS lat. 16943

Tr   Troyes, Bibliothèque municipale, MS 290

V   Vienna, Östereichische Nationalbibliothek, MS lat. 363

Preface

The present study grew out of the question, "What is the *Historia scholastica*?" This work, one of the most copied and cited from the time of its composition and appearance around 1170 through the end of the Middle Ages and beyond, evades simple characterization. Pregnant with the Bible, it is nevertheless not a biblical commentary. It presents the history of salvation from beginning to end but does so in a manner that no modern person would recognize as a history. Composed of lemmata and glosses, like so many medieval works, its lemmata are nonetheless effectively hidden from the view of anyone not intimately familiar with Peter Comestor's unique but durable method of presentation.

Comestor himself, Peter the Eater, remains as much a mystery as his name or his most famous work. We will never know how he received his unique surname, *Comestor* or *Manducator*. His contemporaries were convinced that it had everything to do with the work that made him famous, that he ate the Bible and spit out the *History*. Whatever the truth of the matter, it is a great story, as great as the medieval legend that made him the brother of his master, Peter Lombard, and Gratian. Here again, the work itself was at the center of the story, for these three produced the most famous schoolbooks of the twelfth century.

The *History* was indeed a schoolbook, a quite successful one. The biblical *Gloss* was also a schoolbook, at least in Paris from the time that Peter Lombard got his hands on it until well after Peter Comestor was through with it. Unlike the *History*, it was not a successful schoolbook, at least according to Peter Comestor, even though the biblical *Gloss* was his most important source for the *History*. In fairness, however, it must be admitted that his may not be the last word on the subject of the *Gloss* as schoolbook; since we now know what to look for, we are discovering courses by other masters in which the biblical *Gloss* served as the textbook. There may be a great deal to say on this subject as these courses come to light.

One cannot discuss the *History* as a schoolbook without considering the Lombard's *Sentences*, which went on to become an even more famous schoolbook. Studying the sources of the *Historia scholastica* leads inexorably back to

Comestor's master, the Lombard, for it turns out that Comestor not only mined the *Sentences* in creating the *History* but also took advantage of the Lombard's work on the *Gloss*. For a long time now, ever since the great Ignatius Brady gave up the search for the Lombard's long-lost glosses on most of the Bible apart from those still extant on the Psalms and the Pauline Epistles, scholars have assumed that they are gone forever. They are not, and tracking Comestor's sources for the edition of the *Historia scholastica* will only further underscore the importance of the *Sentences* and the Lombard's own glossed Bible. All signs are that medieval legend had it right in making Peter Lombard and Peter Comestor brothers.

To understand the *History* as a schoolbook, one also has to look ahead, to Comestor's successors as much as to his predecessors, and here Stephen Langton must also be assigned a starring role. Half of this study is devoted to Langton's role in the making of the *History*, and it is no exaggeration to say that without the multiple versions of his course on that work we would be able to know very little for sure about the early history of its text. Langton provides a unique bridge from the Paris schools of the 1160s, when he was a student, to the university that came into being by the close of the twelfth century and beginning of the thirteenth, when he retired from academic life to serve as Archbishop of Canterbury. Like Comestor, Langton was intimately familiar with the Lombard's biblical teaching. Unlike Comestor, he was able to carry it into the thirteenth century. Careful study of his still unedited and unstudied corpus of lectures on the Old Testament is the *sine qua non* not only for editing the *History* and understanding the biblical *Gloss* at Paris during the second half of the twelfth century (how it was used, how its text changed and when, etc.) but also for beginning to study the biblical works of the masters, and especially the friars, during the first half of the thirteenth century.

After an introductory chapter that reviews existing historiography and situates the *History* in four main contexts, the next three chapters are devoted to Peter Comestor's role in the making of the *History*: Chapter Two examines his lectures on the glossed Gospels as background to the making of the *History*; Chapter Three his use of the *Gloss* as a schoolbook; and Chapter Four his applications in the *History* of the lessons learned in teaching using the biblical *Gloss*. The following three chapters feature Langton's role in the making of the *History*: Chapter Five shows why Langton is the key to the early history of the text of the History; Chapter Six explores Langton's relationship with Comestor and the changing roles in that relationship; and Chapter Seven examines the three versions of his course on the History. A brief Chapter Eight concludes the volume.

Out of the many debts incurred in writing this book, I owe the greatest to Steve Brown of Boston College, who first put me on the right track long ago when he taught me how to work with medieval manuscripts and showed me in particular how to use Langton's course to unlock the secrets of the *History*, to my wife, Bernardine, who has patiently supported me and my work while the fruit of this labor slowly ripened, and to our four children, who never tire of teasing their father for his longtime interest in Peter the Eater.

Many of the debts are owed to scholars around the world who have graciously interested themselves in my research. I owe a very substantial debt to Joe Goering of Toronto, whose interest in my work on Comestor and Langton led to my publishing this volume with PIMS Press and will I hope lead to my publishing there my edition and translation of the entire *Historia scholastica*. Joe's careful reading of my drafts combined with his magisterial knowledge of both the history and theology of the twelfth and thirteenth centuries sharpened both my prose and my arguments. Marcia Colish too very generously read through and commented on the entire manuscript, sharing with me the benefits of her considerable wisdom and expertise; her mentorship has been invaluable. Gilbert Dahan has also been so generous in sharing his immense erudition, and I have relied on his judgment time and again, always to my benefit. Numerous conversations and interactions with the late Riccardo Quinto, whose tragic death deprived his family and friends of a wonderful man and the academic world of a peerless scholar, helped me untie thorny knots in unveiling the complicated early history of the manuscripts. It would please Riccardo to know that I have decided at long last to take up his insistent suggestion to immerse myself in the complexities of Langton's surviving works on the Old Testament. And I have benefitted immensely too from the great learning and expertise of his circle of former students and colleagues: Magdalena Bieniak, Caterina Tarlazzi, Francesco Siri, Riccardo Saccenti, Massimiliano D'Alessandro, Fabrizio Amerini, and others. Tracking down the sources of the *History* stuck my nose into the biblical *Gloss* and, serendipitously, into a wonderful and ongoing collaboration with Alexander Andrée, a young but accomplished scholar as gracious as he is learned.

Christoph Egger's unfailingly-gracious help with manuscripts and libraries was invaluable. And there are many others to thank as well, helpful librarians in libraries across Europe and eminent scholars such as David Luscombe and Xavier-Laurent Salvador, who took the time to pose questions that set me on unexpected but fruitful paths. Finally, I would be remiss not to thank publicly Fred Unwalla, Editor in Chief at the Pontifical Institute of Mediaeval Studies, as well as Jeffrey Allen and Megan Jones who assisted him and me so capably with this book. It is a great privilege to be able to work with editors and with a press whose standards are so high.

I owe many debts as well to my colleagues and students here at The Catholic University of America, Susan Wessel, Regis Armstrong, Joshua Benson, Tim Noone, Michael Root, Andrew Cuff, Kevin Augustyn, Fr. Innocent Smith, OP, among others as well, whose support, encouragement, questions, and erudition add so much to my ongoing investigations.

CHAPTER ONE

Formerly Famous but Long Since Forgotten

Peter Comestor's *Historia scholastica*

Although the theological landscape of the later twelfth and early thirteenth centuries remains to a great extent *terra incognita*, Peter Comestor's *Historia scholastica* stands out in that landscape as a conspicuous yet overlooked landmark. I say conspicuous, because, like the *Sentences* of Peter Lombard, the *History* towers over the early scholastic period, and it was the extraordinary success of these twin works that ensured the joint ascendancy of the reputations of the two Peters. Indeed, we find one medieval writer after another testifying to the greatness of Comestor and the *History*; many link Peter Comestor with Peter Lombard, praising with one voice the *Sentences* and the *History*.

The sole entry of Robert of Auxerre's chronicle for 1173 records: "Peter Comestor is considered renowned in France, the foremost of the Parisian Masters, a most eloquent man excellently instructed in the divine Scriptures, who joining together in one volume the histories of both Testaments, produced a work, useful and pleasing enough, compiled from diverse histories."[1] Stephen Langton, one of the most prominent teachers of Scripture and theology at Paris during the last decades of the twelfth century, praised both Peters for their mastery of Sacred Scripture when, referring to Wisdom, he wrote: "Blessed is the man ... that lodgeth near her house and fasteneth a pin in her walls [Eccles. xiv, 22–5] as they do who hand down some writing on Scripture, the Manducator who compiled the *Histories*, the Lombard who established [statuit] the *Sentences*."[2] The chronicler Otto of St. Blaise noted the joint ascendancy of both Peters when he wrote that "[i]n those days Peter Lombard and Peter

---

1 "Petrus Comestor celebris habetur in Francia, Magistrorum Parisiensium primus, vir facundissimus et in scripturis divinis excellenter instructus, qui utriusque testamenti historias uno compingens volumine, opus edidit satis utile, satis gratum, ex diversis historiis compilatum." Robert of Auxerre, *Chronicon* (MGH, Scriptores in folio 26: 240), cited by Saralyn R. Daly, "Peter Comestor: Master of Histories," *Speculum* 32 (1957): 62–73, at 67 n45. Unless otherwise stated, all translations are my own.
2 Quoted and translated by Beryl Smalley, *The Study of the Bible in the Middle Ages*, 3rd rev. ed. (1941; Oxford: Basil Blackwell, 1984), 214 and n1.

Comestor shone forth as distinguished masters at Paris."[3] Another chronicler, Godfrey of Viterbo, started the resilient medieval legend that Comestor was the brother of Peter Lombard and Gratian, the authors of the two most celebrated works in theology and canon law, respectively.[4]

Twentieth-century scholars too, especially those most familiar with the theological works of the later twelfth and early thirteenth centuries, were struck by just how famous the *History* made Comestor. Landgraf, for example, wrote of Comestor that "[h]e owes his extraordinary celebrity to the *Historia scholastica* which, in the scholasticism of the twelfth and thirteenth centuries, counts among the most often cited works."[5] And Martin, who together with Landgraf made the most serious attempt to find the basis for Comestor's authoritative status among his theological successors in the schools, referred to Comestor as "this doctor *famosissimus*" who was "above all known by his *Historia scholastica*."[6] Beryl Smalley too found that the *History* was well-known and cited by Parisian theologians such as Peter the Chanter, in the late twelfth century, and Alexander of Hales and John of La Rochelle, in the early thirteenth.[7] She identifed Peter Comestor and his followers as the unnamed targets of Peter the Chanter's pointed criticism of colleagues who focus on "places, dates, genealogies, and descriptions of buildings such as the tabernacle and the temple image."[8]

3   "His diebus Petrus Lombardus et Petrus Manducator apud Parisiensum magistri insignes claruerunt." Otto of St. Blaise, *Continuatio Sanblasiana* (continuation of Otto of Freising's *Chronicon*) 12 (MGH, Scriptores in folio 20: 308), cited by Marcia L. Colish, *Peter Lombard*, Brill's Studies in Intellectual History 41, 2 vols. (Leiden: Brill, 1994), 1: 31 n51.

4   See Joseph de Ghellinck, *Le mouvement théologique du XIIe siècle*, 2nd rev. ed., Museum Lessianum, Section historique 10 (Bruges: De Tempel, 1948), 214, 285. See also Colish, *Peter Lombard*, 1: 16 and n5.

5   "Sa célébrité extraordinaire, il la doit à l'*Historia scholastica*, qui, dans la scolastique du XIIe et du XIIIe siècle, compte parmi les œuvres les plus souvent citées." Artur Michael Landgraf, "Recherches sur les écrits de Pierre le Mangeur," *Recherches de théologie ancienne et médiévale* 3 (1931): 292–306, at 292.

6   "Pierre le Mangeur est un grand nom dans l'histoire littéraire de la seconde partie du XIIe siècle ... . Ce *famosissimus doctor* ... est surtout connu par son *Historia scholastica*." Raymond-M. Martin, "Notes sur l'oeuvre littéraire de Pierre le Mangeur," *Recherches de théologie ancienne et médiévale* 3 (1931): 54–66, at 54–55.

7   Beryl Smalley, *The Gospels in the Schools, c. 1100 – c. 1280* (London and Ronceverte: The Hambledon Press, 1985), 32, 103, 166, and 180.

8   Smalley, *Gospels in the Schools*, 102–103. The Chanter's insistence that "Scripture was given to us that we should seek out not the vain and superfluous, but faith and moral doctrine and counsels and answers to the countless matters arising in Church affairs"

Like their medieval predecessors, modern scholars also recognized the close relationship between Peter Lombard and Peter Comestor.[9] Recalling the medieval legend that Peter Lombard and Peter Comestor were brothers, the great twentieth-century historians of scholastic thought emphasized the close kinship of the Lombard and Comestor, the *Sentences* and the *History*.[10] In the words of Marie-Dominique Chenu, "the legend of the brotherhood in the flesh of Comestor and of Lombard is a symbol full of truth."[11] Brady established that the *Magister Historiarum* was closely connected to the *Magister Sententiarum* not only in legend but in life, for Comestor, who studied with the Lombard, proved to be our best source for the Lombard's oral teaching.[12] Moreover, I have proven not only that the Lombard's *Sentences* are connected to Comestor's *History* but also that Comestor had and used in his own lectures on John's Gospel an introduction composed by the Lombard to the glossed

provides the context for his critique. The translations given, from a passage in the *Verbum Abbreviatum* (PL 205: 27–28), are Smalley's. I cite here the PL edition of the Chanter's *Verbum Abbreviatum*, since that is the edition which Smalley used. For a modern edition of the same work, see: *An Edition of the Long Version of Peter the Chanter's Verbum Abbreviatum: Petri Cantoris Parisiensis Verbum adbreviatum* (CCCM 196). See also: David Luscombe, "Peter Comestor," in *The Bible in the Medieval World: Essays in Memory of Beryl Smalley*, ed. Katherine Walsh and Diana Wood (Oxford: Basil Blackwell, 1985), 109–129, at 127–128.

9 For a recent and authoritative overview of Peter Comestor's career and works, see the collection of studies in *Pierre de Troyes, dit Pierre le Mangeur, maître du XIIe siècle*, ed. G. Dahan, Bibliothèque d'histoire culturelle du moyen âge (Turnhout: Brepols, 2013).

10 Joseph de Ghellinck repeatedly recalled the legend of the fraternity of the three men, emphasizing the complementarity of their three great works in the development of twelfth-century scholasticism. See de Ghellinck, *Le mouvement théologique*, 213–214; and also *L'essor de la littérature latine au XIIe siècle*, 2 vols., Museum Lessianum, Section historique 4–5 (Paris: Desclée de Brouwer, 1946), 1: 71, 95. For the origins and subsequent *fortuna* of the legend, see *Le mouvement théologique*, Appendix 3: 285, and for a more recent discussion, Colish, *Peter Lombard*, 1: 16 and n5.

11 "... la légende de la fraternité charnelle de Comestor et du Lombard est un symbole plein de vérité." Marie-Dominique Chenu, *Introduction à l'étude de saint Thomas d'Aquin*, 2nd ed. (Montreal: Institut d'études médiévales; Paris: Vrin, 1954), 205. See also Chenu, *La théologie au douzième siècle*, 2nd ed. (Paris: Vrin, 1966), 69 n3 and 328. Henri de Lubac held a similar view of the *History*; see his *Exégèse médiévale: Les quatre sens de l'écriture*, 2 parts, each in 2 vols. (Paris: Aubier, 1961–1964), 2.1: 379.

12 See Ignatius C. Brady's introduction to *Magistri Petri Lombardi Parisiensis Episcopi sententiae*, 2: 39*–44*. See also Ignatius C. Brady, "Peter Manducator and the Oral Teachings of Peter Lombard," *Antonianum* 41 (1966): 454–490.

John.[13] Finally, Martin and Landgraf long ago established a close connection between the works of the two Peters in showing Comestor's dependence on the Lombard's *Sentences*.[14]

In short, therefore, neither Comestor's celebrity, nor his exalted reputation as a theologian among his contemporaries and successors in the schools, nor his close connection to Peter Lombard and the *Sentences* can be doubted. Nonetheless, in sharp contrast to the *Sentences*, the *History* remains overlooked. The words of George Lacombe, written in 1930, still ring true today: "There was a time when the *Historia Scholastica* was one of the most widely used books in Christendom. Today it is almost a miracle to find any one who has read it."[15] As a consequence, Comestor himself, in spite of his exalted medieval reputation, remains as LeGoff put it: "little studied and poorly known."[16] The obvious question is why. In this chapter, therefore, after a brief survey of the *History*'s illustrious *fortuna*, I review the historiography with the goal of explaining how such a famous work – Comestor's *Historia scholastica* was a bestseller from its first appearance in the twelfth century, which continued to be printed into the eighteenth century – fell as it were through the historiographical cracks. In reviewing the relevant historiography, I advance a thesis as to what Comestor's project actually was and how the *History* fits into the various twelfth-century theological currents.

---

13   On the connection between the masterworks of the two Peters, see Mark J. Clark, "Peter Comestor and Peter Lombard: Brothers in Deed," *Traditio* 60 (2005): 85–142. I prove the connection between their lectures on the glossed John in an article, "The Biblical *Gloss*, the Search for the Lombard's Glossed Bible, and the School of Paris," *Mediaeval Studies* 76 (2014): 57–113.

14   Landgraf, speaking for himself and for his collaborator, Martin, concluded: "We have been able to establish that the substance of these citations corresponds closely to that of the *Sentences* of Peter Lombard." Artur Michael Landgraf, "Recherches sur les écrits de Pierre le Mangeur: Le traité *De Sacramentis*, *Recherches de théologie ancienne et médiévale* 3 (1931): 341–372, at 372.

15   George Lacombe, "Studies on the Commentaries of Cardinal Stephen Langton, Part 1," *Archives d'histoire et littéraire du môyen age* 5 (1930): 5–151, at 24.

16   Jacques LeGoff, *La Naissance du Purgatoire* (Paris: Gallimard, 1981), 213.

I. Fortuna

There is no longer any doubt that Comestor produced the *Historia scholastica* in Paris and not in Troyes, where he served as Dean of the cathedral church.[17] Brady established that Peter Comestor went to Paris prior to the end of Peter Lombard's teaching career in 1158–1159, that he witnessed and reported the Lombard's teaching, and that he himself began teaching in the Paris schools after the Lombard's death in 1160.[18] At Paris, Comestor served as Chancellor of Notre Dame and Dean of the cathedral school, which gave him the option of holding or delegating the chair of theology, a position that he held with distinction before turning it over to Peter of Poitiers in 1169.[19]

Sometime between 1168/1169 and 1173, at the peak of a long and productive career as a teacher, theologian, and administrator, Peter Comestor dedicated the *Historia scholastica* to William of Champagne, Archbishop of Sens, better known as William of the White Hands.[20] This dedication constitutes the sole internal evidence for dating the *History*; the beginning of William's tenure as Archbishop of Sens establishes the earlier boundary, while a reference to the

---

17 Daly, "Master of Histories," 65. Because the record of Comestor's duties in Troyes stretches into the 1160s, his tenure as Dean of the Cathedral at Troyes must have overlapped to some extent with his residence in Paris. Sandra Rae Karp, who assumed that Comestor's official business in Troyes precluded his residing or teaching in Paris until quite late in life, argued that Comestor produced the *History* in Troyes. See Karp, "Peter Comestor's *Historia scholastica*: A Study in the Development of Literal Scriptural Exegesis" (Ph.D. diss., Tulane University, 1978), 1–55, esp. 42–55.

18 See Brady's comments in *Magistri Petri Lombardi Parisiensis Episcopi sententiae*, 2: 39*–44*, esp. 39* ("Non sine scandalo (minimo quidem) quosdam modernos invenimus qui adhuc credant quod Magister Petrus Comestor, decanus Trecensis, Parisius venerit solummodo post mortem Lombardi (3 maii 1160), et quidem anno 1164, quando Magistro Odoni successerit in officium cancellarii Parisiensis Ecclesiae."). See also Brady, "Peter Manducator"; Luscombe, "Peter Comestor," 109–110; and Jean Longère, "Pierre Le Mangeur" (1986), *Dictionnaire de spiritualité: ascétique et mystique, doctrine et histoire*, 17 vols. in 21 (Paris: Beauchesne, 1932–1995), 12: 1614–1626, at 1614.

19 Philip S. Moore, *The Works of Peter of Poitiers: Master in Theology and Chancelor of Paris (1193–1205)* (Notre Dame: University of Notre Dame Press, 1936), 118–122; Daly, "Master of Histories," 66 and n32.

20 The controversy over the earlier date arises because, although William was appointed to his see in 1168, he did not formally receive his title until 1169. See Gaines Post, "Alexander III, the *Licentia Docendi* and the Rise of the University," in *Haskins Anniversary Essays in Mediaeval History*, ed. Charles H. Taylor and John L. La Monte (Cambridge: Harvard University Press, 1929), 255–277, at 258.

History in Robert of Auxerre's Chronicle for 1173 establishes that the *History* was already in circulation by that year.[21]

Scholars have taken the dedication as a definitive publication, after which the *History* entered the schools.[22] The assumption is that Comestor 'finished' the *Historia scholastica* at this point in time. In fact, I show below that he did not. The most that can be said is that Comestor dedicated the *History*, such as it was at this time, to Archbishop William. Scholars have also assumed that Comestor had by this time retired to the Abbey of St. Victor as a canon, where he wrote the *History*.[23] The claim that Comestor retired to the Abbey at some point is founded upon solid evidence that he was buried there.[24] There is, however, no evidence to support the claim that he retired from teaching as early as 1169. Longère's guess that Comestor retired to St. Victor after he stepped down from the Chancellorship, an event he dates to 1178, seems more plausible, but this too is speculative.[25] Even the tradition that Comestor died in either 1178 or 1179, oft repeated by scholars, is speculative.[26] In short, absent new evidence for where he was at key times in his career, we are likely to remain ignorant of exactly where and when he wrote it.

There is, however, no doubt that the *History* gained immediate acceptance and acclaim. In his four-volumed study of the medieval scriptural tradition, Henri de Lubac declared that "[t]he *Historia Scholastica* ... of Peter the Eater ... knew from the first a prodigious success, which was not to decline before the sixteenth century."[27] The subsequent and enduring success of this work raised

21 I provide the full reference and citation in n1, above.

22 See, for example, Beryl Smalley, "Some Gospel Commentaries of the Early Twelfth Century," *Recherches de théologie ancienne et médiévale* 45 (1978): 147–180, at 150 and n14, reprinted as "Some Early Twelfth-Century Gospel Commentaries," in *Gospels in the Schools*, 1–35, at 4 and n14; Daly, "Master of Histories," 67 and n45; Luscombe, "Peter Comestor," 119 and n28.

23 See, for example: Smalley, *Gospels in the Schools*, 4 and n14; Luscombe, "Peter Comestor," 110; and Daly, "Master of Histories," 68 and n53.

24 Daly, "Master of Histories," 68 and nn54–57; Luscombe, "Peter Comestor," 110–111 and n7.

25 Longère, "Pierre le Mangeur," 1615. We cannot even be sure when exactly Comestor did retire from that office, for although his last official act as chancellor dates to 1178, the first extant document from his successor, Hilduin, does not appear before 1180. Daly, "Master of Histories," 67 and nn41–42.

26 Daly, "Master of Histories," 72 and n96. See also: Longère, "Pierre le Mangeur," 1615; and Luscombe, "Peter Comestor," 110.

27 "L'*Historia scolastica* ... de Pierre le Mangeur ... connut d'emblée un succès prodigieux, qui ne devait pas décliner avant le XVIe siècle." De Lubac, *Exégèse médiévale*, 2.1: 379.

Peter Comestor to the heights of medieval and early modern celebrity. He became the *Magister Historiarum*, the Master of Histories.

The extraordinary success of the *History* and its author's rise to prominence can be documented in a number of contexts. As the name *Historia scholastica* suggests, it was put to good use in the medieval schools. Comestor's successor to the chair of theology at Notre Dame, Peter of Poitiers, paid his predecessor the high compliment of adding to his work. He composed a *Compendium Historiae in Genealogia Christi* to serve as a summary of the primary characters and dates in the *History* and probably also composed the continuation of Comestor's *History* through the Acts of the Apostles.[28] Stephen Langton not only lectured on the entire *Historia scholastica* sometime before 1176 but also revised and edited this first lecture course twice, the first time before 1176 and again before 1193.[29] In the final redaction of his course on the *History*, Langton refers to lectures that he had heard on the *History* by Jean Beleth († ca. 1182).[30] Beleth was by then an acknowledged Master of Theology at the peak of his career.[31] There

28 Moore, *Peter of Poitiers*, 96–117. In addition to being copied together with the *History* in many manuscripts, the *Geneaology* was hung up in plain view during lectures on Scripture. Moore, *Peter of Poitiers*, 108 n20. For a description of the genealogy by Stephen Langton, a contemporary of Peter of Poitiers, see Smalley, *Study of the Bible*, 214.

29 In an earlier study, "The Commentaries on Peter Comestor's *Historia scholastica* of Stephen Langton, Pseudo-Langton, and Hugh of St. Cher," *Sacris erudiri* 44 (2005): 301–446, I updated the pioneering researches of Lacombe in his "Cardinal Stephen Langton," 18–51, showing that Langton first lectured on the *History* not as Lacombe thought before 1186 or so but in fact before 1176. In two subsequent articles "The Commentaries of Stephen Langton on the *Historia Scholastica* of Peter Comestor," in *Étienne Langton: Prédicateur, bibliste, théologien*, ed. Louis-Jacques Bataillon, Nicole Bériou, Gilbert Dahan, and Riccardo Quinto (Turnhout: Brepols, 2010), 373–393, and "Peter Comestor and Stephen Langton: Master and Student, and Co-Makers of the *Historia scholastica*," *Medioevo* 35 (2010): 123–149, I argued on the basis of chronology, circumstantial evidence, and probability that Langton had been Comestor's student and further that he had collaborated with Comestor in making the *History* part of the developing curriculum at the incipient University of Paris. In a more recent study, "Le cours d'Étienne Langton sur *l'Histoire scolastique* de Pierre le Mangeur: Le fruit d'une tradition unifiée," in *Pierre de Troyes,* ed. Dahan, 243–266, I adduce new evidence to show that Langton was indeed Comestor's student, collaborator, and colleague.

30 Lacombe, who cites this passage, notes that Jean Beleth died around 1182. Lacombe, "Cardinal Stephen Langton," 19.

31 Although there is circumstantial evidence that other scholars also produced commentaries on the *History* in the later twelfth century, they are no longer extant. Morey,

is also Pseudo-Langton, the anonymous successor to Langton who in the early thirteenth century composed a remarkable commentary on the *History* in which he made copious and interesting use of the various redactions of Langton's course.[32] The *History*, therefore, must have been taken up generally into the schools immediately following its appearance.

A second and closely related medieval context in which the *History* played a significant role was that of the education and formation of the mendicant friars after their appearance in the early thirteenth century. The Dominicans in the 1230s undertook a host of biblical projects under the direction and supervision of Hugh of St. Cher, Prior Provincial for France and Prior of the Parisian convent from 1230.[33] The *History* figured prominently among such Dominican biblical projects, and Hugh of St. Cher, supervising a team of Dominicans, produced a sizeable commentary on the *History*.[34] The Dominican commentary

---

citing *Nigellus de Longchamp dit Wireker: Tractatus contra curiales et officiales clericos*, ed. André Boutemy (Paris: Presses universitaires de France, 1959), 5, 23–24, 44–45, notes that Nigel Wireker produced a commentary on the *History* around 1194, and gives the manuscript citation as Cambridge, Trinity College, B.15.5. James H. Morey, "Peter Comestor, Biblical Paraphrase, and the Medieval Popular Bible," *Speculum* 68 (1993): 6–35, at 8 n7. Riccardo Quinto, however, who examined this manuscript, told me that it is not a commentary but rather a copy of the *History* with notes in the margins (personal communication, June 2012). Joseph Goering suggests that William de Montibus may also have lectured on the *History*; see Goering, *William de Montibus (c. 1140–1213): The Schools and the Literature of Pastoral Care*, Studies and Texts 108 (Toronto: Pontifical Institute of Mediaeval Studies, 1992), 35 and n26. Martin cites a *Summa super Magistrum historiarum* in a manuscript at Cambridge, Trinity College, B.16.31; Martin, "Notes," 55 n4. I have examined this manuscript cursorily online, and it seems to contain a straightforward copy of the *History*, nothing more.

32 Clark, "Commentaries on Peter Comestor's *Historia scholastica*," 324–334.

33 For the latest research on Hugh of St. Cher in general, the best place to start is *Hugues de Saint-Cher (†1263), bibliste et théologien*, ed. Louis-Jacques Bataillon, Gilbert Dahan, and Pierre-Marie Gy, Bibliothèque d'histoire culturelle du Moyen Âge 1 (Turnhout: Brepols, 2004), a volume which treats all aspects of Dominican university work supervised by Hugh from 1230–1236 at Paris.

34 Scholars believe that Hugh and the Dominicans working under his supervision produced the commentary on the *History* during the same decade in which they produced the *Postills* on the Bible. See Robert E. Lerner, "Poverty, Preaching, and Eschatology in the Revelation Commentaries of Hugh of St. Cher," in *The Bible in the Medieval World: Essays in Memory of Beryl Smalley*, ed. Katherine Walsh and Diana Wood (Oxford: Blackwell, 1985): 157–189, at 181–83. See also Palémon Glorieux, *Répertoire des maîtres en théologie de Paris au XIIIe siècle*, 2 vols., Études de Philosophie Médiévale 17–18 (Paris: Vrin, 1933–1934), 1: 43–51; Thomas Kaeppeli, *Scriptores ordinis praedicatorum medii aevi*, 4 vols. (Rome: S. Sabinae, 1975–93), 2: 269, 273. Friedrich Stegmüller, *Repertorium Biblicum Medii Aevi*, 9 vols. (Madrid: Instituto Francisco Suárez, 1950–1976), 3:118–173.

on the *History*, which is encyclopedic, remains unedited.[35] We know, however, that Hugh and the Dominicans made extensive use of Langton's commentaries on the *History*, incorporating them into their own commentary virtually in their entirety.[36] These commentaries by Langton, Pseudo-Langton, and the Dominicans, therefore, constitute a unified tradition bridging the Paris of the secular masters and that of the friars.[37]

Hugh and the Dominicans under his supervision doubtless produced their commentary on the *History* in response to then Master-General Jordan of Saxony's constitutions, which were implemented by the Dominican Chapter of 1228, a text which made clear that the *History*, together with the Bible itself and the Lombard's *Sentences*, constituted the foundation of a friar's theological education.[38] Twentieth-century scholars took the reference to glosses in the

35 Anja Inkeri Lehtinen, who is reputed to be working on a critical edition of Hugh's commentary, describes in detail all known manuscripts, whether extant or not. See Anja Inkeri Lehtinen, "The Apopeciae of the Manuscripts of Hugh of St. Cher's Works," *Medioevo* 25 (1999–2000): 1–167, at 3–10.

36 For documentation of Hugh's extensive reliance on Langton's two commentaries, see Clark, "Commentaries on Peter Comestor's *Historia scholastica*," 340–342, 431–436. See also Mark J. Clark, "Stephen Langton and Hugh of St. Cher on Peter Comestor's *Historia scholastica*: The Lombard's *Sentences* and the Problem of Sources used by Comestor and His Commentators," *Recherches de Théologie et Philosophie médiévales* 74 (2007): 63–117. For a note of caution, however, about assuming Hugh's reliance on Langton in general, see Riccardo Quinto, "Hugh of St. Cher's Use of Stephen Langton," in *Medieval Analyses in Language and Cognition*, ed. Sten Ebbesen and Russell L. Friedman (Copenhagen: The Royal Danish Academy of Sciences and Letters, 1999), 281–300.

37 Both Langton and Hugh were giants in the medieval biblical firmament, and their commentaries on the *History* form an important part of their work on the Bible. According to scholars, Langton's biblical commentaries served as the primary resource in scholastic biblical studies for a half century until Hugh's *Postills* eclipsed them. Jacques Verger, "L'Exégèse de l'Université," in *Le Moyen Âge et la Bible*, ed. Pierre Riché and Guy Lobrichon, Bible de tous les Temps 4 (Paris: Éditions Beauchesne, 1984), 199–230, at 201–203; Beryl Smalley, "The Bible in the Medieval Schools," in *The West from the Fathers to the Reformation*, vol. 2 of *The Cambridge History of the Bible*, ed. G.W.H. Lampe (Cambridge: Cambridge University Press, 1969), 197–219, at 206–207. Hugh's biblical commentaries served in the same capacity until they were themselves eclipsed by those of the fourteenth-century Franciscan, Nicholas of Lyra. Smalley, "The Bible in the Medieval Schools," 207–208. Gilbert Dahan's comprehensive study of the high medieval biblical commentarial tradition confirms the traditional view. Gilbert Dahan, *L'Exégèse chrétienne de la Bible en occident médiéval, XIIe–XIVe siècle*, Patrimoines Christianisme (Paris: Les Éditions du Cerf, 1999), 102–120.

38 The relevant text is reproduced at *Constitutiones antiquae ordinis Fratrum Praedicatorum*, ed. A.H. Thomas, in *De oudste constituties van der Dominicanen: Voorgescheidenis, tekst, bronnen, onstaan en ontwikkeling (1215–1237)*, Bibliothèque de la Revue d'histoire ecclési-

final phrase – "fratres missi ad studium in ystoriis et sententiis et textu et glosis precipue studeant et intendant" ("brothers sent to a studium should study
and focus especially on the *Histories* and the *Sentences* and the Bible and the
glosses") – to apply only to "the Text" (that is, the Bible, the Text *par excellence*)
and not to the *History* or the *Sentences*; they thus interpreted this phrase to refer
to Comestor's *Histories*, the Lombard's *Sentences*, and the biblical *Gloss*.[39] That
the Dominicans, however, meant otherwise is clear from the amended version
published in 1256 under the leadership of Raymond of Peñafort.[40] The revised
Dominican constitutions, implemented before mid-century, made plain what
was somewhat ambiguous in the originals, namely that all Dominican friars
were to study not only the *History*, the *Sentences*, and the Bible but also available glosses on those works.[41] Doubtless, one such gloss was meant to be Hugh
of St. Cher's commentary on the *History*. Comestor's *History* continued to
enjoy a privileged place in the educational system of the Dominican order well
into the thirteenth century.[42] Humbert of Romans, for example, who served

---

astique 42 (Leuven, 1965), 304–369, at 361, and also at *Chartularium Uniuersitatis parisiensis*, ed. P. Heinrich Denifle and Émile Chatelain, 4 vols. (Paris: Delalain, 1889–1897),
1: 112, no. 57: "In libris gentilium et philosophorum non studeant, etsi ad horam inspi-
ciant. Seculares scientias non addiscant, nec etiam artes quas liberales vocant, nisi aliquando circa aliquos magister ordinis vel capitulum generale voluerit aliter dispensare,
sed tantum libros theologicos tam juvenes quam alii legant. Statuimus autem, ut que-
libet provincia fratribus suis missis ad studium ad minus in tribus libris theologie
providere teneatur, et fratres missi ad studium in ystoriis et sententiis et textu et glosis precipue studeant et intendant."

39 See, for example Daly, "Master of Histories," 71, and Morey, "Peter Comestor," 6.

40 Thomas, *De oudste Constitutiones*, 83–89 and 119–123, cited by Michèle Mulchahey,
"First the Bow is Bent in Study …": Dominican Education before 1350," Studies and Texts 132
(Toronto: Pontifical Institute of Mediaeval Studies, 1998), 47. See also "Constitutiones
Ordinis Fratrum Predicatorum," 29–68, in Raymond Creytens, "Les Constitutions
des Freres Precheurs dans la Redaction de s. Raymond de Penafort (1241)," *Archivum
Fratrum Praedicatorum* 18 (1948): 5–68; Heinrich Denifle, ed., "Die Constitutionen des
Predigerordens in der Redaction Raimunds von Peñafort," *Archiv für Literatur und
Kirchengeschichte des Mittelalters* 5 (1889): 530–564; and G.R. Galbraith, ed., "The Con-
stitutions of the Dominican Order 1216 to 1360," based upon British Library, Add.
MS 23,935, *Publications of the University of Manchester: Historical Series* 44 (1925): 203–253,
at 251 (Appendix I).

41 *Chartularium Uniuersitatis parisiensis* (ed. Denifle and Chatelain, 1: 113, no. 57 n1): "…
teneatur providere, videlicet in bibliotheca (biblia), hystoriis et sententiis, et ipsi in hiis
tam in textu quam in glossis praecipue studeant et intendant."

42 Mulchahey provides a useful overview of the educational legislation put in place by the
Dominicans during the first half of the thirteenth century. *"First the Bow is Bent in
Study,"* 36–47.

from 1254 as the fifth master general of the Dominican Order, urged friars to impress on their audience knowledge of the Bible, the *History*, and the *Sentences*.[43] It is not, therefore, surprising that the Dominican commentary on the *History* continued to serve the order's educational needs.[44]

There is substantial evidence that the *History* also figured prominently in the formation of Franciscan friars.[45] Balduin has shown that such friars as Alexander of Hales, Saint Bonaventure, Salimbene of Parma, and Roger Bacon knew and frequently cited the *History* and its author by name.[46] He considered Anthony of Padua's use of the *History* in sermons extensive enough to warrant the conclusion that "in the composition of his sermons Saint Anthony had Comestor's *Historia scholastica* continually before his eyes."[47] Chenu cited Anthony of Padua's frequent citation of and extensive reliance upon the *History* in his sermons as evidence of the importance of Comestor's work in the evangelical movement of the twelfth and thirteenth centuries.[48]

---

43 "Officium boni lectoris est ... [d]are operam ut ex lectionibus suis proficiant auditores, aut circa veritatem librorum, aut circa quaestionum utilium intelligentiam, aut circa aliqua quae possint ad morum aedificationem esse; litteram tantum legere, relicta multitudine eorum quae dici possunt ad singula; quod auditores sub eo proficiant ad sciendum *Bibliam*, et *Historias*, et *Sententias* ... ." *Opera de vita regulari*, ed. Joachim Joseph Berthier, 2 vols. (Rome: Typis A. Befani, 1888–1889), 2: 254, cited by Morey, "Peter Comestor," 6 n1. Mulchahey observes that the Dominicans continued to accord the *History* a privileged place in their educational system well into the 1260's. See *"First the Bow is Bent in Study,"* 137–139.

44 It is, therefore, no coincidence that three of the ten manuscripts of this commentary that survived into the twentieth century belonged to Dominican convents: 1) Magdeburg, Bibliothek des Domgymnasium, 238, a manuscript lost during World War II, was produced by the Dominicans in Magdeburg in the fourteenth century; 2) Uppsala C 134, written in France between 1233 and 1248, was given as a gift to the Dominican Convent in Sigtuna by Bishop Thomas of Finland; and 3) Vienna, Dominikaner, MS B 42, a manuscript that is also no longer extant, belonged to the Viennese Dominicans. See Clark, "Commentaries on Peter Comestor's *Historia scholastica*," 397–402.

45 For a treatment of Comestor's influence on Franciscan education in general, see Bert Roest, *A History of Franciscan Education (ca. 1210–ca. 1517)* (Leiden: Brill, 2000).

46 P[ater] Balduinus ab Amsterdam, "*Historia Scholastica* Petri Comestoris in *Sermonibus* S. Antonii Patavani," *Collectanea Franciscana* 24 (1954): 83–109, at 89–90 and notes 39–43, in which the citations are given.

47 "... S. Antonium in *Sermonum* compositione Manducatoris *Historiam Scholasticam* continue prae oculis habuisse ... " (ibid., 106). See also Anthony of Padua, *S. Antonii Patavini Sermones dominicales et festivi*, ed. Beniamino Costa et al., 3 vols. (Padua: Centro studi antoniani, 1979), 3: 311.

48 Chenu, *La théologie au douzième siècle*, 259–260.

The mendicants, of course, modeled their program of studies in theology after that at the University of Paris.[49] They naturally pursued the same program at Oxford, where the *History* also formed part of the theological curriculum. An Oxford University statute of 1253 stipulated that "no one could incept in theology ... unless he lectures on some book from the canon of the Bible or a book of the *Sentences* or of the *Histories*, and preaches publicly in the university."[50] As we should expect, Oxford Masters of Theology, like their counterparts at Paris, knew and cited the *History*. Robert Kilwardby, for example, a Dominican and Regent Master in theology at Oxford until 1261, cited Comestor's *History* repeatedly in his commentary on the *Sentences*.[51]

Although the friars named were scholars, the role of the *History* in their training also points to its importance to religious in a variety of contexts. Besides copies of the *Historia scholastica* in mendicant convents, Stegmüller lists copies originating in Augustinian, Benedictine, Camaldolese, Carthusian, and Cistercian monasteries.[52] Stegmüller's *Repertorium* also lists manuscripts of the *History* in such extra-monastic religious communities as the canons regular, and the number of copies in cathedral churches suggests that bishops too took an active interest in the work.[53] The breadth of its appeal is also shown by its influence on writers as diverse as the canonist Huguccio of Pisa (†1210), who knew

49   Mulchahey, "*First the Bow is Bent in Study*," 67 notes that the *History*, together with the Bible and the Lombard's *Sentences*, had a central place in the formation of young friars, because "Dominican education had become wedded to Parisian theology." Because 1200 is the end term for this monograph, I do not here consider the importance of the *Historia scholastica* for the *studia* of the friars, which were arguably as important and perhaps even more so for medieval theology as the university. This constutes a fruitful subject for future research into the *History's fortuna*.

50   The text of the statute, the relevant part of which reads, "(De theologis licendiandis ad incipiendum). Statuit universitas Oxoniae, et, si statutum fuerit, iterato consensu corroborat quod nullus in eadem universitate incipiat in theologia nisi ... legerit aliquem librum de canone Biblie vel librum sentenciarum vel historiarum et predicaverit publice universitati ..." is reproduced in *Statuta Antiqua Universitatis Oxoniensis*, ed. Strickland Gibson (Oxford: Clarendon Press, 1931), 49, and also in A.G. Little and F. Pelster, *Oxford Theology and Theologians, c. A. D. 1282–1302* (Oxford: Clarendon Press, 1934), 25 and n2.

51   See, for example, the numerous references to Comestor's positions in the *History* in Robert Kilwardby, *Quaestiones in librum secundum Sententiarum*, 8 and 12, ed. Gerhard Liebold, Veröffentlichungen der Kommission für die Herausgabe Ungedruckter Texte aus der Mittelalterlichen Geisteswelt16 (Munich: Verlag der Bayerischen Akademie der Wissenschaften, 1992).

52   Stegmüller, *Repertorium Biblicum*, 4: 6543–6565.

53   Ibid.

and cited the work, and the mystic John Ruysbroec (†1381), who also knew the *History* well and referred to Comestor as the *Magister Historiarum*.[54]

The *History*'s success was not limited to religious communities, nor was its *fortuna* restricted to the Latin-speaking world. One could argue that the *History* exercised far greater influence outside of those institutions, scholastic and religious, in which Latin was the privileged language. It certainly remained relevant far longer, for long after the universities and the religious orders had abandoned study of the *History* in theology, vernacular translations ensured the continued vitality of Comestor's work well into the modern era.[55] Morey argues that "the *Historia* was the single most important medium through which a popular Bible took shape, from the thirteenth into the fifteenth century, in France, England, and elsewhere."[56] Translated into an impressive number of vernacular languages – medieval Castilian, Catalan, Czech, Dutch, English, French, German, Old Norse, Portuguese, and Saxon – it was also abbreviated, excerpted, versified, paraphrased, and adapted for dramatic purposes.[57] Grab-

---

54 For Huguccio's citation of the *History*, see de Ghellinck, *Le mouvement théologique*, 501 n2. On the influence of Comestor on Ruysbroec, see F. van den Berghe, *De invloed van Petrus Comestor op de Schriftuurverklaring van Jan van Ruusbroec*, Mededelingen van de Koninklijke Vlaamse Academie voor Wetenschappen, Letteren en Schone Kunsten van België; Klasse der Letteren 11.10 (Brussels: Paleis der Academiën, 1949).

55 On the *History*'s continuing vitality in French, see P.-M. Bogaert, "La Bible française au moyen âge, des premières traductions aux débuts de l'imprimeri," in *Les Bibles en français: Histoire illustrée, du moyen âge à nos jours*, ed. P.-M. Bogaert (Turnhout: Brepols, 1991), 13–46, where Père Bogaert cites the influential *Bible historiale* of Guyart des Moulins, a translation and adaptation of Comestor's *History*, at 25–27. On the *Bible historiale*, see R. Pozt McGerr, "Guyart Desmoulins, the Vernacular Master of Histories, and the *Bible historiale*," *Viator* 14 (1983): 211–244. Dahan, who cites both these studies, points out in the same footnote that "[o]n attend la publication de la belle these de B. Michel, 'La Bible historiale de Guiart des Moulins,' soutenue à Dijon en octobre 2004, et qui contient une excellente edition de la Genèse." Gilbert Dahan, "Une leçon biblique au XIIe siècle: le commentaire de Pierre le Mangeur sur Matthieu 26, 26–29," in *Ancienne Loi, Nouvelle Loi*, ed. J.-P. Bordier, Littérature et revelation au Moyen Âge 3 (Paris: Université de Paris-Ouest Nanterre-La Défense, 2009), 19–38, at 20 n4.

56 Morey, "Peter Comestor," 6.

57 Stegmüller, *Repertorium biblicum*, 4: 6567–6572, lists translations into medieval French, German, Saxon, Dutch, Portuguese, and Czech. Morey, whose article focuses on the impact of the *History* on medieval vernacular Bibles, cites in addition translations into Castilian, Catalan, and Old Norse; the second part of his article is devoted to numerous Old French and Middle English translations. Morey, "Peter Comestor," 9 and n11, and 17–35. For the many uses to which the *History* was put, see in addition to Morey's article, Karp, "Peter Comestor's *Historia Scholastica*," 228–234; Martin, "Notes," 55 and n5.

mann and, more recently, Longère have taken note of its substantial and lon-glasting influence on art and literature.[58]

The wide-ranging interest in the *History* in the centuries following its appearance in the twelfth century has bequeathed to scholars a lasting testament to its extraordinary success: an impressive number of extant manuscripts and printed editions. More than eight hundred manuscripts of the *History* are extant, copied from the twelfth to the sixteenth centuries.[59] A rapid glance through Stegmüller's *Repertorium* shows the wide geographical diffusion of the *History*, which was carried to the far corners of Europe.[60] So too, the number of printed editions provides tangible evidence for continuing interest in the *History* after the advent of the printing press and indeed for centuries thereafter.[61] Between 1471 and 1486 there were eight printings, and the *History* continued to be published, though less frequently, through the sixteenth and seventeenth centuries. The last printed edition appeared in 1728.[62]

Tributes to Comestor continued into the modern era, as can be seen by reading the notices prefixed to the edition of the *History* reprinted in the *Patrology* of J.P. Migne.[63] But perhaps the best measure of the heights to which Comestor's reputation ascended is his place in Dante's Heaven of the Sun together with Hugh of St. Victor, St. John Chrysostom, Anselm of Canter-

---

58 "Auch Kunst und schöne Literatur sind hiervon mannigfach beeinflußt." Martin Grabmann, *Die Geschichte der scholastischen Methode*, 2 vols. (Freiburg in Breisgau: Herder, 1911), 2: 477 and n6. Longère notes the familiarity of both Langland and Chaucer with the *History*, and cites a play written by Thomas Chandler in 1460, meant for production by students, in which Comestor along with Bernard of Clairvaux, Hugh of St. Victor, and Peter Lombard figured as prominent sources. Longère, "Pierre le Mangeur," 1616 and sources cited therein.

59 See Peter Comestor, *Scolastica historia Liber Genesis* (CCCM 191: xxxi–xxxii). Stegmüller, *Repertorium biblicum*, 4 and 9: 6543–6565 lists two hundred and thirty-four manuscript copies of the *History*, most of them complete.

60 Longère remarks that Polish students carried it back to Poland together with the Lombard's *Sentences*. Longère, "Pierre le Mangeur," 1617, citing "La pensée théologique polonaise jusqu'à la fondation de la Faculté de théologie à Cracovie," in *Le millénaire du catholicisme en Pologne*, ed. Marian Rechowicz (Lublin: Société des Lettres et des Sciences de l'Université Catholique de Lublin, 1969), 2223–2243.

61 The edition of the *History* presented in PL 198 is but one of many, none of which to my knowledge have been examined for light that they could shed on the earlier manuscript tradition.

62 Stegmüller, *Repertorium biblicum*, 4 and 9: 6543–6565.

63 PL 198: 1046–1644.

bury, and other distinguished saints and scholars in the group headed by Thomas Aquinas and Bonaventure.[64]

II. Historical Contexts and Historiography

Why have scholars overlooked the *History*, in spite of its long-lasting fame and, more specifically, in spite of its central importance for understanding theological developments in the later twelfth century? Although there are many possible reasons, two come to mind immediately. The first is the lack of a reliable edition.[65] The second is historiographical. I divide my review in this chapter of relevant historiography into four broad categories. The first two are traditional and familiar, for they are the historiographical contexts into which Comestor's *History* has long been situated and discussed, even if superficially. The last two are not quite new, yet their importance has not been fully understood or appreciated until now. Taken all together, these four considerations provide a proper context for understanding not only Comestor's project in composing the *Historia scholastica* but also his work's place in the theological program that developed as the University of Paris took shape in the final decades of the twelfth century.

a. Comestor and the Lombard

I noted at the beginning of this chapter Comestor's undoubted connection to Peter Lombard and the *Sentences*, recognized both by Comestor's successors in the schools and by modern scholars. Yet the *fortunae* of the two Peters and, in particular, of their two famous works could not have been more different in the historiography of the twentieth and twenty-first centuries. The Lombard, his *Sentences*, and the commentarial tradition spawned by that work have all received sustained scholarly attention for more than a cen-

---

64   Dante, *Paradiso*, 12.134, trans. Charles S. Singleton, 2 vols., Bollingen Series 80 (Princeton: Princeton University Press, 1975), 1: 136.

65   The sole modern text is Agneta Sylwan's recently published edition of the first part cited in n59 above. I document the many problems with Sylwan's edition in Mark J. Clark, "How to Edit the *Historia scholastica* of Peter Comestor," *Revue Bénédictine* 116 (2006): 83–91. In Chapter Five ("The Case for a 'Langton' Edition of the *History*"), below, I discuss the assumptions underlying Sylwan's edition in the context of a broader discussion of the problems attendant upon editing the *History*.

tury.[66] Indeed, the wealth of recent publications suggests that scholarly interest in the Lombard and his work only continues to grow.[67] In stark contrast, Comestor and his *Historia scholastica* have remained in obscurity.

One reason for this is that twentieth-century historians of scholastic thought, while recognizing the link between Comestor and the Lombard and even between Comestor and the *Sentences*, nevertheless established a clear separation between the *Sentences* and the *History* itself. Martin Grabmann was the first and most influential link in this historiographical chain. In his *Die Geschichte der scholastischen Methode*, Grabmann strictly separated the two Peters and their famous works.[68] He also coined a phrase, "biblical-moral," that would become extremely influential in subsequent discussions of both the Lombard's and Comestor's work.[69] Grabmann grouped Peter Lombard with Hugh of St. Victor, Peter Abelard, Robert of Melun, and Peter of Poitiers, whom he deemed "the truest student of the Lombard."[70] These thinkers represented, in Grabmann's estimation, "the theoretical side of theology" in the twelfth century.[71] Grabmann, although he mentioned in passing the *History*'s extraordinary popularity, nevertheless dismissed it as belonging more "in the realm of popular theology."[72] He grouped Peter Comestor with Peter the Chanter and others

66 For recent, general introductions to the Lombard and his *Sentences*, see Philipp W. Rosemann, *Peter Lombard* (New York: Oxford University Press, 2004), and the same author's *The Story of a Great Medieval Book: Peter Lombard's "Sentences"* (Toronto: University of Toronto Press, 2007). For a comprehensive study of the Lombard's *Sentences*, see Colish, *Peter Lombard*. For recent introductions to the commentarial tradition on the Lombard's *Sentences*, see *Mediaeval Commentaries on the "Sentences" of Peter Lombard*, vol. 1, ed. Gillian R. Evans, and vol. 2, ed. Philipp W. Rosemann (Leiden: Brill, 2002 and 2010).

67 A sign of this is the recent translation of all four volumes of the *Sentences*. See *Peter Lombard, The Sentences*, trans. Guilio Silano, 4 vols., Mediaeval Sources in Translation 42, 43, 45, 48 (Toronto: Pontifical Institute of Mediaeval Studies, 2007–2010).

68 Grabmann, *Die Geschichte der scholastischen Methode*, 2: 393.

69 Grabmann, however, did not speak of a school but rather of a "biblical-moral direction" originating with Peter the Chanter: "Die von Petrus Cantor ausgehende biblisch-moralische Richtung der Theologie" (ibid., 2: 476–477).

70 "... von Petrus von Poitiers,dem treuesten Schüler des Lombarden ..." (ibid., 2: 476).

71 "Die theoretische Seite der Theologie ... ist im letzten drittel des 12. Jahrhunderts ..." (ibid.).

72 Grabmann acknowledged the extraordinary success of Comestor's *History* in the Middle Ages but hardly paused to consider what he characterized as more in the realm of popular theology: "Die Bedeutung dieses Werkes, welches im Mittelalter unzähligemal abgeschrieben und auch mehrfach übersetzt wurde und seinem Verfasser den Namen *Magister Historiarum* eintrug, liegt mehr auf populärtheologischen Gebiete" (ibid., 2: 476–477).

whose distinguishing feature was a shared interest in biblical study and practical moral concerns.[73] Grabmann's remarks not only served to separate the *Sentences* and the *History*, but they also established a clear division between twelfth-century theologians whose work was speculative and those whose work was practical.[74]

There was, however, a salient difficulty in Grabmann's characterization of Comestor and his work, which Landgraf was the first to notice. Having discovered that an impressive list of late twelfth- and early thirteenth-century theologians (for example, Praepositinus, Peter the Chanter, Peter of Capua, Guy of Orchelles, Stephen Langton, and Godfrey of Poitiers) and theological works (for example, the Bamberg *Summa* and the *Sentences* attributed to Peter of Poitiers), many of which were considered speculative by Grabmann, cited Comestor's teaching as authoritative, Landgraf set out to account for "the circumstance that, in the literature of the end of the twelfth and of the beginning of the thirteenth centuries, we find an astonishing number of citations of the Eater, which cannot be identified either in the *Historia scholastica* or in his sermons."[75] Landgraf's findings led Martin to question whether Grabmann's characterization of Comestor's interests was too restrictive: "A professor of Sacred Scripture and a moralist, did Peter Comestor also treat theoretical or speculative theology?"[76]

A definitive answer to Martin's question proved elusive. On the one hand, their research first established beyond question Peter Comestor's close ties to Peter Lombard.[77] On the other, Martin and Landgraf differed over whether Comestor had in fact glossed the *Sentences*.[78] Nonetheless, their work on Comestor's preface to the *Sentences*, which circulated independently and was

73 Ibid., 2: 477.

74 "Neben dieser theoretischen Richtung wußte sich in der zweiten Hälfte des 12. Jahrhunderts zu Paris auch eine mehr positiv-praktische Strömung Geltung zu verschaffen, welche die Theologie vornehmlich unter dem Gesichtspunkte des Schriftstudiums und der Moral auffaßte" (ibid.).

75 Landgraf, "Recherches sur les écrits de Pierre le Mangeur," 292.

76 Martin, "Notes," 55.

77 Brady would later prove that Comestor was in the Lombard's classrooms; see his comments in *Magistri Petri Lombardi Parisiensis Episcopi sententiae*, 2: 39*–44*. See also: Brady, "Peter Manducator," 454–490. Scholars have accepted Comestor's status as "a close follower of Peter Lombard" ever since; see Luscombe, "Peter Comestor," 109–110, where all of the evidence for Peter Comestor's relationship to Peter Lombard is reviewed.

78 Martin concluded: "Et c'est tout. Jusqu'à nouvel inventaire, il n'est plus permis de parler d'un commentaire de Pierre le Mangeur sur les Sentences de Pierre Lombard.

attached to later commentaries such as that of Hugh of St. Cher, established an indisputable connection between the theological works of the two Peters.[79] The findings of Landgraf and Martin, therefore, subjected Grabmann's characterization to critical scrutiny and, at least in one respect, overruled him. Landgraf himself and Joseph de Ghellinck, both writing in the 1940s, restored Comestor to the school of Peter Lombard. Paradoxically, however, the essence of Grabmann's view prevailed. Although Joseph de Ghellinck put Comestor in the Lombard's school, he followed Grabmann's lead in treating the *History* separately from the *Sentences* in a section entitled, "L'Activité Biblico-Théologique Des Écoles De Paris."[80] Landgraf placed Comestor with the Lombard but ignored the *History*, devoting one small paragraph to it in his *Introduction à l'histoire de la littérature théologique de la scolastique naissante* and passing over it entirely in his *Dogmengeschichte der Frühscholastik*.[81]

Nous en possédons une introduction, un prologue, rien de plus." Martin, "Notes," 62. Landgraf, however, left open the possibility of finding the sought-for gloss: "Il semble cependant que précisément ce court fragment attribué par un ms au Manducator nous fournisse un moyen de lui attribuer un Glose sur les Sentences." Landgraf, "Recherches sur les écrits de Pierre le Mangeur: Le traité 'De Sacramentis,'" 351.

79 For a recent, magisterial study together with a critical edition of this text, see Riccardo Saccenti, "The *Materia super libros Sententiarum* attributed to Peter Comestor: Study of the Text and Critical Edition," *Bulletin de philosophie médiévale* (2011): 155–215. See also: Artur Michael Landgraf, *Introduction à l'histoire de la littérature théologique de la scolastique naissante*, rev. Albert M. Landry, and translated from the German, *Einführung in die Geschichte der theologischen Literatur der Frühscholastik* (Regensburg: Gregorius-Verlag, 1948), by Louis-B. Geiger (Montreal: Institut d'études médiévales, 1973), 137. Comestor's preface to the *Sentences* is considered in Nancy Spatz, "Approaches and Attitudes to a New Theological Textbook: The *Sentences* of Peter Lombard," in *The Intellectual Climate of the Early University: Essays in Honor of Otto Gründler*, ed. Nancy van Deusen (Kalamazoo: Medieval Institute Publications, Western Michigan University, 1997), 27–52, which is cited and discussed with approval in Marcia Colish, "Scholastic Theology at Paris around 1200," in *Crossing Boundaries at the Medieval Universities: Intellectual Movements, Academic Disciplines, and Societal Conflict*, ed. Spencer A. Young, Education and Society in the Middle Ages and Renaissance (Leiden: Brill, 2011), 31–50, at 47 and n47. For Comestor's other extant theological work, see his *De sacramentis*, ed. Raymond-M. Martin, as appendix to *Maître Simon et son groupe De sacramentis*, ed. Heinrich Weisweiler (Louvain: Spicilegium Sacrum Lovaniense, 1937).

80 De Ghellinck, *L'essor*, 1: 93–95. De Ghellinck did mention Comestor on a number of occasions in *Le mouvement théologique* but discussed the *Historia scholastica* only in connection with the legend of the fraternity of Comestor, the Lombard, and Gratian; see de Ghellinck, *Le mouvement théologique*, 214.

81 Landgraf, *Introduction à l'histoire de la littérature théologique*, 140; cf. also his *Dogmengeschichte der Frühscholastik*, 4 vols. (Regensburg: Friedrich Pustet, 1952–1956).

Subsequently, therefore, even though Grabmann had made only passing mention of Comestor and the *History*, his descriptive label, "biblical-moral," has proven to be highly influential in all subsequent discussions of Comestor's work. For most of the twentieth century, scholars accepted without question Grabmann's view of Comestor's *History* and took his descriptive phrase, "biblical-moral," as a convenient historiographical starting-point. In the mid-twentieth century, for example, both Smalley and Chenu published widely read works that accepted and elaborated Grabmann's division of twelfth-century theology.[82] Smalley's work in particular proved influential in subsequent discussions of the *History*.[83] Perhaps the best example of an influential monograph in the second half of the twentieth century that reinforced Grabmann's biblical-moral demarcation as filtered through Smalley's work was Baldwin's pioneering study of Peter the Chanter.[84] Baldwin preserved Grabmann's characterization of Comestor's work as biblical, while adopting Smalley's substitution of Andrew of St. Victor for Peter the Chanter as an appropriate "biblical" reference point for Comestor.[85] Grabmann's strict demarcation of twelfth-century theologians into two camps, the speculative and the biblical-moral, continues to be repeated and uncritically endorsed by scholars up to the present day.[86]

82 Smalley, *Study of the Bible*, 196–197, and Chenu, *Thomas d'Aquin*, 201–202.

83 Grabmann had actually treated Stephen Langton separately from Comestor and the Chanter. Moreover, he had not actually used the term "school" in his classification of Comestor and the Chanter. Instead, he spoke in terms of a theological "Richtung" ("direction"). See Grabmann, *Geschichte der scholastischen Methode*, 2: 497–501 and 476–477. It was Smalley who, though hesitant to use the term "school," nevertheless grouped the Chanter, Comestor, and Langton together. Smalley, *Study of the Bible*, 197. I discuss Smalley's characterization of the *History*, below, in connection with my discussion of the historiography connecting Comestor and the *History* to the Victorines.

84 John Baldwin, *Masters, Princes, and Merchants: The Social Views of Peter the Chanter and His Circle*, 2 vols. (Princeton: Princeton University Press, 1970), 1: 25–29 and 43–46.

85 "Finally, the Biblical approach of the school of Saint-Victor was perpetuated by Richard of Saint-Victor, Andrew of Saint-Victor, and Peter Comestor" (ibid., 1: 48). According to Baldwin, Langton too followed the school of Saint-Victor as represented by Andrew of Saint-Victor and Peter Comestor" (ibid., 1: 17–18 and 25 n83, citing Smalley, *Study of the Bible*, 196–199). Smalley's work had placed Comestor squarely back into Grabmann's biblical domain, but under the shadow of Andrew of St. Victor instead of Peter the Chanter (*Study of the Bible*, 196–199).

86 According to Colish, "Scholastic Theology at Paris around 1200," 41 n37, Phillippe Buc's monograph, *L'Ambiguïté du livre: Prince, pouvoir, et people dans les commentaires de la Bible au moyen âge* (Paris: Beauchesne, 1994) amplifies Grabmann's classification "with respect to political ethicists." For a more recent endorsement of Grabmann's classification, see Rosemann, *Peter Lombard*.

There have, however, been dissenting voices, especially in recent decades, as new research has called into question the conventional division of twelfth-century theologians into those who engaged in speculative theology and those who did not. Jean Longère showed some time ago that such a division did not fit a number of twelfth-century theologians whose range of interests encompassed the whole range of theology, from speculative to practical.[87] More recently, Joseph Goering, in his study of the work of William de Montibus, called into question the validity of Grabmann's classification.[88] Goering, who calls Comestor "the most famous theologian of the period," thinks that the *History* deserves the attention of modern historians of scholastic theology.[89] More recently still, two up-to-date surveys of scholastic theology in the later twelfth century make the case for discarding altogether what is now a century-old view. Riccardo Quinto has demonstrated in some detail that most of the theologians in the later twelfth century do not fit well into Grabmann's strict demarcation and that the conventional lines need to be redrawn.[90] And Marcia Colish points out that "Grabmann's classification has been modified from two directions."[91] Like Quinto, Colish notes that our understanding of the various theologians working in the later twelfth century has changed as scholars have approached these thinkers on their own terms.[92] My own study, therefore, in which I seek to explain Comestor's project in the *History* in the context of the entire spectrum of theology during the second half of the twelfth century, is in line with these more recent historiographical trends.

In some respects, therefore, the tide is clearly starting to turn. With respect to Comestor and his work, however, Grabmann's classification has continued

---

87 Jean Longère, *Oeuvres oratories des maîtres parisiens au XIIe siècle: Étude historique et doctrinale*, 2 vols. (Paris: Études Augustiniennes, 1975), 1: 155–174.

88 Goering, while he accepts Grabmann's basic descriptive label, "die biblisch-moralische Richtung," argues that this orientation began not, as Grabmann supposed, with the Chanter but with Peter Comestor (*William de Montibus*, 36–41).

89 Ibid., 40.

90 Riccardo Quinto, "La teleogia dei maestri di Parigi e la prima scuola domenicana," in *L'Origine dell'Ordine dei Predicatori e l'Università di Bologna = Divus Thomas* 44 (2006): 81–104, at 84–94.

91 Colish, "Scholastic Theology at Paris around 1200," 42 n37, citing Longère and Quinto and noting that Luisa Valente, in her study *"Phantasia contrarietatis": Contradizzioni scritturali, discorso teologico e arti del linguaggio nel De tropis loquendi di Pietro Cantore (†1197), Testi e studi per il "Corpus philosophorum Medii Aevi"13; Fonti per la storia della logica 2 (Florence: Leo S. Olschki, 1997),* has shown that the Chanter "applied technical semantic analysis to contradictions in the biblical text."

92 Colish, "Scholastic Theology at Paris around 1200," 31–50.

to frame discussion, even among specialists, up to the present day.[93] Indeed, with respect to the *Historia scholastica* in particular, no scholar has challenged until recently the received view that the Lombard's *Sentences* and Comestor's *History* were wholly unrelated.[94] The consensus has been that, although Comestor knew the *Sentences* well, whatever works he may have composed in that theological tradition have been lost. As a result, scholars interested in what Grabmann referred to as speculative theology overlooked the *History*.

They did so in spite of tantalizing hints of an integral connection between the *Sentences* and the *History*, which led Landgraf to speculate that in composing the *History*, Comestor "had the Lombard's *Sentences* under his eyes."[95] My own research has confirmed Landgraf's speculation, for it turns out that Comestor did have the *Sentences* under his eyes, at least in places, in composing the *History*.[96] We are, therefore, no longer justified in separating the *History* from the *Sentences*. The two works themselves, like their authors, were connected not only in legend but in fact.

The historiography just reviewed explains, at least in part, why Comestor's *History* has been overlooked by scholars. It also shows that a salient historiographical omission in scholarly discussions of the *Historia scholastica* has been rectified. Joseph de Ghellinck and Landgraf may have restored Peter Comestor to the "school" of Peter Lombard, but they continued to view the *History* as a work apart. My research establishing a direct connection between the cele-

---

93 See, for example, Dahan, "Une leçon biblique," 20–21 and 33 where, referrring to Comestor's commentaries on the four Gospels, Dahan concludes his article by writing that "... ils sont une source privilégiée pour l'histoire de l'enseignement au XIIe siécle et une illustration remarquable de cette fameuse "école biblique-morale" qui devait, elle aussi, faire progresser l'exégèse de la Bible."

94 Dahan, for example, reviewing comprehensively relevant scholarship, accepts without question the conventional demarcation between the *Sentences* and the *History*. Dahan, *L'Exégèse chrétienne de la Bible*, 102–109.

95 Landgraf cited explicitly theological passages on Baptism and the Eucharist in the *History* that paralleled other works including the *Sentences*. Landgraf, "Recherches sur les écrits de Pierre le Mangeur," 303 and n45. See also Landgraf, "Recherches sur les écrits de Pierre le Mangeur: Le traité 'De Sacramentis,'" 348. And he ultimately concluded: "Dans l'*Historia scholastica* nous lisons en effet une remarque qui semble légitimer la conclusion que, précisément dans la doctrine du baptême, le Comestor a eu sous les yeux les *Sentences* du Lombard." Landgraf, "Recherches sur les écrits de Pierre le Mangeur: Le traité 'De Sacramentis,'" 346.

96 I have shown that Comestor followed the Lombard's *Sentences* closely in composing the first twenty-five chapters of the *Historia Genesis*. Clark, "Peter Comestor and Peter Lombard."

brated works of the two Peters amends what we now know to have been a historiographical lacuna. Scholars have recognized many scholastic chains running out from Peter Lombard and the *Sentences* into the Parisian schools. We must now acknowledge that among them is one whose first link connects both Comestor and the *History* to the Lombard and the *Sentences*.

Historiography on theology during the second half of the twelfth century, therefore, should henceforth reflect this continuity between the two Peters and their most famous works, for the context for understanding Comestor's teaching and writing in the Paris of the 1160s starts with the Lombard's teaching and writing in Paris during the 1150s. We now know that even in the *Historia scholastica* Comestor put to good use his time spent studying the *Sentences* under the Lombard, for he used that work not only as a source but more importantly as an inspiration. Indeed, like his mentor, Comestor went on to create a new form well-suited for passing on part of the theological tradition. It turns out that Chenu, writing in the mid-twentieth century, had it right when he wrote that "point ne faut disjoindre le *Magister historiarum* et le *Magister sententiarum*."[97]

It remains, however, to consider the precise nature of the relationship of the *Sentences* to Comestor's project in composing the *History*. Since Landgraf's time, historians have known that the *Sentences* were a source for Comestor's *History*. My own research has established that they were a not insignificant one. Moreover, like the *Sentences*, the *History* was part of a broader twelfth-century movement in theology away from strict adherence to the biblical text. As many scholars have noted, it complemented and paralleled the *Sentences* in theological education.

At the same time, however, it must be admitted that the two works were essentially different, as were the ends of their authors.[98] Those scholars who classified the *History* and the *Sentences* in separate twelfth-century theological categories were not far off the mark, for it can be seen that Peter Lombard's project in the *Sentences* was not that of Peter Comestor in the *Historia scholastica* and vice versa. Ultimately, therefore, although Comestor and the *History* are connected to the Lombard's legacy in the Parisian schools, we must for now look elsewhere to understand the nature of Comestor's project in the *History*. And the first place scholars have looked is the School of St. Victor.

---

97 Chenu, *La théologie au douzième siècle*, 259.
98 Clark, "Peter Comestor and Peter Lombard," 119.

b. Comestor and the Victorines

Any historiographical discussion of the *History* and the Victorines must start with Beryl Smalley, who saw the *Historia scholastica* in the context of the biblical work of the Victorines and in particular of Hugh of St. Victor's emphasis on the literal/historical sense of Scripture.[99] Indeed, for Smalley, Comestor's *History* represented a pinnacle of sorts for Hugh's program of education: "The greatest triumph for the Victorine tradition was the success of the *Histories*."[100] I shall argue herein that Smalley was surely right, yet for a variety of reasons, which I discuss at the end of this section, below, scholars have not followed up on her insights into the connection between the success of the *History* and the Victorine program.

Like scholars before her, Smalley saw the *History* as a direct response to Hugh of St. Victor's emphasis on history as the foundation for his proposed program of education: "It is often said that the *Historia Scholastica* of Peter Comestor fulfils (sic) an express wish of the *Didascalicon*."[101] Hugh had counseled students of Scripture first to learn history and "the truth of the events that have taken place" from beginning to end and to memorize what has taken place, when, where, and by whom.[102] Reprising Gregory the Great's enduring image comparing the senses of Scripture to a tripartite building, he taught that history was the foundation for theological study: "fundamentum autem et

---

99 Smalley, *Study of the Bible*, 178–180 and 196–215. Smalley showed Comestor's use of Hugh's lecture material on Genesis not preserved in published writings (*Study of the Bible*, 98–99). Hugh's classic defense of the historical/literal sense of Scripture is well known to historians: "Tous les historiens le répètent: pour Hugues, le principe de la doctrine sacrée, son fondement, c'est l'histoire" (De Lubac, *Exégèse médiévale*, 2.1: 287). On Hugh's corpus and influence in general, see notably Dominique Poirel, *Hugues de Saint-Victor* (Paris: Les Éditions du Cerf, 1998). For a more recent overview of Hugh's thought and works, see Paul Rorem, *Hugh of St. Victor*, Great Medieval Thinkers (Oxford: Oxford University Press, 2009).

100 Smalley, *Study of the Bible*, 214.

101 Ibid., 198.

102 See Hugh of St. Victor, *Didascalicon de studio legendi*, 6.3, ed. and trans. into German as *Studienbuch* by Thilo Offergeld, Fontes Christiani 27 (Freiburg im Breisgau: Herder, 1997), 360.3–7, and *Didascalicon de studio legendi*, ed. Henry Buttimer (Washington, DC: Catholic University Press, 1939), 113.24–114.5. There is also a new English translation of the *Didascalicon*, with introduction, in the recently published volume, *Interpretation of Scripture: Theory – A Selection of Works of Hugh, Andrew, Richard, and Godfrey of St. Victor, and of Robert of Melun*, ed. and trans. Franklin T. Harkins and Frans van Liere, Victorine Texts in Translation 3 (Turnhout: Brepols, 2012).

principium doctrinae sacrae historia est."[103] To understand, however, the connection between Comestor's *History* and Hugh's program of education, we must understand what each author meant by history.[104]

The seminal discussion of the meaning of history in the works of Hugh of St. Victor is that of Grover Zinn who, speaking of Hugh's dictum that "history is the foundation and beginning of sacred teaching," writes that "[t]his phrase sums up Hugh of St. Victor's attitude toward the role of history and the literal, historical sense of Scripture in biblical exegesis."[105] Zinn points out that by history Hugh meant not only the traditional signification, namely the quest to understand the primary meaning of the letter by means of grammar and other arts, but also the "intention to understand the text as *history*, as the account of an ordered series of events."[106] As Zinn puts it, "Hugh proposed that the historical exegesis of Scripture be considered a discipline," the first in a series of disciplines – history, then allegory, then tropology – that must be mastered to understand Sacred Scripture.[107]

According to Zinn, the key passage for understanding history as a discipline in Hugh's program is found in the *Didascalicon* in Book 6, Chapter 3 ("De historia"):

103 Hugh of St. Victor, *Didascalicon de studio legendi*, 6.3 (ed. Offergeld, 366.25–26; ed. Buttimer, 116.20–21). Cf. Gregory the Great, *Moralia in Iob* (CCSL 143: 4). See also Rorem, *Hugh of St. Victor*, 32–33. Rorem too makes frequent reference to the various nuances of the meaning of history in Hugh's works. Rorem, *Hugh of St. Victor*, 20–21, 31–33, and throughout.
104 On the significance of history in the theology of Hugh of St. Victor, see Franklin T. Harkins, *Reading and the Work of Restoration: History and Scripture in the Theology of Hugh of St. Victor*, Studies and Texts 167 (Toronto: Pontifical Institute of Mediaeval Studies, 2009).
105 Grover A. Zinn, "'Historia fundamentum est': The Role of History in the Contemplative Life according to Hugh of St. Victor," in *Contemporary Reflections on the Medieval Christian Tradition: Essays in Honor of Ray C. Petry*, ed. George H. Shriver (Durham, NC: Duke University Press, 1974), 135–158, at 138.
106 Ibid., 139.
107 Ibid. Like Comestor, Hugh of St. Victor preferred a threefold understanding – history, allegory, and tropology – of Scripture: "De hac autem materia tractat divina Scriptura secundum triplicem intelligentiam: hoc est historiam, allegoriam, tropologiam." Hugh of St. Victor, *De sacramentis*, prol. (PL 176: 173–618, at 184–185). I continue to cite the text in PL because Rainer Berndt's modern edition, *De sacramentis Christianae fidei*, Corpus Victorinum: Textus historici 1 (Münster: Aschendorff, 2008), is difficult to use owing to the manner of its formatting.

First you learn history and diligently commit to memory the truth of the deeds that have been performed, reviewing from beginning to end what has been done, when it has been done, where it has been done, and by whom it has been done. For these are the four things which are especially to be sought for in history – the person, the business done, the time, and the place. Nor do I think that you will be able to become perfectly sensitive to allegory unless you have first been grounded in history.[108]

Zinn's estimate of this passage is itself worth quoting in full:

The exegete is not simply being trained with an adequate knowledge of grammar and other tools which will enable him to read the text and understand the sense of the words. Something more important is going on in Hugh's program of introductory studies. The student is being taught to examine the biblical text from a particular point of view: history.[109]

In support of his interpretation, Zinn notes that Hugh had listed those biblical books "most useful for the study of *exegesis ad litteram*":[110] "Genesis, Exodus, Josue, the Book of Judges, and that of Kings, and Paralipomenon; of the New Testament, first the four Gospels, then the Acts of the Apostles. These eleven seem to me to have more to do with history than do the others."[111] Zinn also cites Hugh's statement that "[t]he same order of (biblical) books is not to be kept in historical and allegorical study," because the former "follows the order of

---

108 "Sic nimirum in doctrina fieri oportet, ut videlicet prius historiam discas et rerum gestarum veritatem, a principio repetens usque ad finem quid gestum sit, quando gestum sit, ubi gestum sit, et a quibus gestum sit, diligenter memoriae commendes. haec enim quattuor praecipue in historia requirenda sunt, persona, negotium, tempus et locus. neque ego te perfecte subtilem posse fieri puto in allegoria, nisi prius fundatus fueris in historia." *Didascalicon de studio legendi*, 6.3 (ed. Offergeld, 360.1–10; ed. Buttimer, 113.24–114.5). The translation quoted by Zinn, "'Historia fundamentum est,'" 139, is from *The Didascalicon of Hugh of St. Victor: A Medieval Guide to the Arts*, trans. Jerome Taylor (New York: Columbia University Press, 1961), 135–136.

109 Zinn, "'Historia fundamentum est,'" 140.

110 Ibid.

111 Ibid. The relevant text, from *Didascalicon* 6.3 (ed. Offergeld, 364.19–24; ed. Buttimer, 115–116; trans. Taylor, 137), reads: "... Genesim, Exodum, Iosue, librum Iudicum, et Regum, et Paralipomenon; Novi Testamenti, primum, quattuor evangelia, dehinc Actus apostolorum. hi xi magis ad historiam mihi pertinere videntur, exceptis his quod historiographos proprie appellamus."

time" while the latter "the order of knowledge."[112] Taken all together, these texts represent in Zinn's view the conscious articulation of a program of historical studies in reading the Bible, in which history as narrative is the foundation.[113]

At the same time, Zinn sees in Hugh a twofold understanding of history, one that synthesizes what Zinn calls "the narrative and literal aspects of the 'historical' sense of Scripture."[114] In the *Didascalicon*, for example, Hugh makes clear that history means not only historical narrative but in a broader sense the literal sense of all Scripture: "not only the recounting of actual deeds but also the first meaning of any narrative which uses words according to their proper nature."[115] Zinn also quotes Hugh's similar definition in the *De sacramentis christianae fidei*, where the Victorine articulated a twofold understanding of *historia* as historical narrative and literal sense: "History is the narration of deeds done, expressed by the signification of the letter."[116]

Although in citing these passages Zinn acknowledges Hugh's twofold understanding of history, he remains convinced of the primacy of the Bible – seen as historical narrative – as the first discipline in Hugh's program of studies: "Nevertheless, the sense of historical narrative and order remains the basic perspective for the discipline of *historia*. The Bible itself is primarily historical ... ."[117] Zinn

---

112 Zinn, "'Historia fundamentum est,'" 140, citing *Didascalicon* 6.6 (ed. Offergeld, 384.11–13; ed. Buttimer, 123.9–11; trans. Taylor, *Didascalicon*, 145).

113 Zinn, "'Historia fundamentum est,'" 139–141.

114 Ibid., 140.

115 Ibid., 140, citing *Didascalicon*, 6.3: "... non tantum rerum gestarum narrationem, sed illam primam significationem cuiuslibet narrationis, quae secundum proprietatem verborum exprimitur" (ed. Offergeld, 366.1–3; ed. Buttimer, 115.28–116.1; trans. Taylor, 137).

116 Zinn, "'Historia fundamentum est,'" 140, citing *De sacramentis*, prol. (PL 176: 184D), and the translation by Roy J. Deferrari, *On the Sacraments of the Christian Faith* (Cambridge, MA: The Medieval Academy of America, 1951), 5. The translation, however, is not entirely accurate. Hugh actually wrote: "Historia est rerum gestarum narratio, quae in prima significatione litterae continetur" (*De sacramentis*, prol. 4; PL 176: 184–185). Deferrari's translation of the first phrase is fine, but his rendering of the second is imprecise. It should be translated: "History is the narration of deeds done, which [narration] is contained in the first signification of the letter."

117 Zinn, "'Historia fundamentum est,'" 140–141, citing *Didascalicon* 4.1: "Rursus Veteris et Novi Testamenti seriem percurrentes, totam paene de praesentis vitae statu et rebus in tempore gestis contextam cernimus ..." (ed. Offergeld, 270.6–9; ed. Buttimer, 70.9–11). In support of this conclusion, Zinn quotes Hugh's statement that "as we run through the series of books in the Old Testament and the New, we see that the collection is devoted almost entirely to the state of this present life and to deeds done in time" (ibid., citing Taylor's translation, 102).

concludes this portion of his article with an exhortation that could have been penned by Hugh of St. Victor himself: "The foundation of history must be firmly laid, and that foundation consists of a narrative or series of events (*narratio* or *series rerum gestarum*)."[118] Significantly, Zinn cites in support of this conclusion the views of Marie-Dominique Chenu.[119]

Chenu was the only twentieth-century historian of scholastic theology to situate Comestor's *History* within an explicitly theological framework. He called attention to the fact that twentieth-century historians of theology had overlooked a central theological development in the twelfth century: historical theology.[120] In Chenu's view, twelfth-century historical theology, organized not logically but chronologically, sought to render intelligible the divine initiatives in human history recorded in Sacred Scripture; for Chenu, as for Zinn afterwards, the key word was history as *series*, a sequence of ordered events presented in such a way as to render intelligible divine initiatives in human history, or in modern language, salvation history.[121] According to Chenu, Augustine had been the greatest architect of such a theology in the patristic era, while in the twelfth century, Hugh of St. Victor became its most articulate proponent.[122] Like Smalley, Chenu viewed Comestor's *Historia*

---

118 Zinn, "'Historia fundamentum est,'" 141.

119 Ibid., n119.

120 "L'attention des historiens de la théologie, plus sensible aux éclats des polémiques doctrinales ... ne s'est pas suffisamment portée sur un domaine alors étranger au programme des écoles, mais essentiel à l'équilibre général de la pensée chrétienne: celui de l'histoire, comme expression du Christianisme économie temporelle du salut. Ce n'est cependant pas la moindre grandeur du XIIe siècle d'avoir vu nâitre, dans la Chrétienté occidentale, une conscience active de l'histoire humaine ... . On a trop souvent traité ces auteurs comme de simple érudits, en marge des courants du siècle, alors qu'en vérité ils élaborent une théologie, étroitement solidaire de l'enseignement de l'Écriture, dont l'*historia* était la base de la formation des clercs." Chenu, *La théologie au douzième siècle*, 62–63.

121 "... le trait caractéristique d'une histoire par opposition à la connexion logique des disciplines théoriques: c'est une *series*, une succession, et une succession organisée, une continuité articulée, dont les liaisons ont un sens, qui est précisément l'objet de l'intelligibilité de l'histoire ... des initiatives de Dieu dans les temps des hommes, des événements de salut ... . Le temps n'est donc pas seulement une durée cosmique, mais une succession historique d'événements, un *processus saeculi*: la conjonction des deux mots *mundus* et *saeculum* souligne la dimension humaine, voire religieuse *decurrentibus temporibus usque ad finem saeculi*, de cet ordre mystérieux et intelligible ... ." Ibid., 66–67.

122 Ibid., 69 and n3.

scholastica as the crown jewel of this tradition, referring to it as "le livre de base du siècle."[123]

We are now in a position to consider the meaning of history in Comestor's *History*. Comestor's language reveals in many ways his conscious imitation of the tradition, so well described by Chenu and Zinn, that blossomed anew in the twelfth century under Hugh of St. Victor. Indeed, in his epistolary prologue, in which he dedicated the *History* to Archbishop William of the White Hands, Comestor repeatedly uses language that echoes Hugh's discussion of history in various contexts. Of prime importance for Comestor, as for Hugh, is history as narrative. Explaining why he undertook to compose the *History*, Comestor wrote that "[t]he cause of my undertaking this work was the insistent entreaty of colleagues who, because they would often read the history of Sacred Scripture scattered in the scriptural text and glosses, too concise and insufficiently explained, pressed me to compose a work to which they might have recourse for grasping the truth of history."[124] Comestor here refers to "the history of Sacred Scripture" read by colleagues but "scattered in the scriptural text and glosses" ("in serie et glosis diffusam"). I have here rendered the word "serie" as "scriptural text," following Hugh of St. Cher's gloss in the Dominican commentary on the *History*.[125] But it is evi-

---

123 Chenu, *La théologie au douzième siècle*, 259. Chenu returned repeatedly to this theme of the centrality of history in twelfth-century theology and of the corresponding importance of Comestor's *History* in various contexts. See, for example, Chenu, *Thomas d'Aquin*, 41 and 203–205.

124 "Causa suscepti laboris fuit instans petitio sociorum. Qui cum historiam Sacre Scripture in serie et glosis diffusam lectitarent brevem nimis et inexpositam opus aggredi me compulerunt ad quod pro veritate historie consequenda recurrerent." *Petri Comestoris Historia scholastica, prologus epistolaris* (ed. Clark, Textual Appendix A.1 below, lines 4–7). As here, in citing Comestor or Langton, I will sometimes refer the reader to textual appendices at the end of the volume, which reproduce samples from my working editions of the *History* and of the various versions of Langton's course on that work. For the most part, however, I shall refer the reader directly to the manuscripts themselves, since those editions are not yet published.

125 "... IN SERIE id est in textu ... ." Uppsala, University Library, MS C 134, fol. 3vb. I cite this manuscript for Hugh's commentary, because it is the one favored by Lehtinen, Hugh's prospective editor; see Lehtinen, "Hugh of St. Cher's Works," 3–10. In Hugh of St. Cher's time, the Bible, the Text *par excellence*, was often referred to simply as *textus*. Comestor's use of the phrase *in serie* to refer to the scriptural narrative was common in the twelfth century. Hugh of St. Victor, for example, commonly used *seriem narrationis* or *historiae seriem* to refer to *historia*: see *De scripturis et scriptoribus sacris* 5 (PL 175: 9–28, at 15), and *Didascalicon*, 5.2 (ed. Buttimer, 96.8).

dent that Comestor's use of the word "series" hearkened back to Hugh's program.[126]

It is equally obvious from Zinn's examination of history in the works of Hugh of St. Victor that Comestor's references to "the history of Sacred Scripture" and to "the truth of history" also clearly mirrored Hugh's thought. There are, however, several passages in Hugh's works not considered by Zinn that provided likely inspiration for Comestor's juxtaposition of "the history of Sacred Scripture" with "the truth of history." In the first, speaking of the Bible, Hugh wrote: "And in this book two things especially must be sought out: namely, the truth of deeds done, and the form of the words, since just as through the truth of the words we come to know the truth of things, so also the contrary is true: when once we have come to know the truth of things, we know more easily the truth of the words."[127] In the second, Hugh tied the integrity of the writer to the truth of the history recorded:

Sacred Scripture is expounded according to a threefold understanding. The first exposition is historical, in which is considered the first signification of the words with regard to the things themselves about which we are treating ... . History is so called from the Greek word *hystoreo*, which means I see and I recount, for the reason that among the ancients no one was allowed to write about events, unless they had been witnessed by the writer himself, lest falsehood be mixed in with truth through the fault of the writer. In accordance with this understanding history is so called properly and strictly. But it is customarily understood in a broader sense, such that

---

126 Hugh had used this same word many times and in multiple contexts in refering to *historia*. See, for example, his references to *simplicem sensum historiae* and *historiae seriem et litterae soliditatem* in the *Didascalicon de studio legendi*, 5.23 (ed. Buttimer, 95), and his reference to "*seriem narrationis*" in *De scripturis* (PL 175: 15). According to Chenu, "*series narrationis* est une expression favorite d'Hugues de Saint-Victor ... c'est une *series*, une succession, et une succession organisée, une continuité articulée, dont les liaisons ont un sens, qui est précisément l'objet de l'intelligibilité de l'histoire ... des initiatives de Dieu dans le temps des hommes, des événements de salut." Chenu, *La théologie au douzième siècle*, 66–67.

127 "In hoc autem libro duo praecipue attendenda sunt: scilicet veritas rerum gestarum, et forma verborum; quia sicut per veritatem verborum cognoscimus veritatem rerum ita contra, cognita veritate rerum, facilius cognoscimus veritatem verborum ... ." Hugh of St. Victor, *Adnotationes elucidatoriae in Pentateuchon, In Gen.* 3 (PL 175: 29–114, at 32–33).

history is called that sense which is applied to things in the first place from
the signification of the words.[128]

Comestor's explanation that he intended to produce a work that would render
accessible and in a truthful manner "the history of Sacred Scripture" certainly
corresponds to Hugh's ideals for truthful historical exposition of Scripture.
Indeed, Comestor's reference in his prologue to "the truth of history" echoes
Hugh's use of the same words.[129] It is, therefore, exceedingly likely that Hugh's
very language inspired Comestor's own.

Comestor's explanation also corresponds well to the situation facing
would-be expositors of history in the Bible in the second half of the twelfth
century. His assessment that "the history of Sacred Scripture" was scattered
throughout Sacred Scripture itself is first of all consistent both with Hugh of
St. Victor's handpicked list of the most historical books of Scripture and
Comestor's own selective treatment of the Scriptures.[130] So too, his statement
that it was also scattered *in glosis* accords well with what we know about the
study of the Bible in the second half of the twelfth century.[131] Expositors of
the Bible in the second half of the twelfth century were working principally
with the biblical *Gloss*;[132] this originated earlier in the twelfth century and,

128 "Secundum triplicem intelligentiam exponitur sacrum eloquium. Prima expositio est
historica, in qua consideratur prima verborum significatio ad res ipsas de quibus agitur
... . Historia dicitur a verbo graeco historeo quod est video et narro. Propterea quod
apud veteres nulli licebat scribere res gestas, nisi a se visas, ne falsitas admisceretur
veritati peccato scriptoris ... . Secundum hoc proprie et districte dicitur historia; sed
solet largius accipi, ut dicatur historia sensus qui primo loco ex significatione verborum
habetur ad res." Hugh of St. Victor, *De scripturis*, 3 (PL 175: 11–12).

129 "... sicut historiae veritas ... ." *Didascalicon*, 5.2 (ed. Offergeld, 320.25; ed. Buttimer,
96.19).

130 Comestor, of course, did not produce a history of every biblical book. Besides the
Historia Genesis, he composed histories for the following books of the Bible: Exodus,
Leviticus, Numbers, Deuteronomy, Joshua, Judges, Ruth, the four Books of Kings
(our 1 and 2 Samuel and 1 and 2 Kings), Tobit, Ezekiel, Daniel, Judith, Esther, 1 and 2
Maccabees, and the four Gospels treated collectively (the *Historia Evangelica*).

131 Although I here analyze the words *in serie* and *in glosis* separately in order to emphasize
both contexts for the diffusion of "the history of Sacred Scripture" that his colleagues
faced, Comestor clearly connected them. The entire passage – "Qui cum historiam
Sacrae Scripturae in serie et glosis diffusam lectitarent brevem nimis et inexpositam
..." – forms a natural unity in Comestor's elegant Latin.

132 Throughout this study, I refer to this work as the *Gloss*, omitting the standard but
thoroughly misleading adjective, *ordinaria*. I have never seen any author from the
twelfth, thirteenth, and fourteenth centuries refer to this work as *Glossa ordinaria*,

although it was still undergoing significant development, was well-known in Paris at the time Comestor produced his *History*.[133] Comestor himself had lectured on each of the four Glossed Gospels and knew firsthand the extent to which history, whether understood as literal sense or as historical narrative,

---

although I cannot speak to the whole fourteenth century, since the latest authors I am editing are Antonius Andreas and William of Alnwick, neither dating to after the first third of the fourteenth century. Instead, it is universally referred to simply as *Glossa*. Moreover, my own ongoing work on the biblical *Gloss*, and on Peter Lombard, Peter Comestor, and Stephen Langton convinces me that the biblical *Gloss* was anything but ordinary right up to the close of the twelfth century. Indeed, whereas the text of the *Gloss* for certain books became stable earlier in the twelfth century – Alexander Andrée tells me that this is the case for John's Gospel – for many other books (Matthew, Mark, Luke, etc.) there are so many versions that we will need multiple editions to approximate the situation facing the Lombard, Comestor, Langton, and other biblical expositors during the second half of the twelfth century. For Genesis, which I cite abundantly throughout this study, my study of Langton's Old Testament commentaries, which is barely underway, is sufficient to persuade me that the *Gloss* on Genesis was still undergoing significant change during the closing decades of the twelfth century. I use the Rusch edition -- *Biblia Latina cum Glossa Ordinaria: Facsimile Reprint of the Editio Princeps Adolph Rusch of Strassburg 1480/81*, introd. Karlfried Froehlich and Margaret T. Gibson, 4 vols. (Turnhout: Brepols, 1992) – throughout this study, which although it is very late is nevertheless adequate for my purposes here, because it contains so many levels and layers of the biblical *Gloss*, compiled over the course of the twelfth century and perhaps beyond. But for my edition of Comestor's *Historia scholastica*, I shall have to cite different versions of the *Gloss*, and for some books of the Bible many different versions, from the manuscripts themselves, if only to make sense of what Comestor and Langton were doing with the *History* itself.

133 The contemporary of Comestor who attempted to trace the "history of Sacred Scripture" by recourse to the *Gloss* would find the entire text of the Bible set out continuously in a central column spaced so as to accomodate a condensed, outline summary of standard commentary – literal, allegorical, tropological, and anagogical – placed between the lines of the biblical text. Although this interlinear commentary did in fact provide literal or historical commentary on the biblical text, such a manner of exposition presented many difficulties to the reader interested primarily in reading "history." The literal or historical commentary was terse to begin with and was rarely identified as literal or historical. It lay buried in and among the other three levels of commentary. A reader would have to search patiently and carefully to extract it, and what could be extracted was not much. Besides this centered interlinear text and commentary, the reader of the *Gloss* would find an outer layer of marginal commentary consisting of excerpts, largely patristic, bearing on the proximate biblical text. In many cases these excerpts bear an attribution to a particular author. Many are labeled historical, allegorical, tropological, or anagogical, but quite a few of these are not trustworthy. Furthermore, excerpts labeled as historical or literal are interspersed among other types of commentary and are by no means comprehensive or cogent. Many are

was scattered ("diffusam") throughout the biblical *Gloss*. This is precisely how Chenu interpreted Comestor's prologue.[134] The reported complaint of Comestor's colleagues, therefore, fit the facts quite well.

The middle portion of Comestor's epistolary prologue corroborates the view that Comestor set out in the *History* to fulfill Hugh's express wish, as Smalley put it, for a clear and cogent presentation of the historical narrative in the Bible:

> Furthermore, beginning then from the cosmography of Moses, I have composed an historical rivulet reaching up to the ascension of our Savior, leaving to those more skilled than I the ocean of mysteries, in which it is permitted to pursue old matters and to forge new ones. I have also inserted for chronological purposes certain events concerning the histories of the heathen peoples, in the manner of a rivulet which, although it fills the side-streams that it comes upon along its riverbed, nevertheless does not cease to flow onward.[135]

Comestor's image of a historical rivulet, whose source is the creation account left by Moses at the beginning of the book of Genesis and which runs through the

---

simply redundant. For a more precise description of the format of the *Gloss*, which includes exact measurements of the page lay-out, see Margaret Gibson, "The Twelfth-Century Glossed Bible," in *Papers Presented to the Tenth International Conference on Patristic Studies Held in Oxford 1187*, Studia Patristica 23, ed. Elizabeth A. Livingstone (Leuven: Peeters, 1989): 232–244, at 233. She traces the history of the format's development in a line of technical manuscript expertise going back to Carolingian scriptoria of the ninth century. Ibid., 233–237. See also: C.F.R. de Hamel, *Glossed Books of the Bible and the Origins of the Paris Book Trade* (Woodbridge, England: D.S. Brewer, 1984); and Patricia Stirneman, "Où ont été fabriqués les livres de la Glose ordinaire dans la première moitié du XIIe siècle?" in *Le XIIe siècle: Mutations et renouveau en France dans la première moitié du XIIe siècle*, ed. Françoise Gasparri, Cahiers du Léopard d'Or 3 (Paris: Le Léopard d'Or, 1994), 257–301.

134 "Voici son intention explicite: Face à la discontinuité croissante des gloses, retrouver la *veritas historiae* … ." Chenu, *Thomas d'Aquin*, 204; Chenu, *La théologie au douzième siècle*, 69 n3 ("… selon l'intention même de Comestor, voulant retrouver, face au morcelage des gloses, la *veritas historiae* …").

135 "Porro a cosmographia Moysi incipiens rivulum historicum deduxi usque ad ascensionem Domini Salvatoris, pelagus mysteriorum peritioribus relinquens, in quibus et vetera prosequi et nova cudere licet. De historiis quoque ethnicorum quedam incidentia pro ratione temporum inserui, instar rivuli qui secus alveum diverticula que invenerit replens, preterfluere tamen non cessat." *Petri Comestoris Historia scholastica, prologus epistolaris* (ed. Clark, Textual Appendix A.1 below, lines 8–13).

Gospels to Christ's Ascension into heaven, underscores both the importance of history as narrative in the *History* and that narrative's essential connection to Sacred Scripture. The fact that Comestor justifies his inclusion of details from the histories of the Gentiles on chronological grounds, comparing these to side-streams that do not divert the course of this scriptural historical rivulet, only serves to emphasize the integral connection between historical narrative and Sacred Scripture in the *History*. Both Stephen Langton and Hugh of St. Cher, Comestor's most distinguished commentators, took care to emphasize the marginal character of these extra-scriptural historical inserts in the *History*.[136]

At the same time, Comestor's remarks in his letter to William of the White Hands make plain that history in the *History* also meant the literal sense of Scripture, as opposed to the figurative senses. Comestor compares the historical rivulet that he has composed to "the ocean of mysteries." His choice of words for the image used here is no accident, for in his lectures on the four Glossed Gospels, Comestor not only spent a great deal of time explicating the daunting number of figurative glosses contained in the biblical *Gloss* but habitually used the word "mistice" to signal to his students that he was ready to turn his attention to the figurative senses of Scripture.[137] His use, therefore, of the substantive form of the same word in his epistolary prologue clearly signifies

136 Langton, following up on Comestor's image of the *History* as a rivulet, was careful to note in both of his commentaries on the *History* that Comestor's inclusion of such material did not interfere with the *History*'s proper, essentially scriptural course. Glossing Comestor's image of a scriptural rivulet in his lecture course on the *History*, Langton told his students: "INSTAR RIVULI quia sicut rivulus non dimittit cursum suum propter incidentia, sic nec ego propositum id est historie cursum." *Prima Stephani glosa scilicet lectiones a Stephano viva voce ante 1176 datae supra Historiam Genesis* (ed. Clark, Textual Appendix A.2 below, lines 8–10). In the final redaction of his revised course on the *History*, Langton provided a more polished version of the same explanation: "Historie vero dicit se principaliter insistere, licet quedam incidentia ethnicorum id est gentilium ut historiam Troianorum et huiusmodi frequentius interponat, ubi comparat se Magister rivulo qui, licet diverticula que secus alveum invenit repleat, cursum tamen solitum non dimittat." *Tertia Stephani glosa scilicet magistralis anno 1193 recensa supra Historiam Genesis* (ed. Clark, Textual Appendix A.4 below, lines 27–31). Hugh of St. Cher was more concise but even more explicit about the distinction between history proper in the *History* and Comestor's inclusion of episodes from the histories of the Gentiles: "Historiam puram texit, sed incidentia ethnicorum interserit aliquando." Uppsala, University Library, MS C 134, fol. 3vb. These passages make clear that *historia* in the *History* meant *historia Sacrae Scripturae*; any other history was secondary at best.

137 Comestor speaks from experience in using the image of an ocean for the figurative senses. I discuss Comestor's lectures on the Glossed Gospels at some length in Chapters Two and Three, below.

his intention to stick to the primary signification of words in the *History* to the exclusion of the various figurative senses.

Although Comestor alludes to the second of the two principal meanings of history in his epistolary prologue, this understanding takes center stage in Comestor's preface to the *History*, where he compares Sacred Scripture to the divine emperor's dining hall, in which there are intoxicating beverages and food is served that renders those being fed sober:

> It is characteristic of the majesty of an emperor to have three dwelling places in his palace: a courtroom or place of assembly, in which he decrees the laws; a dining hall, in which he distributes food; a bed-chamber, in which he rests. In this way our Emperor, who commands the winds and the sea, has the universe for his courtroom, where at his nod all things are arranged. Whence that [passage of Sacred Scripture]: *I fill heaven and earth.* According to this, he is called Lord. Whence: *for the Lord's is the earth and its fullness.* [He has] the soul of the just for his bed-chamber, since *his delight is to be with the sons of men.* According to this, he is called a spouse. For his dining hall, [he has] Sacred Scripture, in which he so inebriates his own that he renders them sober.[138]

Following this introduction, Comestor proceeds to transform the image of Scripture as a three-story building, passed down from Gregory the Great to Hugh of St. Victor, in such a way as to fit his chosen image of a dining-hall: "Of this dining hall there are three parts: the foundation, the wall, and the roof."[139] Finally, in completing his preface, Comestor uses language and imagery that leave no doubt of the *History*'s filial debt to Hugh of St. Victor:

---

138 "Imperatorie maiestatis est tres in palatio habere mansiones: auditorium vel consistorium in quo iura decernit; cenaculum in quo cibaria distribuit; thalamum in quo quiescit. Ad hunc modum Imperator noster, qui *imperat ventis et mari*, mundum habet pro auditorio, ubi ad eius nutum omnia disponuntur; unde: *celum et terram ego adimplebo.* Secundum hanc dicitur Dominus; unde: *Domini est terra et plenitudo eius.* Animam iusti pro thalamo, quia *delicie sunt ei esse cum filiis hominum.* Secundum hanc sponsus dicitur. Sacram Scripturam pro cenaculo, in qua suos sic inebriat, ut sobrios reddat ... ." *Petri Comestoris Historia scholastica, Praefatio* (ed. Clark, Textual Appendix A.1 below, lines 19–26).

139 "Cenaculi tres sunt partes: fundamentum, paries, tectum." *Petri Comestoris Historia scholastica, Praefatio* (ed. Clark, Textual Appendix A.1 below, line 28).

The foundation is history ... . Allegory is the wall built upon it, which through one event signifies another. Tropology [is] the roof placed on the summit, which through an event signifies what should be done by us. The first is plainer, the second sharper, the third sweeter. Let us take up the beginning from the foundation of speaking, rather from the beginning of that foundation, with the help of God who is the ruler and beginning of all things.[140]

For Comestor, therefore, as for Hugh, history is the foundation, and the final sentence of the *History*'s preface, a rhetorical play on the words "beginning" and "foundation," emphasizes both the fundamental character of history and of the various beginnings crucial for understanding Sacred History: Genesis, the beginning of Sacred Scripture; the creation account that begins Genesis, which recounts the beginning of all creation; and finally God himself, the beginning of all things. Thus, with his exhortation, "Let us take up the beginning," Comestor meant to refer, among other possibilities, to the book of Genesis, the beginning of Scripture.[141] By "the foundation of speaking" Comestor clearly meant the historical or literal sense, the foundational sense of Scripture. By "the beginning of that foundation," he again referred to Genesis, which as the beginning of Scripture constitutes the beginning of history, as Langton's gloss in his lectures on the *History* makes plain: "AB IPSIUS FUNDAMENTI PRINCIPIO id est a libro Genesis, qui est principium historie."[142] Comestor's preface left no doubt that history in the *History* also meant the literal sense of Scripture.[143]

---

140 "Historia fundamentum est ... . Allegoria paries superinnitens, que per factum aliud figurat. Tropologia doma culminis superpositum, que per factum quid nobis sit faciendum insinuat. Prima planior, secunda acutior, tertia suavior. A fundamento loquendi sumamus principium, immo ab ipsius fundamenti principio eo iuvante qui omnium princeps est et principium." *Petri Comestoris Historia scholastica, Praefatio* (ed. Clark, Textual Appendix A.1 below, lines 29 and 33–38).

141 See the gloss of Hugh of St. Cher: "A FUNDAMENTO SUMEMUS PRINCIPIUM a libro Genesis, qui est principium." Uppsala, University Library, MS C 134, fol. 3vb. Comestor could just as well have meant the hexameral account of creation that opens Genesis, since it recounts the beginning of all creation.

142 *Prima Stephani glosa scilicet lectiones a Stephano viva voce ante 1176 datae supra Historiam Genesis* (ed. Clark, Textual Appendix A.2 below, lines 34–35).

143 Both Langton and Hugh of St. Cher took Comestor's preface in precisely this way. In both his lectures on the *History* and in his initial revision of that course, Langton interpreted Comestor's preface as an exclusive focus on the historical/literal sense: "IMPERATORIE. Prefatio est in qua fit <descensus> ad litteram per quoddam simile." *Prima Stephani glosa scilicet lectiones a Stephano viva voce ante 1176 datae supra Historiam Genesis*

It is evident from this examination of the meaning of history in the *History* that for Comestor, as for Hugh of St. Victor, history was the foundation for study of the Bible. For both authors, history had a twofold meaning that was reflected in the various names that they gave to the historical/literal sense of Scripture.[144] So too, although we have seen that both Hugh of St. Victor and Comestor distinguished clearly the senses of *historia*, they each recognized

---

(ed. Clark, Textual Appendix A.2 below, lines 12–13). Cf. *Secunda Stephani glosa scilicet editio recensa augmentataque supra Historiam Genesis effecta a Stephano ipso ante 1176 et tradita in codice H*: "IMPERATORIE. Prefatio est in qua *est* *descensus* ad litteram per quoddam simile." (ed. Clark, Textual Appendix A.3 below, lines 14–15). In the preface that he added to the final version of his revised course, after discussing the various senses of Scripture – unlike Hugh of St. Victor and Peter Comestor, who used a tripartite division of the senses of Scripture, Langton used a fourfold division – Langton concluded: "Tribus omissis agit Magister de sola historia." *Tertia Stephani glosa scilicet magistralis anno 1193 recensa supra Historiam Genesis* (ed. Clark, Textual Appendix A.4 below, lines 23–24). Langton also distinguished in his revised course on the *History* between Comestor's two prologues on the basis of the Magister's intended focus: "Hec epistola est prologus ante rem; demum ponit proemium in re, in quo Sacram Scripturam dividendo ad illam speciem de qua intendit descendit." *Tertia Stephani glosa scilicet magistralis anno 1193 recensa supra Historiam Genesis* (ibid., lines 31–33). Hugh of St. Cher, whose preface to his commentary on the *History* consisted of a lengthy discussion of the four senses of Scripture, echoed Langton's assessment of the historical sense as the principal focus of the *History*: "Hos quattuor modos expositionis possumus in hoc vocabulo Jerusalem invenire. Jerusalem enim historice est civitas illa transmarina in qua Dominus est mortuus; allegorice ecclesia militans; anagogice ecclesia triumphans; tropologice anima fidelis. Tribus ergo ultimis omissis Magister de sola historia prosequitur ... " (Uppsala, University Library, MS C 134, fol. 3vb). Hugh also took over almost verbatim Langton's gloss in his first commentary of Comestor's emperor image: "IMPERATORIAE ETC. Incipit prologus sive prefatio ubi fit descensus ad litteram per quoddam simile." Uppsala, University Library, MS C 134, fol. 3vb.

144 As we have seen, Hugh recognized two related senses of history and indeed referred to *historia* by a variety of different names that made manifest this twofold sense. See, for example, his use of the phrases "simplicem sensum historiae" and "historiae seriem et litterae soliditatem" in his *Didascalicon*, 5.2 (ed. Offergeld, 320.6–7, 12–13; ed. Buttimer, 96.3, 8–9) and his use of the similar phrase "seriem narrationis" in his *De scripturis et scriptoribus sacris*, 5 (PL 175: 15): "Quid sit necessaria interpretatio litteralis et historica." Comestor, who routinely used both names in his lectures on the Glossed Gospels, made his twofold understanding of history in the *History* plain enough that neither Langton nor Hugh could mistake his meaning. Each commentator spoke of *historia* and *littera* in referring to history in the *History*. Throughout this study, therefore, following the lead of Comestor, his predecessors and successors, I refer to the primary sense of Scripture interchangeably as the historical or literal sense of Scripture.

an intrinsic connection between the two principal meanings.[145] Finally, just as Zinn has made the case that for Hugh of St. Victor, history as narrative was of paramount importance, I shall make the case in this study that Comestor also followed Hugh in privileging this sense of history in the *History*. As Smalley proved, Comestor knew the works of Hugh of St. Victor and cited them in his own.[146] Comestor's language in his epistolary prologue and in the preface to the *History* leaves little doubt that he was following in the footsteps of the Victorine in undertaking to compose the *History*.

It is, therefore, no surprise that most historians have agreed with Smalley in viewing Comestor's *History* as an extension of the Victorine emphasis on the historic or literal sense.[147] What is somewhat surprising, however, is that Smalley's insight has not spurred further research into the nexus between

---

145 We have already seen several passages showing that the two meanings of history were intimately related in Hugh's thought, such that true knowledge of the one led to true knowledge of the other and vice versa. See for example *Adnotationes elucidatoriae in Pentateuchon, In Gen.* 3: "In hoc autem libro duo praecipue attendenda sunt: scilicet veritas rerum gestarum, et forma verborum; quia sicut per veritatem verborum cognoscimus veritatem rerum ita contra, cognita veritate rerum, facilius cognoscimus veritatem verborum ..." (PL 176: 32–33). See also the definition of history given in the *De sacramentis,* prol.4: "Historia est rerum gestarum narratio, que in prima significatione littere continetur" (PL 176: 184–185).

146 Smalley, *Study of the Bible*, 98–99.

147 "Cette 'histoire' consacre et étend dans l'usage courant de l'école et de la prédication, la méthode historico-littérale de Saint-Victor." Chenu, *La théologie au douzième siècle*, 259. See also: Longère, "Pierre le Mangeur," 1616: "On peut voir aussi dans l'*Historia scolastica* une application des principes formulés par Hugues de Saint-Victor ... dont le *Didascalicon* ... prône le recours à l'*historia* comme fondement de toute exégèse et condamne ceux qui veulent exposer le contenu théologique d'un texte sans étude préalable du sens littéral"; and Luscombe, "Peter Comestor," 119: "Many years earlier Hugh of St. Victor had urged the study of the whole Bible in its literal and historical sense before attempting an allegorical interpretation. Peter Comestor was in effect fulfilling Hugh's wish for a continuous and comprehensive commentary which took the form of an *historia*." Jean Châtillon, citing Chenu above, declared: "On a dit très justement de ce livre, qu'il consacrait et étendait 'dans l'usage courant la méthode historico-littérale de Saint-Victor.'" Châtillon, "La Bible dans les Écoles du XIIe siècle," in *Le Moyen Age et la Bible*, ed. Pierre Riché and Guy Lobrichon, Bible de tous les temps 4 (Paris: Éditions Beauchesne, 1984), 163–197, at 195. Henri de Lubac disagreed with Chenu's estimate, because he did not consider "la méthode de Saint-Victor" to be "historico-littérale": "Nous ne serons pas non plus tout à fait d'accord avec le R.P. Chenu, pour qui cette *Histoire* 'consacre et étend dans l'usage courant de l'école et de la prédication la méthode historico-littérale de Saint-Victor.'" De Lubac, *Exégèse médiévale*, 2.1: 380.

Comestor's *History* and the Victorine tradition. Indeed, the sole context for scholarly discussion of Comestor's *History* vis-à-vis the Victorines has been the ongoing investigation of the biblical commentaries of Andrew of St. Victor, who in Smalley's view took the lead role among the Victorines in rescuing the literal sense in the Middle Ages.[148] Smalley's interest in Andrew of St. Victor's work has borne sustained fruit in large part because scholars have critically edited his works.[149] Furthermore, her estimate of Andrew's importance within the Victorine tradition has been embraced by scholars.[150]

Smalley's emphasis on Andrew of St. Victor's unique approach to the letter of Scripture has been most emphatically ratified by Rainer Berndt in his monograph, *André de Saint-Victor: Exégète et Théologien.*[151] In the same study, however, Berndt called into question two of Smalley's ideas about the *History*'s connection to the Victorines. The first was Smalley's suggestion that Andrew's commentaries were a principal source for the *History*.[152] More importantly for

148 Smalley, *Study of the Bible*, esp. chapter 4, 112–195. This chapter was based in large part upon an earlier article: Beryl Smalley, "Andrew of St. Victor, Abbot of Wigmore: A Twelfth-Century Hebraist," *Recherches de théologie ancienne et médiévale* 10 (1938): 358–373.

149 To date, editions for the following works have appeared: *Expositio super Heptateuchum* (CCCM 53); *Expositio super Danielem* (CCCM 53F); *Expositio in Ezechielem* (CCCM 53E); *Expositiones historicae in libros Salomonis* (CCCM 53B); *Expositio hystorica in librum regum* (CCCM 53A); and *Super duodecim prophetas* (CCCM 53G).

150 See, for example, Châtillon, "La Bible dans les Écoles du XIIe siècle," 183–184. For a more recent example, see Franklin T. Harkins, "Following with Unequal Step: Andrew of St. Victor, the *Glossa ordinaria*, and Compilatory Exegesis in the Twelfth Century," in *Transforming Relations: Essays on Jews and Christians throughout History in Honor of Michael A. Signer*, ed. Franklin T. Harkins (Notre Dame: University of Notre Dame Press, 2010), 150–178.

151 Rainer Berndt, *André de Saint-Victor: Exégète et Théologien*, Bibliotheca Victorina 2 (Paris and Turnhout: Brepols, 1991). As the title suggests, Berndt not only focuses on Andrew as a literal expositor of Scripture but also argues that Andrew deserves consideration and recognition as a theologian. Berndt's study, which is based on critical editions of several of Andrew's commentaries on Scripture, in most respects completes and extends the picture of Andrew first drawn by Smalley. See esp. his Chapter 5, "La conception du commentaire scripturaire d'André de Saint-Victor," 164–175.

152 Smalley, "The School of Andrew of St. Victor," *Recherches de théologie ancienne et médiévale* 11 (1939): 146–151. Although Smalley, who based her conclusion on textual parallels in different biblical books, had acknowledged the need for further research, subsequent scholarship accepted the *History*'s dependence on Andrew as a given: see Karp, "Peter Comestor's *Historia scholastica*," 182; Longère, "Pierre le Mangeur," 1616; Luscombe, "Peter Comestor," 112; Châtillon, "La Bible dans les Écoles du XIIe siècle," 196. Mark Zier's study of Andrew on *Daniel* seemed to confirm this dependence. Zier,

the purposes of this study, Berndt questioned the validity of Smalley's view of the *History* as the high point of the Victorine tradition of interest in the literal or historical sense of Scripture, asserting that the method and aims of Peter Comestor in the *History* and those of Andrew of St. Victor in his commentaries on Scripture were essentially different.[153] His view is that, whereas Andrew of St. Victor preserved the bond affirmed beforehand by Hugh of St. Victor between the letter of Scripture and its literal sense, Comestor broke it.[154]

While I agree with Berndt that Andrew of St. Victor and Peter Comestor had different ends, I do not agree that the former was faithful to Hugh of St. Victor while the latter was not. As I showed above, Comestor, like Hugh, understood by history both an ordered narrative, grounded emphatically in Scripture, and the literal exposition of Scripture. There is in fact an indissolu-

---

"The *Expositio super Danielem* of Andrew of St. Victor" (Ph.D. diss., University of Toronto, 1983), 105. Berndt, however, called into question Comestor's dependence on Andrew. After systematic study of the textual convergences between Andrew's works and Comestor's *History*, Berndt first concluded that Andrew was not a principal source of Peter Comestor. Berndt, *André de Saint-Victor*, 102. In a later article, however, Berndt seemed to retreat from his earlier conclusion. Speaking of the same 174 textual convergences without identifiable sources, he says: "Une dépendance de Pierre le Mangeur à l'égard du commentaire d'André de Saint-Victor ne rendrait-elle pas mieux compte de ces rencontres?" Rainer Berndt, "Pierre le Mangeur et André de Saint-Victor: Contribution à l'étude de leurs sources," *Recherches de théologie ancienne et médiévale* 61 (1994): 88–114, at 111.

153 Berndt contrasts Comestor's approach, which he calls historiographical, with Andrew's more traditional exposition of the Bible: "Avec l'*Historia scholastica*, Pierre le Mangeur a choisi de conduire son étude biblique d'après un modèle que nous appellerions historiographique ... . En revanche, André de Saint-Victor est resté fidèle au genre littéraire de l'*expositio*." Berndt, *André de Saint-Victor*, 282. But one obvious problem with Berndt's view is that the *History* is organized according to standard biblical divisions: books (Genesis, Exodus, etc.); collections of books (the Pentateuch, the Gospels, etc.); and Testaments (the New and the Old).

154 "... il nous semble que Pierre se démarque considérablement d'André: si celui-ci a eu pour intention, comme nous nous proposons de l'établir au cours de ce travail, de développer le rapport entre la *littera* et l'*historia*, et s'il s'est, dans cette mesure même, éloigné des préoccupations de Hugues, il demeure que le lien entre le texte et l'histoire, affirmé par Hugues, est sauvegardé chez André. Ce lien, Pierre l'a rompu en donnant la préférence à la *veritas historiae* sur la *littera*. Sous ce rapport donc, et quoi qu'il en soit des emprunts ponctuels, aussi nombreux et littéraux soient-ils, les visées des deux auteurs sont essentiellement diverses, et il n'existe pas de dépendance de Pierre par rapport à l'exégèse d'André. S'il fallait parler de rupture dans la tradition exégétique inaugurée par Hugues, il serait sans doute moins erroné de la placer au niveau de Pierre plutôt qu'à celui d'André." Berndt, *André de Saint-Victor*, 104.

ble link in the *History* between the Bible and history understood in both senses. On the one hand, Comestor organized his narrative according to the Bible, as each individual history therein corresponds to a biblical book (for example, *Historia Genesis, Historia Exodi*, etc.) or collection of books (the *Historia evangelica* is based on all four Gospels).[155] On the other, every chapter of the *History* is filled with literal *expositiones*, which make up the greater part of the *History*'s text. Like Andrew, Comestor was an expert expositor of the literal sense, one who drew constantly and carefully on the abundant precedent tradition of historical commentary.

Although my purpose here is not to compare Andrew and Comestor as scholars, one example will serve to make my point. In the tenth chapter of the *Historia Genesis* ("De institutione coniugii"), glossing Genesis 1.31 (*"ET VIDIT DEUS CUNCTA QUE FECERAT ET ERANT VALDE BONA"*), Comestor preferred the original text of Augustine's *De Genesi ad litteram* to the extract found in the biblical *Gloss*. He focused on the word *valde* and cited an example used by Augustine but not incorporated into the *Gloss* – eyes are more beautiful in an animal than when separated from the animal's body – to illustrate the point that while individual things in creation were good, taken collectively they were all exceedingly good.[156] Comestor, therefore, did not sever the link between Scripture and literal exposition, as Berndt asserts. He did, however, change the relation-

---

155 In this connection it is interesting that in several early manuscripts the title of Comestor's work refers explicitly to the Old and New Testaments, as in one of our two earliest: "Item Praefatio Magistri Petri Manducatoris in Historia Veteris et Novi Testamenti." Paris, BnF, MS lat. 16943, fol. 2ra, hereinafter cited as P. In another the epistolary prologue is headed by a similar title: "Incipit prefatio epistolaris in Historiam scholasticam de Veteri et Novo Testamento." St. Albans, England, British Library, Royal 4 D.VII, fol. 9ra. Perhaps the most cogent statement about the matter is that of Hugh of St. Cher who, commenting on Comestor's dedication, declared simply that "the subject matter of this book is the same as that of the entire Bible." "Materia quidem huius libri est eadem que et totius Biblie." Uppsala, University Library, MS C 134, fol. 3vb.

156 *Petri Comestoris Historia Genesis*, 10, in Vienna, Östereichische Nationalbibliothek, MS 363, fol. 10rb, hereinafter cited as V, where Comestor was relying on Augustine, *De Genesi ad litteram libri duodecim*, 3.24 (CSEL 28.1: 91–92). By contrast, Andrew was content to rely on the *Gloss* extract which, although attributed to Augustine, was actually from Bede. Andrew of St. Victor, *Expositio super Heptateuchem* (CCCM 53: 24.634–642), and GM, 1: 16a, marginal gloss 5. The gloss in question is based on Bede, *Libri quattuor in principium Genesis*, 1, Gn 1.31 (CCSL 118A: 31–32). Andrew's editors mistakenly cite Augustine, an understandable error given that Bede himself relied on Augustine.

ship between biblical text and literal commentary owing to an adaptation in form and method.[157]

I make the case in this study that Comestor adapted the traditional format, both in terms of form and method, out of necessity owing to the lack of materials suitable for introducing the Bible to students in the Paris of the 1160s. There was as yet no text available that answered Hugh of St. Victor's *desideratum* for a cogent presentation of salvation history grounded in the Bible. Therefore, even if Berndt were right that Andrew of St. Victor's traditional exposition of the literal sense of Scripture was more faithful to Hugh's vision than Comestor's adaptation – and it is by no means clear that he is – nevertheless, one would have to acknowledge that Comestor's realization rendered Hugh's vision of a historical foundation for the study of the Bible a living reality, one deserving of the kind of sustained scholarly attention devoted to the works of Andrew of St. Victor.

At the same time, scholarly enthusiasm for Andrew of St. Victor is insufficient by itself to account for why historians have not pursued the tantalizing insights of Smalley and Chenu into the *History*'s starring role in the continuation of the Victorine program of education. The most obvious reason, of course, has been the lack of a reliable, modern edition of Comestor's *History* and the difficulties attendant upon producing one.[158] So too, as Chenu himself noted, twentieth-century historians of theology, more interested in explicitly doctrinal works during the early scholastic period, overlooked the central importance of history in the theology of the second half of the twelfth century.[159] But

---

157 Berndt does acknowledge that Comestor did change the form of the traditional biblical commentary: "Le Mangeur renonce à la forme traditionnelle qui consiste à suivre un livre biblique en l'expliquant pas à pas, en faveur d'un récit historique qui s'organise lui-même, au lieu de se laisser conduire par le fil d'un texte qui fait autorité." Berndt, *André de Saint-Victor*, 282.

158 See my discussion of these difficulties, below in Chapter Seven, where I show that Stephen Langton is the key to any edition of Peter Comestor's *Historia scholastica*.

159 "L'attention des historiens de la théologie, plus sensible aux éclats des polémiques doctrinales ... ne s'est pas suffisamment portée sur un domaine alors étranger au programme des écoles, mais essentiel à l'équilibre général de la pensée chrétienne: celui de l'histoire, comme expression du Christianisme économie temporelle du salut. Ce n'est cependant pas la moindre grandeur du XIIe siècle d'avoir vu nâitre, dans la Chrétienté occidentale, une conscience active de l'histoire humaine ... . On a trop souvent traité ces auteurs comme de simple érudits, en marge des courants du siècle, alors qu'en vérité ils élaborent une théologie, étroitement solidaire de l'enseignement de l'Écriture, dont l'*historia* était la base de la formation des clercs." Chenu, *La théologie au douzième siècle*, 62–63.

arguably the single most important reason is that historians have failed to recognize that Comestor's *History* carried Hugh's program into the university.

Even Chenu seems to have missed the central importance of history to the study of theology in the schools.[160] Zinn too was convinced that Hugh's sense of the importance of history played no part in the schools: "The sense of history which Hugh shows in his writings was characteristic of a particular segment of twelfth-century society: monks and canons regular. History had no place in the liberal arts and consequently in the later university curriculum."[161] Like so many historians, Zinn assumed that the curriculum established in the developing university revolved around systematic exposition of theological *quaestiones*.[162]

It turns out, however, that this was not in fact the case. The truth is more complex, for there was a long interim period of development in which both Peter Lombard's *Sentences* and Peter Comestor's *Historia scholastica* played crucial roles. Colish has shown that, before the Lombard's *Sentences* became the basis for systematic magisterial exposition of independent theological *quaestiones* starting with Alexander of Hales in the 1220s, *magistri* teaching the *Sentences* in the schools used the Lombard's work in a much more straightforward, modest manner.[163] Moreover, I show in this study that this period of interim scholastic gestation was in fact longer than scholars have realized. Langton came to Paris ten to fifteen years earlier than scholars have supposed; he was already lecturing in Paris on the *Historia scholastica* prior to 1176. And he was Comestor's student long before that.[164]

Comestor's *History*, therefore, served *magistri* teaching in the schools of Paris for at least the last three decades of the twelfth century and well into the thirteenth as the standard text for introducing students to the Bible. By means of the *History*, therefore, the Victorine program of history-centered education

160   Thus, for example, in the passage quoted in the preceding footnote, Chenu speaks of history as "un domaine alors étranger au programme des écoles." Ibid.

161   Zinn, "'Historia fundamentum est,'" 143.

162   "The masters in the schools tended to move away from the practice of integral biblical reading in *lectio divina* with its historical frame to a program oriented around collections of *quaestiones* covering theological topics in a systematic, objective manner." Ibid.

163   Marcia L. Colish, "The Pseudo-Peter of Poitiers Gloss," in *Mediaeval Commentaries on the Sentences of Peter Lombard*, 2: 1–34.

164   See the following studies: Clark, "Peter Comestor and Stephen Langton"; and Clark, "Le cours d'Étienne Langton." In Chapter 7, below, I document both Langton's multi-faceted relationship with Comestor and the outlines of his career in Paris.

was borne straight into the heart of the university and subsequently into popular culture throughout Europe, first through the preaching of the friars who adopted that university curriculum for their formation, and second through the vernacular translations that made Comestor's textbook into a medieval and early modern bestseller. Smalley, it turns out, was right after all about the *History* as the "greatest triumph for the Victorine tradition."[165] But that tradition does not by itself account for Comestor's undertaking to write the *History*, which owed as much to another celebrated twelfth-century text, the biblical *Gloss*.

c. Comestor and the Glossatores

For commentators on the Bible during the second half of the twelfth century, the fundamental text *par excellence* was the biblical *Gloss*.[166] Twentieth-century scholarship on the *Gloss* evolved from portraying it as a conservative text, which preserved and presented in a convenient manner the antecedent Christian tradition of commentary on the Bible, to recognizing its innovative character.[167]

---

165 Smalley, *Study of the Bible*, 214.

166 The most recent general treatment is Lesley Smith's survey of available scholarship in *The "Glossa ordinaria": The Making of a Medieval Bible Commentary* (Leiden: Brill, 2009). Smith relies especially on the researches into the *Gloss* of Beryl Smalley, whose articles dating back to the 1930s have remained authoritative. See, for example: Beryl Smalley, "Gilbertus Universalis, Bishop of London (1128–34) and the Problem of the 'Glossa ordinaria' I," *Recherches de théologie ancienne et médiévale* 7 (1935): 235–263; "Gilbertus Universalis, Bishop of London (1128–34) and the Problem of the 'Glossa ordinaria' II," *Recherches de théologie ancienne et médiévale* 8 (1936): 24–60; and "La *Glossa ordinaria*: Quelques prédécesseurs d'Anselme de Laon," *Recherches de théologie ancienne et médiévale* 8 (1937): 24–60. Alexander Andrée, however, who takes Smith (as well as scholars in general) to task for her uncritical reliance on Smalley and who insists on the need for new research, has shown that much if not most scholarship on the *Gloss* will have to be rethought. Alexander Andrée, "Anselm of Laon Unveiled: The *Glosae svper Iohannem* and the Origins of the *Glossa Ordinaria* on the Bible," *Mediaeval Studies* 73 (2011): 217–260. See also his review of Smith's monograph: Alexander Andrée, "Laon Revisited: Master Anselm and the Creation of a Theological School in the Twelfth Century," *The Journal of Medieval Latin* 22 (2012): 257–282.

167 Margaret Gibson, for example, referred to it as "first and foremost a work of reference ... the best tool yet devised for quick access to the Fathers ... ." Gibson, "The Twelfth-Century Glossed Bible," 243–244. See also Margaret Gibson, "The Place of the *Glossa Ordinaria* in Medieval Exegesis," in *Ad litteram: Authoritative Texts and their Medieval Readers*, ed. Mark D. Jordan and Kent Emery, Jr. (Notre Dame: University of Notre Dame Press, 1992), 5–27. By contrast, speaking of the *Gloss*, Signer wrote: "It is a work of exegesis with an independent agenda." Michael A. Signer, "The *Glossa Ordinaria*

Nevertheless, most scholarly work on the *Gloss*, following Smalley's ground-breaking researches into its provenance, has continued to focus "on the problems of the layout of the page and the place of the *Gloss*'s final editing."[168] The little work that has been done on the actual use of the *Gloss* by twelfth-century expositors of the Bible has confirmed its central importance as the source of first resort.[169] Not surprisingly, therefore, most historians who have taken note of the *History* have recognized the biblical *Gloss* as a principal source for Comestor.[170]

As with Comestor's relation to the Victorines, however, the key figure in understanding existing historiography on Comestor and the *Gloss* remains Beryl Smalley, for it was she who first showed how fundamental the *Gloss* was to the work of Peter Comestor and to that of his near contemporaries, Andrew of St. Victor, Peter the Chanter, and Stephen Langton.[171] Smalley documented the fact that in their generation "lectures on Scripture began to take the form

---

and the Transmission of Medieval Anti-Judaism," in *A Distinct Voice: Medieval Studies in Honor of Leonard E. Boyle O.P.*, ed. Jacqueline Brown and William P. Stoneman (Notre Dame: University of Notre Dame Press, 1998), 591–605, at 598. More recently, I have supported Signer's view, arguing that both Andrew of St. Victor and Peter Comestor used the *Gloss* as a vehicle for impressing their own distinctive exegetical stamp on the tradition of literal commentary mediated by the compilers of the *Gloss*. Mark J. Clark, "Glossing Genesis 1.2 in the Twelfth Century, or How Andrew of St. Victor and Peter Comestor Dealt with the Intersection of *nova* and *vetera* in the Biblical *Glossa ordinaria*," *Sacris erudiri* 46 (2007): 241–286.

168 See especially the following key studies: De Hamel, *Glossed Books of the Bible*; and Stirnemann, "Où ont été fabriqués les livres," 257–301.

169 Thus, for example, while Andrew of St. Victor's use of the *Gloss* has long been recognized, Frans van Liere has shown the extent of Andrew's dependence on it, writing that "in his commentaries on the Heptateuch and Samuel and Kings, Andrew excerpted mainly *one* source, the *Glossa ordinaria*." Frans van Liere, "Andrew of St. Victor and the Gloss on Samuel and Kings," in *Media Latinitas: A Collection of Essays to Mark the Occasion of the Retirement of L.J. Engels*, ed. R.I.A. Nip and H. Van Dijk Instrumenta Patristica 28 (Turnhout: Brepols, 1996), 249–253.

170 See, for example, Luscombe, "Peter Comestor," 111, and Daly, "Master of Histories," 64. A curious exception is Agneta Sylwan, who undervalues, in my view, the importance of the *Gloss* among Comestor's sources. Thus, for example, although she notes Comestor's reliance both upon the Vulgate and the *Vetus latina* in her account of his treatment of the biblical text, Sylwan does not discuss Comestor's consistent use of the scriptural text itself of the glossed Bible. Peter Comestor, *Scolastica historia* (ed. Sylwan, xxi, xxx–xxxi).

171 Smalley, *Study of the Bible*, 178–181.

of glossing the *Gloss*, or, on St. Paul and the Psalter, the *Magna Glosatura*."[172] She also noted the fact that the *History*, like the biblical *Gloss*, became a textbook in the schools of Paris.[173] In fact, Smalley was in a unique position to make this scholastic connection between the two works, for as she cautiously observed based upon her own pioneering researches: "So far as we know, the earliest example of a gloss on the *Gloss* is a series of lectures on the Gospels by Peter Comestor ... ."[174]

Smalley herself went on to study Comestor's lectures on the Glossed Gospels as part of a broader study of the Gospels in the schools during the twelfth and thirteenth centuries.[175] In her study, until recently the sole examination of Comestor's Gospel lectures, Smalley focused on Comestor's "attitudes to the precepts of the Sermon on the Mount, to apostolic poverty and to ecclesiology."[176] More relevant to my own study, her article gave "an account of his techniques as a lecturer and of his sources" in order to "provide a framework for his doctrine ... ."[177] Smalley included the *Historia scholastica* in her examination of Comestor's technique in his Gospel lectures, for she asserted that "[m]uch of the lecture material reappears, either verbatim or nearly [so] in the *School History*."[178] Smalley was wrong about this, for in fact very little of the material in Comestor's voluminous lecture courses on the four glossed Gospels made its way into the *History*.[179] She was, however, right in connecting the biblical *Gloss* to Comestor's *Historia evangelica* as its principal source.

---

172 Ibid., 64–65. Smalley, however, was mistaken in supposing that lectures on the *Magna glosatura* were limited to the Pauline epistles and the Psalter, for, as I show below in Chapters Two and Three, Comestor and his students clearly understood that his lectures on the Glossed Gospels were based on the *Magna glosatura* for the Gospels.

173 Speaking of the *History*, she wrote: "It became a 'set book' in the schools and formed the subject of lecture courses, just as did the *Gloss*; hence it got its name, the *Historia Scholastica* ... ." Smalley, *Study of the Bible*, 178–179.

174 Ibid., 65.

175 See Beryl Smalley, "Peter Comestor on the Gospels and His Sources," *Recherches de théologie ancienne et médiévale* 46 (1979): 84–129, quotation at 84, subsequently republished as Chapter Two in Smalley, *Gospels in the Schools*, 37–83, quotation at 37.

176 Smalley, *Gospels in the Schools*, 37.

177 Ibid., 37.

178 Ibid., 62.

179 I show in Chapters Two and Three, below, where I describe the precise relationship between the *Gloss* and Comestor's lectures on the Glossed Gospels, that Smalley was mistaken.

The *History* (and not just the *Historia evangelica*, that part of the *Historia scholastica* that treats the four Gospels as a unified narrative) reveals on every page the imprint of Comestor's lectures on the glossed Gospels, but not in the way that Smalley supposed. Comestor's lectures on the glossed Gospels cannot be fairly said to constitute the matter of the *History*, or to use the Aristotelian-scholastic vocabulary of causation, its material cause. They do, however, reveal its formal cause, for the form, structure, and method of the *History* are the direct product of Comestor's experience using the *Gloss* to teach the Bible in the schools.[180]

Smalley, therefore, was prescient in her observations about the twelfth-century contexts for understanding the *History*, for she recognized that the *Gloss* and the *History* belonged to the same scholastic context, even if she did not realize that the deficiencies of the one as a set text for teaching the Bible led directly to the creation of the other. Comestor's *History*, therefore, is as much the child of the biblical *Gloss* as it is of the Victorine program for the importance of history in the study of the Bible.[181] If the latter provided the proper subject, Comestor's long classroom experience with the former pointed the way to a new form and method for teaching the Bible in the schools.

We are now in a position to consider the overall context for understanding Comestor's project in composing the *History*, for we see clearly that it was grounded in three important but diverse twelfth-century theological currents. The *Sentences* of his teacher, Peter Lombard, provided Comestor both material and inspiration for creating a new kind of *summa* for teaching the Bible, but they did not and indeed could not supply the form, for it was in aim and essence a different project. Another mentor, Hugh of St. Victor, drew a map for theological education and in particular for study of the Bible, and Comestor took that map seriously enough to create a work that made the study of Bible history, understood in both senses, not only feasible but enjoyable in an introductory Bible course.[182] Finally, Comestor's own long experience using the

180 I document this claim in the next three chapters of this study.

181 For a recent study documenting Comestor's reliance on the *Gloss* as a source of first resort and also his ability to go beyond it when necessary in his quest to establish what he calls "the truth of history," see the fine article by David Luscombe, "Peter Comestor and Biblical Chronology," *Irish Theological Quarterly* 80 (2015): 136–148.

182 I do not attempt in this study to deal with another twelfth-century treatment of theology in the context of salvation history, namely that of Rupert of Deutz. See in this connection Rupert of Deutz, *De sancta Trinitate et opus eius* (CCCM 21–24), which is discussed in some detail by John H. Van Engen, *Rupert of Deutz* (Berkeley: University of

Gloss to teach the Bible gave him a blueprint for structuring such a work, for in the course of working around the difficulties presented by the *Gloss* as a set text Comestor forged the method that he would use to structure the *History*.

The very diversity of these three fundamental influences suggests a high degree of difficulty in classifying the *History* and explains, at least in part, why the *History* has so long fallen through the historiographical cracks. Thus, it is easy on the one hand to understand how Grabmann and other distinguished twentieth-century historians of theology interested principally in the history of doctrine could separate the *History* from the *Sentences*. At the same time, Berndt's more recent assertion that, in contrast to Andrew of St. Victor's scriptural *expositiones*, Comestor's *Historia scholastica* was anything but traditional and should be classed separately from biblical commentaries seems equally implausible. The truth is that Comestor's *History* had something of both ends of the twelfth-century theological spectrum in it. It was in fact something altogether new; it did not resemble anything else and has as a result proven difficult for modern historians to classify and to understand. Indeed, as its twelfth-century family tree suggests, the *History* was a hybrid, the offspring of the new and the old, the progressive as well as the traditional.

Like the *Sentences*, the *History* was part of a progressive movement in twelfth-century theology away from the traditional straightforward exposition of the biblical text. In this connection, the fact that Comestor forged the *History*'s method from his classroom experience teaching by means of the *Gloss* is revealing. It is no accident that Comestor and the *History* were criticized by contemporaries who believed that glosses had taken on undue importance relative to the text of the Bible itself.[183] The *Gloss* itself constituted a huge step in this theological trend, yet the immediate success of Comestor's *History*, which lent itself easily to classroom teaching in a way that the *Gloss* did not, institutionalized the practice in the schools. It is, therefore, easy to understand

---

California Press, 1983) and touched upon briefly by Colish in *Peter Lombard*, 1 : 35–37. A comparison of the projects of Peter Comestor and Rupert of Deutz, which would be of undoubted interest for our understanding of this branch of theology in the twelfth century, is beyond the scope of this study, even though there is clear evidence that Peter Comestor was familiar with Rupert's *De divinis officiis*. See Hubert Silvestre, "Le jour et l'heure de la nativité et de la résurrection pour Rupert de Deutz," in *Pascua mediaevalia: Studies voor Prof. Dr. J.M. de Smet,* ed. R. Lievens, E. Van Mingroot, and W. Verbeke, Mediaevalia Lovaniensia, Series 1/Studia X (Leuven: Universitaire Pers, 1983), 619–630 at 619–627.

183 Smalley, *Study of the Bible*, 215–216.

William of Auvergne's complaint that students were "satisfied to have heard the preliminaries to Holy Scripture, such as the *Histories* or some other works. The rest they neglect."[184]

At the same time, the *History* was the fruit of a Victorine program for restoring traditional Bible-centered values in the study of the theology. Chenu, like Smalley, saw this clearly and recognized in this history-centered program an important and overlooked contribution of twelfth-century theology. The fact that the *History* carried this program forward, first into the university, subsequently through the preaching and teaching of the mendicant orders, and ultimately into popular culture itself through translations, versifications, and the like, ensured the continuing vitality of this more traditional theological program.

In short, Comestor's *History* was a product of its time, a janus-like work, forged serendipitously out of necessity and inspiration, which looked backward and forward at the same time. Comestor had taught the Bible for years using the *Gloss* and knew better than anyone the difficulties the use of that text occasioned in the classroom. He thus knew from experience that no existing text answered Hugh of St. Victor's call for an introduction to the Bible centered on history. Moreover, having studied the *Sentences* for years under the Lombard, he also knew firsthand how effective and useful new means for passing on old traditions could be in the schools. His experiences in Paris, therefore, as a student and disciple of the Lombard, as a disciple of Hugh of St. Victor, and as a Master teaching theology at Notre Dame all combined to make him uniquely qualified to produce a work that would answer a pressing need on the eve of the coming-to-be of the University of Paris, namely a textbook that would introduce students to the Bible. Happily, this is precisely what he did, and his contemporaries and successors in the schools recognized immediately both his greatness and the greatness of the *History*.

But the story of the the *History*'s immediate success in the schools does not begin and end with Comestor alone, for just as the Lombard had passed on to his talented student the mantle of leading theologian in the schools of Paris at the start of the 1160s, so too Comestor passed this same baton at the conclusion of that same decade to another talented student, Stephen Langton, who had come to study in Paris, the theological center of Europe.

---

184 Smalley, *Study of the Bible*, 215, citing her article, Beryl Smalley, "Some Thirteenth-Century Commentaries on the Sapiential Books," *Dominican Studies* 2 (1949): 318–355, at 329. The translation is Smalley's.

d. *Comestor in the Schools*

Scholars have long recognized a close affinity between Peter Comestor and Stephen Langton based on their assiduous and expert exposition of the Bible.[185] As with Comestor, however, scholars have tended to overlook Langton's biblical corpus, focusing more on his speculative theological works.[186] In recent decades especially, these latter have attracted more sustained scholarly attention owing to the efforts of Riccardo Quinto.[187] We have just seen the first

---

185 The classic discussion remains Smalley's mid-twentieth-century treatment. Smalley, *Study of the Bible*, 196–263.

186 The seminal studies were those of Lacombe and Smalley eighty years ago: Lacombe, "Cardinal Stephen Langton," 1–151; and Beryl Smalley and Alys L. Gregory, "Studies on the Commentaries of Cardinal Stephen Langton, Part 2," *Archives d'histoire doctrinale et littéraire du Moyen Âge* 5 (1930): 152–266. Quite recently, however, a few important steps have been taken towards establishing some chronological certainties regarding the dating of Langton's biblical commentaries owing to newly discovered data. Thus for example, Riccardo Quinto, relying on internal evidence provided by Louis-Jacques Bataillon for the dating of Troyes, Bibliothèque municipale, MS 1046 to 1203, a manuscript that contains a copy of Langton's commentary on the twelve Minor Prophets, suggests "that the new capitulation of the Bible, for the Minor Prophets at least, was already complete between 1196 and 1201, and that Langton should not be considered as the only author responsible for this undertaking (since in one case at least he does not agree with the way the chapters were subdivided)." Riccardo Quinto, "Stephen Langton," in *Mediaeval Commentaries on the Sentences of Peter Lombard*, 2: 36–76, at 43–44, citing in n39 the study of Louis-Jacques Bataillon, "Les douze prophètes enseignés et prêchés par Étienne Langton," in *Étienne Langton: Prédicateur, bibliste et théologien*, ed. Louis-Jacques Bataillon, Nicole Bériou, Gilbert Dahan, and Riccardo Quinto (Turnhout: Brepols, 2010), 427–448, and again in n42 Bataillon's "prudent conclusions" about Langton's role in establishing the new chapter divisions of the Bible.

187 For a comprehensive listing of scholarship on Langton, the best place to start is the chronological bibliography provided by Riccardo Quinto (from the thirteenth century through 1994, the date of his dissertation) in Riccardo Quinto, *Doctor Nominatissimus: Stefano Langton († 1228) e la tradizione delle sue opere*, Beiträge zur Geschichte der Philosophie und Theologie des Mittelalters, Neue Folge 39 (Münster: Aschendorff, 1994), x–xxv. For more recent bibliography, see Riccardo Quinto, "Stephano Langton e la teologia dei maestri secolari di Parigi tra XII e XIII secolo," *Archa Verbi: Yearbook for the Study of Medieval Theology* 5 (2008): 122–142. For the state of scholarship on Langton's *Quaestiones*, see Quinto's article in the proceedings from the international conference on Langton that took place in Paris in 2008: Riccardo Quinto, "La constitution du texte des *Quaestiones theologiae* d'Étienne Langton," in *Étienne Langton*, 525–562. For a revised estimate of Langton's commentary on the *Sentences*, see Riccardo Quinto, "Stephen Langton," in *Mediaeval Commentaries on the Sentences of Peter Lombard*, 2: 36–76. For Langton as preacher, the seminal work is Phyllis B. Roberts, *Stephanus de Lingua-Tonante: Studies in the Sermons of Stephen Langton*, Pontifical Institute

fruits of the longstanding research of Riccardo Quinto and Magdalena Bieniak into Langton's *Quaestiones*.[188] Because Langton's imposing corpus of biblical commentaries, like Comestor's, remains for the most part unedited and unstudied, scholars have not been in a position to understand more completely the nexus between the works of these two great twelfth-century "Masters of the Sacred Page."[189] It was of course this corpus of biblical work that led scholars following Grabmann and Smalley to group Comestor and Langton together, but no one connected the two twelfth-century masters in life because the assumed chronologies made such a connection impossible.

It turns out, however, that Comestor and Langton were in Paris together for a long time.[190] To avoid repetition, I shall do no more than note the fact of their lengthy collaboration here, since I devote Chapters Five, Six, and Seven of this monograph to establishing that Langton also played a key role, if not the key role, in the institutionalization of the *Historia scholastica* as a text, as a textbook, and as a key part of the developing curriculum of the nascent University of Paris. The evidence presented there not only shows that the scholastic careers and *fortunae* of Comestor and Langton are inextricably intertwined but also that Langton carried on faithfully the scholastic project that Comestor had started with the *History*. This fourth and final historiographical context, therefore, is arguably the most important of all, since Langton was in important respects a co-maker of the *History*.[191]

of Mediaeval Studies: Studies and Texts 16 (Toronto: Pontifical Institute of Mediaeval Studies, 1968). See also Riccardo Quinto, "The Influence of Stephen Langton on the Idea of the Preacher in Humbert of Romans' *De Eruditione Predicatorum* and Hugh of St.-Cher's Postille on the Scriptures," in *Christ Among the Medieval Dominicans: Representations of Christ in the Texts and Images of the Order of Preachers*, ed. Kent Emery, Jr. and J. Wawrikow (Notre Dame: University of Notre Dame Press, 1998), 49–91, in which Quinto demonstrates the connection between Langton's preaching and the evangelical movement that led to the founding of the Dominicans.

188 See Stephen Langton, *Quaestiones theologiae: Liber 1*, ed. Riccardo Quinto and Magdalena Bieniak, Auctores Britannici Medii Aevi (Oxford: Oxford University Press, 2014).

189 The designation is Smalley's; see *Study of the Bible*, 196.

190 I set forth the new chronology in detail in Chapter Seven below.

191 See Clark, "Peter Comestor and Stephen Langton."

III. Concluding Observations

The foregoing review of historiography, while explaining to some extent the *History*'s present obscurity, also serves to situate it in four important twelfth-century historical and theological contexts. Comestor's attendance at the Lombard's lectures on the *Sentences* during the 1150s clearly planted the seeds for creating the *History* in light of the fact that the *Sentences* served Comestor extensively as a foundation for a large portion of the *History*.[192] The works of the two Peters, produced at roughly the same time, were complementary products of the same scholastic milieu. Moreover, if the principal inspiration for the subject matter of the *History* came from the Abbey of St. Victor, Comestor developed the means for turning that inspiration into a useful reality in the classrooms of Notre Dame during the 1160s and well into the 1170s, which he spent lecturing on the *Gloss*. It was in those classrooms that he developed and refined his own method of teaching the Bible to students, which he would concretize in the form and structure of the *History*, which would replace the *Gloss* as the textbook for teaching the Bible in the Parisian classrooms of the 1170s and beyond. I shall show that Comestor himself, a reigning Master of Theology in Paris, used the *History* for just this purpose during that decade, as did others such as Jean Beleth and Stephen Langton.

We shall see that the latter's role is especially important, for Langton undertook to carry on Comestor's legacy in the schools. Indeed, Langton was more than just a teacher of the *History*. Even more than Comestor himself, it was Langton who made the *Historia scholastica* an integral part of the curriculum at the developing University of Paris. His growing reputation as a Master of Theology, his persistent attention to his own course on the *History*, and finally his apparent interest in the text of the *History* itself all show sustained commitment on his part to Comestor's legacy and magnum opus.

192 Clark, "Peter Comestor and Peter Lombard."

CHAPTER TWO

Lessons Learned in the Classroom

Comestor's Lectures on the Glossed Gospels

Besides the *Historia scholastica*, the principal surviving works of Peter Comestor are the student reports of his lectures on each of the four Gospels; each is extensive, ranging from fifty to ninety folios on average in the many extant manuscript copies of each commentary.[1] These are important not only because they constitute the surviving record of Comestor's live teaching in Paris but also, as I show in this and the next chapter, because they served as precursors to the *Historia scholastica* in many different respects. To show this, however, requires a preliminary account of Comestor's method of explicating the Gospels to his students.

In general, scholars have overlooked the classrooms of the second half of the twelfth century.[2] Happily, although Comestor's Gospel commentaries have themselves attracted little scholarly attention, two pertinent specialist studies exist. Beryl Smalley's "Peter Comestor on the Gospels and His Sources" was, until quite recently, the sole study to examine them in any depth.[3] As the title of her article suggests, Smalley's principal concern was to discuss "Peter Comestor as a pioneer of lecturing on the gospels at Paris" by focusing on

---

1   Friedrich Stegmüller, *Repertorium Biblicum Medii Aevi*, 9 vols. (Madrid: Instituto Francisco Súarez, 1950–1976), 4: 293–297 (numbers 6575–6578).

2   As Dahan observes, "Malgré le nombre important d'études récentes sur les écoles du XIIe siècle, on possède très peu de données sur les methods d'enseignement et sur les conditions concretes de cet enseignement." Gilbert Dahan, "Une leçon biblique au XIIe siècle: Le commentaire de Pierre le Mangeur sur Matthieu 26, 26–29," in *Ancienne Loi, Nouvelle Loi*, ed. J.-P. Bordier, Littérature et revelation au Moyen Âge 3 (Paris: Université de Paris-Ouest Nanterre-La Défense, 2009), 19–38, at 22, citing relevant literature. I am grateful to Professor Dahan not only for sharing his insights with me in several private conversations but also for having shared this article with me before publication.

3   Beryl Smalley, "Peter Comestor on the Gospels and His Sources," *Recherches de théologie ancienne et médiévale* 46 (1979): 84–129, reprinted in *The Gospels in the Schools, c. 1100 – c. 1280* (London and Ronceverte: The Hambledon Press, 1985), 37–83.

"patristic teaching on the gospels as it passed down to Comestor in the originals and through intermediaries such as the *Gloss*."[4] After sketching salient aspects of the patristic tradition of commentary on the Gospels as well as later Carolingian contributions, Smalley proceeded to identify Comestor's principal sources from his immediate predecessors in the mid-twelfth century, focusing especially on the unidentified author of the *Enarrationes in S. Mattheum*.[5] Dismissing earlier attributions to Anselm of Laon and Geoffrey Babion, Smalley gave her view that this commentary was written c. 1140 by a religious who made use of the *Gloss* and other Laon material, whom she called B and who was important, "because Peter Comestor made so much use of him."[6]

In the second section of her article, Smalley identified B's principal sources and outlined the chief characteristics of his exegesis, focusing particularly on his treatment of those parts of Matthew's Gospel that deal with poverty.[7] In the remainder of her article, Smalley turned her attention to Comestor's Gospel glosses themselves.[8] Because Smalley's insights about Comestor's Gospel commentaries are especially relevant to my own interest in the nexus between his classroom lectures on the Gospels and the *History*, I discuss them, below, in the course of my own exposition of Comestor's method of lecturing on the Glossed Gospels.

The only other specialist study of Comestor's Gospel commentaries is Gilbert Dahan's study of one of Comestor's lectures on the glossed Matthew.[9] His findings, which complement and expand those established by Smalley, are of special interest and relevance to my own inquiry into the ties linking Comestor's *History* to his Gospel glosses, because one of Dahan's principal aims is to explicate the method and structure of Comestor's lessons on the Glossed Gospels. As with Smalley's conclusions, it will be helpful to relate his findings in the context of my own discussion of the features of Comestor's Gospel lectures most germane to the *History* itself.

For this study of Comestor's lectures on the four Glossed Gospels, I use Troyes MS 1024, mainly because it contains copies of all four of Comestor's Gospel lectures and because of the high quality of the manuscript itself. The choice is not arbitrary, for Comestor was himself from Troyes and maintained

---

4   Smalley, *Gospels in the Schools*, 37.
5   See PL 162: 1227–1500, with Smalley, *Gospels in the Schools*, 37–48.
6   Smalley, *Gospels in the Schools*, 48.
7   Ibid., 49–58.
8   Ibid., 58–82.
9   Dahan, "Une leçon biblique."

close ties to it for his entire life.[10] Nor, however, is it ideal, because having consulted the various manuscripts used by Beryl Smalley for her work, I have first-hand knowledge of textual omissions through *homeoteleuta* in Troyes MS 1024.[11] Nevertheless, its text is perfectly adequate for my purposes of communicating an accurate understanding of the salient features of Comestor's method in his lectures.

Throughout this study, as in the editions I am currently preparing of Comestor's *History* and Langton's commentaries on that work, I demarcate all lemmata, scriptural or otherwise, by SMALL CAPITALS; I follow conventional practice in italicizing scriptural lemmata. Thus, for Comestor's commentaries on the Glossed Gospels that I quote, I set off Comestor's citation to Scripture and to individual glosses in capital letters, italicizing the former. For ease in following his outline, I highlight in bold typeface the word **"glosa,"** which he uses frequently to direct his students' attention to a particular gloss in their text of the *Gloss*. For the sake of convenience I use the Rusch edition of the *Gloss*.[12] I do so in spite of the fact that Comestor's quotations from the *Gloss* make clear that the Rusch edition is only a rough approximation of the version of the Gloss with which Comestor was working in the 1160s and 1170s.

I. *Comestor's Classroom Experience*

Before examining Comestor's lectures on the Glossed Gospels, there are two preliminary and related questions to consider: what exactly was Comestor lecturing on? and how should we classify these works of Comestor? Smalley did not address the first question directly but seemed to assume that Comestor and

---

10   See the evidence presented in Sandra Rae Karp, "Peter Comestor's *Historia scholastica*: A Study in the Development of Literal Scriptural Exegesis" (Ph.D. diss., Tulane University, 1978; Ann Arbor: University Microfilms, 1982), 1–55, esp. 42–55.

11   Smalley, *Gospels in the Schools*, 58–62.

12   Like Dahan, I use the Rusch edition of the *Gloss* for convenience, although Comestor's quotations from the *Gloss* do not always line up with the Rusch edition: see *Biblia Latina cum Glossa Ordinaria: Facsimile Reprint of the Editio Princeps Adolph Rusch of Strassburg 1480/81*, introd. Karlfried Froehlich and Margaret T. Gibson, 4 vols. (Turnhout: Brepols, 1992). I typically cite G for the *Gloss*, and either GM, for the *Glossa marginalis*, or GI, for the *Glossa interlinearis*, so that the reader may be able quickly to locate the gloss that I am citing. It should be noted that Comestor and Langton frequently make the same distinction, so my practice is in line with the authors upon whom this study is based with regard to the *Gloss*.

his students had everything that they needed with the biblical *Gloss* alone, for she related his practice of lecturing first by delivering his own prologue, of devoting his second lecture to the prologue to the particular book of the Glossed Bible at issue, and of proceeding thereafter to lecture on what she called the commentary itself.[13] Smalley was mistaken in attributing to Comestor himself the prologues that head the four Glossed Gospels.[14] Nonetheless, for my purposes here it is sufficient to take note of the basic structure that she identified.

As for the second question, she named these "Comestor's commentaries on all four gospels."[15] Dahan follows Smalley in referring to "son commentaire des quatre Évangiles."[16] He distinguishes, however, between Comestor's works and what he calls the true commentaries on the *Gloss* that appear at the end of the twelfth century, namely the commentaries of Langton and others on the Lombard's *Magna glosatura* of the Pauline epistles and of other books.[17]

For several reasons I am convinced that this distinction is inapposite. First, Comestor's lectures on the Glossed Gospels show already the formal elements for a commentary in the strict sense now supposed by scholars to have been adopted only in the thirteenth century. Second, Comestor and his students had in front of them the *Magna glosatura* for the Gospels, and I have good reason to think that this was Peter Lombard's own work.[18] Here, however, it suffices to document the fact that Comestor and his students were using a Great Gloss for Luke.

Thus, for example, while lecturing on Elizabeth's unexpected pregnancy in her old age, Comestor directs his students to the scriptural words, "occulta-

---

13 Smalley, *Gospels in the Schools*, 62–65.

14 I show Smalley's mistake, showing that Peter Lombard initiated this practice and also that Comestor made use of his master's prologue on the Glossed John in my article: Mark J. Clark, "The Biblical *Gloss*, the Search for the Lombard's Glossed Bible, and the School of Paris," *Mediaeval Studies* 76 (2014): 57–113.

15 Smalley, *Gospels in the Schools*, 58.

16 Dahan, "Une leçon biblique," 20.

17 Ibid., 23: "Cette explication prend appui sur la *Glossa*. Il ne s'agit pas d'un commentaire de celle-ci: à la fin du XIIe siècle, nous trouvons des œuvres qui sont de vrais commentaires de la *Glossa ordinaria*, surtout sur les épîtres pauliniennes (il s'agit en fait de la *Magna glossatura* de Pierre Lombard) mais aussi sur d'autres livres."

18 For evidence that shows the need to reopen the search for the remainder of the Lombard's glossed Bible (that is, all of the books lectured on by the Lombard other than the ones known to scholars, namely the Psalms and the Pauline Epistles), see Clark, "The Search for the Lombard's Glossed Bible."

bat se."[19] He then explicates these words by lecturing on a series of marginal glosses, each of which give an account of Elizabeth's behavior in hiding herself for five months.[20] I am interested here in the last of these, in which Comestor paraphrases the gloss, adding to its explanation of Elizabeth's actions some practical wisdom of his own:

> **Gloss** about the same thing: SHE WAS HIDING HERSELF on account of prudence, that is knowingly and on purpose, not wishing suddenly to reveal her pregnancy. For often women are deceived, thinking that they had conceived when they had not. And therefore she wants to test whether it is true that she had conceived.[21]

Comestor then cautions his students about the middle portion of a gloss that follows, telling them:

> Dismiss the middle portion of the gloss that follows ... . For it is annulled with the *Great Gloss*. Pass over, therefore, for now that middle portion of that gloss and take up there: TO TAKE AWAY MY DISGRACE. And a gloss follows this text: of sterility and conception in her old age ... namely to conceive in her old age was a disgrace among men but not with God.[22]

The text to which Comestor refers his students following his directive to skip over the middle of the gloss appears in the Rusch edition as the last part

---

19 Troyes, Bibliothèque municipale, MS 1024, fol. 144rb, middle, in which Comestor refers to GM, Luc. 1.24 ad loc., 4: 141, col. a, marginal gloss 5. For ease of reference, I follow Dahan's practice of numbering the marginal and interlinear glosses, starting from 1, as here. Cf. Dahan, "Une leçon biblique," 23–24.

20 See Troyes, MS 1024, fol. 144rb, middle, in which Comestor refers to GM, Luc. 1.24 ad loc., 4: 141, col. a, marginal glosses 4, 5, and 6.

21 Troyes, MS 1024, fol. 144rb, middle, in which Comestor refers to GM, Luc. 1.24 ad loc., 4: 141, col. a, marginal gloss 6: "**Glosa** de eodem: OCCULTABAT SE propter prudentiam id est scienter et ex industria nolens subito revelare conceptum. Falluntur enim sepe mulieres putantes se concepisse, cum non conceperint. Et ideo vult probare, si verum esset quod conceperit."

22 Troyes, MS 1024, fol. 144rb, middle, in which Comestor refers to GM, Luc. 1.24 ad loc., 4: 141, col. a, marginal gloss 6: "Meditullium glose quod sequitur dimitte ... . Negetur cum magna Glosa. Transi ergo ad presens illud meditullium et sume ibi: AUFERRE OBPROBRIUM. Et prosequitur **glosa** textum: sterilitatis et conceptionis in senectute ... scilicet concipere in senectute obprobrium apud homines non apud Deum."

of the sixth gloss of the left-hand column of page 141. Although we cannot be certain that the gloss to which Comestor was referring is the middle portion of that same gloss we see in the Rusch edition – "For five months, that is the five ages of the world or the five books of Moses"[23] – for he does not specify the text, it does seem likely, for a short time later in his lecture, while discussing at length problems in dating correctly the conception of the Savior, Comestor tells his students: "From this was taken that middle gloss that you had dismissed."[24] The middle portion of that gloss just quoted does accord perfectly with the context of his remarks: "... by the five months since Elizabeth had conceived ... are signified the five books of Moses ... or the five ages of the world."[25]

Whatever its exact text, however, it is clear from Comestor's words ("For it is annulled with the *Great Gloss*") that the gloss to which he was referring was rendered obsolete by the *Magna glosatura*. The very fact that he and his students had the Great Gloss for the Gospels is news indeed.[26] Moreover, the fact that by the 1160s masters of theology were lecturing on the *Magna glosatura* for the Gospels makes me hesitant to distinguish Comestor's commentaries from those of Langton and others in the later twelfth century, as Dahan does, on the basis that Langton and other late twelfth-century masters were commenting formally on the *Magna glosatura*, while Comestor was not. This is not to deny that real distinctions do exist between Comestor's commentaries and those of Langton on Scripture, but I would be very cautious about coming to any conclusions at this point about what version or versions of the *Gloss* were being used and when in the latter half of the twelfth century.

I also have reservations about Dahan's view that Comestor was using the *Gloss* as a reference text complementing another and separate biblical text, and that since Comestor was not really lecturing on the *Gloss* per se, these are not

23 GM, Luc. 1.24 ad loc., 4: 141, col. a, marginal gloss 6: "Mensibus quinque, hoc est quinque milibus seculi sive quinque libris Moysi."

24 Troyes, MS 1024, fol. 144vb, top: "De hoc sumptum est illud meditullium glose quod dimiseras." This particular directive of Comestor's is all the more fascinating, because it is bracketed and set off as a note to the text. It is easy to imagine the student reporter framing as a note something that Comestor added as an aside to his lecture.

25 Troyes, MS 1024, fol. 144va, bottom – fol. 144vb, top: "per quinque menses quibus conceptus Elisabeth ... significantur quinque libri Moysi ... vel quinque mundi etates ... ."

26 For more evidence that Comestor and his students had a Great Gloss on Luke in front of them, see the text quoted in Chapter Three at n39.

commentaries in the strict sense.[27] I am not sure that Dahan is correct. My view is that neither Comestor nor his students were going back and forth between different volumes, the one the text of the Bible and the other the text of the *Gloss*, but rather between the biblical text set forth in the *Gloss* and the various interlinear and marginal glosses that surrounded it on the same page. Moreover, although Comestor's lectures address both the scriptural text and the attached glosses, it is clear that for Comestor the importance of explicating the glosses rivals, if not supersedes, that of explicating the biblical text itself.

To understand better these questions, to get a feeling for the substance and style of Comestor's classroom teaching, and especially to have a solid understanding of his method of proceeding so as to be able to compare his method in the *History* itself, it would be helpful at this point to see Comestor in action. Because Comestor begins his *Historia evangelica* with three chapters treating in that order the conception of the Baptist, the conception of the Savior, and the birth of the Baptist, all of which are dealt with in the first chapter of Luke's Gospel, it will be convenient to focus here on Comestor's treatment of that same material.

Here too, however, we run into a preliminary obstacle. As Smalley pointed out, Comestor led his students through the Glossed Gospels by means of a series of lectures.[28] There are, however, no indications by the student reporters where one lecture ends and another begins.[29] As Dahan notes, this is a serious impediment for anyone trying to understand the structure of Comestor's courses on the Glossed Gospels, for unlike the student reports that have come down to us from the thirteenth century, which make clear the divisions of the magisterial lectures, these *reportationes* are continuous.[30]

27 Dahan, "Une leçon biblique," 23: "Ici, la *Glossa* sert seulement de texte de référence ou d'aide, dans un mouvement d'aller et retour frequent, de l'évangile à la Glose. Contrairement à ce qui a pu être dit ici ou là, la *Glossa* est matériellement présente: le maître dispose probablement d'un texte de Matthieu avec la *Glossa*."
28 Smalley, *Gospels in the Schools*, 62–65. As the title of his article makes clear, Dahan refers to each lecture as a "leçon": see Dahan, "Une leçon biblique," 23.
29 Both Smalley and Dahan note the ubiquity of the evidence signaling the reporter's presence: Smalley, *Gospels in the Schools*, 61; Dahan, "Une leçon biblique," 24.
30 Dahan, "Une leçon biblique," 22: "Nous nous heurtons à une première difficulté: comment delimiter les leçons? Alors que dans l'exégèse du XIIIe siècle, les reportationes se découpent selon le rythme des leçons du maître – meme si nous sommes parfois surprise des differences parfois considérables dans la dimension de ces leçons – ici, le commentaire est continu, meme pas rythmé par un decoupage en chapîtres." Dahan further notes that Comestor's predecessors, including his near contemporary Zachary of Besançon, divided their treatment of the Gospels into sections as established by Eusebius. Ibid., 22–23 and n14.

Comestor's lectures on the beginning of Luke's Gospel illustrate beautifully the difficulty, for it is well nigh impossible to know for sure where his lecture on Luke's prologue ends and his treatment of the Gospel narrative begins. The reason for this is that, although the textual demarcation in Luke's Gospel is explicit, Comestor does not make a clear distinction between his explication of the prologues, and in particular his portrait of Luke the historiographer, and that part of Luke's Gospel that begins the historical narrative proper, namely the coming of the Baptist and the Savior.[31] Instead, he begins the *Historia evangelica* with the coming of the precursor, John the Baptist, starting with that passage from the first chapter, fifth verse of Luke's Gospel: "Fuit in diebus Herodis Regis Iudeae." For the sake of convenience, therefore, I shall take up my explication of his lectures on the *Gloss* at the same place, even if it is possible that I am stepping into the middle of one of Comestor's lectures. For my purposes, however, this makes no difference; what is important is what Smalley refers to as "Comestor's obsessive care to 'order' the glosses in relation to the text."[32]

a. *Ordering Biblical Text and Glosses*

Comestor's method in his lectures on the Glossed Gospels remains the same throughout; in general, he goes back and forth between the biblical lemmata and the glosses that relate to them.[33] As a rule, the biblical lemmata are brief; Comestor cites just enough of the scriptural text to enable his students to follow his lecture on the various glosses. Often this is just one word, as here, *Fuit*, which Comestor refers to after having just addressed two marginal glosses: that beginning with the word "prolixiorem" and attributed to Ambrose; and the next beginning with the name "Theophilus," attributed to Bede.[34]

At this point in his lecture, Comestor is focusing on Luke as historiographer, as is clear from what he tells his students after introducing the lemma, *fuit*:

---

31   I should note too that Comestor was not yet working with the modern chapter divisions, which as Dahan points out come into common usage in the early thirteenth century with the spread of the so-called "Paris Bibles." Dahan, "Une leçon biblique," 22–23 n14. Nevertheless, for the sake of convenience, I shall make frequent use of the modern chapter divisions to make it easier to follow Comestor.

32   Smalley, *Gospels in the Schools*, 65.

33   Dahan's description – "dans un movement d'aller et retour fréquent" – is both accurate and felicitous. Dahan, "Une leçon biblique," 23.

34   GM, Luc. 1.5 *ad loc.*, 4: 139, col. a, marginal glosses 11 and 12.

He was Luke, who is going to treat the history of the Lord's coming in the flesh, begins from the arrival of the precursor who is not far off from the coming of the Savior. Whence it is clear that he does not begin from too far back, for it is not customary that the arrival of their vanguard anticipate by much the arrival of the lords. For whenever we see the vanguard of a king or some powerful personage enter a city, then we are certain that his arrival will be next. Luke, therefore, begins with the father of the precursor, namely Zachariah, and follows the usage of the historiographer: determining about Zachariah his position and his wife and where he lives and who was king during his lifetime, since historiographers are accustomed to ascertain with precision all of those circumstances that concern those about whom they are writing.[35]

Comestor here takes pains to justify as historiographically fitting the evangelist's decision to start with the coming of the Baptist, the precursor to the coming of the Lord. In particular, he situates Luke's decision to begin his narrative with the Baptist's father, Zachary, about whom he supplies the most important circumstances of his life and times, in the context of the standards of historiography. Comestor cites another marginal gloss that supports what he has just said about Luke as historiographer: "**Gloss**: HE FULFILLED THE ORDER, that is, the convention of a historiographer."[36] Comestor has evident respect for the methods of those writing history, and he makes sure that his students know that Luke meets their high standards.

Comparing Comestor's words to the *Gloss* itself reveals that Comestor paraphrased it: "*A CERTAIN PRIEST ETC.* HE FULFILLED THE ORDER. He named the king and the region in which he was; he speaks about the priest and his people

---

35   Troyes, MS 1024, fol. 142va, bottom – 142vb, top: "*FUIT* Tractaturus Luchas hystoriam dominici adventus in carnem, inchoat ab adventu precursoris, qui non multum est alienus ab adventu Salvatoris. Unde patet quod non incipit a nimis remoto, quia non solet adventus precursoris multum alienus esse ab adventu dominorum. Cum enim videmus precursores regis vel alicuius potentis ingredi civitatem, iam certi sumus de proximo eius adventu. Incipit ergo a patre precursoris scilicet Zacharia et sequitur ydioma hystoriographi, determinando circa Zachariam officium eius et uxorem et regionem et regem cuius tempore fuit, quia has omnes circumstantias circa eos de quibus narrant solent hystoriographi determinare."

36   Troyes, MS 1024, fol. 142vb, top: "**Glosa**: IMPLEVIT ORDINEM, id est morem hystoriographi."

and his wife."[37] We see further that in his remarks Comestor attached the substance of this marginal gloss to a different scriptural lemma than that provided by his predecessor, the glossator.[38] Finally, we note as well that he first paraphrased the gloss before citing it in support of what he had just said.

Comestor next directed his students to an interlinear gloss after specifying another word of Scripture:

> OF HEROD. **Gloss**: ALREADY THERE WAS REIGNING A FOREIGNER, as if the glossator were saying that Luke does not begin from too far back, since the anointing, which was a sign of the coming of the Lord in the immediate future, had already ceased, already I say both anointings had ceased, namely the royal and the priestly. For the Kingdom of the Jews had already been transferred to Herod, who was a foreigner and an Idumean by race, even though he had undertaken circumcision. And the legal privileges of the priests were also being sold by the Romans, and so in a certain way the anointing of the priesthood had already ceased.[39]

We here notice several new things. First, Comestor does not refer to the interlinear gloss by another name but calls it simply a gloss, as with his references to marginal glosses.[40] Second, he continues with the theme that he had been developing in his lecture, namely that Luke's choice of beginning for the Gospel narrative was not too far removed from his principal subject, that is, the com-

---

37 GM, Luc. 1.5 *ad loc.*, 4: 139, col. a, marginal gloss 14: "*SACERDOS QUIDEM ETC.* IMPLEVIT ORDINEM: Dixit regem et regionem in qua fuit; sacerdotem et gentem eius et uxorem illius indicat."

38 As Smalley notes, Comestor routinely distinguishes between the *glosator*, who was responsible for compiling and editing the individual glosses, and the *expositor*, the original commentator whose gloss the former excerpted. Smalley, *Gospels in the Schools*, 65.

39 Troyes, MS 1024, fol. 142vb, top: "*HERODIS* **Glosa**: IAM REGNABAT ALIENIGENA, quasi diceret glosator non incipit a nimis remoto, quia iam cessabat unctio, quod erat signum dominici adventus in proximo futuri, iam inquam cessabat utraque unctio scilicet et regalis et sacerdotalis. Iam enim translatum erat regnum Iudeorum ad Herodem, qui erat alienigena et Ydumeus genere, licet susceperit circumcisionem. Et legalia sacerdotium etiam iam vendebatur a Romanis, et ita quodammodo cessabat iam unctio sacerdotii."

40 Dahan points out that elsewhere Comestor does distinguish between marginal and interlinear glosses, referring to the former as *glosa* and the latter as *interlinearis*. Dahan, "Une leçon biblique," 24. I am not sure what to make of the difference in practice. It may be that at some point in his career as a lecturer Comestor changed practices, or it may be that his own classroom practices differed from time to time.

ing of the Savior. Third, Comestor injects himself into the scene ("inquam") and adds a good bit of explanation to what his students had before them in the pithy marginal gloss.

Comestor then notes a third word of Sacred Scripture from the same line: "*PRIEST*" ("sacerdos" in Latin); this lemma precedes another ("A PRIESTLY SACRIFICIAL CALF").[41] Comestor's citation to the marginal gloss in question serves as prelude to his own paraphrased version of its substance: both Luke and his Gospel were prefigured in the Old Testament, which also takes its point of departure from the priesthood, and in the New, by the Passion of Christ, who offered up himself for us as it were as a sacrificial calf.[42] Comestor then explicates for a second time the same word ("sacerdos") in Luke's text, lecturing on King David's expansion of the priesthood.[43] After his remarks, Comestor refers his students to the marginal gloss whose substance he had just greatly expanded.[44]

We see in these two segments of Comestor's lecture several more salient features of his method of proceeding in the classroom. First, as in the *Gloss* itself, the theme of the congruence of the Old and the New Testaments is never far from Comestor's thoughts, and he takes every opportunity, as here, to develop it. Interestingly, the substance of the first marginal gloss cited and subsequently paraphrased by Comestor was attached in the *Gloss* not to "sacerdos" but to "fuit," which Comestor had already cited and discussed.[45] This suggests that Comestor was re-ordering the glosses, both marginal and interlinear, in relation to Scripture.

After this brief survey, we are poised to understand the salient features of Comestor's method of ordering and re-ordering both the scriptural text and the glosses set forth in the *Gloss*. Comestor cites either a word from Scripture or a few words from a gloss, marginal or interlinear, to signal to his students the

---

41 Troyes, MS 1024, fol. 142vb, top: "*SACERDOS* **Glosa**: VITULUS SACERDOTALIS HOSTIA."

42 Troyes, MS 1024, fol. 142vb, top: "*SACERDOS* **Glosa**: VITULUS SACERDOTALIS HOSTIA, quasi diceret glosator hoc evangelium inchoat a sacerdote, ideo congrue per vitulum, qui erat oblatio sacerdotum. In Veteri Testamento prefiguratum est hoc evangelium, id est hic evangelista, quod et a sacerdote inchoatur, et in Novo Testamento, id est in passione Christi, qui quasi vitulus pro nobis immolatus est."

43 Troyes, MS 1024, fol. 142vb.

44 Troyes, MS 1024, fol. 142vb, top-middle, referring to GM, Luc. 1.5 *ad loc.*, 4: 139, col. b, marginal gloss 5: "**Glosa**: CUM DAVID ETC."

45 Troyes, MS 1024, fol. 142vb, top-middle, referring to GM, Luc. 1.5 *ad loc.*, 4: 139, col. a, marginal gloss 13: "*FUIT IN DIEBUS*. Ambrosius. VITULUS SACERDOTALIS HOSTIA: Per vitulum ergo hoc evangelium figuratum, in quo a sacerdotibus inchoatur et in vitulo consummatur id est in Christo qui pro mundi vita immolator."

end of one thought and the beginning of another. As we have seen, this does not mean that Comestor changes topics or themes. To the contrary, he often continues to develop the same themes. Nevertheless, these lemmata, scriptural or taken from the glosses in the *Gloss*, constitute directional signposts. They are the skeletal framework of his lectures. Sometimes, as we have seen, they initiate a new direction or explication. At other times, they bring it to a close. Comestor often cites a gloss in support of what he has just said. Just as often he cites a gloss before he explicates its substance. To better understand how Comestor integrates in his lectures this treatment of Scripture and gloss, it would be helpful first to look more closely at each separately.

Taking first his method of dealing with Scripture, Comestor proceeds slowly through the text of Scripture that he is discussing, even though he frequently backtracks to pick up either texts that he missed or to treat a different sense of the same texts. Thus, Comestor proceeds in order through Luke 1.5 ("Fuit in diebus Herodis regis Iudeae sacerdos quidam nomine Zacharias de vice Abia"), lecturing on most of these words.[46] After skipping ahead to "apparuit ei angelus" – his own paraphrase of a phrase from Luke 1.11 – Comestor returns several times to discuss alternative interpretations of "de vice Abia."[47] He then picks up and discusses scriptural phrases that he had initially passed over: "Erant autem ambo iusti ante Deum," "incedentes in omnibus mandates et iustificationibus Dei," "Et non erat," "Factum est autem," etc.[48] In doing so, however, he switches from literal to figurative explication of these scriptural lemmata.[49] The important point here is that in each case, both in his initial literal explication and his subsequent figurative elaboration, Comestor works slowly and surely forward through Luke's text.

By contrast, Comestor's ordering of the various glosses displayed in the *Gloss* is much less predictable; one never knows to which gloss he will go next. Nonetheless, what is patent is the care that he takes to order them for his students.[50] A typical example that illumines both points is Comestor's discussion of the exchange between Zachary and Gabriel following the angel's promise

46 Troyes, MS 1024, fol. 142vb, bottom.
47 Ibid.
48 Troyes, MS 1024, fol. 142vb, bottom – fol. 143ra, top.
49 Troyes, MS 1024, fol. 143ra, top: "Hee omnes <glose> sunt de littera. De mistico intellectu habes ... ." I discuss this feature of Comestor's method of lecturing in the next section: "History and Mystery."
50 Like Smalley, Dahan is struck by Comestor's constant solicitude to order the text for his students: "Ce qui est fascinant dans ce texte (comme dans l'ensemble des

that Elizabeth would bear him a son, which Luke goes into at great length but which Comestor relates concisely: "the angel promised Zachary that a son would be born ... ."[51] Comestor, having summarized Gabriel's promises to Zachary (Luke 1.13–17), proceeds to gloss separately and preliminarily the scriptural phrases in Luke 1.18 that relate Zachary's response: "How may I know this?"; "I am an old man"; "my wife is advanced in years."[52] He then tells his students that Gabriel's twofold response, namely that he stands before the throne of God and also that he was sent to Zachary, seems to be impossible: "Note that he says two things that seem unable to be at the same time, namely 'I stand before God' and 'I was sent to you.' Note therefore that to wherever an angel be sent, everywhere he finds the presence of God, since God is everywhere."[53]

At this point, Comestor refers his students to the first of three successive glosses on this issue. Paraphrasing the ninth marginal gloss on the right-hand column, he notes: "About this you have **the gloss**, SINCE TO US ETC. Even if an angel is a circumscribed spirit, that is, a being such that it is in one place and not in another, it is not circumscribed <in another sense>, that is, restricted by the boundary of a place ... ."[54] Comestor next directs his students to the preceding marginal gloss, the eighth set forth on the page, telling them: "... now read that one: ON ACCOUNT OF THE ALTITUDE ETC."[55] Last of all,

---

commentaries sur les évangiles de Pierre le Mangeur) est le va-et-vient constant, du texte biblique à la *Glossa*. Le reportateur a conserve les consignes très concretes du maître à ses disciples. Presque toutes invitent à se reporter au texte biblique ou à la glose." Dahan, "Une leçon biblique," 24.

51 Troyes, MS 1024, fol. 143vb, bottom: "Promisit angelus Zacharie filium nasciturum ... ."

52 Troyes, MS 1024, fol. 143vb, bottom: "Unde hoc sciam," "ego sum senex," "uxor mea processit in diebus suis."

53 Troyes, MS 1024, fol. 143vb, bottom – 144ra, top: "Nota quia duo dicit que videntur non posse simul esse scilicet 'assisto ante Deum' et 'missus sum ad te'. Ideo nota quia quocumque mittatur angelus ubique invenit presentiam Dei, quia Deus ubique est."

54 Troyes, MS 1024, fol. 144ra, top: "De hoc habes **glosam**, cum ad nos etc. Etsi angelus est spiritus circumscriptus id est ita ens in uno loco quod non in alio, non circumscriptus id est loci termino clausus ... ." The marginal gloss paraphrased by Comestor (GM, Luc. 1.19 *ad loc.*, 4: 140, col. b, marginal gloss 9) reads follows: "*ANTE DEUM*. Beda. CUM AD NOS veniunt angeli, sic exterius implent ministerium ut tum ante deum interius per contemplationem assistant. Quia et si angelus est spiritus circumscriptus, summus spiritus qui deus est incircumscriptus est, intra quem currit angelus quocumque movetur vel mittatur."

55 Troyes, MS 1024, fol. 144ra, top: "... modo lege illam, PROPTER ALTITUDINEM ETC." Comestor's reference is to GM, Luc. 1.19 *ad loc.*, 4, p. 140, col. b, marginal gloss 8: "Beda. Propter altitudinem promissorum dubitat signum inquirens quomodo credere valeat ... ."

Comestor directs his students to the seventh marginal gloss, placing the last first and the first last, saying simply: "... after that one this one: IF IT WERE A MAN ETC."[56] Comestor has turned the glossator's order upside down, taking three successive marginal glosses in reverse order, in order to present the material of the *Gloss* in a way he thinks best suited to his students' understanding. Moreover, it is evident that to follow his directions, his students must have in front of them some version of the text of the *Gloss*; this suggests that some version of the *pecia* system was already in place by the 1160s.[57]

Taking then Comestor's treatment of the scriptural text and glosses as an integrated whole, we find a mixed priority. Comestor uses Scripture to organize the themes of his lectures but devotes considerably more time to explicating the many glosses that surround the scriptural text. In part, of course, this was a practical result of lecturing on the *Gloss*, whose pages contained far more gloss than Scripture. But reading through Comestor's commentaries on the four Glossed Gospels has persuaded me that something else was at work as well: his desire to reorganize, expand upon, or abbreviate the *Gloss*. Comestor was not just making use of ready-to-hand glosses to shed light on Scripture, although as we have already seen he did so frequently, repeating those glosses by means of paraphrase. He also devoted a great deal of time to lecturing on the glosses themselves, in the process focusing the attention of his students more on the glosses in question than on the scriptural text to which they were attached.

Comestor's lectures on the various episodes in Luke's infancy contain many typical examples, but two will suffice here to make the point. Although both come from Comestor's lecture on the Annunciation, I will present them here in reverse order, beginning with Mary's question to Gabriel: "How will this take place, since I do not yet know man?"[58] Comestor has just cited Gabriel's promise that Mary's son will reign "in eternum," referring his students to the corresponding interlinear gloss and restating it for them: "*FOR EVER*. **Gloss**: IN THE PRESENT LIFE, truly as it were for ever, since both here and in the

---

56 Troyes, MS 1024, fol. 144ra, top: "... post ea illam: SI HOMO ETC." Comestor's reference here is to GM, Luc. 1.19 *ad loc.*, 4: 140, col. b, marginal gloss 7: "unde hoc sciam. Beda. Si homo esset qui promittebat impune liceret querere signum ... ."

57 Dahan agrees that Comestor's students must also have had in front of them a copy, however modest, of the *Gloss*. Dahan, "Une leçon biblique," 23.

58 GM, Luc. 1.34 *ad loc.*, 4: 142, col. a: "Quomodo fiet istud, quoniam virum non cognosco?"

future ... ."[59] He now introduces Mary's question with his own gloss, explaining that she does not doubt that Gabriel's words will come true but only questions the manner of their fulfillment.[60] To support his position, Comestor directs his students to a marginal gloss, whose substance he concisely paraphrases: "**Gloss**: SHE HAD READ, namely in Isaiah that a virgin would give birth, and she knew that she was a virgin. Therefore, she did not doubt that this could be fulfilled in her own person. Therefore, she seeks to know the manner, which had not been prophesied but which had been reserved to the angel."[61]

Having already introduced, cited, and paraphrased one marginal gloss addressing Mary's question, Comestor now refers his students to another, which preceded the one just discussed and in which the glossator raised the following question: "*HOW WILL THIS HAPPEN*. Ambrose. Since Sarah laughed about God's promise and Mary said — *how will this happen, since I do not know man?* — why were they not mute like Zachary?"[62] Comestor did not here summarize or paraphrase the gloss but instead re-presented the whole thing to his students in his own words and in a more scholastic format:

> **Another gloss**: CUM SARAH ETC. The glossator poses the question why, since each woman, namely both Mary and Sarah, had hesitated about the promise, was the punishment of silence not inflicted on them as on Zachary? For we read about Sarah that ... she burst into laughter at the angel's promise and that, laughing under her breath, she said, how could this happen for me such that we could conceive? The solution is that neither of the women had doubts about the fulfillment but about the manner, but Zachary did not believe in the fulfillment but admitted openly that he

59 Troyes, MS 1024, fol. 145va, middle-bottom: "*IN ETERNUM*. **Glosa**: IN PRESENTI, quasi vere in eternum quia et hic et in futuro ... ." Comestor here refers to GI, Luc. 1.34 *ad loc.*, 4: 142, col. a, interlinear gloss 1.

60 Troyes, MS 1024, fol. 145va, middle-bottom: "*QUOMODO FIET ISTUD, QUONIAM VIRUM NON COGNOSCO* id est non agnoscere in proposito ... ecce non dubitat quin impleatur sed de modo implecionis; ideo ait, *quomodo*, ut sint due dictions quasi modum quero sed de impletione non hesito ... ."

61 Troyes, MS 1024, fol. 145va, middle-bottom: "**Glosa**: legerat scilicet in Ysaya virginem parituram, et sciebat se virginem. Ideo non dubitabat hoc in se posse impleri. Ideo modum querit, qui non erat prophetatus sed angelo reservatus." Comestor here refers to GM, Luc. 1.34 *ad loc.*, 4: 142, col. a, marginal gloss 4.

62 GM, Luc. 1.34 *ad loc.*, 4: 142, col. a, marginal gloss 3: "*QUOMODO FIET*. Ambrosius. Cum Sara risit de promissione dei et Maria dixit, quomodo fiet istud quum virum non cognosco, cur non fuerunt mute sicut Zacharias?"

did not know, asking how will I know this, as if to say, I do not know that this will be fulfilled ... .[63]

Both the gloss and Comestor's restatement are of special interest, for they show clearly that the practice of raising and answering questions was already in use, even among the makers of the *Gloss*. Indeed, Comestor's re-presentation reveals a more developed format, namely that of an explicit framework of question posed and solution offered, which would become the standard scholastic format by the end of the century.[64] Moreover, Comestor's re-presentation of the marginal gloss betrays his own keen interest in the question posed; his version is not only differently organized but also more complete in the substance and development of each point. Indeed, his whole treatment of Mary's question centers on the glosses surrounding this scriptural text in the *Gloss*, and his method goes far beyond merely repeating the substance of those glosses. Instead he directs the attention of his students from the scriptural text to the glosses themselves, explicating to be sure the scriptural text at issue but also unpacking for his students in a variety of ways the content of the glosses themselves. He is in fact lecturing on the *Gloss* and not on Scripture, on the Glossed Luke and not on Luke.[65] The consequence is that Comestor spends considerably more time explicating the glosses than he does Scripture.

The second example arises in the context of Comestor's lecturing on the many layers of significance attached to Gabriel's having appeared to Mary in the sixth month of Elizabeth's pregnancy ("Mense autem sexto"). Comestor first directs his students' attention to Mary herself, beginning with the lemma, "TO

---

63 Troyes, MS 1024, fol. 145va, middle-bottom: "**alia**: CUM SARA ETC. Movet questionem glosator cum utraque scilicet et Maria et Sara de promissione hesitaverit, quare non eis est inflicta pena taciturnitatis sicut Zacharie? De Sara enim legitur quod ... ad promissionem angeli prorupit in chachinnum et subridens ait, quomodo possit hoc fieri de me ut conciperemur. Solutio est quod neutra earum dubitavit de impletione sed de modo, sed Zacharias implendum non credidit sed se nescire professus est, inquirens *unde hoc sciam* quasi nescio implendum ... ." Comestor here refers to GM, Luc. 1.34 *ad loc.*, 4: 142, col. a, marginal gloss 3.

64 There are sufficient question/response texts in Comestor's lectures to question Dahan's rather sharp distinction between Comestor and his successors in the schools: "Contrairement à ce qui sera le cas chez Pierre le Chantre et, surtout, chez Étienne Langton, ces difficultés ne sont pas énoncées dans la forme proper de la question (*Queritur utrum* ou simplement *questio*) mais ce sont bien des interrogations qui sont à chaque fois sous-entendues." Dahan, "Une leçon biblique," 28.

65 Dahan emphasizes this very point. Ibid., 22–25.

A VIRGIN," and commenting that the marginal gloss, "WOMAN BY THE DEVIL ETC.," attached by the glossator to these words was "an elegant adaptation through antithesis."[66] Citing the next word from the Gospel, "betrothed," Comestor again directs his students to a corresponding marginal gloss.[67]

This time, however, Comestor is not content simply to refer his students to the somewhat lengthy gloss in question but instead organizes it for them, telling them to distinguish in it six separate causes why the Lord wished to be born from a mother betrothed to Joseph. Although Comestor expands considerably what the glossator had pithily written, he nevertheless lists the first five without much explication apart from several additional lines clarifying the meaning of each cause: first, that Jesus would be from Joseph's line; second, that Mary might not be found pregnant without a husband, which would make her seem like an adulteress; third, that she would have someone to console her, for a woman needs the consolation of a man; fourth, that Joseph would be able to bear witness to her status as a virgin; fifth, that the mystery of the Incarnation would remain hidden from the Devil, who would think Mary pregnant by Joseph.[68] All five reasons can be found in the marginal gloss itself, albeit more concisely stated, yet Comestor makes sure that his students not only focus on but also distinguish clearly each of the five causes listed by the glossator.

In restating, however, the sixth cause why Jesus wanted to be born from a betrothed mother, Comestor not only expanded what was written in the *Gloss* but also arguably read into it far more than was there. The glossator had written: "Also, greater credence is ascribed to the words of Mary and reason for a lie removed. For it would seem that an unmarried virgin had meant to cover up

---

66   Troyes, MS 1024, fol. 144vb, top: "*AD VIRGINEM.* **Glosa**: MULIER A DYABOLO ETC. Elegans adaptio per antitesin." Comestor here references GM, Luc. 1.27 *ad loc.*, 4: 141, col. b, marginal gloss 3.

67   Troyes, MS 1024, fol. 144vb, top: "*DESPONSATAM.* **Glosa**: DE DESPONSATA ETC." Comestor here refers his students to GM, Luc. 1.27 *ad loc.*, 4: 141, col. b, marginal gloss 4.

68   Troyes, MS 1024, fol. 144vb, middle-bottom – fol. 145ra, top: "Et distingue in glosa sex causas quibus voluit nasci de desponsata. Prima est ut per Ioseph series generationis texeretur ... . Secunda causa est ne quasi adultera gravida inveniretur sine viro ... quod non est infamata tanquam rea adulterii ... Tercia causa est ut haberet qui eam consolaretur. Mulier namque solatio viri indiget. Quarta causa est ut Ioseph preberet testimonium integritati eius qui desponsaverat eam virginem ... . Quinta causa est ut Diabolo celaretur mysterium incarnationis, ut videns eam desponsatam Ioseph putaret Christum filium Ioseph."

blame with a lie."[69] The clear sense is that were Mary pregnant but not betrothed to Joseph, anything she might say about her pregnant condition could be construed as a lie, an attempt to deflect blame from herself. Comestor, however, was far more specific in what he told his students: "the sixth cause is that greater credence might be given to the words of Mary, who said that she had conceived by the Holy Spirit. It is not, however, written in the Gospel that Mary said this, but it is intimated from the gloss. And not everything is read in the Gospel, for Mary would seem to be hiding blame, were she to say that she had conceived by the Spirit ... ."[70]

Comestor's reading of the gloss is fascinating, for by no means according to the glossator did Mary say precisely that she had conceived by the Holy Spirit. Indeed, to have said so would not in fact have been a lie but rather the truth, however hard to believe. If we take the glossator at his word, Mary's legitimate betrothal to Joseph removed from her an occasion for lying, for one can easily imagine the temptation to any ordinary unmarried virgin to lie about being pregnant. Mary, of course, was no ordinary unmarried virgin, and the glossator's use of "videretur" makes clear that there would have been only the appearance of a lie in Mary's case. Giving Comestor every benefit of the doubt, we can imagine that his students heard what seemed a reasonable inference in Comestor's way of reading the gloss: had Mary said anything under such circumstances, she would have said that she had conceived by the Holy Spirit.

What makes Comestor's words so striking, however, is his bald use of the indicative in saying of Mary that "she said that she had conceived of the Holy Spirit." Comestor admits that Mary did not say this anywhere in the Gospel. But, intimating that she did so, he uses the factual indicative of the verb. One wonders if this grammatical distinction was lost on his students. Even more interesting is his next observation: "And not everything is read in the gospel." Here, he offers his own crisp rationale for expanding on the glosses, as well as on the historical and theological content of Scripture itself, since the Bible does not convey everything relevant to salvation history.

69 GM, Luc. 1.27 *ad loc.*, 4: 141, col. b, marginal gloss 4: "Fides etiam Marie verbis maior ascribitur et mendacii causa removetur. Videretur enim culpam obumbrasse voluisse mendacio innupta virgo."

70 Troyes, MS 1024, fol. 145ra, top: "Sexta causa est ut maior fides adhiberetur verbis Marie dicentis se concepisse de Spiritu Sancto. Non tamen legitur in Evangelio istud dixisse sed ex glosa innuitur. Nec omnia leguntur in Evangelio. Videretur enim tegere culpam, si diceret se de Spiritu concepisse ... ."

We cannot of course see how Comestor's students heard these words, for we have no record of their response. It is possible that they seemed novel and progressive, or alternatively it may be that Comestor was repeating what was already a commonplace in the Paris of the 1150s and 1160s. But whether this principle was a theological and exegetical commonplace in the 1150s and 1160s or was an innovation of Comestor's, it is a hallmark of his approach. Either way, we see that already in Comestor's mid-twelfth-century classroom in Paris the practice of theological inquiry had moved one big step away from attention to *sacra pagina* by itself. We are far from what would become a widening gulf between Scripture and theological inquiry in the pedagogy and magisterial disputation of the thirteenth century. Nevertheless, already in the Parisian classrooms of the mid-twelfth century, magisterial attention was being diverted to a significant extent from Scripture itself to the tradition of glosses that has grown up around *sacra pagina*.

Comestor's creative use of the *Gloss*, and specifically his giving pride of place more to explicating the glosses attached to Scripture itself, and the grounds on which he does so, should give us pause about the longstanding scholarly consensus that the *Gloss* and the twelfth-century masters who made use of it belong squarely in the traditional, conservative, "biblical-moral" theological camp.[71] There can be no doubt that Comestor's use of the *Gloss* in his lectures on the Glossed Gospels was progressive and emphatically not conservative. His lectures clearly constituted a step away from traditional commentaries that focused on Scripture itself. As such, Comestor's lectures on the glossed Gospels should be viewed as part of the same twelfth-century movement in theology away from strict adherence to the biblical text as the Lombard's *Sentences* and, as I argue more fully, below, Comestor's own *Historia scholastica*. For now, however, it is sufficient that Comestor's pithy statement to his students – "And not everything is read in the Gospel" – serve as a bracing reminder that his method in lecturing and the structure of those lectures reflected the fact that the Bible by itself furnished an incomplete record of sal-

---

71 See, for example, Beryl Smalley, *The Study of the Bible in the Middle Ages*, 3rd rev. ed. (1941; Oxford: Basil Blackwell, 1984), 46–66; Guy Lobrichon, "Une nouveauté: Les gloses de la Bible," in *Le Moyen Âge et la Bible*, ed. Pierre Riché and Guy Lobrichon, Bible de tous les Temps 4 (Paris: Éditions Beauchesne, 1984), 95–114; and Dahan's overview of the state of biblical textual criticism in the twelfth century in Gilbert Dahan, *L'exégèse chrétienne de la Bible, XIIe–XIVe siècle, Patrimoines Christianisme* (Paris: Les Éditions du Cerf, 1999), 167–191.

vation history. More was needed, and Comestor was already working in these lectures to meet that need.

b. *History and Mystery*

Having described in some detail the first salient feature of Comestor's lectures on the Glossed Gospels, it remains to set forth an account of the other, namely the clear and constant demarcation Comestor makes between history, the literal sense of Scripture, and what he routinely refers to as *mistice*, the various figurative senses. On the one hand, this hardly requires explanation, for like Comestor's habitual referring of the New and the Old Testaments to each other, the interplay between literal explication and figurative explication is so ubiquitous in his lectures that one can find it on virtually every folio left by the student reporters. Its sheer volume, therefore, requires no demonstration. On the other hand, the care that Comestor takes to distinguish between literal and the figurative explication deserves attention here for two reasons above all. First and most obviously, we see the magnitude of the task that Comestor faced in re-ordering the *Gloss* on a second level for his students in making sure that they differentiated clearly between the literal and figurative glosses that were everywhere juxtaposed and intermingled therein. The *History* itself would be the fruit of this laborious work. Second, we get a close look at the wonder-inducing fluidity between the literal and the figurative for Comestor and his auditors. As I show below, precisely because of the permeability of the boundary between the two, it would prove impossible to keep the two entirely separate, even in the *History*.

In the epistolary prologue to the *History*, Comestor wrote that "beginning then from the cosmography of Moses, I have composed a historical rivulet reaching up to the ascension of our Savior, leaving to those more skilled than I the ocean of mysteries, in which it is permitted to pursue old matters and to forge new ones."[72] Comestor's use of the ocean as an image to express the extent of the tradition of figurative interpretation was no idle imagining, nor was it an exaggeration, for having lectured on all four of the Glossed Gospels he had immersed himself and his students in that tradition; and thus he knew firsthand just how broad and deep it was. Moreover, in contrast to the *History*,

---

72 *Petri Comestoris Historia scholastica, prologus epistolaris* (ed. Clark, Textual Appendix A.1 below, lines 8–11): "Porro a cosmographia Moysi incipiens rivulum historicum deduxi usque ad ascensionem Domini Salvatoris, pelagus mysteriorum peritioribus relinquens, in quibus et vetera prosequi et nova cudere licet."

in which he stated from the beginning his own conscious effort to restrict the scope of the project to the literal/historical sense, in his lectures on the Glossed Gospels Comestor dove willingly into "the ocean of mysteries," for not only did the text of the Gospels provide countless opportunities for figurative interpretation, but the *Gloss* itself was well endowed with readings directed to the various senses of Scripture. Since Comestor was lecturing on the *Gloss* and not on the Gospels per se, he had constant occasion to explicate those mysteries for his students.

At the same time, however, Comestor had to explicate the literal sense of the text of the Gospels, and this was no easy task. As Smalley noted long ago, the "gospels put special difficulties in the way of an exegete wishing to expound the literal sense. Jesus spoke and acted in parables; the evangelists used metaphorical language; the gospels, St. John's in particular, were meant to be read on two levels."[73] In lecturing on the *Gloss* Comestor constantly had to treat both the literal/historical sense and the various figurative senses; his great challenge was to ensure that his students distinguished clearly between them.

Another look at Comestor's treatment of Gabriel's appearance to Zachary will suffice to show Comestor's habitual concern with distinguishing for his students between what should be understood *ad litteram* and what should be classified as *mistice*. Zachary's entry into the temple, and in particular his entry as high priest, gave Comestor ample occasion to tease out for his students various figurative implications. He told his students, for example, that Zachary's entrance into the Holy of Holies prefigured Christ's ascension into heaven.[74] Moreover, just as the High Priest entered into the Holy of Holies to pray for the people standing and praying outside of the Temple, so Christ, after all those things that he had decreed from all eternity had been fulfilled, ascended into heaven to intercede on our behalf with God the Father.[75] In like fashion, the people whom Luke describes as praying outside of the Temple waiting for the priest to leave the Holy of Holies stand for us, as we wait for the coming of the Lord.[76] Comestor concluded this brief figurative explication with a bit of

---

73   Smalley, *Gospels in the Schools*, 38.

74   Troyes, MS 1024, fol. 143rb, middle: "... et vide quia introitus in Sanctam Sanctorum prefigurabat ascensionem Christi in celum."

75   Ibid.: "Sicut enim summus sacerdos intrabat Sanctam Sanctorum, ut interpellaret pro populo foris stante, sic Christus impletis omnibus que ab eterno disposuerat implenda in carne ascendit in secreta celi et interpellat pro nobis ad patrem."

76   Ibid.: "... quia quasi pre foribus stantes expectamus adventum eius, sicut populus foris stans expectabat egressum sacerdotis de Sancta Sanctorum."

remarkable history, telling his students that Zachary's entry into the Holy of Holies, which took place on the same day as Gabriel's announcement of the Incarnation to Mary, prefigures Christ's ascension into heaven.[77]

In general, in navigating between the historical and the figurative, Comestor most often addresses his remarks to one level of the text at a time. Such is the case here. Having just reviewed a number of figurative understandings, he now tacked back to the historical sense, narrating and describing in some detail for his students what Zachary did after entering the Temple. According to Comestor, Zachary walked in, carrying both the thurifer filled with coals and the incense, which he then sprinkled over the coals and lit.[78] Since there is nothing in the Glossed Luke itself providing such details, it is easy to imagine Comestor relying on twelfth-century liturgical practice at this point. He explains that Zachary lit the incense so that its smoke would impede his eyesight, lest, looking upwards, he might spy the two Cherubim and lest the glory of the Lord might appear between them and blind him.[79]

Although to modern ears Comestor's explication may seem fanciful, nonetheless it is clear from the context that he was still sticking to the historical sense. He was still proposing what he thought had happened historically, explaining that it was at the very moment when Zachary had just dealt with the incense that Gabriel appeared.[80] Comestor now injected his own opinion into a longstanding question over the position in the Temple of the altar of incense, telling his students that he agreed with those holding as certain that the altar of incense was outside of the Holy of Holies, that is, outside of the veil.[81]

---

77 Ibid., middle-bottom: "Eadem ergo die prefiguratus est eius ascensus in celum per introitum sacerdotis in Sanctam Sanctorum, et descensio eius in carnem nuntiata est per angelum."

78 Ibid., bottom: "Postea intrabat sacerdos Sanctam Sanctorum cum pulvere timiamatis deferens turibulum in manibus plenum prunis. Et statim postquam intraverat ponebat pulverem super prunas in turibulo ... ."

79 Ibid.: "ut sic caligo fumi oculos eius involveret, ne sursum aspiciens posset intueri duo cherubin, ne si forte gloria Domini inter duo cherubin appareret et eius visione statim expiraret."

80 Troyes, MS 1024, fol. 143rb, bottom, referring to GM, Luc. 1.11 *ad loc.*, 4:140, col. a: "Factum est ergo quod Zacharias posuerat incensum, et cum egressus esset posito incenso et staret iuxta altare incensi *APPARUIT* ei *ANGELUS.*"

81 Troyes, MS 1024, fol. 143rb, bottom: "Nos, inquit, enim ita prosequimur tamquam pro constanti habentes quod altare incensi sive timiamatis erat extra Sanctam Sanctorum scilicet extra velum." The reporter, who inserts the word *inquit*, here indicates that Comestor is giving his own position.

Comestor made sure that his students knew that his view accorded with the majority: "For Josephus bears witness to this, and Bede and all the Fathers except Augustine agree about this."[82]

Comestor would now bring this particular excursus into the literal sense to a close. After telling his students that another altar, the altar of sacrifices, was located outside under the sky, Comestor returns to consider once more the phrase: "he appeared."[83] About this word, he first defines apparition properly speaking as something said of God or of angels, when they appear suddenly before our eyes.[84] He then refers his students to a marginal gloss on point, directing them especially to its final sentence: "And it is good that he appears in the Temple next to the altar and on the right-hand side, since he foretells the coming of the true priest and the mystery of the universal sacrifice and the joy of the heavenly gift that is signified through 'right-hand side.'"[85] Whereas the glossator had compressed a tripartite consideration of Gabriel's location in the Temple into one sentence, correlating each position to a significant feature of salvation history, Comestor wanted his students to consider each correlation individually.[86] Comestor's explication is worth quoting in full; speaking about Gabriel, he said:

> Thus his appearance in the Temple is good, since he foretells the coming of the true priest, that is, Christ; it is also good that he is next to the altar, since he foretells the mystery of the universal sacrifice, that is, he foretells

82   Troyes, MS 1024, fol. 143rb, middle: "Hoc enim testatur Iosephus, et Beda et omnes auctores in hoc concordant Augustino excepto."

83   Troyes, MS 1024, fol. 143rb, bottom, referring to GM, Luc. 1.11 *ad loc.*, 4: 140, col. a: "Altare autem holocaustorum erat in atrio exterius sub divo. *APPARUIT.*"

84   Troyes, MS 1024, fol. 143rb, bottom to fol. 143va, top: "Nota quia apparicio proprie dicitur Dei vel angelorum aspectibus nostris repentina oblatio quando scilicet aliquis se offert et presentat subito visibus nostris. De quo tamen non est in potestate nostra ut appareat.".

85   Troyes, MS 1024, fol. 143va, top: "De hoc habes **glosam**: DE DEO ETC." The marginal gloss to which Comestor refers, the last line of whose text I have translated, reads in part as follows: "*APPARUIT.* Ambrosius. Beda: De deo vel de angelis dicitur … . Et bene in templo iuxta altare et a dextris apparet, quia veri sacerdotis adventum et ministerium sacrificii universalis et caelestis doni gaudium quod pro dexteram significatur predicat." GM, Luc. 1.11 *ad loc.*, 4: 140, col. a, marginal gloss 3. Note that I have substituted "mystery" for "ministry," because the text quoted below in n87 makes clear that Comestor and his students had "mysterium" and not "ministerium" in their text.

86   Troyes, MS 1024, fol. 143va, top: "Et nota diligenter quia in fine glosse tribus reddit tria, et tu redde singula singulis … ."

the sacrifice that must be celebrated generally by the Church, which at that time was hidden; it is good that he appears on the right side, since he foretells the joy of the heavenly gift, that is, the joy of eternal beatitude to be given from heaven.[87]

One might reasonably suppose that Comestor had here returned to the figurative in directing his students to this marginal gloss and in explicating its final sentence. But Comestor's next remarks make it clear that he at least did not think that he was doing so. Recalling Zachary's disturbed emotional state after Gabriel had suddenly appeared, Comestor refers his students to the next marginal gloss.[88] He again unpacks in a straightforward manner its contents, explaining what *turbatio* is, how it feels, and adding that, whereas angels generally bring the remedy of consolation to those experiencing fright from their appearance, demons do the opposite.[89] Comestor concludes thus: "In this way all of these things are explained according to the literal sense."[90]

On the one hand, Comestor's words seem to indicate unambiguously that it was at this point, and not earlier, that he wished to redirect his students' attention to the figurative. On the other, one cannot help but puzzle over Comestor's treatment of the marginal gloss relating Gabriel's position in the Temple, a matter of historical consideration, to three seemingly allegorical understandings. Did Comestor really deem that marginal gloss and his remarks on it part of an ongoing historical explication? We can of course never know for sure. Yet it is difficult to take his words providing a directional signpost to his students, in which he signals the end of "ad litteram" explication, in any other way. Perhaps one might say that the brief flight into the figurative arose in the context of literal of historical explication. Nevertheless, it reveals beau-

---

87 Troyes, MS 1024, fol. 143va, top: "Ita bene apparet in templo, quia predicat adventum veri sacerdotis id est Christi; bene iuxta altare, quia predicat mysterium universalis sacrificii, id est predicat sacrificium generaliter ab Ecclesia celebrandum quod tunc occultum erat; bene in dextera, quia predicat gaudium celestis doni id est gaudium eterne beatitudinis de celo dandum." Comestor is here explicating GM, Luc. 1.11 *ad loc.*, 4: 140, col. a, marginal gloss 3.

88 "*TURBATUS* **glosa**: SOLEMUS ETC." Troyes, MS 1024, fol. 143va, top, where Comestor refers to GM, Luc. 1.11 *ad loc.*, 4: 140, col. a, marginal gloss 4.

89 Troyes, MS 1024, fol. 143va, top: "Vide quia turbatio debet intelligi quedam mentis alienatio qua patitur homo ex improviso alicuius occursu. Et tunc quodammodo perstringimur id est quandam angustiam patimur. Angeli autem de sui visione pavescentibus consolationis remedio timorem excutiunt, demones terrorem amplius incutiunt."

90 Ibid.: "Ita ad litteram hec omnia exponuntur."

tifully just how thin the line was between the literal and the figurative for Comestor and his students.

The example just given, in which Comestor first explicated in an ongoing way one sense of Scripture before shifting his attention to develop another at some length, is typical of these lectures. As a rule, he tended to develop one line of reasoning fully before changing course. It often happens, however, that Comestor comes across texts that necessitate a more rapid back and forth between the literal and the figurative senses, as in his next few remarks:

> Mystically, through THE TEMPLE into which Zachary entered is understood ... the Blessed Virgin, who was the temple of the Holy Spirit into which the Son of God entered. **Gloss**: ZACHARY, HAVING ENTERED ... THE PEOPLE PRAYS ... FROM THEIR CAPTIVITY. This can be understood literally, since the Jewish people were praying at that time spiritually to be freed from captivity, when the Son descended into the Virgin, since <the Jewish nation> was at that time a tributary to the Romans, and it can also be understood spiritually through their praying for a messiah; the Son of God appeared, when he descended into the Virgin ... . The disturbed state of Zachary stands for the disturbed state of the Jews who were remaining in a state of disbelief.[91]

Comestor's comment here shows that this was one gloss that could be understood either way. It is not immediately clear why the student reporter inserted the word "spiritually," which is also included in other manuscripts, into Comestor's explication of the first and literal sense.[92] If Comestor in fact said it in this place, it was a strange thing to say, for no doubt there were many intertestamental Jews literally praying for freedom from the Roman yoke. After all, to pray spiritually is redundant. One can, however, easily imagine a stu-

---

91 Troyes, MS 1024, fol. 143va, top-middle: "Mistice per TEMPLUM in quod intravit Zacharias, mistice significatur beata virgo, que fuit templum Spiritus Sancti in qua intravit Dei filius. **Glosa**: INGRESSUS ZACHARIAS ... POPULUS ORAT ... DE CAPTIVITATE, Hoc potest intelligi ad litteram, quia populus iudaicus tunc spiritualiter orabat liberari a captivitate, cum Dei filius descendit in virginem, quia tunc erat tributarius Romanis, et de spirituali per messiam; apparuit Dei filius, cum descendit in virginem ... . Turbatio Zacharie significat turbationem iudeorum manentium in incredulitate." Note that I omit in my translation the duplication of "mistice," which is omitted in other manuscripts. See, for example, Avranches, MS 36, fol. 112va, middle.

92 See, for example, Avranches, MS 36, fol. 112va, middle.

dent reporter trying to keep up with Comestor's rapid-fire back and forth between the senses. Whatever the truth of this detail, a clear picture emerges of Comestor's occasional need to shift back and forth from one sense to another on the spot as it were.

Comestor's solicitude that his students distinguish clearly between the tradition of literal interpretation handed down in the *Gloss* and the tradition of figurative interpretation is patent. Moreover, his few remarks on the subject of Zachary's entrance into the Temple show well the daunting task he faced in sorting out the various senses in the *Gloss*. Indeed, in the brief portion of his lecture just quoted, Comestor distinguished for his students a number of interpretations, both literal and figurative, that had been packed pithily by the glossator into a single, brief marginal gloss without any indication as to which was which.[93] Finally, Comestor's constant care to sort out the literal from the figurative is a sure sign of how closely related they oftentimes were. From our vantage point, of course, Comestor sometimes seems to be engaging in figurative explication while telling his students that he is doing just the opposite. But even for twelfth-century students of the Bible, it was not easy to keep them separate; perhaps it might be truer to say that there was on occasion ample reason not to do so.

We can see this dynamic at work even in the *Historia scholastica*, in which Comestor is explicit about his intention to stick exclusively to the literal sense.[94] Stephen Langton, glossing Comestor's words in the second version of his commentary on the *History*, also reports Comestor's having disregarded the figurative senses in favor of the literal as a matter of fact: "Having omitted the three figurative senses, the Master treats history alone."[95] Langton even tells his students that although Comestor had proposed devoting a work to allegorical readings he had found no indication that the Master of Histories had actually done so.[96] Nevertheless, although it can be truly said that Comestor eschewed the allegorical for the literal and that he was highly selective in his choice of materials for the *History*, the dynamism of the schools coupled with the very

---

93 The gloss in question is at GM, Luc. 1.11 *ad loc.*, 4: 140, col. a, marginal gloss 2.

94 The relevant text is reproduced in n72 above.

95 "Tribus omissis agit Magister de sola historia." *Tertia Stephani glosa scilicet magistralis anno 1193 recensa supra Historiam Genesis* (ed. Clark, Textual Appendix A.4 below, lines 23–24).

96 "Proposuerat enim forsitan componere allegorias. Quod tamen non invenimus fecisse Magistrum." *Tertia Stephani glosa scilicet magistralis anno 1193 recensa supra Historiam Genesis* (ed. Clark, Textual Appendix A.4 below, lines 59–60).

structure of the *History* made possible changes to its text, including those that seemed to contradict Comestor's original aims.

A prime example can be seen in the second chapter ("De conceptione Salvatoris") of the *Historia evangelica*. In the manuscript, Paris, BnF, lat. 16943 ("P"), this chapter ends with the line: "And he is believed to have been conceived on March 25, and after thirty three years had passed he died on the same day."[97] In the manuscript, Vienna, Östereichische Nationalbibliothek, MS 363 ("V"), however, the same second chapter ends with a gloss that has been added to the line just quoted: "Whence the Jews transgressed that <saying of the Old Testament>: *thou shalt not cook a young goat in the milk of its mother*, that is, thou shalt not kill Christ on the day of his conception."[98] In fact, P represents a more pristine version of the *History*'s textual tradition than V, and so the fact that V includes an additional gloss is not surprising.[99] The inclusion of this particular gloss, however, is surprising, for not only does it seem wholly out of context in the historical narrative, but it also seems to appear out of the blue.

In fact, however, it is not as far removed as one might suppose, for what makes the inclusion of this particular gloss especially interesting is that Comestor seems to have been its author and source, at least proximately, for he had made this very point in lecturing on the Glossed Gospel of Luke. After speaking of God's removing Elizabeth's disgrace in Luke 1.25 ("respexit auferre opprobrium meum inter homines"), Comestor for the first time in his lectures on the Glossed Luke left the text and glosses behind to deliver a long discourse juxtaposing, comparing, and contrasting the Old and the New Testaments. As always in his lectures on the Gospel glosses, Comestor attended carefully to the distinction between literal and allegorical interpretations.[100] Leaving behind

---

97 "Creditur autem conceptus octavo Kalendas Apriles, et revolutis triginta tribus annis eadem die mortuus est." *Petri Comestoris Historia evangelica*, 2 (ed. Clark, Textual Appendix B.1 below, lines 27–28).

98 [Unde Iudei transgressi sunt illud: *non coques hedum in lacte matris sue*, id est non occides Christum in die conceptionis sue.] *Petri Comestoris Historia evangelica*, 2 (ed. Clark, Textual Appendix B.1 below, lines 28–30). The Old Testament quotation is from Exodus 23.19.

99 I discuss these two manuscripts, P and V, in Chapter Five; I show that although P preserves an earlier version of the *Historia scholastica*, V not only preserves many changes made to the *History* by Peter Comestor himself but also more closely approximates the version that Stephen Langton used in making the *History* part of the curriculum of the incipient University of Paris.

100 Troyes, MS 1024, fol. 144rb, bottom: "... quia nondum revelatur ei mysterium conceptionis sue, pro quo misterio daturum esset ei in senectute concipere quod postea revelatum est ei in adventu Beate Virginis. Haec omnia, que ad litteram prosecuti sumus, mistice exponuntur."

literal interpretation for the allegorical, he cited Zachary as the symbol of the Levitical priesthood and Elizabeth as the symbol of the law.[101] Like Zachary and Elizabeth, both the priesthood and the law had grown old; Elizabeth is an especially fitting symbol for the law, for like women, who cannot conceive without the help of men, the law needs the priesthood to produce spiritual offspring.[102] Furthermore, just as Elizabeth was sterile, so too the law was barren, for it could bring no one to perfection, nor could it open the door of the Kingdom of heaven.[103]

At this point, Comestor introduces the New Testament into his analysis, comparing the Gospel to the Law. Indeed both were sterile and for the same reason, for neither could open the door to the Kingdom of Heaven, which was opened only by the blood of Christ.[104] Unlike the law, however, which could not lead to fruit either by itself or by proxy, the Gospel did in fact serve as precursor to the opening of the Kingdom of Heaven.[105] Comestor continues his allegorical exposition with a parallel allegory: Zachary represents the legal priesthood, and his entry into the Temple signifies the penetration of priests into the profundity of the mysteries; the people standing outside represent the simple folk, who wait upon the learning of the doctors.[106] The burning of the incense stands for the fervor of divine love, and Comestor interprets this for his students with an ardent recommendation of *lectio divina*: "such that this is the sense: by however much ardent zeal they apply themselves to *lectio divina*, to

---

101 Ibid.: "Per Zachariam ergo potest intelligi sacerdocium Leviticum, per Elisabet potest intelligi lex ... ."

102 Ibid.: "... quia sicut illi ambo processerant in diebus suis, sic et sacerdocium vetus senuerat, et lex inveterata erat. Sacerdocium quipped legale circum tempus Christi incurvabatur ad senium, cum Simoniace vendebatur. Lex quoque inveterata erat, cum tradicionibus Phariseorum post ponebatur. Bene autem per mulierem exprimitur lex, quia sicut mulier non potest per se concipere sine opere et exercicio viri, sic lex sine doctrina et exercicio sacerdotum non potest duos spirituales filios generare."

103 Troyes, MS 1024, fol. 144rb, bottom – fol. 144va, top: "Et sicut Elisabet sterilis, ita lex infecunda, quia neminem ad perfectum ducebat. Nec ianuam regni aperiebat ... ."

104 Troyes, MS 1024, fol. 144va, top: "Si ianuam non aperiebat, eadem ratione evangelium sterile est, quia nec lex nec evangelium ianuam regni aperivit sed sanguis Christi."

105 Ibid.: "Vide ergo quia lex merito dicta est sterilis, quia nec ex se fecit fructum nec habuit fructum consecutum. Evangelium vero licet ex se non aperuit ianuam regni, tamen apercio ianue consecuta est evangelium."

106 Troyes, MS 1024, fol. 144va: "Et legale sacerdotium per Zachariam, qui intrat in templum, significatur, quia sacerdotes debent penetrare per funditatem misteriorum; per plebem foris stantem exprimuntur simplices. Qui autem doctoribus erudicionem expectant."

that extent <they will receive> more fully the grace of God."[107] Whatever else Comestor's classroom was, it was no stale academic discussion.

Comestor concludes with a stirring peroration on the mystical synchronicity and parallelism between the Old and the New Testaments regarding the births of John the Baptist and Jesus: "since through all that took place in the five ages about which the law treats the incarnation of Christ was prefigured, and in the sixth age completed, or since the law contained in the five books of Moses was consummated in the Incarnation of Christ, it is very fitting that it was announced in the sixth month from the conception of the Baptist. Whence it follows: *and in the sixth month etc.*"[108] After this transition back to the text of Luke's Gospel, however, Comestor dealt with a seeming difficulty in chronology: "… but this does not appear to hold, for since in September the Baptist was conceived, if in the sixth month from September our Lord was conceived, therefore in February. Skip over therefore, that last little bit of September and begin your calculation from October, and the sixth month will be March, on the twenty-fifth day of which our Lord was conceived, and on the same day suffered."[109] Comestor, however, in telling his students to ignore the last part of September (from September 25 to October 1), was simply having them count from the twenty-fifth of each month: from September 25 to October 25, from October 25 to November 25, from November 25 to December 25, from December 25 to January 25, from January 25 to February 25, and finally from February 25 to March 25, for the requisite six months.

It is at this point, namely at the juncture of the transition in his lecture between the conception of the Baptist and the conception of the Lord, that Comestor introduced in his lecture the seemingly incongruous text with which the second chapter of the *Historia evangelica*: "Whence the Jews transgressed that <saying of the Old Testament>: *thou shalt not cook a young goat in the milk of*

---

107 Ibid.: "Per accensionem timiamatis exprimitur fervor divine dilectionis … ut sit sensus: quanto ardentiori studio divine lectioni insistunt, tanto amplius gratiam Dei."

108 Troyes, MS 1024, fol. 144vb, top-middle: "… quia per ea que facta sunt in quinque etatibus de quibus agit lex Christi incarnatio est prefigurata, et in sexta etate completa, vel quia lex in quinque libris Moysi contenta in Christi incarnatione est consummata, bene congruit quod sexto mense a conceptione Iohannis est adnuntiata. Unde sequitur: *In sexto autem mense etc.*"

109 Troyes, MS 1024, fol. 144vb, top-middle: "… sed non videtur stare, nam cum in Septembri conceptus sit Baptista, si sexto mense a Septembri conceptus est Dominus, ergo in Februario. Ideo pretermitte illud residuum Septembris et incipe computationem ab Octobri, et erit sextus mensis Martius, cuius vicesima quinta die conceptus est Dominus et in eadem passus."

its mother, that is, thou shalt not kill Christ on the day of his conception."[110] In his lectures on the Glossed Luke, he had glossed the text from Exodus in a slightly more elaborate fashion: "Whence allegorically there was prohibited in the Law: *thou shalt not cook a young goat in the milk of its mother*, as if to say, beware O Jews, lest you cook, by the fire of the passion, a young goat, that is the Christ, who is signified by a young goat, in the milk of its mother, that is, on the day of his conception."[111]

The early introduction of this text into the *History* raises a number of seemingly intractable questions. Who introduced it? Was it Comestor himself, who had years earlier introduced it in a similar context in his lectures on the Glossed Gospel? If so, why had he not introduced it into the *History* in the first place? Moreover, why would Comestor introduce into the *History* an obviously allegorical text, when he took great pains not to do so elsewhere? Langton provides no guidance here, for he does not gloss this particular text. We are left to wonder at what appears to be at the same time both an insoluble mystery and a rather striking coincidence, namely that we find in the text of Comestor the *Magister Historiarum* another Comestor, namely the *expositor figurarum*.

The presence of this particular text in the *Scholastic History* calls to mind Comestor's words in his epistolary prologue about the ocean of mysteries, namely the various allegorical senses of Scripture.[112] Comestor was himself an accomplished navigator of that ocean, and his choice of metaphor was no accident, for the tradition of Christian allegorical interpretation was indeed an ocean. I would, however, suggest another metaphor to describe the significance of this particular text in the *History*, namely an iceberg, for whatever else it shows, Comestor's explication of Exodus 23.19, both in his lectures on the Glossed Luke and as it appeared in the *Historia evangelica*, makes abundantly clear that the historical sense was truly the tip of an iceberg of glosses. We may never know how this particular text made its way into the *History*, but its very presence, however incongruous, testifies to the proximity of that enormous

---

110 [Unde Iudei transgressi sunt illud: *non coques hedum in lacte matris sue*, id est non occides Christum in die conceptionis sue.] *Petri Comestoris Historia evangelica*, 2 (ed. Clark, Textual Appendix B.1 below, lines 23–24). The Old Testament quotation is from Exodus 23.19.

111 Troyes, MS 1024, fol. 144vb, top-middle: "Unde mistice in lege prohibitum est: *ne coques edum in lacte matris sue*, ac si diceretur: cave o Iudee, ne hedum, id est Christum, qui significatur per hedum, decoques – igne passionis – in lacte matris sue, id est in die conceptionis sue."

112 The relevant text is reproduced in n72 above.

allegorical tradition and also to the porousness of the boundary separating the literal from the figurative senses.

The introduction of this text into the *History* is significant in the context of this study for another reason, for it illustrates the ease in which glosses in general were transferable to the *History*. This particular gloss worked its way into the main text of the scholastic version of the *History* before 1183 at the latest, and it was no exception. Indeed, I have shown that the *History* was from the beginning a dynamic text, in no small part because it entered the schools as soon as it appeared. I have also shown, thanks to Langton's testimony, that Comestor did not stop working on it – there is no conceivable reason why he should have – and have argued that in all likelihood Comestor himself taught the *History* during the 1170s and perhaps even earlier. That Comestor, author and teacher, continued to revise the *History* should surprise no one, but what is fascinating about the teaching of this text in the decades during which the University of Paris took shape is the ease in which it lent itself to revision and adaptation by all those teaching it – Langton and many others.

It is precisely to understand how the *History* came to be so eminently adaptable to classroom teaching and to revision by teachers that I have thought it worthwhile to sketch here in some detail Comestor's method of lecturing on the *Gloss*. Of prime importance is the fact that in lecturing on the *Gloss* Comestor sought above all to recast it for his students. If the *Gloss* provided a new resource for Comestor and his students to work with, his mode of lecturing nevertheless makes plain that it was less than ideally suited to classroom lecturing on the Bible. In his recent study of one of Comestor's lectures on the Glossed Matthew, Dahan emphasized that the great insight afforded by Comestor's teaching with the *Gloss* is the discovery that it became a textbook for the study of Scripture.[113] In his estimate, it was so used during the second third of the twelfth century and less so in the thirteenth.[114] In my view, this version of events and, in particular, this timetable is right. It raises the question, however, of what happened during the final third of the twelfth century.

The short answer is that, in working with the *Gloss*, Comestor did what any expert teacher would do in working with a textbook that was not altogether suitable for his ends: he remade it orally in the course of his teaching.

---

113 Dahan, "Une leçon biblique," 33: "Le plus remarquable est certainement la manière dont il illustre un moment particulier de l'histoire de l'exégèse occidentale. La *Glossa ordinaria* est devenue un outil de base dans l'enseignement de la Bible ... ."

114 Ibid.

Thus, he not only re-ordered the glosses in relation to Scripture and vice versa but also remade their substance, pruning here and expanding there. He took the undifferentiated masses of literal and figurative glosses and separated them for his students, making clear to his students what he held to be of more importance and what of less. In short, in lecturing on each of the Glossed Gospels, Comestor came to know intimately the limitations of the *Gloss* as a set text for the classroom. How Comestor dealt with those limitations in the *Historia scholastica* is the subject of the next chapter.

CHAPTER THREE

From the *Gloss* to the *History*

Comestor's four courses on the Glossed Gospels are eminently worthy of study, opening a window onto the teaching of the Bible at the school of Notre Dame in Paris in the 1160s.[1] Moreover, they provide a valuable record of the use of the *Gloss* as an introductory biblical textbook in the classroom by a distinguished twelfth-century *magister*. Dahan captures well the significance of this latter point for those interested in how the Bible was taught in the twelfth century:

> Thus, this text of Peter Comestor's seems instructive in several regards. The most remarkable is certainly the manner in which it illustrates a particular moment in the history of western exegesis of the Bible. The *Glossa ordinaria* became a fundamental tool in the teaching of the Bible: very much used in this second third of the twelfth century, it will be less so in the thirteenth, without ceasing to be present on the desk of the master preparing or giving his courses.[2]

In this chapter, through Comestor's use of the *Gloss* in his lectures on the glossed Gospels I show why it had such a short shelf life as a biblical textbook

---

1 Gilbert Dahan, "Une leçon biblique au XIIe siècle: Le commentaire de Pierre le Mangeur sur Matthieu 26, 26–29," in *Ancienne Loi, Nouvelle Loi*, ed. J.-P. Bordier, Littérature et revelation au Moyen Âge 3 (Paris: Université de Paris-Ouest Nanterre-La Défense, 2009), 19–38, at 19 and 33.

2 Ibid., 33: "Ainsi, ce texte de Pierre le Mangeur paraît instructif à plusieurs titres. Le plus remarquable est certainement la manière dont il illustre un moment particulier de l'histoire de l'exégèse occidentale. La *Glossa ordinaria* est devenu un outil de base dans l'enseignement de la Bible: très utilisée en ce deuxième tiers du XIIe siècle, elle le sera moins au XIIIe, sans cesser d'être presenter sur la table du maître, préparant ou donnant ses cours."

and how Comestor ameliorated its deficiencies in the *History*.[3] Indeed, I argue that Comestor, in using the *Gloss* as a textbook in his courses on the four Gospels, not only recognized its deficiencies as a basic text but also discovered the principles that he would use to create a new textbook preeminently suited to introducing students to the Bible, namely the *Historia scholastica*.

I. *The* Gloss *as Introductory Biblical Textbook*

Comestor's Gospel lectures reveal right away two salient defects of the *Gloss* as introductory biblical textbook. The first is the problem of scale, for the *Gloss* is massive and hence difficult to use in many respects both for master and students. The second and related problem is that of organization, for the *Gloss* and indeed the Gospels themselves were ill-suited both to systematic treatment of topics and to cogent narrative. The reader of his lectures sees Comestor dealing with both problems constantly.[4]

The student reports of Comestor's lectures on the Glossed Gospels, however, were not themselves the answer to the difficulties posed in teaching the Bible by means of the *Gloss*, for since Comestor based his courses on the *Gloss*, the resulting collection of lectures suffered from the same problems. Indeed, it is difficult to imagine that any other master could have made use of Comestor's courses on the four Gospels apart from using them as an encyclopedic companion to teaching the *Gloss*.[5]

---

3   By saying that the *Gloss* had a short life as a biblical textbook, I mean only that it would not be used again as the textual basis for comprehensive in-class lectures. It would of course be used extensively by thirteenth-century scholastics as a handy authoritative reference, and indeed would become in the thirteenth century "ordinaria."

4   Although I provide some in-depth analysis of the *Gloss* in this chapter, I focus more on Comestor's use of the *Gloss* and his attempt to remedy these two defects in his lectures on the glossed Gospels.

5   This, I have argued in a series of articles, is precisely how Stephen Langton used them. See Mark J. Clark, "Peter Comestor and Stephen Langton: Master and Student, and Co-makers of the *Historia scholastica*." *Medioevo* 35 (2010): 123–150; "The Commentaries of Stephen Langton on the *Historia scholastica* of Peter Comestor," in *Étienne Langton: Prédicateur, bibliste, théologien*, ed. Louis-Jacques Bataillon, Nicole Bériou, Gilbert Dahan, and Riccardo Quinto (Turnhout: Brepols, 2010): 373–393; and "Le cours d'Étienne Langton sur *l'Histoire scolastique* de Pierre le Mangeur: Le fruit d'une tradition unifiée," in *Pierre de Troyes, dit Pierre le Mangeur, maître du XIIe siècle*, éd. G. Dahan, Bibliothèque d'histoire culturelle du moyen âge (Turnhout: Brepols, 2013), 243–266.

As Beryl Smalley showed long ago, however, Comestor used them himself in fashioning the *History*.[6] Her view was that Comestor made extensive use of these courses: "Much of the lecture material reappears, either verbatim or nearly so in the School *History*."[7] In fact, however, the truth is nearly the opposite. In the *Historia evangelica* Comestor uses only the tiniest fraction of the material contained in his lectures on the four Gospels. Nonetheless, Smalley's basic impression of the importance of Comestor's Gospel lectures to the *History* was just, for as I show herein those lectures contained the seeds not only of the *Historia evangelica* but also of the *Historia scholastica* itself.

For my purposes, therefore, Comestor's lectures on the Glossed Gospels are of keen interest not so much for the quantity of material taken over into the *Historia evangelica* as for understanding the method and structure Comestor would employ so fruitfully in the *History*.

a. *The Problem of Scale*

I am convinced with Dahan that Comestor and his students had in front of them copies, whether in whole or in part, of the *Gloss* for each Gospel that he was lecturing on. Their textbook, therefore, was to a great extent comprehensive, containing as it did both literal and figurative glosses. Moreover, despite the imposing size of the *Gloss*, the surviving reports make plain that Comestor's lectures on the Glossed Gospels were not in any sense cursory. On every folio the reader of those reports sees Comestor examining in depth one or more questions. Indeed, a salient feature of these lectures is that Comestor consistently returns to treat certain themes again and again. Not surprisingly, the resulting corpus of lectures is quite substantial, such that Comestor's lectures on Luke, for example, while not nearly so large as the Glossed Luke itself, are nevertheless copious.

Nevertheless, Comestor's coverage of the *Gloss*, although extensive, cannot fairly be described as comprehensive. In fact, Comestor routinely skips over large sections of Scripture, and although he addresses himself to numerous glosses on every folio of the *Gloss*, he also skips over very many of these. Doubtless, he did so of necessity, for to have treated them all would have resulted in lectures as encyclopedic as the *Gloss* itself; there are just too many glosses to treat them all. Already, however, in his lectures on the Glossed

6 Smalley, *The Gospels in the Schools, c. 1100 – c. 1280* (London and Ronceverte: The Hambledon Press, 1985), 62–83.
7 Ibid., 62.

Gospels, we see Comestor shrinking the *Gloss*, both scriptural text and glosses attached thereto, to a more manageable size.

Comestor's chief means of abridging the *Gloss* was scriptural paraphrase, artfully integrated with the already-existing elements of the *Gloss*. Moreover, although he made frequent and effective use of such scriptural paraphrase in his lectures on the Glossed Gospels, Comestor would make scriptural paraphrase in the *History* itself far more central, for he would use it to fashion the lemmata that would serve throughout as the backbone of that work.

A fitting example to introduce Comestor's artful use of scriptural paraphrase can be found near the start of his lectures on the Glossed Matthew. He first lectured at length on the long genealogy that opens Matthew's Gospel (Matt. 1.1–17).[8] Comestor then turned his attention to the material from Matthew's Gospel – "cum esset desponsata mater eius Maria Ioseph antequam convenirent inventa est in utero habens de Spiritu Sancto" (Matt. 1.18) – that he would subsequently weave together with Luke's account to provide the pre-history to the birth of Jesus.[9] In both his Gospel lectures and the *History*, Comestor cites the opening words of this scriptural text ("cum esset desponsata"), which also introduce a marginal gloss in the *Gloss*.[10] In his lectures on the glossed Matthew, however, he does not at first address either directly. Instead, after a few last words on the substance and the significance of Matthew's genealogy, Comestor digresses to provide his students a summary of the Lucan material that serves as the backdrop to what Matthew has to say. Comestor, who both in his Gospel lectures and in the *History* treats each episode or chapter in the early history of Christ's life discretely, begins by telling his students that Luke takes up this particular chapter earlier than Matthew: "And it must be noted that Luke begins this chapter earlier."[11]

This one-sentence introduction leads to his own summary account of Luke's material, in which Comestor weaves together phrases taken verbatim from Luke's Gospel with both scriptural paraphrase and gloss. We do not know for sure in what order Comestor lectured on the four Glossed Gospels, for there

---

8   See *Glose Comestoris in Mattheum glosatum*, Troyes, Bibliothèque municipale, MS 1024, fol. 1–6.

9   Comestor's treatment of the material from Matthew's Gospel begins in the third chapter of the *Historia evangelica*: "**De ortu precursoris**." *Historia evangelica* (ed. Clark, Textual Appendix B.1 below, lines 31–77).

10   GOM, Matt. 1.18 *ad loc.*, 4: 6, col. b, marginal gloss 4.

11   *Glose Comestoris in Mattheum glosatum*, Troyes, MS 1024, fol. 6va, middle: "Et notandum quia hoc capitulum Lucas inchoat altius."

is to my knowledge no decisive internal evidence. Presumably, he took them in the order in which they are presented in the New Testament: Matthew, Mark, Luke, and John. This is in fact the order in which they are copied in many manuscripts, including the one that I rely on chiefly for this study, Troyes MS 1024. It seems likely, therefore, that Comestor was providing a capsule summary of this portion of Luke's Gospel to students who had not yet heard him lecture on the Glossed Luke. But whatever the truth of the matter, his summary constituted a digression, properly speaking, and one that was necessary to fill in the gaps in Matthew's account. I reproduce here Comestor's summary in full, for we can see in it the rough outline of what would become Comestor's characteristic method and style in the *History* itself:

> For he hands down that *the angel, Gabriel, was sent by God to a city, Nazareth, to a virgin betrothed to Joseph* and greeted by the angel. And as soon as she responded, *behold the handmaid of the Lord,* immediately by the working of the Holy Spirit one part of the flesh of the Virgin was separated from the remaining flesh of the Virgin and formed into the body of Christ. And immediately there was in her womb the Word made man, thus perfect God, perfect man. And when it had been told to her by the angel about her kinswoman, Elizabeth, that she had conceived a son in her old age and that this was the sixth month for her who was called sterile, *Mary set forth at once with haste into the mountains, and she entered into the home of Zachary* and was taking care of her pregnant relation. And she gave of herself diligently to Elizabeth as she was giving birth, and as we read in the Book of the Just the Blessed Virgin with her own hands first lifted up the newborn Baptist from the ground. And after three months had passed Mary returned from the mountains, and since her belly had already swollen a little bit she was found by Joseph to be with child, that is, pregnant. Matthew, therefore, begins after the Blessed Virgin's return from the mountains, when she was discovered by Joseph through the distension of her belly to be pregnant. About this you have a gloss that says that these matters, which have been thoroughly treated outside of his Gospel, are omitted untouched by Matthew.[12]

12 *Glose Comestoris in Mattheum glosatum,* Troyes, MS 1024, fol. 6va, middle, in which Comestor is referring to GM, Matt. 1.18 *ad loc.,* 4: 7, col. a, marginal gloss 1: "Tradit enim quia missus est angelus Gabriel a Deo in civitatem Nazareth ad virginem Ioseph desponsatam et ab angelo salutatam. Et quam cito respondit, ecce ancilla Domini, sta-

Comestor here combines Scripture, scriptural paraphrase, and glosses on Scripture in a condensed narrative that moves along briskly. Thus, for example, where Luke has Gabriel explain to Mary, following her question about how this will come about, that the Holy Spirit and the power of the Most High will overshadow her, Comestor skips ahead to her words of assent – "behold the handmaid of the Lord" – and not only narrates the Holy Spirit's immediate operation but also goes into the particulars of the instantaneous formation of the Lord's body – "perfect God, perfect man" – in the Virgin's womb. Making use of scriptural paraphrase enables Comestor to cover large swaths of scriptural narrative – "And when it had been told to her by the angel about her kinswoman, Elizabeth, that she had conceived a son in her old age and that this was the sixth month for her who was called sterile" – without leaving the scriptural text, which he can at any time take up again verbatim: "... *Mary set forth at once with haste into the mountains, and she entered into the home of Zachary ... .*"

At the same time, scriptural paraphrase freed Comestor to relate important and interesting details omitted by Scripture. Thus we learn that Mary herself served as midwife to her kinswoman, Elizabeth, as she was giving birth, and also that Mary was the first to pick up the newborn John the Baptist. It also gave Comestor considerable leeway to emphasize one thing rather than another. He tells us here, for example, several times what Scripture leaves implicit, namely that Joseph discovered her pregnancy in the most natural way possible, for Mary was herself showing after her time visiting Elizabeth and Zachary in the mountains. Finally, Comestor's integration of Scripture, scriptural paraphrase, and scriptural gloss allowed him to move seamlessly between Scripture and gloss. In the example just cited, Comestor began by directing his students both to Matthew's text and to a particular gloss on point, and ended

---

tim opere Spiritus Sancti separata est particula carnis virginee a reliqua Virginis carne et formata in corpus Christi. Et statim fuit in utero eius verbum homo, sic perfectus Deus, perfectus homo. Et cum dictum esset ei ab angelo de Elizabeth cognata sua quod concepisset filium in senectute sua et quod ille mensis sextus esset ei que vocatur sterilis, statim abiit in montana cum festinatione et intravit in domum Zacharie et ministrabat cognate pregnanti. Et diligenter obsecuta est parienti, et ut traditur in Libro Iustorum Beata Virgo manibus propriis de terra levavit Baptistam natum. Transactis autem tribus mensibus rediit de montanis, et quia iam aliquantulum intumuerat venter eius inventa est a Ioseph in utero habens id est gravida. Inchoat ergo Mattheus post reditum Beate Virginis de montanis, quando cognita est a Ioseph gravida pro tumore ventris. De hoc habes glosam que dicit hec a Mattheo preteriri intacta que extra litteram sunt pretaxata. QUOMODO HOC FACTUM SIT ETC."

by directing them to another, pithy gloss, whose contents were now readily intelligible in the light of his own digression.

Comestor's chosen means of rendering intelligible for his students the nexus between the Gospels of Luke and Matthew introduces well the salient features of his use of scriptural paraphrase in his lectures on the Glossed Gospels: integration of Scripture and scriptural paraphrase; integration of traditional interpretation found in glosses with Scripture and scriptural paraphrase into a single narrative; facility of transition between Scripture and discrete glosses; and, finally, the historical and theological amplification of both Scripture and of the *Gloss* at some points, along with the radical abridgment of the *Gloss* at others.

It is this last point that I wish to focus on here, for Comestor made frequent use of these techniques to reduce the *Gloss* to a manageable scale for his students, and it would be a short step to putting the same method to good use in composing the *History*. A few typical examples comparing Comestor's treatment of a topic in his Gospel lectures and his treatment of the same in the *Historia evangelica* will suffice to show both the radical change in scale from the former to the latter and the continuity in method.

One such example is Comestor's treatment of the interaction and conversation between the angel Gabriel and Zachary. In his lectures on the Glossed Luke, Comestor returns repeatedly and at some length to the issue of Zachary's punishment by Gabriel and treats his muteness up to the time of the Baptist's birth in several different contexts.[13] In the midst of this discussion he introduces and glosses Gabriel's actual words delivering the punishment – "et ecce <eris tacens> ... ."[14] Even though he dwells at some length on Zachary's punishment, Comestor abridges substantially the scriptural narrative, in part by skipping over entirely Luke's account of the remainder of Gabriel's speech and the fulfillment of the promised threat (Luke 1.20–23). But he also renders succinct whatever he includes. Thus, for example, Comestor glosses in a straightforward way the first portion of Gabriel's address to Zachary, directing his students to Luke's text by citing a few words of each scriptural phrase, that is, to God's answering Elizabeth's prayer, to the proper naming of the child, and to the many wondrous things that his gifted son would accomplish and directing them to the appropriate glosses.[15] He then succinctly summarizes Luke's

13   *Glose Comestoris in Lucam glosatam*, Troyes, MS 1024, fol. 143vb– fol. 145va.
14   *Glose Comestoris in Lucam glosatam*, Troyes, MS 1024, fol. 144ra, top-middle.
15   *Glose Comestoris in Lucam glosatam*, Troyes, MS 1024, fol. 143v, columns a and b.

account of Gabriel's promises and Zachary's responses: "The angel promised Zachary that a son would be born and related many things that would be true about the boy, so that in the conception of so great a son his father would rejoice. But Zachary, considering that he was little suited to generating a son, and considering too that his wife was infertile and had already entered *into old age*, believed impossible what had been promised by the angel. He responded therefore: *How will I be sure of this?*"[16]

Several things stand out about this passage integrating brief phrases of Scripture into a larger passage of Comestor's own making. First, Comestor's scriptural paraphrase makes plain what Scripture does not say, namely that Zachary considered the angel's promises impossible. This explains why Zachary was punished, transferring the explanations offered for his punishment in the glosses into a scriptural paraphrase. We see here again, therefore, that scriptural paraphrase lends itself well to integration with the interpretations of Scripture enshrined in the glosses. Indeed, we have now seen that Comestor had multiple ways to integrate scriptural text and glosses, for he could choose to integrate those interpretations into the paraphrase itself, or he could move easily back and forth between Scripture and discrete glosses.

Second, Comestor's paraphrase leads up to and ends with another quotation of Scripture. We saw above in his summary paraphrase of the Lucan material in his lectures on the Glossed Matthew that Comestor began and ended this part of his lecture with glosses. In the present instance, he began and ended with verbatim scriptural quotations. In both examples, Comestor moved easily back to his ordinary *modus operandi* in his lectures of citing Scripture and ordering glosses, for scriptural paraphrase could be easily integrated both with Scripture and gloss.

Third and finally, Comestor's paraphrase substantially abridged the scriptural narrative, even as it incorporated parts of it verbatim.[17] Comestor summarized in a few sentences what Luke covered at great length in the first chap-

---

16 *Glose Comestoris in Lucam glosatam*, Troyes, MS 1024, fol. 143v, column b: "Promisit angelus Zacharie filium nasciturum et multa circa puerum futura congessit, ut in conceptione tanti filii pater exultaret. Ille autem considerans se minus idoneum ad generandum, considerans etiam quod uxor sua infecunda esset et iam processiset *in diebus suis*, credidit impossibile quod ab angelo promittebatur. Ideo respondit: *unde hoc sciam?*"

17 Comestor restates Zachary's question verbatim: "Et dixit Zacharias ad angelum: Unde hoc sciam? Ego enim sum senex, et uxor mea processit in diebus suis." G, Luc. 1.18 *ad loc.*, 4: 140, col. b.

ter of his Gospel.[18] We see that scriptural paraphrase gave Comestor great flexibility in treating both Scripture and the tradition of interpretation. He was able to go in a variety of directions, while at the same time preserving cogency. Comestor had the option of remaking the scriptural narrative wholly into paraphrase, or incorporating snippets of Sacred Scripture, as he did here. Doubtless, for men like Comestor whose minds were steeped in the Scriptures, it would be second nature to incorporate scriptural phrases into their lectures, consciously or not, and so the line between Scripture and scriptural paraphrase might often be hard to discern. But in either case we see the development of a supple tool for treating Scripture and gloss together, one that Comestor here used to render manageable the scale of the material in the *Gloss* for his students.

We see Comestor putting this same tool to effective use in the *History*, where his paraphrased version of this particular episode in the second chapter of the *Historia evangelica* is even more succinct: "When on the day of propitiation Zachary *was placing the incense*, an angel foretold to him that a son would be born to him from his wife. Zachary, considering the sterility of his wife and the old age of them both, did not believe, and on account of this he was rendered mute up to the day of the birth. The angel also made known to him the name of the boy as well as the boy's magnificence together with his abstinence." A side-by-side comparison of this passage in Latin with Comestor's treatment of the same material in his lectures on the Glossed Luke reveals that Comestor, while using the same method, had sharpened his razor by the time that he composed the *History*:

Historia evangelica, Chapter 1 (ed. Clark, lin. 9–13):

> Cum in die propiciacionis INCENSUM PONERET, PREDIXIT EI ANGELUS NASC-
> ITURUM SIBI FILIUM DE UXORE. QUI CONSIDERANS STERILITATEM UXORIS
> SUE ET UTRIUSQUE SENECTUTEM NON CREDIDIT, ET OB HOC OBMUTUIT
> USQUE AD DIEM PARTUS. NOMEN QUOQUE PUERI ET MAGNIFICENTIAM CUM
> ABSTINENTIA EI INDICAVIT.

Glose Comestoris in Lucam glosatam (Troyes, MS 1024, fol. 143v, column b):

> Promisit angelus Zacharie filium nasciturum et multa circa puerum futura
> congessit, ut in conceptione tanti filii pater exultaret. Ille autem consider-

18   Luke 1.5–18.

ans se minus idoneum ad generandum, considerans etiam quod uxor sua infecunda esset et iam processiset *in diebus suis,* credidit impossibile quod ab angelo promittebatur. Ideo respondit: *unde hoc sciam?*

The relationship between the two passages is clear, for we see Comestor incorporating into the *Historia evangelica* some of the same words and phrases used in his classroom lectures. So too, we find in the *History* the same salient characteristics of Comestor's use of paraphrase in his lectures: seamless integration of Scripture and scriptural paraphrase; easy incorporation of glosses into the narrative; facility of transition between Scripture and gloss; and radical abridgement of Scripture itself.

What is most striking about the version in the *Historia evangelica* is its cogency. Comestor has here reduced what was an enormous amount of material in the *Gloss,* both Scripture and glosses, to a pithy episode. His use of scriptural paraphrase, artful already in his lectures on the Glossed Gospels, has become literary. Some of the difference can be explained by the gap between oral and written expression. In his lectures, although Comestor had doubtless prepared thoroughly beforehand, he was speaking to a class. In the *History,* he was writing for posterity. Nevertheless, it is clear that he has applied the same method to good effect, producing a narrative at once concise, polished, and pleasing.

Another typical example is afforded by Comestor's treatment of the six causes why the Lord willed that his mother be betrothed to Joseph. This example is particularly apt, for it occurs in the middle of Comestor's transition in the *Historia evangelica* from Luke's Gospel to Matthew's in his own account of the infancy narrative. I have already in Chapter Two discussed Comestor's lengthy remarks on this topic in lecturing on the Glossed Luke, during which Comestor told his students that "not everything is read in the Gospel."[19] Comestor also dwelled at some length on this same point in his lectures on the Glossed Matthew, bringing it up in the form of a question: "It is asked why God had willed that the Blessed Virgin be betrothed?"[20] As in his lectures on the Glossed Luke, Comestor here points out that a multifaceted answer to this question lay to hand in a marginal gloss: "A manifold cause is reported in the gloss: IDEO

---

19 See Chapter Two, 69–71. The quotation, "Nec omnia leguntur in Evangelio," may be found at *Glose Comestoris in Lucam glosatam,* Troyes, MS 1024, fol. 145ra, top.

20 *Glose Comestoris in Mattheum glosatum,* Troyes, MS 1024, fol. 6vb, middle: "Queritur quare voluerat Deus Beatam Virginem desponsari?"

DESPONSATA."[21] The marginal gloss itself does not elaborate these causes but rather presents them concisely:

SINCE SHE WAS BETROTHED. ORIGEN. THUS BETROTHED, in order that she might signify the Church, which is a virgin and one betrothed, and that through Joseph Mary's family tree might be made manifest, or that Joseph would be a witness of her chastity, defending her from the ignominy of suspicion, and lest she be condemned for adultery, and that the Virgin might be supported by the consolation of a man, and that the birth [of the Christ child] might be hidden from the Devil, who was not able to find out from what seed he was born, whether from a virgin, and lest the virgins have an excuse for their disgrace, since the Mother of Christ would have been disgraced.[22]

Quoting from and incorporating small phrases and parts of phrases from the marginal gloss, Comestor lectured on Matthew 1.18. Moreover, just as he had done in his lectures on the Glossed Luke, Comestor unpacked for his students at some length the causes in the marginal gloss. The first cause listed, namely that Mary's betrothal referred allegorically to the Church, was the only one not found in the Glossed Luke. Comestor devoted more class time to this, a mystical or allegorical cause, than to the others, explaining to his students the various ways in which Mary's betrothal to Joseph prefigured that of the Church to Christ. Comestor told his students:

The first cause is mystical, namely that she may more elegantly signify the Church, WHICH IS A VIRGIN, that is, not having the corruption of sin, AND A SPOUSE, not a wife .... For spouse is said from espousal. Therefore, before the coming of Christ in the flesh, the Church was the spouse of Christ, not the wife, since the union of Christ and his Church had been accom-

---

21 *Glose Comestoris in Mattheum glosatum*, Troyes, MS 1024, fol. 6vb, middle, citing GM, Matt. 1.18 *ad loc.*, 4: 6, col. b, marginal gloss 3: "Et redditur multiplex causa in glosa."

22 *Glose Comestoris in Mattheum glosatum*, Troyes, MS 1024, fol. 6vb, middle: "*CUM ESSET DESPONSATA. ORIGENES. IDEO DESPONSATA*, ut significare (sic) ecclesiam que virgo sit et sponsa, et ut per Ioseph origo Marie ostenderetur, vel ut Ioseph esset testis castitatis defendens eam ab infamia suspitionis, et ne ut adultera damnaretur, et ut virgo viri solatio sustentaretur, et ut Dyabolo partus occultaretur, qui nequit satis dinoscere an ex semine natus sit, an de virgine, et ne virginibus esset excusatio infamie, quia mater Christi infamata fuerit."

plished through the consent of souls but had not yet been accomplished through the union of natures .... Or since spouse properly speaking means before the handing over ... .[23]

It is worth noting that Comestor here preserves the lexical meaning of *sponsa* as *fiancée* and not as wife (then current among contemporary theologians and canonists).[24]

Comestor's treatment of the other causes was less elaborate yet still more comprehensive than that found in the marginal gloss upon which he was lecturing. He explained that the second cause was that Mary's genealogy might be firmly and fittingly established through Joseph, as was customary.[25] The third was that Joseph, a just man, would be in a position to testify to Mary's chastity and to defend her from suspicion or reproach.[26] At this point, however, Comestor once more found it necessary to reorganize the marginal gloss for his students:

Now switch to that [lemma], LEST THE VIRGINS HAVE THE EXCUSE OF IGNOMINY. For this [is] about this cause, and this marginal gloss is not well organized. And read it thus: that is, so defending her from disgrace, lest the foolish virgins have an excuse for their disgrace. For if the Blessed Virgin had been disgraced, the foolish virgins, if they were caught deflowered and accused, would have an excuse, saying: it is no wonder, if we have been

---

23 Ibid.: "IDEO DESPONSATA ETC. Prima causa mistica est scilicet ut elegantius SIGNIFI-CARET ECCLESIE (sic), QUE VIRGO EST, id est non habens macule corruptionem, ET SPONSA, non uxor .... Sponsa enim a sponsione dicitur. Ergo ante adventum Christi in carnem, ecclesia erat sponsa Christi, non uxor, quia facta erat unio Christi et ecclesie per consensum animorum, sed nondum facta erat unio naturarum .... Vel quia sponsa proprie dicitur ante traductionem ... ."

24 See Marcia L. Colish, *Peter Lombard*, 2 vols., Brill's Studies in Intellectual History 41 (Leiden: Brill, 1994), 2: 653–654, where Colish provides citations to the pertinent texts in the notes. Colish's summary of twelfth-century debates surrounding marriage provides useful background to Comestor's discussion. Ibid., 628–648.

25 *Glose Comestoris in Mattheum glosatum*, Troyes, MS 1024, fol. 6vb, middle-bottom: "ET PER IOSEPH Ecce secunda causa scilicet ut per Ioseph contribulem suum origo Beate Virginis ostenderetur, quia non solent series genealogiarum texi per nomina feminarum."

26 *Glose Comestoris in Mattheum glosatum*, Troyes, MS 1024, fol. 6vb, bottom: "VEL UT IOSEPH Tercia causa scilicet ut testimonium viri iusti fidem faceret eius castitati, quia habuerat eam in custodia sua. DEFENDENS EAM AB INFAMIA SUSPITIONIS scilicet ne fieret infamis."

subjected to abuse and blasphemy, since the mother of Christ did not lack the signs of disgrace ... .[27]

Comestor here may be referring to the foolish virgins of the Gospel spoken of in the twenty-fifth chapter of Matthew's Gospel, five of whom were wise and five of whom were foolish, for they were without oil for their lamps.[28] But whatever his intended reference, the lack of order in the marginal gloss meant that he had to reorder it for his students, taking more time than he otherwise would have. Comestor now summarily disposed of the three remaining causes, directing his students to go back to the earlier portion of the marginal gloss: that Mary might not be accused of adultery; that she would have Joseph to care for her; and that the birth of Jesus might remain hidden from the Devil.[29]

I have reproduced most of this portion of his lecture on Matthew 1.18 to emphasize that for Comestor Mary's betrothal was an important point and one

---

27   Ibid.: "Modo transi ad illud: NE VIRGINIBUS ESSET EXCUSATIO INFAMIE. Hoc enim de hac causa, nec glosa bene ordinata est, et iunge ita: id est ideo defendens eam ab infamia, ne virginibus fatuis esset inde excusatio. Si enim esset infamata Beata Virgo, virgines fatue, si deprehenderentur corrupte et arguerentur, possent habere excusationem dantes: non est mirum, si exposite sumus contumeliis et blasphemie, quia nec mater Christi caruit nota infamie." I should note that Joseph Goering suggests the more felicitous "nostra" for "nota" here, which would in fact be a better reading, according to which the foolish virgins would be saying that Mary "did not share our infamy." But "nota" is the reading in Troyes MS 1024 and Bodleian MS, Laud. misc. 291, at fol. 7vb, and therefore until I have had the chance to check other manuscripts I must stick with the less elegant version.

28   Since Comestor is lecturing on Matthew's Gospel, this is a reasonable assumption. On the other hand, he may simply be speaking of "foolish virgins" of whatever sort, since there is nothing that explicitly identifies them as the more famous group spoken of by Jesus in his well-known parable.

29   *Glose Comestoris in Mattheum glosatum*, Troyes, MS 1024, fol. 6vb, bottom – fol. 7ra, top: "Modo redi: VEL NE ADULTERA DAMPNARETUR. Si queratur utrum virgines, si deprehenderentur corrupte, lapidarentur ... adultere. De virgine inquit filie familias scilicet filia sacerdotis. Hoc expressum habeo in Deuteronomio, et forte quia Beata Virgo erat de genere Aaronitarum ... de tribu sacerdotali, si ante desponsionem corrupta deprehenderetur ad modum adultere, lapidaretur. De aliis autem virginibus expressum non habeo. ET IDEO VIRGO Alia causa scilicet ut haberet virum qui ei provideret. ET UT DIABOLO Alia causa ideo scilicet desponsata est, ut non deprehenderet Diabolus eam virginem esse, et sic nesciret filium Dei natum de virgine. Voluit enim Deus celare Diabolo secretum incarnationis usque ad tempus passionis ..."

for which the summary treatments in the marginal glosses of the *Gloss*, both in Matthew and in Luke, were insufficient by themselves. It is not surprising that he includes this material in his *Historia evangelica*. What is noteworthy is the dramatic change in scale from his classroom lectures to that of his own textbook.

Comestor made the transition from Luke's narrative to Matthew's in the third chapter of the *Historia evangelica*, "On the Birth of the Precursor."[30] In the first several portions of this chapter, Comestor covered the material presented in Luke 1.39–80, from Mary's hastening off to the hill country of Judea to visit with and assist Elizabeth, through her *Magnificat*, to the wonders surrounding the birth of John the Baptist, and finally to the Canticle of Zachariah.[31] Comestor brought this portion of his narrative to a close with a verbatim quotation from Luke's Gospel: "*AND THE BOY GREW UP AND GREW STRONG IN THE SPIRIT. AND HE REMAINED IN THE DESERT UNTIL THE DAY OF HIS COMING FORTH OPENLY TO ISRAEL.*"[32]

In the third and final portion of Chapter Three of his *Historia evangelica*, Comestor employs the same mix of Scripture, scriptural paraphrase, and gloss that he had used to summarize the Lucan material in his lectures on the Glossed Matthew to summarize Matthew's account of Joseph's discovery upon Mary's return that she was pregnant:

MEANWHILE MARY, RETURNING TO NAZARETH *WAS FOUND* BY HER FIANCÉ *TO BE PREGNANT BY THE HOLY SPIRIT.* JOSEPH, DETERMINED NOT *TO TAKE HER* AS HIS WIFE, *MADE UP HIS MIND TO DISMISS HER SECRETLY.* BUT HE WAS ADVISED *IN A DREAM* BY AN ANGEL TO ACCEPT HER *AS HIS WIFE.* AND SO THAT JOSEPH MIGHT NOT SUSPECT ADULTERY, THE ANGEL MADE CLEAR TO HIM THAT THE BOY HAD BEEN CONCEIVED *BY THE HOLY SPIRIT.* AND HE INSTRUCTED HIM TO NAME HIM *JESUS*, SINCE HE WOULD *SAVE HIS PEOPLE FROM THEIR SINS.* From this Joseph understood that God, who alone forgives sins, would be born. AND TAKING HIS FIANCÉE AS HIS WIFE, he remained a virgin with the Virgin. Mary indeed had a husband, lest being pregnant she be disgraced, and that she might enjoy the dedicated service

---

30 *Historia evangelica*, 3 (ed. Clark, Textual Appendix B.1 below, lines 31–77): "De ortu precursoris."

31 Ibid., lines 32–45.

32 Ibid., lines 55–57, where Comestor reproduces Luke 1.80: "*PUER AUTEM CRESCEBAT ET CONFORTABATUR SPIRITU. ET ERAT IN DESERTIS LOCIS USQUE AD DIEM OSTENSIONIS AD ISRAEL.*"

and the consolation of a husband, and that the birth of God might be kept hidden from the Devil.[33]

Although Comestor here incorporates words and phrases from Matthew's Gospel, Comestor makes more use of scriptural paraphrase than he does of Scripture itself. Moreover, although he tells the same story, his use of scriptural paraphrase enables him both to provide more detail and to abridge Matthew's narrative. It also enables him to integrate effortlessly into his narrative the causes why Jesus wanted Mary to be betrothed to Joseph. Thus, for example, where the glossators, both in Matthew and in Luke, had given as one cause that Mary might not be suspected of adultery, Comestor, making explicit what Scripture leaves implicit, relates that the angel made sure that Joseph himself did not suspect her of adultery. The change is subtle but effective, for whereas the glossators were vague about who might suspect Mary of adultery, Comestor's paraphrase brought the gloss more in line with the text of Scripture itself in identifying Joseph as the principal actor in the drama.

Using the same technique of integrating Scripture and scriptural paraphrase with glosses, Comestor makes explicit several other matters that are implicit in Matthew's account. Each of them centers on St. Joseph and provides a fuller account of his transformation from surprised spouse to supportive husband. Thus, Comestor tells us that Joseph learned from the angel that "God, who alone forgives sins, would be born" of Mary. It is immediately apparent why Comestor included the parenthetical remark that God alone forgive sins, for Joseph, by learning that the child would forgive sins (Matthew 1.21), understood that the child was God, because (he reasoned) only God can forgive sins. Moreover, Joseph would be the guardian of this divine child, born of the Holy Spirit, truly God with all of God's unique powers including forgiveness of sins.

---

33 Ibid., lines 58–67, where Comestor reproduces Matthew 1.18–25: "REVERTENS AUTEM MARIA NAZARETH *INVENTA EST* A SPONSO *IN UTERO HABENS DE SPIRITU SANCTO*. QUI NOLENS *EAM TRADUCERE* IN CONIUGEM, *OCCULTE VOLUIT EAM DIMITTERE*. *IN SOMNIS AUTEM ADMONITUS EST AB ANGELO, UT ACCIPERET EAM IN *CONIUGEM*. Et ne suspicaretur adulterium, CONCEPTUM PUERUM *DE SPIRITU SANCTO* INDICAVIT. ET UT *IESUM* VOCARET PRECEPIT, QUIA *SALVUM* FACERET *POPULUM SUUM A PECCATIS EORUM*. Ex hoc cognovit Ioseph Deum nasciturum, qui solus peccata dimittit, ET ACCIPIENS SPONSAM IN UXOREM, CUM VIRGINE VIRGO PERMANSIT. Habuit autem Virgo virum, ne gravida infamaretur, et ut viri solatio ministerioque frueretur, et ut Diabolo occultaretur Dei partus."

Comestor's pithy phrase conveys something of the wonder Joseph must have experienced at the prospect of the birth of the Christ child.

Comestor further tells us that after taking Mary as his wife Joseph "remained a virgin with the Virgin Mary." Again, the phrase, a gloss on the paraphrased scriptural text that precedes it, conveys pithily the doctrine of Mary's perpetual virginity, while at the same time jarring the reader out of any complacency he might feel about Joseph. Comestor's narrative once more makes Joseph – who would not only take Mary as his wife and care for her and the child but would himself contrary to all expectation remain a virgin – a central actor in the drama.

At the close of the chapter, having succinctly related Mary's transition in status from betrothed to wife, as well as Joseph's corresponding transformation from fiancé to husband, Comestor gets to the causes for the divine will that Mary be betrothed to Joseph. He lists three: that the pregnant Mary not be disgraced, that she have a husband to look after and console her, and that the birth of the Savior remain hidden from the Devil. But in contrast to his lectures on the Glossed Matthew and the Glossed Luke, where for the good of his students he had to digress, reorganizing the material presented in the *Gloss*, Comestor here integrates these glosses in the context of a flowing but cogent narrative. He also once again changes subtly the context for their discussion, for in place of a discussion of Mary's betrothal and all that such a status implied under Jewish law, Comestor re-presents these glosses as an integral part of God's plan in giving Joseph to Mary, first as spouse and then as husband.[34]

The two examples just considered, Comestor's treatment of Gabriel's interaction with Zachary and his account of the divine causes for Mary's betrothal to Joseph, show Comestor feeling his way towards a more concise means of presenting the biblical narrative and the tradition of glosses on the scriptural text to students. Comparison of his treatment of the same material in his lectures on the *Gloss* and in the *History* reveals the development of a method that could be used with subtlety and finesse to abridge radically the scriptural narrative and tradition of interpretation attached thereto. Comestor's

---

34 For a magisterial explication of the contemporary discussion of the status of Joseph and Mary under Jewish law, which makes plain the influence of his teacher, Peter Lombard, on Comestor with respect to this issue, see Giulio Silano's discussion in his translation of Peter Lombard, *The Sentences, Book 4: On the Doctrine of Signs*, trans. Guilio Silano, Mediaeval Sources in Translation 48 (Toronto: Pontifical Institute of Mediaeval Studies, 2010), xlvi–xlvii.

re-presentation in the *Historia evangelica* of the same material is distinguished chiefly by its cogency. Indeed, the examples just considered show clearly Comestor's solving one of the salient difficulties in using the *Gloss* as a textbook, namely the problem of its enormous scale. These same examples, however, also show that Comestor constantly had to grapple with the organization of the material presented in the *Gloss*. How he applied the same basic principles to solve that fundamental problem is the subject of the next section.

b. *The Problem of Organization*
That the problem of scale just considered was to a certain extent inseparable from the problem of organization for Comestor is evident from the examples just considered. We have seen that Comestor extracted a few details from his lectures, in themselves a tiny proportion of the material that he had covered in the *Gloss* with his students in the lecture hall, and incorporated them into chapters in his *Historia evangelica*. We have further seen that this process was not a simple matter of removing material from one work and grafting it onto another. Indeed, in incorporating those details into the *History*, Comestor not only reduced vastly their scale but also changed both their form and their context.

There are several plausible explanations for this change in form and context. In part, of course, Comestor's doing so was necessary to restrict the scope of the *History* to the literal sense of Scripture. So too, it was in part the natural result of the transition from lecturing to writing. In the lecture hall, Comestor had the time to dwell at length on a detail, if he so pleased, and the opportunity to return to the same topic, as he did repeatedly with the reasons for the divine will that Mary be betrothed to Joseph. In the *History*, by contrast, there was neither need nor opportunity for repetition or digression. Moreover, in composing the *History* Comestor had the opportunity to revise and to polish his work.

But in large part the changes wrought had to do with the deficiencies of the *Gloss* as a set text for lecturing on the Bible. Even apart from the fact that its folios included and mixed together indiscriminately all the various senses for interpreting Scripture, it is clear from Comestor's repeated complaints to his students that the *Gloss* was an imperfect vehicle for teaching Scripture. Even had Comestor not said anything about imperfect organization in the *Gloss*, the fact that he constantly reorganized it for his students shows well enough his view as to its organization. Comestor's remark to his students that a particular marginal gloss was not well organized – "Modo transi ad illud: NE VIRGINIBUS ESSET

EXCUSATIO INFAMIE. Hoc enim de hac causa, nec glosa bene ordinata est" – could legitimately be applied to the biblical *Gloss* as a whole.[35] Happily, however, there is no need to divine Comestor's thoughts in general from his comments about a single gloss, for he himself makes plain his views about the salient defect of the *Gloss* as a textbook for teaching the Bible to students. He does so while speaking of Mary's *Magnificat*, and in taking his students through the text of Mary's canticle, Comestor gives his students a short but revealing lesson on how to read the *Magna glosatura*.

To follow Comestor's lecture, it would be helpful to reproduce here the marginal gloss in the *Gloss* that forms the crux of his remarks:

MY SOUL MAGNIFIES THE LORD. BEDE. First she declares publicly the gifts that have been granted spiritually to her, then she enumerates the blessings of God by which he has never ceased to care for the human race, as if to say, God has raised me up by so great a gift, that by no use of the tongue could I unfold [what he has done for me] but I offer every feeling of my inner being with great praises of thanks. All that I live, all that I feel, all that I see in contemplating his greatness I devote to observing his commandments.[36]

Comestor first points out to his student auditors that, although the canticle is not divided in the scriptural text, the marginal gloss at issue makes clear a tripartite division.[37] Comestor next explicates that tripartite division for his students:

For there is a tripartite partition of this canticle, namely as the partitions of the psalms are distinguished: in the first partition, Mary gives thanks

---

35 For the entire quotation, see n27 above.

36 GM, Luc. 1.46 *ad loc.*, 4: 143, col. a, marginal gloss 4: "*MAGNIFICAT ANIMA MEA DOMINUM*. BEDA. Primo dona sibi spiritaliter concessa profitetur, deinde beneficia Dei quibus generaliter humano generi in eternum consulere non desistit enumerat quasi tanto munere me Dominus sublimavit, ut nullo lingue officio explicare possim sed totum animi interioris affectum magnis gratiarum laudibus offero. Totum quod vivo, totum quod sentio, totum quod discerno in eius magnitudine contemplanda in eius preceptis observandis impendo."

37 *Glose Comestoris in Lucam glosatam*, Troyes, MS 1024, fol. 146rb: "... et licet in litera non habeas distinctum, nota tamen in glosa diligenter triphariam distinctionem."

for the gifts bestowed spiritually on her; in the second, she gives thanks
for the benefits bestowed generally on the human race, that is with reference to the humble and about the rejection of the proud, so that you may
call benefits the scourges with which God corrects the proud, in that text,
namely in *his mercy*; in the third part, she gives thanks for the singular dis-
pensation by which it was arranged that the Word of God should become
incarnate, in that text, namely *he has taken up Israel for his own son*.[38]

Comestor's explication thus far is straightforward, and with the aid of this particular marginal gloss his students have at their disposal a simple outline for
understanding the *Magnificat*.

It is at this point, however, that Comestor makes his remarks about how to
read the *Gloss* in general. He is prompted to do so because, once again, he has
to organize the various elements of the *Gloss* for his students:

> See, therefore, that the *Magna Glosa* must be read in piecemeal fashion, and
> first he distinguishes partitions as if to say that there are three segments of
> this canticle: FIRST, that is, in the first segment, THEN, that is, in the second,
> ENUMERATES ETC. There you have your distinct segments. About the third
> you have it towards the end of the gloss. At this point leave this gloss, in
> order to read piece-by-piece, and read that interlinear gloss: IN SOUL AND
> IN SPIRIT ETC. And you can distinguish which gloss intimates somewhat
> that distinction, that you call the soul sensual life etc … . And now return
> to the gloss, AS IF ETC. And it is a summary … . Now you have an exposi-
> tion of what was said, *in God … salvation*, but you do not yet have an expo-
> sition of what was said, *my*, and this is what follows … . Whence also *my* is
> said figuratively. Before you go on, read that gloss: *whichever soul believes*.
> And it is the moral sense … .[39]

---

38   *Glose Comestoris in Lucam glosatam*, Troyes, MS 1024, fol. 146rb: "Est enim triplex par-
     ticio huius cantici scilicet distinguuntur particiones psalmorum: in prima particione
     agit gratias de beneficiis spiritualiter sibi collatis; in secunda agit gratias pro beneficiis
     humano generi generaliter collatis id est de respectu humilium et de eiectione super-
     borum ut beneficia etiam apelles flagella quibus corripit superbos ibi scilicet in *miseri-
     cordia*; in tercia parte agit gratias pro singulari dispensatione qua dispensatum est ut
     verbum Dei incarneretur ibi scilicet *suscepit Israel puerum suum*."

39   Ibid.: "Vide ergo quia Magna Glosa legenda est intercise, et principium distinguit
     particiones quasi tres sunt particiones huius cantici: PRIMO id est in prima particione,
     DEINDE id est in secunda ENUMERAT ETC. Ecce habes distinctas suas particiones. De

The interlinear gloss to which Comestor here refers in the middle of these remarks reads as follows: "AMBROSE. In soul and in spirit devoted to God the Father and the Son, one God from whom all things, and through whom all things are venerated with holy affection."[40] As Comestor makes plain, it is this interlinear gloss that sheds light on Mary's reference to her inner soul and to her life in the marginal gloss. He is, therefore, forced as it were to redirect his students' attention to this interlinear gloss before refocusing their attention on the marginal gloss that he had been discussing. Finally, before moving on from considering this marginal gloss, Comestor tells his students to read the next marginal gloss on the page.[41]

Comestor's reorganization of the material in the *Gloss* is nothing new at this point, for in this and the last chapter we have seen him doing so repeatedly. Indeed, one can find multiple examples of his reorganizing the *Gloss* in precisely this fashion on almost every folio of the manuscripts preserving his lectures on the Glossed Gospels. What he says here, however, about what he is doing is of capital importance for two reasons. First, he gives voice to what he is constantly forced to do in teaching students by means of the *Gloss*. In telling his students that the *Gloss* had to be read *incisive*, which I have rendered into English as "piece-by-piece," Comestor shared with them the principal reason for his labor-intensive method of teaching with it in the classroom. Comestor ceaselessly reorganized the various "pieces" of the *Gloss* for his students, and indeed, as we have seen, the biblical *Gloss* had to be read in this piecemeal fashion for many reasons. The literal had to be distinguished from the figurative. The marginal glosses had to be collated with the interlinear glosses, as in the example just considered, and the scriptural text properly related to both. Above

---

tercia habes in fine. Hic dimitte glosam, ut legas incisive, et lege illam interlinearem: ANIMA ET SPIRITU ETC. Et potes distinguere que glosa aliquantulum innuit distinctionem, ut animam dicas vitam sensualem etc ... . Et modo revertere ad glosam QUASI ETC. Et est summa ... . Ecce habes expositum quod dictum est, *in deo salutari*, sed nondum habes expositum quod dictum est *meo*, et hoc est quod sequitur ... .Unde et spiritualiter *meus* dicitur. Antequam progrediaris lege illam: QUECUMQUE ANIMA CREDIT. Et est moralis ... ." I have shown (above, in Chapter Two) that Comestor and his students were using what they considered to be the Great Gloss on Luke, doubtless authored by Peter Lombard. Here is another clear reference to that *Magna Glosa*.

40 GI, Luc. 1.46 *ad loc.*, 4: 143, col. a, interlinear gloss 2: "Ambrose. Anima et spiritu Deo patri devota et filio, unum Deum ex quo omnia et unum Deum per quem omnia pio venerator affectu."

41 GM, Luc. 1.46 *ad loc.*, ed., 4: 143, col. a, marginal gloss 5: "Moyses. Quecumque anima credit etc ... ."

all, the glosses themselves, all of them treated by Comestor, had to be placed in proper order to correspond not only to the biblical narrative and text but also and even more importantly to Comestor's ordered presentation of history and mystery. The *Gloss*, in short, was not by any means a text that lent itself easily to classroom explication.

The second reason for the importance of what Comestor says in his lecture about how the *Gloss* must be read is even more significant, for it enables us to connect explicitly his project in composing the *History* to his lectures on the Glossed Gospels.[42] The reason for this is that we are now in a position to understand more fully Comestor's explanation, in his epistolary prologue to the *History*, for why he undertook to compose that work, which can now be read in the light of his remarks to his students that the *Gloss* must be read *incisive*. Speaking of the *History*, Comestor wrote: "The cause of my undertaking this work was the insistent entreaty of colleagues who, because they would often read the history of Sacred Scripture scattered in the scriptural text and glosses, too concise and insufficiently explained, pressed me to compose a work to which they might have recourse for grasping the truth of history."[43]

Here we get to the heart of Comestor's stated reasons for writing the *History*. The claim that he wrote only because his brethren begged him to do so is a conventional aspect of the modest author topos. It does not necessarily

---

42 In discussing relevant historiography in Chapter One, I noted that while Smalley observed that both the biblical *Gloss* and the *History* served as textbooks for teaching the Bible, she did not perceive that the *History* was the actual fruit of Comestor's teaching by means of the *Gloss* apart from identifying it as a source. I here provide the evidence for Comestor's understanding of the causal relationship between the two school-texts.

43 Prologus Magistri epistolaris (ed. Clark, Appendix A.1, lines 4–7): "Causa suscepti laboris fuit instans petitio sociorum. Qui cum historiam Sacre Scripture in serie et glosis diffusam lectitarent brevem nimis et inexpositam opus aggredi me compulerunt ad quod pro veritate historie consequenda recurrerent." In translating Comestor's phrase *in serie* as "in the text of Scripture itself," I follow Hugh of St. Cher's gloss: "IN SERIE id est in textu." Uppsala, University Library, MS C 134 (Dominican Convent of Sigtuna, 1233–1248), fol. 3va. In Hugh's time the Bible, the Text *par excellence*, was often referred to simply as *textus*. Comestor's use of the phrase *in serie* to refer to the scriptural narrative was common in the twelfth century. Hugh of St. Victor, for example, commonly used *seriem narrationis* or *historiae seriem* to refer to *historia*. See, for example, *De scripturis*, 5 (PL 175: col. 15), and *Didascalicon de studio legendi*, 5.2, ed. and trans. into German as *Studienbuch* by Thilo Offergeld, Fontes Christiani 27 (Freiburg im Breisgau: Herder, 1997), 320.6–7, 12–13, and *Didascalicon de studio legendi*, ed. Henry Buttimer (Washington, DC: Catholic University Press, 1939), 96.3, 8–9, 48.

describe what really happened. But the specific complaint is important, for we can now understand precisely what it was that his colleagues meant in complaining that "they would often read the history of Sacred Scripture scattered in the scriptural text and glosses, too concise and insufficiently explained ... ." It is true of course that history understood as historical narrative was featured more in certain biblical books than in others, as Hugh of St. Victor and Comestor had clearly recognized. Yet Comestor's words here fit the biblical *Gloss* far better than the Bible by itself, for he uses a phrase – "historiam Sacre Scripture in serie et glosis diffusam" – that could only refer to the former. Moreover, as we have seen in this and the preceding chapter, the "history of Sacred Scripture" spoken of here by Comestor, whether understood as the literal sense of Scripture or as a biblically-based narrative of salvation history, was indeed "scattered in the scriptural text and glosses" throughout the *Gloss*. This is precisely why the *Gloss* had to be read *incisive*, and "Comestor's obsessive care to 'order' the glosses in relation to the text," as Smalley so aptly put it, testifies eloquently to how thoroughly he did so in teaching by means of the *Gloss*.[44] Moreover, if I am correct in maintaining that his reference to *"socii"* must naturally be understood to refer to his colleagues in the schools generally, which would of course include the Victorines as well as the *magistri* teaching alongside Comestor in the Parisian schools, then they too would have faced the same problems in using the *Gloss* as a tool for teaching and understanding the various riches in the Bible.

Comestor's words in his epistolary prologue, therefore, juxtaposed both with his explanation to his students that the *Gloss* must be read *incisive* and his solicitude to do so in his teaching, make perfect sense of the reality that he and his students faced in seeking to understand that history, both fundamental sense and historical narrative, in the *Gloss*. This is precisely how Chenu interpreted Comestor's prologue: "Here is his explicit intention: faced with a growing discontinuity of glosses, rediscover *the truth of history* ... ."[45] I argued in Chapter One that Comestor's references to "historiam Sacre Scripture" and "pro veritate historie consequenda" in this same passage support the view championed by Smalley and to some extent by Chenu that one branch of the *History*'s family tree

44 Smalley, *Gospels in the Schools*, 65.
45 Chenu, *Introduction à l'étude de saint Thomas d'Aquin*, 2nd ed. (Montreal: Institut d'études médiévales; Paris: Vrin, 1954), 204: "Voici son intention explicite: Face à la discontinuité croissante des gloses, retrouver la *veritas historiae* ... ." See also Chenu, *La théologie au douzième siècle*, 2nd ed. (Paris: Vrin, 1966), 69 n3 ("... selon l'intention même de Comestor, voulant retrouver, face au morcelage des gloses, la *veritas historiae* ... ").

was the vision of a discipline of history set forth by Hugh of St. Victor.[46] We can see here that this same passage reveals just as clearly the other branch, for in the light both of Comestor's pithy but revealing phrase and of his experience in the classroom it is evident that the *History* was also the child of the *Gloss*. To continue with the analalgy of parentage, Hugh's Victorine program of education can be said to represent the paternal side of that genealogy, for in composing the *History* and in making history the foundation of Bible study, Comestor dutifully followed Hugh's counsels.[47] The *Gloss* can be said to represent the maternal side, for Comestor's *History* was literally born from the body of the *Gloss* itself, not only in terms of its matter but more importantly in terms of its very form.

We are now in a position to see how Comestor solved this salient difficulty in teaching by means of the *Gloss*, so accurately described in his epistolary prologue to the *History*. As with the problem of scale, comparison of Comestor's treatment of the same material in his lectures on the glossed Gospels and in the *Historia evangelica* reveals how Comestor remedied the problem of organization. First and most obviously, he took what was a problem in the *Gloss* and made of it a virtue in the *History*, for in the latter work it was Comestor himself who ordered the "pieces" (both from Scripture and from the various glosses in the *Gloss*) into a cogent narrative.

We have already seen Comestor making use of scriptural paraphrase to do just this, and in fact paraphrase, both of Sacred Scripture and the glosses attached thereto, was his chief tool for refashioning the disparate elements of history into a concise narrative. Often a single, well-placed paraphrase would serve in the *History* to replace what Comestor had labored long to cover in teaching with the *Gloss*. A typical example is Comestor's treatment of Zachary's silence, imposed by the angel as a punishment for disbelief.[48] In his lecture on this portion of the Glossed Luke, Comestor discoursed at great length on the reasons for Zachary's silence, leading his students through a variety of glosses, interlinear and marginal, that had to be re-ordered.[49] In the *His-*

---

46   See my discussion in Chapter One at 28-37.
47   Comestor, of course, had ready access to the entire Victorine corpus, which was not only well preserved but made readily available. See Rudolf Goy, *Die Überlieferung des Werke Hugos von St. Viktor* (Stuttgart: Hiersemann, 1976).
48   I quote at 90–93 above, portions of related passages from Comestor's Gospel lectures and the *Historia evangelica* in showing Comestor's use of scriptural paraphrase to abridge the story of Gabriel's interaction with Zachary in the *History*.
49   *Glose Comestoris in Lucam glosatam*, Troyes, MS 1024, fol. 144ra, middle-bottom, in which Comestor refers to GI AND GM, Luc. 1.24 *ad loc.*, ed., 4: 141, col. a, interlinear gloss 1, marginal glosses 1, 2, and 7.

toria evangelica, by contrast, Comestor used a taut paraphrase – "ET OB HOC OBMUTUIT USQUE AD DIEM PARTUS" – to replace not only these various glosses but also the scriptural passage to which they were attached.[50]

Frequently, though, Comestor would make surgically precise use in the *History* of the language in the glosses that lay to hand in the *Gloss.* In lecturing on Luke's account of the Annunciation, for example, Comestor had at first skipped over Gabriel's reference to Elizabeth as Mary's cousin, omitting the words "*cognata tua.*"[51] He did return to these words subsequently, first quoting Luke and then repeating these very words in the course of his discussion of the remarkable fact that Mary and Elizabeth were related: "... precursorem nasciturum de *cognata tua,* sed mirum videtur quod cognate fuerunt ... ."[52] Comestor concluded this part of his lecture by directing his students without explication to the first word ("Legimus etc.") of a marginal gloss on point: "We read that Aaron, who was of the tribe of Levi, took his wife from the tribe of Judah, Elizabeth, the sister of Naason. And among the ancestors of David we read that Joiada the priest had a wife from the regal tribe, Josabet, the daughter of Jorah. Whence it is that both tribes, the priestly and the regal, were joined."[53]

In the *Historia evangelica,* by contrast, Comestor actually used these lines to connect his own paraphrase of the annunciation to Luke's words recounting Mary's humble assent: "And he indicated to her that her kinswoman, Elizabeth, had also conceived. For the priestly and the regal tribes were conjoined, because not only did Aaron have a wife from Judah, Elizabeth, the sister of Naason, but also Joiada the priest had a wife, Jocabat, who was the daughter of King Joram. AND *MARY* SAID: *LET IT BE DONE TO ME ACCORDING TO THY WORD.*"[54] What makes Comestor's use of this marginal gloss in the *History* especially interesting is the fact that it connects the *Historia evangelica* to

---

50 Luke 1.20.

51 *Glose Comestoris in Lucam glosatam,* Troyes, MS 1024, fol. 145vb, middle, referring to Luke 1.36: "*ET ECCE,* angelus dixerat virgini, *CONCEPIT* ...."

52 *Glose Comestoris in Lucam glosatam,* Troyes, MS 1024, fol. 145vb, bottom.

53 GM, Luc. 1.36 *ad loc.,* 4: 142, col. b, marginal gloss 1: "Legimus quod Aaron, qui de tribu Levi erat, accepit uxorem de tribu Iuda, Elizabeth sororem Naason. Et in posteris David legimus quod Ioiada pontifex uxorem habuit de tribu regali Iosabet, filiam Ioram. Unde utreque tribus, regalis et sacerdotalis, erant coniuncte."

54 *Historia evangelica,* 2 (ed. Clark, Textual Appendix B.1 below, lines 21–25): "ET ETIAM CONCEPISSE COGNATAM SUAM ELIZABETH SIBI INDICAVIT. Permixte enim erant tribus sacerdotalis et regia, nam et Aaron uxorem habuit de Iuda Elizabeth sororem Naason, et Ioiada pontifex Iocabet filiam regis Ioram. ET AIT *MARIA: FIAT MIHI SECUNDUM VERBUM TUUM* ...."

his lectures but indirectly, for the intersection of material is incidental. Comestor did no more than cite this gloss in his lectures but quoted it in the *History*, where it evidently served his ends as part of the narrative.

We see clearly, therefore, that Comestor's long experience lecturing on the four Glossed Gospels in the cathedral school of Notre Dame during the 1160s, and in particular his success in coming to grips with the salient difficulties of the biblical *Gloss* as textbook, namely the problems of massive scale and poor organization, bore considerable fruit in the form of two governing principles that Comestor would use to create a new and much-improved, introductory biblical textbook. The first of these principles, namely that Sacred Scripture does not by itself tell us everything that we need to know, makes plain the importance of the precedent tradition of interpretation enshrined by the *glossatores* in the glosses, marginal and interlinear, found in the biblical *Gloss*. The second principle, however, completes the first, for it is plain that those glosses themselves needed to be properly organized not only in relation to Sacred Scripture but also in relation to each other.

What was needed, therefore, was a method for forming both Scripture and gloss into a cogent format, one that would transmit in pleasing form the twin aspects of history as literal interpretation and as historical narrative. How well Comestor succeeded in meeting that need is well illustrated by the *Historia scholastica* itself, in which Comestor forged a multifarious tradition into one cogent expression of history, understood both as the literal sense of Scripture and also as narrative. In the next chapter, I address both meanings, respectively, showing Comestor's method in the *History* for bringing order out of the chaos of the Church's seemingly limitless treasury of literal or historical glosses and his success in achieving a unified historical narrative.

CHAPTER FOUR

Towards a Better Textbook

The Making of the *Historia scholastica*

We saw in Chapter Three that Peter Comestor, dissatisfied with the *Gloss* as a textbook, developed a different way of introducing students to biblical study in the *Historia scholastica*. In this work he both amplified and streamlined biblical exposition, melding into a readable text Holy Scripture, glosses derived from previous authors and commentators, extra-biblical as well as post-biblical material, and his own interpolated comments. Leaving to others "the ocean of mysteries" as well as the extrapolation of dogmatic and moral theology from biblical exegesis, Comestor made explicit his goal to illuminate the literal/historical sense of Scripture and its meaning for salvation history.[1]

History, as we have seen, had a twofold sense: the primary, literal sense of Scripture, and the narrative itself. Comestor chose a simple and felicitous structure for combining both in his *History*, following to some extent the plan of Hugh of St. Victor's *Didascalicon*. Emphasizing the primary importance of mastering the historical sense as the foundation for all study of the Bible, Hugh had listed those biblical books that he considered most useful for the study of history: Genesis, Exodus, Joshua, the Book of Judges, the Books of Kings, Paralipomenon, and in the New Testament the four Gospels and the Acts of the Apostles.[2] Comestor, however, enlarged Hugh of St. Victor's list of the biblical books requiring historical study, adding Leviticus, Numbers, Deuteronomy, Ruth, Tobit, Ezekiel, Daniel, Judith, Esther, and First and Second Maccabees. The Acts

---

1   *Petri Comestoris Historia scholastica*, Prologus epistolaris (ed. Clark, Textual Appendix A.1 below, lines 8–10): "Porro a cosmographia Moysi incipiens rivulum historicum deduxi usque ad ascensionem Domini Salvatoris, pelagus misteriorum peritioribus relinquens ... ."

2   Hugh of St. Victor, *Didascalicon de studio legendi*, 6.3, ed. and trans. into German as *Studienbuch* by Thilo Offergeld, Fontes Christiani 27 (Freiburg im Breisgau: Herder, 1997), 364.19–24; *Didascalicon de studio legendi*, ed. Henry Buttimer (Washington, DC: Catholic University Press, 1939), 115–116; *The Didascalicon of Hugh of St. Victor: A Medieval Guide to the Arts*, trans. Jerome Taylor (New York: Columbia University Press, 1961), 137.

of the Apostles, the one book on Hugh's list omitted by Comestor, was subsequently added to the *History*.[3] The *History*'s range was so comprehensive that Hugh of St. Cher, whose team of Dominicans put together an encyclopedic commentary on the *History* in the 1230s, hailed it as equivalent to the entire Bible.[4]

The names given to Comestor's *Historia scholastica* by scholars reflect its general structure. Smalley habitually referred to Comestor's book as the *Histories*, because Comestor wrote each of the Old Testament books that he treated as a separate history (*Historia Genesis*, *Historia Exodi*, etc.). He even harmonized the four Gospels into a separate *Historia evangelica*. Nevertheless, there can be no doubt that Comestor viewed his work as a unified whole, "a historical rivulet ... running from the cosmography of Moses to the Ascension of our Lord and Savior."[5] For this reason I refer to it as Comestor's *History*.

As a pedagogical text, the *History* remained a work in progress; the version dedicated to William of the White Hands between 1169 and 1173 was not the final one. Our earliest manuscripts show that the chapter divisions remained in flux during the 1170s and into the 1180s. Even the overall structure of the work remained unsettled. Thus Langton, lecturing on the *History* sometime during the first half of the 1170s, noted that there was disagreement over where the Old Testament portion of the *History* ended and the New Testament portion began.[6] Nevertheless, the broad outlines are clear: the *Historia scholastica* is

3   Acts was added to the *History* before 1183 at the latest, in all probability after Langton's lecture course and his revision of the same, both of which predate 1176, since Langton did not address it in these works.

4   "Materia quidem huius libri est eadem que et totius Biblie." Uppsala, University Library, MS C 134, fol. 3vb.

5   For the Latin text, see n1 above. Thus, Comestor commonly begins a succeeding biblical book with the words "prosequitur historia."

6   *Prima Stephani glosa scilicet lectiones a Stephano viva voce ante 1176 datae supra Historiam Genesis* (ed. Clark, Textual Appendix B.2 below, lines 1–3): "Capitulum. FUIT IN DIEBUS ETC. Sic incipit Lucas evangelium suum, et incipit hic Historia evangelica secundum distinctiones huius voluminis. Alii distinguunt aliter, ibi scilicet MORTUO SYMONE ETC." In his second, magisterial revision of this lecture course in 1193, Langton explained that the earlier division was actually based on material taken over in its entirety from Josephus and Hegessipus, which Comestor appended to the end of the Book of Machabees to provide a suitable transition between the Old and the New Testaments: "*FUIT IN DIEBUS ETC*. Sic incipit Lucas evangelium suum, et hic incipit Historia evangelica secundum distinctiones huius voluminis. Alii *altius* incipiunt, ibi scilicet MORTUO SIMONE ETC. +Et notandum quod quicquid dictum est a fine libri Machabeorum usque ad hunc locum scriptum est de Iosepho et Egessipo historiographo, et non continetur in Veteri Testamento, sed ideo interseruit Magister ut Vetus Testamentum congrue

composed of a series of individual histories, each of which is subdivided into chapters organized topically. Together these histories make up a single narrative of salvation history from the beginning of creation to Christ's Ascension into heaven, the last event recorded in Comestor's *Historia evangelica*.

By contrast, the *History*'s internal structure is not readily apparent, since underlying its unified narrative is a framework of lemmata and gloss whose outlines are difficult to see, especially for the modern reader. Comestor used a great many sources in compiling this narrative, but in general they can be reduced to three main categories: the Bible itself, the Christian tradition of literal/historical glosses on the Bible, and extra-biblical sources.[7] In contrast to other medieval biblical commentaries and works, in which the lemmata, composed exclusively of quotations from the Bible, are clearly distinguished in the manuscripts from the commentary proper (by red ink, underlining, larger lettering, etc.), no such visual aids are present in the manuscripts of the *History*.[8] Of the fifty or so manuscripts of the *History* that I have examined in person, only in one, Dijon MS, Bibliothèque Municipale 566, are the lemmata distinguished from the glosses attached to them. Complicating matters further is the fact that Comestor used not only biblical but also extra-biblical sources for his lemmata, something to my knowledge unprecedented in the Christian commentarial tradition.[9]

This made no difference to medieval schoolmen and their pupils, who were intimately acquainted with Comestor's sources. Indeed, we know for a fact that the twelfth- and thirteenth-century *magistri* who taught the Bible, using the

---

continuaretur Novo+." *Tertia Stephani glosa scilicet magistralis anno 1193 recensa supra Historiam Genesis* (ed. Clark, Textual Appendix B.4 below, lines 1–6).

7 For the first two categories, the biblical *Gloss* is by far the most important source, since it is Comestor's preferred access way into the tradition. See Mark J. Clark, "Peter Comestor's *Historia Genesis* and the Biblical *Gloss*," *Mediaeval Studies* 76 (2014): 57–113. For the last category Josephus is the one most often used by Comestor.

8 Typical examples of the format traditional in conventional Christian biblical commentaries are those of Comestor's near predecessor, Andrew of St. Victor, critical editions of which have been appearing since 1986: *Expositio super Heptateuchum* (CCCM 53); *Expositio super Danielem* (CCCM 53F); *Expositio in Ezechielem* (CCCM 53E); *Expositiones historicae in libros Salomonis* (CCCM 53B); *Expositio hystorica in Librum Regum* (CCCM 53A); *Super duodecim prophetas* (CCCM 53G). In each of these editions, the scriptural lemmata, italicized by convention, are readily recognizable.

9 Among such extra-biblical sources substituted for Scripture by Comestor are the *Sentences* of his master, Peter Lombard. See Mark J. Clark, "Peter Comestor and Peter Lombard: Brothers in Deed," *Traditio* 60 (2005): 85–142.

History, had no difficulty recognizing the boundaries between its lemmata and glosses, because the manuscripts reveal a continuous process of addition, subtraction, and substitution of individual glosses; these were exchanged with surgical precision.[10] Moreover, by contrast, the lemmata remained remarkably stable; to my knowledge only Comestor and his star pupil, Langton, altered them.[11] Over time, however, the framework of the *History*, once so plainly evident to his contemporaries and successors in the medieval schools, became hidden, as familiarity with the Latin biblical tradition and with the storehouse of glosses attached to it waned. A sign of how difficult it ultimately became to recognize the boundaries between lemmata and gloss in the *History* is that neither the editors of the Patrology edition of that work nor Agneta Sylwan in her edition of the *Historia Genesis* make any distinction between lemmata and gloss.[12] Biblical quotations in these are italicized, but since Comestor utilizes more biblical paraphrase than verbatim quotation, the skeletal framework of the *History*'s lemmata remains mostly invisible in both editions.

To show clearly the distinction in the *History* between the lemmata and the glosses attached to these, in my edition I make use of the following typographical conventions. First, I set off all lemmata in capital letters. As is customary, I italicize all Scriptural quotation, which means that some portion of the lemmata are italicized capital letters. I do not, however, italicize scriptural

10   I document this process in the following series of articles: Mark J. Clark, "Peter Comestor and Stephen Langton: Master and Student, and Co-makers of the *Historia scholastica*," *Medioevo* 35 (2010): 123–150; "The Commentaries of Stephen Langton on the *Historia scholastica* of Peter Comestor," in *Étienne Langton: Prédicateur, bibliste, théologien*, ed. Louis-Jacques Bataillon, Nicole Bériou, Gilbert Dahan, and Riccardo Quinto (Turnhout: Brepols, 2010), 373–393; and "Le cours d'Étienne Langton sur *l'Histoire scolastique* de Pierre le Mangeur: Le fruit d'une tradition unifiée," in *Pierre de Troyes, dit Pierre le Mangeur, maître du XIIe siècle*, éd. G. Dahan, Bibliothèque d'histoire culturelle du moyen âge (Turnhout: Brepols, 2013), 243–266.

11   See my discussion of Langton's revision of the *History*'s opening lemma, a juxtaposition of Genesis 1.1 and the prologue to John's Gospel, in Mark J. Clark, "The *Fortuna* of the Prologue to the *Gospel of John* in Four Important, Twelfth-Century Texts: The Glossed John, Peter Comestor's Lectures on the Glossed John, Comestor's *Historia scholastica*, and Langton's Course on the *History*," in *"In principio erat Verbum": Philosophy and Theology in the Commentaries on the Gospel of John (II–XIV Centuries)*, ed. Fabrizio Amerini, Archa Verbi Subsidia 11 (Münster: Aschendorff Verlag, 2014), 111–128. This article revises to some extent my prior discussion of the same texts in "The Commentaries on Peter Comestor's *Historia scholastica* of Stephen Langton, Pseudo-Langton, and Hugh of St. Cher," *Sacris erudiri* 44 (2005): 301–446, at 362–374.

12   See PL 198: 1046–1644, and Peter Comestor, *Scolastica historia Liber Genesis* (CCCM 191).

paraphrase, which Comestor employs constantly. Moreover, since he not infrequently quotes Scripture in glossing the lemmata, there are many instances in my edition of the *History* where italicized scriptural text may be found not in the lemmata proper but in the accompanying glosses. Finally, I underline extrabiblical sources in the *History*'s lemmata.

I base my edition of the *Historia scholastica* on the early manuscript, Vienna, Österreichische Nationalbibliothek MS 363, that most closely approximates the version which Langton and his students used in the early 1170s.[13] Thus, I am calling this the "Langton" or "University" edition of the *History*.[14] In this and the remaining chapters of this study, I rely on the two parts of the *History*, the *Historia Genesis* and the *Historia evangelica*, that I am preparing first for publication.[15] My goal herein is solely to illuminate the making of the *History*, and these two parts are sufficient to shed ample light on that work's interior structural framework. Because they are also representative of the *History* as a whole in terms of its method and structure, I can speak with confidence herein in general terms both of the *History*'s components and of Comestor's method in putting them together.[16]

To manifest the *History's* interior structural framework, I discuss in the first part of this chapter Comestor's creative use of the three principal building blocks of the *History*: Bible, gloss, and extra-biblical sources. I then show in Chapters Five through Seven how the *History* encapsulated and transmitted in one convenient volume the twofold meaning of *historia*: the Christian tradition of literal/historical biblical exposition, and history understood as narrative, namely that of the history of salvation.

---

13 This edition, along with the corresponding English translation in multiple volumes, as well as a supplementary volume of my editions of all three versions of Langton's course on the *Historia scholastica* and that of the anonymous commentator whom I call Pseudo-Langton, will all be published by the Pontifical Institute of Mediaeval Studies. For a description of the latter author, see Clark, "Commentaries on Peter Comestor's *Historia scholastica*," 324–334 and 396–397.

14 I make the case for a "Langton" or "University" edition of the entire *Historia scholastica* in Chapter Five below.

15 For the reasons why I am not making use of Sylwan's edition of the *Historia Genesis*, see Mark J. Clark, "How to Edit the *Historia scholastica* of Peter Comestor," *Revue Bénédictine* 116 (2006): 83–91. I also discuss the principles of Sylwan's edition at some length, below, in Chapter Five, where I provide the rationale for my own edition of Comestor's *History*.

16 Once my editions of the entire *Historia scholastica* have appeared, we will be in a position to assess Comestor's treatments of different parts of the Bible and its commentarial tradition.

I. *The Building Blocks of the* History

Comestor built the *History* out of an impressive list of sources, many of which he referred to by name, but the biblical *Gloss* was his source of first resort both for the Bible itself and for the tradition of Christian literal/historical glosses on the Bible.[17] Nonetheless, his use of both Bible and gloss was creative and personal enough to warrant separate treatment of Bible and gloss here. So too, his integration of extra-biblical sources into his *History*, both as lemmata and gloss, also warrants separate treament.[18]

a. The Bible
Peter's Latin surname, Comestor or Manducator (in English, Peter the Eater) is said to have been derived from his having eaten or devoured the entire Bible. Comestor, however, does not simply quote the biblical text verbatim but, as often as not, he paraphrases it, combines quotation with paraphrase, and interweaves the biblical text thus manipulated with his chosen commentary. A good example is his treatment of Genesis 1.1–14, visible when we juxtapose it with the actual biblical text:

Genesis 1.14–18:

> (**Gen 1.14**) Dixit autem Deus fiant luminaria in firmamento caeli ut dividant diem ac noctem et sint in signa et tempora et dies et annos (**Gen 1.15**) ut luceant in firmamento caeli et inluminent terram et factum est ita (**Gen 1.16**) fecitque Deus duo magna luminaria luminare maius ut praeesset diei et luminare minus ut praeesset nocti et stellas (**Gen 1.17**) et posuit eas in firmamento caeli ut lucerent super terram (**Gen 1.18**) et praeessent diei ac nocti et dividerent lucem ac tenebras et vidit Deus quod esset bonum.

---

17   See Clark, "Peter Comestor's *Historia Genesis* and the Biblical *Gloss*," *Medioevo* 39 (2014): 135–170.

18   By lemmata in the *History*, I mean the structural framework of texts that Comestor explicates. In most biblical commentaries, the lemmata are the scriptural passages commented upon by the expositor. In the *History*, they are both scriptural, verbatim and paraphrased, and extra-scriptural.

Historia Genesis:

FECIT ENIM IN EO DIE *LUMINARIA*: SOLEM ET LUNAM *ET STELLAS* ... . Sol et luna dicuntur *MAGNA LUMINARIA* ... . LUNAM *ET STELLAS* VOLUIT ILLUMINARE NOCTEM ... UT *IN SIGNA ET TEMPORA ET DIES ET ANNOS* ... . FACTA ERGO *LUMINARIA POSUIT* DEUS *UT LUCEANT IN FIRMA-MENTO CAELI ET ILLUMINENT TERRAM*, sed non semper, ET *DIVIDANT LUCEM AC TENEBRAS*.[19]

Comestor here eliminates duplication by reorganizing Scripture, beginning with a paraphrase of Genesis 1.16, followed by an extra-biblical comment on the sun and moon.[20] He then follows with another, partial, reworked scrip-tural paraphrase ("LUNAM ET *STELLAS* VOLUIT etc."), which he cou-ples with the verbatim text of Genesis 1.14 ("*IN SIGNA* etc."). Comestor then inserts a single word from Genesis 1.17 ("*POSUIT*") with text from Genesis 1.15 and 1.18. He also interposes his own comment ("but not always") to make better sense of the final combination of biblical text and paraphrase. The result is a cogent blend of gloss and Scripture, reorganized by means of paraphrase.

In fashioning such blends of Scripture, scriptural paraphrase, and gloss, Comestor made use of the entire Latin biblical tradition at his disposal in the twelfth century: the biblical *Gloss*, which encapsulated one version of the Vul-

---

19   V, fol. 8vb–9ra–b.
20   This portion of Comestor's paraphrase was likely inspired by one of three frequently consulted sources. The first is that of Haimo of Auxerre, *Commentarius in Genesim*, Gen 1.14 (PL 131: 56C): "Luminaria solem, et lunam, et caeteras stellas accipimus." Until quite recently, this commentary on Genesis was mistakenly attributed to Remigius of Auxerre. See the introduction by Edwards to his edition, Remigius, *Expo-sitio super Genesim* (CCCM 136: xiii–xx). See also Burton Van Name Edwards, "In Search of the Authentic Commentary on Genesis by Remigius of Auxerre," in *L'É-cole carolingienne d'Auxerre de Murethach à Rémi*, ed. Dominique Iogna-Prat, Colette Jeudy, and Guy Lobrichon (Paris: Beauchesne, 1991), 399–412. The second is Josephus, *Antiquitates Judaicae: The Latin Josephus: Genesis*, 1.31, ed. Franz Blatt (Aarhus: Univer-sitetsvorlaget, 1958), 127: "quarta enim die ornavit caelum sole et luna aliisque sideribus." This passage from Josephus may also have been the inspiration for the third source, Peter Lombard, *Sent.* 2. d. 14. c. 9 (ed. Brady, 1.2: 389–399): "Quarta enim die ornatum est firmamentum sole et luna et stellis."

gate tradition; other versions of the Vulgate; and the *Vetus latina*, largely available through the many patristic citations of it that circulated.[21] Moreover, his use of variant textual traditions recorded in the critical editions of the Vulgate and *Vetus latina* suggests that he had access to multiple manuscripts recording different traditions of each version.[22]

Comestor's treatment of Genesis 2.7 ("Therefore, the Lord God formed man from the mud of the earth") in the thirteenth chapter of the *Historia Genesis* is a good example of his precise use of multiple textual traditions. Relying on Peter Lombard as his principal authority, Comestor wrote:

And since there are two parts to man, Moses treats both. For that which is written — "*HE FORMED MAN FROM THE MUD OF THE EARTH*" — is directed towards the flesh, and that which follows — "*AND HE BREATHED INTO*" — looks towards the soul, as if to say that God made man's body from the earth, his soul from nothing. Another translation has "*he blew into*" or "*he blew*," which is not incongruously said of God, as some have thought, even though God does not have a throat or breath. For God "*BREATHED INTO*," that is, made the breath of life. Similarly, "*he blew into*," that is, he made both breath and the soul.[23]

21   In addition to Beryl Smalley, *The Study of the Bible in the Middle Ages*, 3rd rev. ed. (1941; Oxford: Basil Blackwell, 1984), see also: Raphael Loewe, "The Medieval History of the Latin Bible," and Beryl Smalley, "The Bible in the Medieval Schools," both in *The West from the Fathers to the Reformation*, The Cambridge History of the Bible, vol. 2, ed. G.W.H. Lampe (Cambridge: Cambridge University Press, 1969), 102–154 and 197–219, and more recently, Jacques Verger, "L'Exégèse de l'Université," in *Le Moyen Âge et la Bible*, ed. Pierre Riché and Guy Lobrichon, Bible de tous les temps 4 (Paris: Éditions Beauchesne, 1984), 199–232.

22   See Laura Light, "Versions et révisions du texte biblique," in *Le Moyen Age et la Bible*, 55–93. Comestor in this regard followed the practice of all twelfth-century scholastics, who did not have a standard text of the Vulgate until the arrival of the thirteenth-century Paris Bible.

23   V, fol. 10vb: "Et quia due sunt hominis partes, de utraqua agit. Ad carnem enim spectat quod dicitur, *FORMAVIT HOMINEM DE LIMO TERRAE*, ad animam, *ET INSPIRAVIT ETC.*, quasi diceret, corpus fecit de terra, animam de nichilo. Alia translatio habet *insufflavit* vel *sufflavit*, quod non est incongruum de Deo, ut quidam putaverunt, cum fauces et spiritum non habeat. Deus enim *INSPIRAVIT* id est spiritum fecit. Similiter *insufflavit* id est flatum et animam fecit."

The Lombard had cited in the *Sentences* the Septuagint (LXX) readings given by Augustine: "vel secundum aliam litteram *flavit* vel *sufflavit.*"[24] Comestor, however, not content simply to repeat the biblical text quoted by either the Lombard or Augustine, controlled the text of both by going directly to the *Vetus latina* itself, where he found and used "insufflavit vel sufflavit," doubtless because "insufflavit" accorded better with the Lombard's gloss.

Another fine example is Comestor's incorporation of an alternative reading (from the *Vetus latina*) into the opening lemma of his chapter on the four rivers of paradise: "Et FONS vel FLUVIUS EGREDIEBATUR AD IRRIG-ANDUM PARADISUM id est ligna paradisi. FONS potest intellegi ... ."[25] *Fons* (spring or source) was a variant reading for Genesis 2.10 in the *Vetus latina*; *flumen* (river) the principal reading.[26] Both the principal reading in the Vulgate tradition and the text of the *Gloss* had *fluvius* (river), which Comestor also reproduced. A few lines later, Comestor cited his tailored version of the rest of Genesis 2.10 – "QUI FONS DIVIDITUR IN QUATTUOR FLUMINA" – this time using only *fons* from the Old Latin.[27] He also substituted another LXX variant (*flumina*, rivers) – the principal *Vetus latina* readings were *partes* (parts) or *principia* (beginnings) – for the Vulgate's *capita* (heads or, in this case, sources).[28] The result of his tinkering was a sensible introduction – "WHICH SPRING IS DIVIDED INTO FOUR RIVERS" – to his subsequent discussion of the four rivers of paradise.

Comestor is not unique among patristic and medieval commentators, who typically cite alternative translations of the biblical text not only to shed light on it but also to buttress their own theological desiderata. Generally speaking, however, his reasons for doing so are narrative rather than doctrinal. A good

---

24 See Peter Lombard, *Sent.* 2. d. 17. c. 1.2 (ed. Brady, 1.2: 410.7–13), where the Lombard relies on Augustine, *De Genesi ad litteram libri duodecim*, 7.1 (CSEL 28.1: 201.14–22); see *partim Sent.* 2. d. 17. c. 1.3 (ed. Brady, 1.2: 410.14–411.2), and cf. Bede, *Libri quattuor in principium Genesis* I, Gn 2.7 (CCSL 118A: 44.1385–1395). See also Peter Lombard, *Sent.* 2. d. 17. c. 1.5 (ed. Brady, 1.2: 411.10–13), where he relies on GOM, Gn 2.7 *ad loc.*, 1: 20, col. b, marginal gloss 3. Bede, who also relied on Augustine and made the same points, did not mention the Septuagint.

25 V, fol. 11va: "And a spring or river went out to irrigate paradise, that is, the trees of paradise. The spring of paradise is able to be understood ... ."

26 See Gn 2.10 in *Genesis*, ed. Bonifatius Fischer, Vetus Latina: Die Reste der Altlateinschen Bibel 2 (Freiburg: Herder, 1951–1954), 43.

27 V, fol. 11va.

28 See Gn 2.10–11 in *Genesis* (ed. Fischer), 43.

case in point is his consideration of three different translations of the passage relating the sacrifices of Cain and Abel, which he gives a distinctive treatment.

The first passage relates God's approval of Abel's sacrifice and his disapproval of Cain's: "*AND GOD LOOKED WITH FAVOR ON ABEL AND ON HIS GIFTS, BUT ON CAIN AND ON HIS GIFTS HE DID NOT LOOK WITH FAVOR.*"[29] Comestor remarks: "Since Abel was himself pleasing to God, his offering was also pleasing on his behalf. As to how this was known, another translation makes plain: '*God made it fiery hot above Abel and above his gifts.*' For fire from heaven burned up his offering ... ."[30] Comestor's source was an excerpt taken from Jerome's *Hebrew Questions on Genesis* in the *Gloss*, which reproduced this line from the translation of Theodotion.[31] In both the *Gloss* and Jerome, however, the alternative translation cited reads as follows: "*inflammavit Dominus ... super sacrificium eius.*"[32] Unlike Bede, who copied this passage verbatim, Comestor altered the passage in two places, substituting *Deus* for *Dominus* and *munera* for *sacrificium.*[33] By changing these words, Comestor kept the focus on *inflammavit*, the key word in the alternative translation, which explained how Moses knew about God's pleasure with Abel and his offering.[34] The two word changes also harmonized the alternative translation with the passage from the Vulgate just cited, in which both *Deus* and *munera* appeared.

The second example also centers on a phrase from Theodotion preserved through Jerome and the *Gloss*. Comestor inserted it into a narrative composed of dialogue (between God and Cain) and explanatory glosses:

> Cain's gifts, however, born from the avarice of man, did not please God. *AND CAIN WAS ANGRY AND HIS FACE FELL* from shame, seeing his younger brother elevated above him. Scolding Cain, therefore, GOD

---

29 V, fol. 14va: "*ET RESPEXIT DEUS AD ABEL ET AD MUNERA EIUS, AD CAIN VERO ET AD MUNERA EIUS NON RESPEXIT.*"

30 Ibid.: "Quia placuit Deo Abel, et pro ipso placuit oblatio eius. Quod quomodo cognitum fuerit, alia translatio aperit: *inflammavit Deus super Abel et super munera eius.* Ignis enim de caelo oblationem eius incendit ... ."

31 GM, Gn 4.4 *ad loc.*, 1: 31, col. a, marginal gloss 7, which is taken from Jerome, *Quaestiones hebraicae in Genesim*, Gn 4.4 (CCSL 72: 6).

32 Ibid.

33 Bede's source was Jerome. See Bede, *Libri quattuor in principium Genesis*, Gn 4.5 (CCSL 118A: 74.69–71).

34 Like other patristic and medieval exegetes, Comestor considers Moses the author of the Pentateuch.

SAID: *WHY ARE YOU ANGRY? WILL YOU NOT, IF YOU ACT WELL, RECEIVE* a reward, namely from me? Alternatively, for *YOU WILL RECEIVE*, Theodotion put it instead: *your gift will be acceptable.*[35]

The last line, quoted as an excerpt from Theodotion, did not reproduce what was in Comestor's likely source, the *Gloss* version of Jerome. That passage, which was close to the original, read: "Alternatively, according to Theodotion – 'it will be acceptable' – that is, I will take up your gift."[36] Comestor altered the wording of the quotation, in this case by conflating Theodotion's two-word translation with Jerome's gloss for purposes of grammatical clarification. The change made no difference in sense yet produced a sentence with the same direct object already mentioned twice in the immediately preceding narrative. Comestor's paraphrase of Theodotion, therefore, fit smoothly into his treatment, serving as a concise but complete bridge between two quotations from the Vulgate tradition.

At first glance, the third passage looks to be different, since Comestor gives a mostly accurate version of an alternative translation: "Another translation has: *why did your face fall? Have you not, if you offer rightly but do not rightly divide your offering, sinned?*"[37] What makes it similar to the previous two examples, however, is how Comestor uses it. Jerome produced this translation from the Septuagint at the beginning of his commentary on Genesis 4.6–7 in order to explain why it did not faithfully accord with the Hebrew original. This text actually preceded Theodotion's "*acceptabile erit*" in Jerome and the *Gloss*. Yet

35 V, fol. 14va–b: "Munera vero <Cain> ex avaritia hominis nata Deo non placuerunt. *IRATUSQUE EST CAIN ET CONCIDIT VULTUS EIUS* pre verecundia minorem sibi prelatum videns. Increpans ergo DOMINUS Cain AIT: *QUARE IRATUS ES? NONNE SI BENE EGERIS, RECIPIES* praemium, scilicet a me? Vel pro *RECIPIES* posuit Theodotion: *acceptabile erit munus tuum?*"

36 "Vel secundum Theodotion acceptibile erit hoc est munus tuum suscipiam." GM, Gen. 4.7 *ad loc.*, 1: 31, col. b, marginal gloss 1. Jerome's commentary has: "... sive, ut Theodotion ait, *acceptabile erit*, id est munus tuum suscipiam." Jerome, *Quaestiones hebraicae in Genesim*, Gn 4.7 (CCSL 72: 7).

37 V, fol. 14vb: "Alia translatio habet: *quare concidit vultus tuus? Nonne si recte offeras, non recte autem dividas, peccasti? Quiesce, ad te conversio eius et tu dominaberis illius.*" I have reproduced in this footnote the fuller version of the gloss to show that it seems to come straight out of a marginal gloss in the *Gloss* ("... *quare concidit vultis etc.* Hier., *Nonne si recte offeras non autem recte dividas peccasti. Quiesce, ad te conversio eius et tu dominaberis illius.*" GI, Gen. 4.7 *ad loc.*, 1: 31, col. b, interlinear gloss 1, which is itself close to the original in Jerome, *Quaestiones hebraicae in Genesim*, Gen 4.7 (CCSL 72: 7).

Comestor puts it to use precisely as worded, since it enables him to bring the twenty-seventh chapter to a close with several suitable glosses: "He had offered rightly, since he was offering to God as a creature to his creator, but he did not divide rightly, since he was offering himself, who was a better offering, to the Devil. Alternatively, he did not divide rightly, since he kept the better parts for himself. For he offered to God worn and gnawed ears of grain [picked up] along the road."[38] Comestor here employs a translation that Jerome had criticized as defective, because it fits in well with glosses arranged by him in a particular order in the *History* itself. In changing the context rather than the wording of this particular scriptural quotation from Jerome, Comestor smoothly incorporates this alternative translation as well to his narrative framework. In all three cases, whether he retains, changes, or eliminates their wording, Comestor uses his combination of reworked Scripture and literal commentary as raw materials for the narrative account that he so painstakingly pieces together.

Finally, several short examples will suffice to show the range of Comestor's creative use of the Bible generally. In the first, he puts Scripture to work, using it to interpret scriptural lemmata already cited. Discussing God's blessing of the seventh day, Comestor changes slightly Genesis 2.3 ("*et benedixit dei septimo et sanctificavit illum*"): "*ET BENEDIXIT DIEI SEPTIMO* id est *SANCTIFICAVIT EUM.*"[39] Here is the letter as gloss; paraphrased slightly, Scripture interprets itself.

In the second, Comestor again relies on Scripture, in this case a combination of Genesis 2.4 and Genesis 1.27, which he uses as a means of critiquing authoritative interpretation:

THESE ARE THE GENERATIONS OF HEAVEN AND EARTH ETC.
Certain commentators fix the end of the six days here. Others there: *Adam knew his wife.* (Genesis 4.25) Others where Scripture has: *here is the book of the generation of Adam.* (Genesis 5.1) Leaving out however what is doubtful, we stand on the letter. Since Moses had spoken of the creation of husband and

---

38 V, fol. 14vb: "Recte obtulerat, quia Deo quasi creaturam creatori, sed non recte diviserat, quia se, qui melior oblatio est, Diabolo <offerebat>. Vel non recte divisit, quia meliora sibi retinuit. Spicas vero attritas et corrosas secus viam Domino obtulit." Comestor took the first gloss from Haimo, a favorite source. Haimo of Auxerre, *Commentarius in Genesim*, 4.7 (PL 131: 69B–C).

39 V, fol. 10va. Comestor seems to have substituted the reading "eum" from the *Vetus latina*.

wife simultaneously, which however did not take place simultaneously, in order to explicate that which he had included concisely, he repeats also the point about the remaining generations.[40]

Here Comestor uses Scripture to interpret both Scripture and other commentators. He rests the case that the letter of Scripture resolves the doubts engendered by conflicting commentaries on another scriptural passage (Genesis 1.27: "so God created mankind in his own image ... male and female he created them"), which he cites to explain the repetition by analogy.

Examples could be multiplied to illustrate what the passages just cited reflect: Comestor uses Scripture in a variety of ways, paraphrased or not, as text to be glossed, or as text glossing itself, or as text invoked to mediate, to opt among, or to dismiss previous interpretations. To what degree did his method presume knowledge of the Bible in his readers and hearers? While medieval Christians often knew some parts of the Bible by heart, such as the Psalms, prayed daily in the *opus dei,* and were familiar with passages read repeatedly in the liturgy of the Mass, the same cannot be said for much of the *History.* It would thus appear that Comestor intended this work to be studied side by side with a text of the Bible. Indeed, in a number of places he seems to have assumed that his readers either had the Bible in front of them or knew it by heart.

Scriptura subintellecta

Good evidence that Comestor made that assumption can be found in the opening lines of Chapter Seven, which I juxtapose with several of Comestor's principal sources for purposes of comparison:

Historia Genesis:

ON THE FIFTH DAY GOD ADORNED THE AIR AND THE WATER, GIVING FLYING CREATURES TO THE AIR AND SWIMMING CREATURES TO THE WATER, AND BOTH

---

40 V, fol. 10va–b: "*ISTE SUNT GENERATIONES CELI ET TERRE.* Quidam hic determinant opera sex dierum. Quidam ibi: *cognovit Adam uxorem suam.* Alii ibi: *hic est liber generationis Ade.* Pretermisso autem quod dubium est littere insistamus. Quia creatione maris et femine simul dixerat, que tamen simul facta non fuit, ut explicet quod sub brevitate concluserat repetit et de reliquis generationibus."

CAME OUT OF THE WATERS. For water turns easily into air by becoming less dense, and the reverse is true by becoming more dense. Moses called fish *REPTILES, BECAUSE BY A CERTAIN IMPULSE THEY DRAG THEMSELVES ALONG LIKE SNAKES. THEY ARE NOT BORNE ALONG BY FEET LIKE WILD ANIMALS. NOTE THAT FROM THAT WHICH WAS SAID – FLYING CREATURES OVER THE EARTH – PLATO ERRED.*[41]

Peter Lombard, *Sent.*2, dist. 14, ch. 1 (ed. Brady, 1. 2:400.17–20):[42]

De opere quinti diei, quando creavit Deus ex aquis volatilia et natatilia ... et de eadem materia, id est de aquis, pisces et aves creavit, volatilia levans in aera, et natatilia remittens in gurgiti.

Josephus, *Antiquitates Judaicae*, 1.31 (ed. Blatt, 127.14–15):

quinto die animalia natatilia et volatilia, alia quidem in profundo, alia vero in aere esse constituit.

Genesis 1.20:

Dixit etiam Deus producant aquae reptile (reptilia *VL*) animae viventis et volatile super terram sub firmamento caeli.

Comestor here paraphrases Genesis 1.20, substituting language common to the Lombard and Josephus ("volatilia" and "natatilia") for the scriptural

---

41 V, fol. 9rb: "QUINTO DIE DEUS ORNAVIT AËREM ET AQUAM, **VOLATILIA** DANS AËRI, **NATATILIA** AQUIS ET UTRAQUE EX AQUIS ORTA SUNT. Facilis enim transitus est aque in aëra tenuando et aëris in aquam spissando. Pisces vocavit Moyses *REPTILIA, QUIA IMPETU QUODAM TOTOS SE RAPIUNT UT SERPENTES; NON FERUNTUR PEDIBUS UT FERE. NOTA QUOD EX HOC QUOD DICTUM EST – VOLATILE SUPER TERRAM – ERRAVIT PLATO.*" On the subject of Plato's errors about creation, see the comprehensive discussion of the various twelfth-century contexts in Marcia L. Colish, *Peter Lombard*, 2 vols., Brill's Studies in Intellectual History 41 (Leiden: Brill, 1994), 1: 303–341.

42 I provide the Latin text for the Lombard, Josephus, and Genesis 1.20, to emphasize the key Latin words ("volatilia," "natatilia," and "volatile").

language ("aquae reptile animae viventis et volatile").[43] He does, however, use scriptural language in several glosses. In the first, noting that Moses referred to fish as reptiles ("Moses called fish reptiles ..."), Comestor makes use of the *Vetus latina* reading (*"reptilia"*) rather than that in the *Gloss* (*"reptile"*). In the second, he quotes part of the Vulgate text – ("Note that from that which was said – *volatile super terram* – Plato erred") – that he had omitted in his opening paraphrase.

Two things stand out in Comestor's almost casual asides introducing the scriptural text. First, Comestor's paraphrase and commentary inverted the traditional format of text and gloss. His opening lemma made clear the meaning of the letter, while his two glosses introducing scriptural texts served as commentary. Second, in referring to scriptural text, *"volatile super terram,"* which he himself had not quoted, Comestor seems to have assumed that his readers knew the text of Genesis 1.20. He himself did not bother to provide that text in a lemma, yet he felt free to quote it as already known.

Language in the next several chapters lends support to the view that the *History* was read with the Bible as a companion piece.[44] In Chapter Nine ("De opere sexte die"), Comestor follows an opening paraphrase of Genesis 1.24–25, in which he uses just three words from Scripture (*"iumenta, reptilia, bestias"*), with a lengthy sequence of glosses and questions, in which he incorporates various scriptural citations into his commentary.[45] In Chapter Ten ("De hominis creatione"), however, he returns to Genesis 1.24–25, paraphrasing Scripture as follows: "MOREOVER, GOD GAVE TO MAN PRECEDENCE OVER

43 On Comestor's systematic use of the Lombard's *Sentences* to structure his own treatment of the Hexameron in the *History*, see Clark, "Peter Comestor and Peter Lombard," 90–122.

44 The chapter divisions are different in our two earliest manuscripts: V and P. The former has two chapters, adding a new chapter with a separate heading ("Auctoritate Augustini probat pisces animas habere"), where the latter has only one. Cf. V, fol. 9rb–9va and P, fol. 4rb. In this monograph, unless I specify otherwise, I am referring to the chapter divisions in V. I set forth my reasons for privileging V in the Chapter Five.

45 V, fol. 9va: "SEXTA DIE **ORNAVIT** DEUS TERRAM. PRODUXIT ENIM TERRA OMNIA GENERA ANIMALIUM: *IUMENTA, REPTILIA, BESTIAS.*" The remainder of the chapter consists of commentary. Comestor quotes Luke 21.18 (*"nec capillus de capite eius peribit,"* at V, fol. 9vb) without attribution and also Genesis 3.18 (*"spinas et tribulos germinabit tibi terra,"* V, fol. 10ra), which he returns to subsequently, when he discusses the curses assigned by God to the serpent, the woman, and the man.

ALL OTHER LIVING BEINGS. In three things, therefore, the dignity of man is noted. First, since he was not only made *according to his own kind*, as has been said above, but also since he is the image of God."[46]

Comestor's reference to the phrase, *"in genere suo,"* is odd, since he had omitted it in covering Genesis 1.24–25. How are we to understand Comestor's words, "ut predicta," given that he himself had said nothing about the phrase in question to this point in the *History*? This wording poses the same problem as the phrase that he had used in Chapter Seven: "Nota quod ex hoc quod dictum est." In each case Comestor spoke as if he had already used the words of Scripture at issue, yet the fact is that he had not. In some fashion the text of Genesis was being read along with the *Historia Genesis*: the students either had its text in front of them or knew it by heart. How else to explain Comestor's phrasing?

Other passages also suggest Comestor's assumption that his readers have a text of the Bible in front of them. In Chapter Twenty-Four ("De maledictionibus viri et serpentis"), recounting Eve's attraction to the fruit (in Genesis 3.6), Comestor incorporated into his opening lemma language from Genesis 2.9 (*"pulchrum visu"* and *"ad vescendum suave"*) that he had omitted from his coverage of that verse in his treatment (in Chapter Fifteen) of Eden and its special trees.[47] From a narrative standpoint, Comestor's editorial decision made good sense. It was when Eve looked at it that she noticed the physical attributes of the apple. Nonetheless, in incorporating key language from Genesis 2.9 into his treatment of Genesis 3.6 after omitting it in the first place, Comestor assumed the scriptural fluency of his readers.

In the example just considered, Comestor wove previously omitted Scripture into a scripturally based lemma. He also frequently made use of previously omitted Scripture for commentary. A good example can be seen in Comestor's treatment of the Tower of Babel, a condensed version of Genesis 11.1–9.[48] The key passage is as follows:

---

46 V, fol. 10ra: "DEDIT AUTEM DEUS HOMINI UT PREESSET CETERIS ANIMANTIBUS. In tribus ergo notatur hominis dignitas: primo quia non solum factus est *in genere suo*, ut predicta, sed etiam quia ymago Dei est."

47 V, fol. 13ra. For chapter fifteen, see V, fol. 11ra–b.

48 V, fol. 19ra: "Post obitum vero Noe MOVENTES PEDES SUOS *AB ORIENTE* CONVENERUNT DUCES IN UNUM CAMPUM *SENNAAR*. **ET TIMENTES DILUVIUM CONSILIO NEMROTH VOLENTES REGNARE CEPERUNT EDIFICARE** TURRIM, QUE PERTINGERET USQUE AD CELOS HABENTES *LATERES PRO SAXIS ET BITUMEN PRO CEMENTO. DESCENDIT AUTEM DOMINUS UT VIDERET TURREM* id est animadvertit ut puniret. ET AIT AD

Nor do I think that what Moses says about Regma, the son of Chus, should be overlooked, namely that he had two sons, Saba and Dodan. Josephus though says Saba and Judas, the latter of whom, *living among the Egyptian people of the West, left his own name to the Jewish people.* As to what is added – *Assur went out from the land of Sennaar* – it must be understood that Nimrod drove him by force out of that land and from the tower that was his by hereditary right. Alternatively, Assur, the son of Sem, who discovered purple and the ointments for the head and body, for whom Chaldea and Assyria were named, must not be understood, but Assur, that is, the kingdom of the Assyrians, went out from there, which happened at the time of Sarug, great-grandfather of Abraham.[49]

Comestor here interposes three separate scriptural texts, which he had already passed over in silence, into a carefully structured sequence of lemmata and glosses based mainly on Josephus's narrative. Comestor's first comment ("Nor do I think …") recalled Genesis 10.7 ("Filii Chus, Saba et Hevila et Sabatha et Regma et Sabatacha; filii Regma, Saba et Dadan"), which he had entirely omitted in the previous chapter.[50] So too, his interposed phrase ("Assur went out from the land of Sennaar") introduced yet another scriptural text omitted in the previous chapter, in this case a line from Genesis 10.11: "de terra illa egressus est Assur." Finally, the third alternative understanding that he proposed, beginning with "must not be understood," implicitly recalled a third text passed over in the previous chapter, namely Genesis 10.22: "Filii Sem, Aelam et Assur et Arfaxad et Lud et Aram."

ANGELOS: *VENITE, CONFUNDAMUS LINGUAM EORUM, UT NON INTELLEGAT QUISQUAM VOCEM PROXIMI.*" Comestor took the first sentence of this passage verbatim from the last sentence of Josephus, *Antiquitates Judaicae*, 1.118 (ed. Blatt, 138.15–17) and the second from a combination of *Antiquitates Judaicae*, 1.117 (ed. Blatt, 138.12–13) and Genesis 11.9. The phrases from Josephus are in bold.

49 V, fol. 19ra–b: "Nec pretereundum puto quod Moyses dicit Regma, filium Chus, duos habuisse filios Saba et Dodam. Iosephus vero dicit Saba et Iudan, quorum Iudas *Egyptiacam gentem Hesperiorum inhabitans, Iudeis cognomen suum reliquit.* Quod autem subditur – *de terra Sennaar egressus est Assur* – intellegendum est quod Nemroth eum expulit vi de terra illa et turre que eius erat iure hereditario. Vel non est intellegendum de Assur filio Sem, qui invenit purpuram et unguenta crinium vel corporum, de quo Chaldea et Assiria dicta est, sed Assur id est regnum Assiriorum, inde *egressum est*, quod tempore Saruch, proavi Abrahe, factum est."

50 V, fol. 18va–b and 19ra.

In this chapter on the Tower of Babel, Comestor's editorial decisions served to strengthen the narrative structure. He made Josephus a primary source and to some extent Moses a secondary one, presumably since the former had more specific information. His subordination of Scripture to the role of commentary enhanced the narrative, since in each case Moses provided information ancillary to the main story. What Moses said about Regma's two sons served to introduce Josephus's insight about the naming of the Jewish people. The quotation about Assur and the land of Sennaar complemented information provided by Josephus about Nimrod's role in building the tower. It also served to introduce Assur, the son of Sem, as well as an important set of actors on the historical stage: the Assyrians.

This precise and careful treatment of all his sources suggests that Comestor had intentionally passed over these passages in the previous chapter, in which he had recounted the history of the sons of Noah and also that of Nimrod. In other words, he thought through his use of the Bible before deciding where each piece of the historical puzzle and each source would best fit. Moreover, in this particular case the manner in which he introduced as commentary scriptural texts that he had previously passed over in silence lends support to the idea that familiarity with the Vulgate was the stage on which the *History* was set. Comestor's seemingly nonchalant use of phrases such as these – "nor do I think that what Moses says ... should be overlooked" and "as to what is added" – suggests a classroom conversation between parties thoroughly familiar with the text of the Latin Bible.

One detail in particular underscores how much scriptural fluency Comestor was assuming. The passage quoted above discusses at some length Assur, one of the sons of Sem mentioned in Genesis 10.22. That same text introduced Arfaxad, another son of Sem. Comestor began the chapter following his treatment of the Tower of Babel with a verbatim extract from Genesis 11.10: *"SEM WAS ONE HUNDRED YEARS OLD WHEN HE BEGAT ARFAXAD IN THE SECOND YEAR AFTER THE FLOOD."*[51] Arfaxad, it turns out, was a noteworthy character among Noah's descendants, who lived at a pivotal time. Comestor, mentioning Assur the son of Sem and thereby recalling implicitly Genesis 10.22, brought Arfaxad to the attention of his scripturally adept readers. It was no accident that he felt comfortable using this passage as a transition to his discussion of Arfaxad in the next chapter, for his

---

51 V, fol. 19va: *"SEM CENTUM ERAT ANNORUM QUANDO GENUIT ARFAXAT BIENNIO POST DILUVIUM."*

subtle use of Scripture presupposed a great deal of familiarity with it. Even admitting that the *History* was a self-contained work, which could be read by itself, we must take seriously the possibility that it was read and studied alongside the Bible itself.

b. *The Glosses*
Comestor's use of traditional literal/historical commentary was innovative, not least because he yokes it to the various manipulations of the biblical text discussed above, in large part to clarify the literal sense. In Chapter Five of the *History*, for example, he alternates between the Vulgate and the *Vetus latina* as part of a well-organized sequence of glosses:

And he added to that another work, when *HE SAID, LET THE EARTH GERMINATE*, and it is not only about the work of germinating that this must be understood, but about the potency as well, as if he said, let it be able to germinate. FOR *THE EARTH BROUGHT FORTH* FROM THE EARTH *VEGETATION BLOOMING AND MAKING SEED AND FRUIT-BEARING TREES MAKING FRUIT EACH ACCORDING TO ITS KIND*. It is obvious that the earth produced its own plants not over a period of time, as now, but immediately in the fullness of its verdure, in which they are filled with both seed-bearing vegetation and fruit-bearing trees. Whenever *BLOOMING* is said must also be noted. Certain thinkers say that the world was made in spring, since verdure and fruitfulness are characteristic of that time of year. Others, since they read, *TREE ... MAKING FRUIT*, and what was added, *VEGETATION HAVING SEED*, say that it was made in August under the sign of the lion, but the Church holds it as certain that it was made in March. Note that when he first says, *MAKING SEED*, he also adds, *HAVING EVERY SEED*, since ... ."[52]

<hr>

52 V, fol. 8va–b: "Et addidit illi opus aliud, cum *DIXIT, GERMINET TERRA*, nec de opere germinandi intellegendum est tantum, sed de potentia quasi diceret potens sit germinare. *EDUXITQUE DE TERRA HERBAM VIRENTEM ET FACIENTEM SEMEN ET LIGNUM POMIFERUM FACIENS FRUCTUM SECUNDUM GENERA SUA*. Patet quia non per moras temporum, ut modo, produxit terra plantas suas, sed statim in maturitate viridi, in qua et herbe seminibus et arbores pomis onuste sunt. Notandumque cum dictum est *VIRENTEM*. Quidam dicunt mundum factum in vere, quia viror illius temporis est et fructificatio. Alii quia legunt, *LIGNUM...FACIENS FRUCTUM*, et additum est, *HERBAM HABENTEM*

After first citing the Vulgate's *facientem semen*, Comestor substitutes *habentem semen* from the *Vetus latina* to set up an alternative interpretation: trees and plants already have seeds in August.[53] He immediately returns, however, to *facientem semen* and also introduces the phrase – *HABENS UNUMQUODQUE SEMENTEM* – to set up a gloss from Haimo on the various ways in which "seed" can be understood: "… since it is properly called *sementis*, when it is still ready to be sown; but *semen* when it is sown, and *seminium* when it has been sown. It is, however, distinguished otherwise as well: *sementis* of fruits and trees; *semen* of animals; *seminium* the beginning of anything whatsoever."[54] The well-ordered sequence of scriptural lemmata and glosses and, in particular, the timely juxtaposition of the two Vulgate phrases mentioning (different) seeds introduce seamlessly the material from Haimo. Throughout this passage Comestor makes Sacred Scripture the handmaid of the literal sense by using alternative scriptural readings to match alternative glosses.

Another example of Comestor's innovative blend of gloss, Scripture, and scriptural paraphrase is his account of the creation of Eve. After repeating verbatim much of Genesis 2.18 ("And God also said: it is not good for man to be alone: let us make him a helper …") Comestor adds a phrase – "for bearing children that are like to him"– that is one part interposed gloss and one part scriptural paraphrase.[55] The former – God gave man a helper *for the purpose of begetting children* – is clearly an interpretation, the latter a paraphrase of the final two words ("*similem sui*") of Genesis 2.18.[56] Was the gloss meant to be part of the paraphrase? It is hard to say for sure, but whether or not he meant the phrase "ad procreandos liberos" as a gloss or part of the paraphrase is ultimately irrelevant. The important point is that Comestor wove text and gloss into a single

---

SEMEN, factum esse dicunt in Augusto sub leone, sed in Martio factum dogmatizat ecclesia. Nota cum primo ait, *FACIENTEM SEMEN*, et addit, *HABENS UNUMQUODQUE SEMENTEM*, quia … ."

53 Cf. Gn 1.12 in *Genesis* (ed. Fischer), 16.

54 V, fol. 8vb: "… quia sementis proprie dicitur dum adhuc est in sementivo, vel sementum; semen vero cum seminatur; seminium vero cum seminatum est. Distinguitur tamen aliter: sementis frugum et arborum; semen animalium; seminium cuiuslibet rei exordium." Haimo of Auxerre, *Commentarius in Genesim*, Gen 1.11 (PL 131: 56C). The marginal *Gloss* has a similar passage, which may itself be based on Haimo: see GM, Gen. 1.11 *ad loc.*, 1: 12, col. a, marginal gloss 6. Comestor's wording, however, is much closer to that found in the commentary attributed to Haimo.

55 V, fol. 12ra: "AD PROCREANDOS LIBEROS QUOD SIT SIMILE ILLI."

56 Comestor found the interposed gloss both in the interlinear and the marginal *Gloss*. See GI and GM, Gn 2.18 *ad loc.*, 1: 23, col. b and marginal gloss 2.

whole, thereby making the interpretation part of the text. Gloss and scriptural text have equal billing.

On occasion Comestor even gave the glosses top billing, subordinating Scripture entirely to gloss. The best example is his treatment of the diverse colors of the switches and the offspring of livestock in Jacob's negotiations with his father-in-law, Laban, where most of the chapter consists of an inversion of the letter of Scripture and its sense.[57] Scripture recounts how, after fourteen years of serving Laban, Jacob asked leave to depart for his native land with his wives and children. Laban, who had prospered exceedingly owing to Jacob's service, bargained for more time from Jacob and asked his son-in-law to name his salary. Jacob, who needed wealth to care for his clan, agreed to continue caring for Laban's flocks on terms that Laban accepted, provided only that Laban did what he asked.[58] Up to this point, Comestor reproduced the scriptural narrative faithfully, adding only a detail from Jerome's commentary through the *Gloss* that Laban had asked for seven more years.[59]

We know from Jerome that the exact details of Jacob's counter-proposal were controversial among Christian biblical commentators owing to perceived ambiguity in the scriptural text:

> *I will go today through all of your cattle; separate therefrom every spotted and particolored animal and every animal of uniform color among the lambs and the spotted and particolored among the goats, and it will be my share. And my just conduct will answer for me on the following day, when my share will have come before you. For every animal, on which there will not have been spots and particolor among the goats and the lambs, will be counted my theft etc.* To a great extent in the Septuagint the sense is confused, and to this day I have not been able to find one Christian commentator, who could explain clearly what was said in this passage.[60]

---

57 The chapter begins at V, fol. 29vb.

58 Gn 30.25–31.

59 V, fol. 29vb. See also: GM, Gen. 30.27–28 *ad loc.*, 1: 78, column a, marginal gloss 1, which is taken from Jerome, *Quaestiones hebraicae in Genesim*, Gen. 30.32–33 (CCSL 72: 37). The assertion of Josephus that Jacob worked for Laban for twenty years probably also gave credence to Jerome's statement: see Josephus, *Antiquitates Judaicae*, 1.309 (ed. Blatt, 163: 23–24).

60 "*Transibo in universo pecore tuo hodie, separa inde omne pecus varium et discolorum et omne pecus unius coloris in agnis et varium et discolorum in capris et erit merces mea: et respondebit mihi iustitia mea in die crastino, cum venerit merces mea coram te: omne, in quo non fuerit varium et discolor in capris et in agnis, furtum erit apud me* et cetera. Multum apud LXX interpretes

Jerome, however, did not hesitate to provide a solution himself, restating the scriptural text and controversial issue in plain language:

> You desire, said Jacob, that I should serve you even for another seven years; then do what I ask. Separate all the particolored and spotted animals, the sheep as well as the goats, and deliver them into the hands of your sons. Conversely, give to me the animals of uniform color, either white or black, from both flocks. If, therefore, any spotted animal is born of the white and black ones, which are of uniform color, it will be mine, but if any of uniform color, yours. I do not ask a difficult thing. On your side is the nature itself of flocks, such that white animals are born from white, and black animals from black; on my side my just conduct, while God looks down upon my lowliness and work. Laban willingly took Jacob up on his offer and, as Jacob was asking, separated the flocks, making a journey of three days between Jacob and his own sons, lest any fraud should be born out of the proximity of their respective flocks.[61]

Comestor substituted Jerome's account virtually verbatim in place of all but a few words from Genesis 30.32–34.[62] He then added the following postscript: "And so this explanation is clear, except that in the biblical text it says "*THAT LABAN DELIVERED THE SINGLE-COLORED FLOCK INTO THE HANDS OF HIS OWN SONS*. This seems contrary to that which we have said."[63] No clearer example of Comestor's willingness to subordinate the let-

---

confusus est sensus, et usque in praesentem diem nullum potui invenire nostrorum, qui ad liquidum, quid in hoc loco diceretur, exponeret." Jerome, *Quaestiones hebraicae in Genesim*, Gen. 30.32–33 (CCSL 72: 37).

61 Ibid.: "Vis, inquit Jacob, me servire tibi etiam alios septem annos: fac quod postulo. Separa omnes discolores et varias tam oves quam capras et trade in manus filiorum tuorum, rursumque ex utroque grege alba et nigra pecora, id est unius coloris, da mihi. Si quid igitur ex albis et nigris, quae unius coloris sunt, varium natum fuerit, meum erit: siquid vero unius coloris, tuum. Rem non difficilem postulo. Tecum facit natura pecorum, ut alba ex albis et nigra nascantur ex nigris: mecum iustitia mea, dum deus humilitatem meam respicit et laborem. Optionem Laban datam libenter arripuit et ita, ut Jacob postulabat, faciens trium dierum iter inter Jacob et filios suos separavit, ne quis ex vicinitate pecoris nasceretur dolus."

62 V, fol. 29vb. Comestor may have relied on the original or a long excerpt in the marginal *Gloss*. See GM, Gen. 30.32–33 *ad loc.*, 1: 78, col. a, marginal gloss 1.

63 V, fol. 29vb: "... et ita dictum planum est, nisi quod in textu legitur, *QUOD LABAN UNICOLOREM GREGEM TRADIDIT IN MANU SUORUM FILIORUM*. Quod contrarium videtur ei quod diximus ... ." It should be noted that the last line

ter of Scripture to its sense could be found. Comestor openly acknowledged that his narrative in this instance was founded on a gloss that appeared to contradict the text of Scripture. Faced with this problem, he naturally offered several possible ways of reconciling the two conflicting accounts: "It can be said that he, namely Jacob, handed <these single-colored sheep and goats> over into the hands of his sons, that is, of the grandsons of his own sons, who were shepherds under their father. Or it was said through anticipation, that is, that Laban gave the unicolored flock, born afterwards under the guardianship of Jacob, to his sons together with the multicolored flock previously given."[64] He ended, however, with what amounted to a frank admission of ambiguity: "Jerome also says that up to his time this passage was confused."[65] Thus, faced with a problematic biblical text as well as a problematic gloss, Comestor was willing to leave the matter unresolved.

Nonetheless, in the rest of this chapter, Comestor continued to substitute Jerome's commentary for scriptural lemmata in recounting the bizarre tale of Jacob's manipulation of the offspring of his flocks through the use of particolored switches and rods at the drinking troughs, where female animals, mounted by males as they drank, saw the reflections of these switches in the water.[66] To clarify this gloss-based narrative account, Comestor added a number of colorful glosses from Jerome and Augustine through the *Gloss*:

> As for what is said, *in order that they might conceive* among the rods, Jerome says that the force of the Hebrew word cannot be expressed except in a roundabout way. It signifies therefore the final shuddering of the whole body in the last heat of sexual intercourse. Nor is it to be wondered at that offspring similar to the reflected image should come into being in the extreme stage of pleasure, since Jerome says that this very thing takes place

---

("Quod contrarium etc."), present in MS P (BnF lat. 16943) at fol. 20vb, is here added in the margins of V, together with the start of the next line, quoted in n66, below. The biblical text that Comestor here cites is Genesis 30.35. The preceding verses of that text (Gen. 30.32–34) also plainly contradict Jerome's restatement.

64 V, fol. 29vb: "Potest dici eum tradidisse in manu filiorum id est nepotum suorum filiorum, scilicet Iacob, qui sub patre opiliones erant, vel per anticipitationem dictum est id est unicolorem gregem post natum sub custodia Iacob dedit filiis suis cum diversicolore prius dato." It is worth noting that manuscript P (BnF lat. 16943), omits the reference to Jacob ("scilicet Iacob") that makes sense of the first alternative. See P, fol. 20vb.

65 Ibid.: "Ierominus quoque dicit usque ad tempus suum confusum hunc locum fuisse."

66 See Genesis 30.37–42; Comestor's account can be seen at V, fol. 30ra–b.

among herds of horses in Spain. And Quintilian defended a matron, who had been accused because she had given birth to an Ethiopian, arguing that this had happened from the viewing of an image. And in the books of Hippocratis there is reported to have been written that a certain woman was to be punished because she had given birth to a very beautiful boy completely unlike either parent and their families, except that Hippocras advised to search, lest perhaps there should be a picture in the bedroom.[67]

Comestor here relied on patristic authorities, mediated through the *Gloss*, who gave him access to authoritative scientific and medical data, which he understood the Jacob of Genesis to have possessed.[68] These were glosses on a text, however, which Comestor himself had fashioned largely from other glosses. In short, his use of the tradition of historical/literal glosses at his disposal was as flexible and creative as his use of the Bible.

Finally, Comestor himself supplies what is missing in the biblical narrative by means of interposed comments of his own. His interpolations render explicit what is frequently implicit in Scripture. A single example will do duty for the many passages of this sort found in the *History*. Recounting the eating of the apple by Eve and then by Adam, Comestor adds several details of his own in between two biblical lemmata: "AND *THE WOMAN* SAW FIRST THAT THE TREE WAS *BEAUTIFUL TO BEHOLD*, that is, clean, and noting, either from smell or touch, that it [was] *AGREEABLE TO EAT, SHE ATE IT AND GAVE IT TO HER HUSBAND*, perhaps softening him up with persuasive words, which the Bearer of the Law skipped over for the sake of

---

67 V, fol. 30ra: "Quod autem dicitur *UT* in virgis *CONCIPERENT*, dicit Ieronimus vim Hebrei verbi nisi in circuitu exprimi non posse. Significat ergo extremam totius corporis concussionem in fervore coitus extremo. Nec mirum similem conspecte ymagini sobolem fieri in extremo voluptatis, cum hoc ipsum in equarum gregibus apud Hispanos fieri dicat Ieronimus. Et Quintilianus matronam accusatam, quod Ethiopem peperisset, ex ymagine conspecta hoc accidisse argumentans defendisset. In libris Ypocratis scriptum repperitur quandam puniendam, quia pulcherrimum peperisset utrique parenti generi quoque eorum toti dissimilem, nisi monuisset Ypocras querere, ne forte talis pictura esset in cubiculo."

68 Comestor took much of this commentary from GM, Gen. 30.32–33 *ad loc.*, 1: 78, col. a, marginal gloss 1, which is itself excerpted from Jerome, *Hebraicae Quaestiones in Genesim*, Gen. 30.32–33 (CCSL 72: 37–38). It is certain that Comestor here relied on the excerpt attributed to Jerome in the *Gloss* rather than on the original, since the compilers of the *Gloss* took the final story, namely that of Hippocras, from Augustine's *Quaestiones in Heptateuchum*, 93 (CCSL 33: 35.1157–1164).

brevity."[69] Comestor here joins Genesis 3.6 ("The woman, therefore, saw that the tree was good to eat, beautiful to look at, and delightful in aspect, and she took of its fruit and ate, giving some to her husband, who ate of it as well.") and Genesis 2.9 ("And the Lord God brought forth from the earth every tree beautiful to behold and pleasant to eat ..."), a passage which he had omitted in his earlier chapter on the trees of Eden, into a single account. An expert story-teller, he also interpolates several details that bring his readers right into the scene. Eve saw the fruit on the tree, which Scripture says was beautiful to see, and then, according to Comestor either smelling or touching it, led Adam down the path of destruction with seductive words. Adding just a bit to what Moses had written, Comestor makes the scriptural account come alive. At the same time, Comestor excuses Moses's silence about Eve's persuasive words in the usual way: Moses omitted these for the sake of brevity.

These examples show that, as with his treatment of Sacred Scripture, Comestor's use of the tradition of historical/literal glosses at his disposal was characterized chiefly by flexibility. He used them creatively and in conjunction with the Bible to form a single historical narrative. There were, however, significant gaps in the Bible with regards to salvation history, and Comestor did not hesitate to make use of extra-biblical sources to fill in those gaps.

c. *Extra-Biblical Sources*

Like most Christian commentators on the Bible, Comestor frequently takes note of the reticence of Moses. In his chapter "On the four rivers of Paradise," for example, glossing the word "Eufrates," Comestor explains that Moses said nothing about the course of the Euphrates through Chaldea, because it was well known that Abraham had come from Chaldea.[70] A few chapters later, treating the formation of Eve from Adam's rib while the latter slept, Comestor discusses at some length Moses's silence about the soul in his account of the formation of Eve, providing both an explanation of that silence and a resolution of the question.[71] At some points he merely excuses Moses's silence, as for

---

69 V, fol. 13ra: "VIDITQUE *MULIER* PRIUS QUOD LIGNUM ESSET *PULCHRUM VISU* ID EST MUNDUM ET, EX ODORE VEL TACTU NOTANS QUOD *AD VESCENDUM SUAVE, COMEDIT DEDITQUE VIRO,* forte premonens verbis persuadibilis, que transit legis lator brevitatis causa ... ."

70 V, fol. 11vb: "*EUFRATES frugifer* vel *fructuosus,* de quo (per quas transeat regiones) quasi notum tacuit Moyses, quia est in Chaldea unde venerat Abraham."

71 V, fol. 12rb – 12va: "Nota quod de formatione mulieris agendo, de corpore tantum dictum est. Unde quidam ideo tacitum esse voluerunt de anima, ut daretur intelligi sic:

instance in his chapter on Abraham's arrival in Chanaan. Addressing Moses's silence about where Abraham went between the time of the Lord's appearance to him and to his erection of an altar to the Lord once in Canaan, Comestor concisely remarks: "for the sake of brevity or as if already known."[72] Elsewhere, however, Comestor assigns himself the task of filling the gaps in Moses's account of history by recourse to extra-biblical sources.

A good example is Comestor's chapter on the descendants of Adam ("De generationibus Ade").[73] Moses had touched lightly on Adam's many descendants. Fortunately, Comestor has a source that enables him to fill in the gaps:

ADAM KNEW EVE, not in paradise but when he was already guilty and ejected [therefrom]. The Bearer of the Law skips briefly over his progeny, hastening on to the time of Abraham, father of the Hebrews; he is silent about the many sons and daughters of Adam. But Methodius the martyr prayed while he was in prison, and there was revealed to him by the Spirit about the beginning and the end of the world. And that about which he had prayed he also left written, although simply, saying that [Adam and Eve] went out from paradise as virgins and that in Adam's fifteenth year of life there was born to him Cain and his sister, Calmana. For, even though Adam was created as if a thirty-year old, nevertheless he was one day old, and then a year, and after two years, he was three years old, and so on with the rest. And he could have had before Cain many children, who are here passed over in silence by Moses. After another fifteen years, he had Abel and his sister, Debora. When Adam was one hundred and thirty years old, Cain slew Abel, and Adam and Eve mourned him for a hundred years. Then in the thirtieth year of the first chiliad, Seth was born to them. For Methodius begins that era after Adam's two-hundredth year and calls it the first chiliad. And this agrees with what we find in the Septuagint, for the seventy say that Adam was two hundred and thirty years old when he

---

traductam animam mulieris de anima viri sicut carnem de carne. Augustinus etiam hesitare videtur quid sentiendum sit de anima, an ex traduce sit an de nichilo. Sed id ipsum est, quod tacitum est de anima, potius contra eos est. Si enim anima mulieris fuit ex traduce, aliter facta est quam anima viri, que de nichilo. Et si aliter fiebat, taceri non debuit, ne sic facta putaretur, ut iam audieramus de anima viri. Itaque tacendo innuit non aliter putandum factam esse quam didiceramus prius."

72   V, fol. 20rb: "Quo iverit subticuit Moyses brevitatis causa vel quasi notum."
73   V, fol. 14rb.

begat Seth. But nevertheless in the Hebrew it is one hundred and thirty. But let us return to the brevity of Genesis.[74]

Methodius gave him access to information omitted by Scripture.[75] The first four chapters in Genesis, in particular, posed a vexing difficulty, namely how to account for the initial spread of humanity over the earth during the period when Adam and Eve had only two sons, one of whom murdered the other. Pseudo-Methodius knew of details – Adam and Eve left paradise as virgins; Adam, created as a thirty-year-old, nevertheless had plenty of time to bring other children into the world before Cain was born in the fifteenth year of Adam's earthly existence; there were daughters born to Adam and Eve, from whose wombs other descendents would come into being – important to a comprehensive and comprehensible account of history.

Josephus was another source with knowledge of extra-biblical history. Comestor frequently appealed to both authors together to supplement or correct Moses. For instance, one of the details omitted by Moses but supplied by Methodius was important to establishing a reliable early chronology. According to him, since Adam and Eve mourned Abel for one hundred years after Cain had killed Abel in the one hundred and thirtieth year of Adam's life, Seth was born to Adam and Eve in the primal parent's two hundred and thirtieth

---

74   V, fol. 14rb–14va: "*ADAM COGNOVIT EVAM* non in paradiso sed iam reus et eiectus. Legis lator breviter generationes transit, festinans ad tempora Abrahe patris Hebreorum, et plures subticet Ade filios et filias. Sed Methodius martyr oravit dum esset in carcere, et revelatum est ei a Spiritu de principio mundi et fine. Quod et oraverat et scriptum licet simpliciter reliquid dicens quod virgines egressi sunt de paradiso et anno vite Adam decimo quinto natus ei est Cain et soror eius Calmana. Et si enim Adam factus est quasi in etate triginta annorum, tamen fuit unius diei et anni et post duorum annorum <egit> tertium (trium *vid. in cod.*) et sic de ceteris. Et potuit ante Cain multos genuisse, qui tacentur hic. Post alios quindecim annos natus est ei Abel et soror eius Delbora. Anno vite Adam centesimo tricesimo Cain occidit Abel, et luxerunt eum Adam et Eva centum annis. Tunc natus est eis Seth tricesimo anno prime ciliadis. Inchoat enim Methodius secula post ducentos annos Ade et vocat seculam unam ciliadem. Et in hoc consonant in Septuaginta, qui dicunt Adam ducentorum triginta annorum esse cum genuit Seth. Sed tamen in Hebreo est centum triginta. Sed redeamus ad brevitatem Genesis."

75   Comestor, of course, had no idea that Pseudo-Methodius was not really Methodius. His only critical remark was the observation that Methodius's writing was simple. For the text of the Pseudo-Methodius, I use Pseudo-Methodius, *Sermo de novissimus temporibus*, in *Sibyllinische Texte und Forschungen: Pseudo-Methodius, Adso und die Tiburtinische Sibylle*, ed. Ernst Sackur (Halle: Max Niemeyer, 1898), 60–96.

year.[76] Comestor returned to this same topic in his chapter summarizing the generations of Adam, in which he re-presented the account of Moses in the fifth chapter of Genesis as follows:[77]

THIS IS THE BOOK OF THE PROGENY OF ADAM Moses repeats the topic of the descendants of Adam in order to follow an unbroken sequence of genealogies. Certain writers, however, begin the first age from Adam; others from Seth. Methodius agrees with these latter authorities, and therefore he says this, that no-one was born from Abel, and all of the descendants of Cain perished by the flood. ADAM HOWEVER LIVED FOR ONE HUNDRED AND THIRTY YEARS AND BORE SONS AND DAUGHTERS IN HIS IMAGE AND LIKENESS ... . Perhaps Moses left out the hundred years of Adam's mourning since, as we said, the Seventy and Methodius and Josephus write that he was two hundred and thirty years old when he begat Seth.[78]

Relying not only on Methodius but also on Josephus for his chronology of Adam and his descendants, Comestor was thus able to supplement Moses; at the same time, he was able to explain the silence of Moses. The final result was a harmonization of sources, biblical and extra-biblical, that accounted for the whole story.

Both Josephus and Pseudo-Methodius supplied interesting information left out of the scriptural account. At times this information was not only interesting but sensational. For example, Scripture provides little detail about the sins that led to the Flood. According to the Vulgate tradition reproduced in the

---

76 Comestor could also have relied on Jerome for this information. Jerome, *Hebraicae Quaestiones in Genesim*, Gen. 5.3 (CCSL 72: 8).

77 V, fol. 15vb.

78 "*HIC EST LIBER GENERATIONIS ADE*. Repetit de generatione Ade, ut integrum ordinem genealogiarum prosequatur. Tamen quidam ab Adam incipiunt primam etatem; alii a Seth, quibus consentit Methodius. Et ideo hoc dicit, quia de Abel nullus natus est, et generatio Cain tota diluvio periit. *VIXIT AUTEM ADAM CENTUM TRIGINTA ANNIS ET GENUIT AD YMAGINEM ET SIMILITUDINEM SUAM* ... . Forte Moyses centum annos luctus Ade pretermisit quia, ut diximus, Septuaginta et Methodius et Josephus ducentorum triginta annorum eum fuisse scribunt cum genuit Seth." Quoting Genesis 5.1 and 5.3–4, Comestor here names both Josephus and Pseudo-Methodius together with the Septuagint as the sources for the chronology that he presents. See: Josephus, *Antiquitates Judaicae*, 1.68, 83 (ed. Blatt, 132.3–4 and 134.1), and Pseudo-Methodius, *Sermo de novissimus temporibus*, 1 (ed. Sackur, 60–61).

Gloss, after the death of Lamech and after Sem and Ham and Japheth had been born to Noah (Genesis 5.30–31), the world was repopulated thus (Genesis 6.1–4):

> And when men had begun to multiply over the earth and had given birth to girls, the sons of God, seeing their daughters and that they were beautiful, took wives for themselves from all that they had chosen. And God said: my spirit will not endure in man forever, since he is flesh. And his days will be one hundred and twenty years. And giants were over the earth in those days. For after the sons of God went to the daughters of men and the latter bore children, these are the powerful ones, the famous men from that generation.[79]

Comestor's summary of this scriptural narrative ends with a frank admission that Moses had been vague about when various evil deeds had occurred:

> *NOAH, HOWEVER, WHEN HE WAS FIVE HUNDRED YEARS OLD BEGAT SEM, HAM, AND JAPHETH.* Moses, who was about to speak about the flood, skipped over its cause saying: *WHEN MEN BEGAN TO MULTIPLY OVER THE EARTH THE CHILDREN OF GOD*, that is, the pious sons of Seth, SAW *THE DAUGHTERS OF MEN*, that is, from the race of Cain and, overcome by desire, *THEY TOOK THESE AS WIVES, AND FROM THESE UNIONS WERE BORN THE GIANTS.* But Moses does not specify the time when this took place, whether in Noah's time or before, either a long time before or a little.[80]

---

79   G, Gen. 5.32 and 6.1–4 *ad loc.*, 1: 35, col. a: "Noe vero cum quingentorum esset annorum genuit Sem, Cham, et Iaphet. Cumque cepissent homines multiplicari super terram et filias procreassent, videntes filii dei filias hominum quod essent pulchrae, acceperunt uxores sibi ex omnibus quas elegerant. Dixitque Deus: non permanebit spiritus meus in homine in aeternum, quia caro est. Eruntque dies illius centum viginti annorum. Gigantes autem erant super terram in diebus illis. Postquam enim ingressi sunt filii dei ad filias hominum illeque genuerunt: isti sunt potentes a saeculo et viri famosi."

80   V, fol. 16ra: "*NOAH VERO CUM QUINGENTORUM ESSET ANNORUM GENUIT SEM, CHAM, ET IAPHET.* Moyses dicturus de diluvio premisit causam eius dicens: *CUM CEPISSENT HOMINES MULTIPLICARI SUPER TERRAM,* VIDERUNT *FILII DEI* id est filii Seth religiosi *FILIAS HOMINUM* id est de stirpe Cain et victi concupiscentia *ACCEPERUNT EAS UXORES. ET NATI SUNT INDE GIGANTES.* Tempus quidem quando hoc factum fuerit, utrum sub Noe vel ante, vel multum vel parum ante, non determinat."

Moses offers little assistance here, identifying neither the problematic giants whom Comestor finds in this text nor the timing of the unions that produced them. Likewise, the *Gloss* itself provides little help, specifying only that Scripture's "sons of God" were the pious sons of Seth and that "the daughters of men" came from Cain's stock.[81] So Comestor turns to Josephus and Methodius for answers:

> Josephus, however, says that the sons of Seth remained good up to the seventh generation. Afterwards they moved towards evil things, falling away from their paternal religious practices, and on account of this they turned God against themselves. For many angels of God, having sexual relations with women, begat harmful sons. These latter, on account of their confidence in their strength, were called giants by the Greeks. Methodius treats the cause of the flood, namely the sins of men, more expansively, saying that in the five-hundredth year of the first chiliad the sons of Cain abused the wives of their own brothers with excessive fornication. Furthermore, in the six-hundredth year the wives, having fallen into madness, turned the tables and abused their husbands. Upon Adam's death Seth separated his family from that of Cain, who had returned to his native soil. For when his father was alive he had forbidden them from inter-marrying. And Seth lived on a certain mountain close to Paradise, while Cain lived in the field where he had slain his brother. In the five-hundredth year of the second chiliad, men became inflamed for each other and had sexual relations with each other. In the seven-hundredth the sons of Seth lusted after the daughters of Cain, and the giants were born from these unions. And, with the coming of the third chiliad, the flood swamped the earth. Thus Methodius arranges everything.[82]

---

81 See GI, Gen. 6.2 *ad loc.*, 1: 35, col. a.
82 V, fol. 16ra–b: "Iosephus tamen dicit quod usque ad septimam generationem boni permanserunt filii Seth, post ad mala progressi sunt, recedentes a sollempnitatibus paternis, et ob hoc Deum contra se irritaverunt. Nam multi angeli Dei cum mulieribus coeuntes iniuriosos filios genuerunt. Qui propter confidentiam fortitudinis a Graecis gigantes dicti sunt. Methodius causam diluvii, hominum scilicet peccata, diffusius exsequitur dicens quia quingentesimo anno primae ciliadis filii Cain abutebantur uxoribus fratrum suorum nimiis fornicationibus. Sexcentesimo anno mulieres in vesaniam versae supergressae viris abutebantur. Mortuo Adam Seth separavit cognationem suam a cognatione Cain, qui redierat ad natale solum. Nam et pater vivens prohibuerat ne miscerentur (miscentur *in cod.*), et habitavit Seth in quodam monte proximo paradiso. Cain

Filling in his narrative with Josephus and Methodius, Comestor locates the evil cause and the chronology that he was looking for. Incorporating verbatim whole sentences from Josephus and Methodius, Comestor's account does not contradict Scripture but fills in gaps.

The great authority that Comestor accords to Josephus, Pseudo-Methodius, and a few others, chiefly Haimo and Peter Lombard, is shown by the fact that Comestor even uses such extra-biblical sources for the lemmata that make up the skeletal framework of the *History*. Sacred Scripture, quoted verbatim or paraphrased, is the ordinary foundation for the *History*'s lemmata, but Comestor frequently complements or even substitutes altogether for the *History*'s scriptural lemmata. Because I have elsewhere documented his use of the Lombard's *Sentences* to substitute for the *History*'s scriptural lemmata, I shall focus here on Haimo and Josephus.[83]

Comestor's reliance on the author responsible for the commentary attributed to Haimo of Auxerre is complicated owing to that work's relationship to the biblical *Gloss*. There is no doubt that the two works were related. One had to be a primary source for the other, since they share in many cases verbatim extracts of commentary on Genesis.[84] Since Comestor used both extensively, it is frequently difficult to discern which one he relied on in a particular case. Only a detail retained in one or the other permits certain identification.

A good example is Comestor's chapter on Abram's arrival in Chanaan, where his glossing of Genesis 12.6 closely resembles both sources:

AND HE ENTERED *THE LAND OF CHANAAN* AND CAME TO *SICHEM*, which is often corruptly called Sichar, AND *TO THE BRIGHT VALLEY*, which was then called Pentapolis, from the five cities of the Sodomites, and which is now called the Sea of Salt or of the Dead, since nothing lives in it and nothing having a soul is able to submerge in it,

---

autem habitavit in campo ubi fratrem occiderat. Quingentesimo anno secunde ciliadis exarserunt homines in alterutrum coeuntes. Septingentesimo filii Seth concupierunt filias Cain et orti sunt gigantes. Et incepta tertia ciliade inundavit diluvium. Sic ordinat Methodius." Cf. Josephus, *Antiquitates Judaicae* 1.72–73 (ed. Blatt, 132.18–25), and Ps. Methodius, *Sermo de novissimus temporibus*, 1–2 (ed. Sackur, 61–63).

83 For Comestor's extensive reliance on Peter Lombard in his treatment of creation in the *History*, see Clark, "Peter Comestor and Peter Lombard, 90–122."

84 My guess would be that the compilers of the *Gloss* used the commentary attributed to Haimo, since the latter work tends to have details omitted in the former.

or the lake of asphalt that is of pitch, which is called Jewish, or the valley of Salt dwellers.[85]

Haimo of Auxerre, *Commentary on Genesis*, 12.6 (PL 131: 82B–C):

He went through all the way to the place Sichem. Sichem is a city, which is called corruptly by certain people Sichar. But it means shoulder. He calls the bright valley Pentapolin, which is now the Sea of Salt and is called of the dead and the lake of Asphalt and the lake of the salt dwellers.[86]

GOI, Gen 12.6 *ad loc.*, 1: 44, col. a:

Sychem is a city, which is corruptly called Sychar and means shoulder. And all the way up to the bright valley which is now called the Sea of Salt or of the dead and the lake of asphalt and the valley of the salt dwellers.[87]

The relationship between the latter two sources is impossible to mistake owing to the language commonly shared. Yet, as these citations show, Comestor, who read and relied on both, incorporates into his version one detail in Haimo that is not found in the *Gloss*, namely that the *convallis illustris* (or in Comestor's version the *vallis illustris*) was at that time called *Pentapolis*, or "five cities."

There are other passages in which Comestor's Haimo functions as a substitute for Scripture. On the four rivers of Paradise, Comestor writes, discussing Phison, "Here it traversed the land Evilath, that is, India, AND IT CARRIES ALONG GOLDEN SANDS."[88] Comestor used the final clause in place of the last part of Genesis 2.11 – "Nomen uni Phison. Ipse est qui circuit omnem ter-

---

85 V, fol. 20ra–b: "ET INTRAVIT *TERRAM CHANAAN* ET VENIT AD *SICHEM,* que corrupte Sichar sepe legitur, ET *AD* VALLEM *ILLUSTREM,* que *Pentapolis* tunc dicebatur a quinque urbibus Sodomorum, que nunc Mare Salis vel Mortuum dicitur, quia nil in eo vivit et nil in eo mergi potest animam habens, vel lacus aspalti id est bituminis quod dicitur Iudaicum, vel vallis Salinarum."

86 "*Pertransivit usque ad locum Sichem. Sichem* civitas est, quae a quibusdam corrupte *Sichar* dicitur. Interpretatur autem *humerus. Convallem illustrem* Pentapolin dicit, quae nunc est *mare Salis* et *Mortuum* dicitur et *lacus Asphalti* et *lacus Salinarum.*"

87 "*Sychem* civitas quae corrupte dicitur *Sychar* et interpretatur *humerus. et usque ad convallem illustrem* quae nunc mare salis vel mortuum dicitur et lacus asphalti et salinarum vallis."

88 V, fol. 11va: "HIC *CIRCUIT TERRAM EVILATH* id est Indiam, ET TRAHIT AUREAS HARENAS."

ram Evilath, ubi nascitur aurum." – and the first part of Genesis 2.12: "Et aurum terrae illius optimum est ... ." His likely source was the commentary of Haimo, who in glossing Genesis 2.11, had written: "*qui circuit omnem terram Evilath* id est, Indiae trahens aureas arenas."[89] The *Gloss*, at least in the versions accessible to us, has no such reference to the golden sands of India. Likewise, in his chapter on the Ark, Comestor substitutes the exact words of Haimo ("SUMMITAS EIUS PERFICERETUR") in place of two words of Genesis 6.16 ("consummabis summitatem").[90]

Of all the authorities to whom he appeals, Josephus is the one whom Comestor substitutes most often for Moses. Comestor frequently cites him by name and even more frequently uses him without attribution. Scholars familiar with the *History* have taken note of Comestor's extensive reliance on Josephus in that work.[91] My focus here, however, is on Comestor's use of Josephus in place of scriptural lemmata in the *History*. A good example is Comestor's discussion of the respective offerings of Abel and Cain, where he conflates the accounts of Josephus and Moses (Genesis 4.3–4):

AFTER MANY DAYS THEY OFFERED TO GOD *GIFTS: CAIN FROM* THE FRUITS OF THE EARTH, *ABEL,* ACCORDING TO JOSEPHUS, MILK AND THE FIRST-BORN OF HIS LAMBS. Moses says – *AND FROM THEIR FATNESS* – that is from the fattest of the flock he also offered.[92]

---

89 Haimo, *Commentarius in Genesim*, 2.10 (PL 131: 61B).
90 Cf. V, fol. 16vb and Haimo, *Commentarius in Genesim*, 6.16 (PL 131: 75A–B).
91 See, for example, Saralyn R. Daly, "Peter Comestor: Master of Histories," *Speculum* 32 (1957): 62–73, at 64, and David Luscombe, "Peter Comestor," in *The Bible in the Medieval World: Essays in Memory of Beryl Smalley*, ed. Katherine Walsh and Diana Wood (Oxford: Basil Blackwell, 1985), 109–129, at 119. The fundamental study remains Heinz Schreckenberg, *Die Flavius-Josephus-Tradition in Antike und Mittelalter*, Arbeiten zür Literatur und Geschichte des hellenistischen Judentums 5 (Leiden: Brill, 1972). Schreckenberg provides a table of textual parallels between Comestor and Josephus at 148–149.
92 V, fol. 14va: "*POST MULTOS DIES* OBTULERUNT DEO *MUNERA: CAIN DE FRUGIBUS, ABEL*, secundum Iosephum, **LAC ET PRIMOGENITA AGNORUM.** Moyses ait – *ET DE ADIPIBUS EORUM* – id est de pinguioribus gregis etiam obtulit."

Genesis 4.3–4:

And it happened that after many days that Cain offered gifts to the Lord from the fruits of the earth. Abel also offered from the first-born of his flock and from their fatness.[93]

Jos., *Antiquitates Iudaicae*, I.54 (ed. Blatt, 130.13):

For when it had pleased them to offer sacrifice to God, Cain indeed offered the produce from the growths of his fields, while Abel offered milk and the first-born of his flocks.[94]

Comestor here substitutes Josephus's account, which is more specific, for that in Genesis to form the lemma.

In most cases, however, Comestor uses Josephus's account in place of Scripture without attribution. In his chapter on the death of Abel, for instance, Comestor omits the latter half of Genesis 4.9, in which Cain, questioned by God about the whereabouts of Abel, responded that he did not know and asked God: "Am I my brother's keeper?"[95] Instead, Comestor adapts a detail from Josephus, who makes explicit what Scripture only implies, namely that Cain had hidden the body after murdering Abel.[96] Comestor, writing of the exchange between God and Cain, incorporates this detail into the structural framework of his narrative: "**SINCE, WHEN HE WISHED TO HIDE THE DEED,** *GOD SAID: THE VOICE OF THE BLOOD OF YOUR BROTHER CRIES OUT TO ME FROM THE EARTH,* that is, WHAT *YOU HAVE DONE* is notorious ... ."[97] Later in the same chapter, Comestor adds another unattributed detail from Josephus's account:

---

93 "Factum est autem post multos dies ut offerret Cain de fructibus terrae munera Domino. Abel quoque obtulit de primogenitis gregis sui et de adipibus eorum."

94 "Nam cum eis placuisset sacrificare deo, Cain quidem de culturae germinationibus obtulerat fructum, Abel autem lac et primogenita gregum."

95 This chapter begins at V, fol. 14vb.

96 Jos., *Antiquitates Judaicae* 1.55 (ed. Blatt, 130.15–17): "quem cum necasset et mortuum occultasset ... ."

97 V, fol. 14vb: "**QUIA, CUM VELLET OCCULTARE FACTUM,** *DIXIT DEUS: VOX SANGUINIS FRATRIS TUI CLAMAT AD ME DE TERRA* id est notum est quod *fecisti* ... ."

NOW THEREFORE *YOU WILL BE ACCURSED OVER THE EARTH, A WANDERER AND EXILE.* Cain was deservedly cursed, which Adam was not since, knowing the punishment for his first lie, he nevertheless added fratricide. CAIN, therefore, **FEARING** either that **WILD BEASTS WOULD DEVOUR HIM, IF HE WERE TO GO OUT FROM THE COMPANY OF MEN**, or that, if he should remain with them, they would kill him on account of his sin, and condemning himself and despairing, SAID: *MY WICKEDNESS IS TOO GREAT THAT I SHOULD FIND MERCY; EVERYONE WHO FINDS ME WILL KILL ME.* He said this out of fear, or he said it, wishing for it, as if to say: *if only they would kill me.*[98]

In this case, Comestor's incorporation of Josephus's suggestion that Cain was afraid of wild animals lends color to the episode.[99]

Such conflations of Moses and Josephus to form lemmata are routine in the *History*. In the very next chapter, in which he treats the subject of Cain's descendants, Comestor takes the names from Genesis 4.22, Sella and Tubalcain, but preferrs Josephus's account for the precise details of the latter's professional abilities:

"*SELLA BEGAT TUBALCAIN,* WHO NOT ONLY FIRST DISCOVERED THE BLACKSMITH'S ART BUT ALSO PRACTICED DECOROUSLY THE ARTS OF WAR ... ."[100]

---

98 V, fol. 14vb – 15ra: "*NUNC* ERGO *MALEDICTUS ERIS SUPER TERRAM, VAGUS ET PROFUGUS.* Merito iste maledicitur quod non Adam, quia sciens iste penam prime prevaricationis, tamen fratricidium addidit. TIMENS ergo CAIN NE vel **BESTIE EUM DEVORARENT, SI EGREDERETUR AB HOMINIBUS**, vel si maneret cum eis pro peccato suo occiderent eum, damnans se et desperans AIT: *MAIOR EST INIQUITAS MEA QUAM UT VENIAM MEREAR; OMNIS QUI INVENERIT ME OCCIDET ME.* Ex timore hoc dixit vel optando dixit quasi diceret: *utinam occideret me.*"

99 Jos., *Antiquitates Judaicae* 1.59 (ed. Blatt, 131.2–5): "... quo formidante, ne bestiis capiendus incideret et eo modo periret, iussit ut nihil triste de tali cogitatione metueret neque ei propterea malum quicquam per bestias eveniret, ac per omnem terram eum sine formidine."

100 "*SELLA GENUIT TUBALCAIN,* QUI ET **FERRARIUM ARTEM PRIMUS INVENIT, RES BELLICAS DECENTER EXERCUIT** ... ." V, fol. 15rb–15va.

Genesis 4.22:

> "Sella also begat Tubalcain, who was a hammerer and a smith in all the works of bronze and iron ... ."[101]

Josephus, *Antiquitates Iudaicae* 1.64 (ed. Blatt, 131.21–22):

> "But Iobel, who was born of another mother, exercised decorously the arts of war excelling all others in bravery ... he first discovered the blacksmith's art."[102]

Tubalcain, or Iobel in Josephus's version, was not only an expert smith, who forged bronze and iron into pleasing shapes, but also a warrior, who practiced the arts of war with decorum.

As with his creative treatment of Bible and gloss, Comestor integrated extra-biblical sources fully into the *History*, even using them to form the lemmata of his work. His method – the ubiquitous use of paraphrase, blurring lines between sources, inverting the sequence of Scripture and gloss – are by now familiar. To conclude my examination of Comestor's role in the making of the *History*, there remains only to show briefly two things: first, how he remedied the problem of scale, which had rendered the biblical *Gloss* so unsuitable as a textbook for teaching the Bible; and second, how he conveyed in a cogent and accessible manner the two senses of *historia*, literal interpretation and historical narrative.

II. *Method and Structure*

We saw in Chapter Three that the biblical *Gloss* posed two main problems when used by Comestor as a textbook for teaching the Bible: scale and lack of focus. Comestor addressed both in the *History*, focusing on history alone (understood both as the tradition of literal/historical interpretation of the Bible and as the narrative of salvation recorded in the Bible) and making use of a structure that condensed his three principal source-types into a cogent narrative. In the sec-

---

101 "Sella quoque genuit Tubalcain, qui fuit malleator et faber in cuncta opera aëris et ferri."

102 "Iobel autem, qui ex altera natus est, fortitidine cunctos excellens res bellicas decenter exercuit ... ferrarium artem primus invenit."

ond part of this chapter, therefore, we shall look at examples that shed light on two salient aspects of the structure of the *History*: first, the condensing of Scripture and the tradition of Christian commentary on it into a pithy narrative; and second, his exclusive focus on history.[103]

a. *Comestor's Abridgement of Scripture and the Tradition of Glosses*
There is no better example of Comestor's abridging the biblical narrative and the Christian tradition of historical glosses than his treatment of Noah and the Ark. In the first thirty or so chapters of the *Historia Genesis*, he made many cuts in Scripture, condensing its narrative in a variety of places, but in none of these earlier chapters did Comestor make cuts on such a scale as when he got to the subject of Noah, relying on Scripture and Josephus to place Noah in the tenth generation from Adam.[104]

What makes Comestor's account of Noah's genealogy so noteworthy is the speed with which he moves from Seth to Moses, beginning with the opening line of Genesis 5.1: *"THIS IS THE BOOK OF THE DESCENDANTS OF ADAM."*[105] Following a conflation of Genesis 5.3–4, whose last part looked back not only to Genesis 5.1 but also to Genesis 1.26–27, Comestor summarizes all of Genesis 5.6–31 in one line. Speaking of Seth, he writes: "ISTE *GENUIT ENOS*, QUI *CAINAN*, QUI *MALELEHEL*, QUI *IARETH*, QUI *ENOCH*, QUI *MATUSALAM*, QUI *LAMETH*, QUI *NOE*."[106] This is addition by subtraction. Most of the scriptural material omitted by Comestor centers on the lifespans of those named. Moreover, the language in Scripture used to account for each individual is redundant. Comestor, by contrast, simply moves his story along from one key character to the next by cutting any extraneous material.

The same economy of expression characterizes his whole account of the Ark. He begins his chapter on the cause of the Flood, for instance, with the report in Genesis 5.31 that Noah was five hundred years old when he begat

---

103 Since Comestor's method remains the same throughout the *Historia scholastica*, the structure of which is consistent from beginning to end, I provide here examples taken from the *Historia Genesis* that are representative of the structure of the *History* as a whole.
104 V, fol. 16ra: **"PORRO NOE FUIT DECIMUS AD ADAM."** The quotation is based on Josephus *Antiquitates Judaicae* 1.79 (ed. Blatt, 133: 11–14).
105 V, fol. 15vb: *"HIC EST LIBER GENERATIONIS ADE."*
106 V, fol. 15vb–16ra.

Sem, Ham, and Japheth.[107] He ends the same chapter with snippets from Genesis 6.9 and 6.13, which enables him to skip over the largely redundant material covered in Genesis 6.8–13.[108] After a brief chapter on the features of the Ark itself, Comestor provides an abbreviated account of the procession onto the Ark, eliminating considerable redundancy in Scripture by skipping back and forth between the sixth and seventh chapters of Genesis.[109] Each of these changes, which presuppose on Comestor's part a comprehensive reorganization of the biblical text, eliminate repetition and render cogent Comestor's narrative. They are in fact typical of his editorial work throughout the *History*.

Comestor's way of organizing topics also facilitates his streamlining of the scriptural account. The *History*'s next four chapters (on the timing of Noah's entry onto the Ark, on the Flood itself, on the timing of Noah's exit from the Ark, and on the rainbow) illustrate how selective he was in his choice of scriptural texts and in his organization of the scriptural story.

Comestor introduces the whole story with his own version of Genesis 6.22, Genesis 7.5, or both, which serves as a transition into this phase of the tale: "AND NOAH DID EVERYTHING THAT *THE LORD HAD COM-MANDED*."[110] There follows a concise account of the entry onto the Ark: "*IN THE SIX HUNDREDTH YEAR OF HIS LIFE NOAH WENT ONTO THE ARK* WITH EVERYTHING THAT THE LORD HAD TOLD HIM.

---

107 V, fol. 16ra: "*NOE VERO CUM QUINGENTORUM ESSET ANNORUM GENUIT SEM, CHAM, ET IAPHET.*"

108 V, fol. 16va: "*NOE VERO IN GENERATIONIBUS SUIS PERFECTUS ERAT* quasi diceret non illius perfectionis est que est in patria, sed secundum modum generationis sue id est terrene. *ET DIXIT DOMINUS AD NOE: FINIS UNIVERSE CARNIS VENIT CORAM ME.* Preter eos qui in archa erant salvandi *DISPERDAM EOS CUM TERRA* id est cum fertilitate terre. Tradunt enim vigorem terre et fecunditatem longe inferiorem esse post diluvium. Unde esus carnium homini concessus est, cum antea fructibus terre victitarent."

109 Thus, for example, he uses a line from Genesis 6.18 but omits Genesis 7.1, both of which recount God's command to get on board. See V, fol. 17ra–b. Comestor does, however, quote verbatim a large chunk of God's instructions in Genesis 6.21 to bring on board food to be eaten for man and beast, an order of priority understandable enough for one named "The Eater." V, fol. 17ra: "*TOLLESQUE TECUM EX OMNIBUS QUE MANDI POSSUNT, UT SINT TAM TIBI QUAM ILLIS IN ESCAM.*"

110 V, fol. 17rb: "FECITQUE *NOE CUNCTA QUE SIBI DEUS PRECEPERAT.*" Comestor here draws from Genesis 6.22 ("Fecit ergo Noe omnia quae praeceperat ei Deus."), Genesis 7.5 ("Fecit ergo Noe omnia quae mandaverat ei Dominus."), or both. G, Gen. 6.22 and 7.5 *ad loc.*, 1: 37, col. a and b.

At the divine signal all of these were led with the help of angels ON THE SEV-
ENTEENTH DAY OF THE SECOND MONTH."[111] To show the extent to
which Comestor abridged and reorganized the scriptural account, it will be
helpful to set forth the scriptural verses upon which Comestor drew for his
concise summary in the order in which he used them. In the examples that follow, I highlight in bold those scriptural passages that Comestor either quoted
or paraphrased:

Genesis 7.11: **In the six hundredth year of his life Noah ... .**[112]
Genesis 7.6: And Noah was six hundred years old when the waters of the Flood
covered the earth.[113]
Genesis 7.7: And on account of the waters of the Flood, **Noah went onto the
Ark**, and his sons, his wife, and the wives of his sons entered with him.[114]
Genesis 7.8: Also from all living things, clean and unclean, from all flying crea-
tures, and from everything that moves upon the earth.[115]
Genesis 7.9: Two by two they went to Noah onto the Ark, male and female,
just as the Lord had instructed Noah.[116]
Genesis 7.10: And after seven days had passed the waters of the Flood covered
the earth.[117]
Genesis 7.11 (continued): **in the second month, on the seventeenth day of
the month** there erupted all the sources of the great abyss, and the floodgates
of heaven were opened.[118]

---

111 V, fol. 17rb: "*SEXCENTESIMO ANNO VITE SUE INGRESSUS EST NOE
ARCHAM* CUM OMNIBUS, QUE DIXERAT EI DOMINUS. Que et nutu divino
et ministerio angelorum adducta sunt IN *MENSE SECUNDO, DIE DECIMA
SEPTIMA.*"

112 G, Gen. 7.11 *ad loc.*, 1: 37, col. b: "Anno sescentesimo vitae Noe ... ."

113 G, Gen. 7.6 *ad loc.*, 1: 37, col. b: "Eratque sexcentorum annorum quando diluvii aquae
inundaverunt super terram."

114 G, Gen. 7.7 *ad loc.*, 1: 37, col. b: "et ingressus est Noe et filii eius uxor eius et uxores
filiorum illius cum eo in arcam propter aquas diluvii."

115 G, Gen. 7.8 *ad loc.*, 1: 37, col. b: "De animantibus quoque mundis et immundis et de
volucribus caeli et ex omni quod movetur super terram."

116 G, Gen. 7.9 *ad loc.*, 1: 37, col. b: "duo et duo ingressa sunt in arcam ad Noe masculus
et femina, sicut praeceperat Deus Noe."

117 G, Gen. 7.10 *ad loc.*, 1: 37, col. b: "cumque transsissent (*sic*) septem dies aquae diluvii
inundaverunt super terram."

118 G, Gen. 7.11 *ad loc.*, 1: 37, col. b: "mense secundo septimodecimo die mensis rupti sunt
omnes fontes abyssi magne et catharactae caeli apertae sunt."

In abridging Genesis 7.6–11, Comestor first excerpts snippets of scriptural text and reorganizes them, starting with the beginning of a chronological precision in Genesis 7.11 and going back to Genesis 7.7 (*"IN THE SIX HUNDREDTH YEAR OF HIS LIFE NOAH WENT ONTO THE ARK"*). He then paraphrases in a one-phrase summary the remainder of Genesis 7.7 and all of Genesis 7.8 and 7.9 ("WITH EVERYTHING THAT THE LORD HAD TOLD HIM"). He interposes a gloss ("At the divine signal all of these were led with the help of angels"), part of which comes straight from an interlinear gloss.[119] Comestor concludes with the remainder of the chronological precision in Genesis 7.11 (*"ON THE SEVENTEENTH DAY OF THE SECOND MONTH"*).[120] He is able to skip entirely Genesis 7.13–16, much of which is redundant.[121] Once again, Comestor accomplishes a lot with a little. Passing over the long lists of people and animals in Noah's train, Comestor moves the narrative quickly to the flood itself, his next topic.

Comestor's account of the flood itself is equally concise, as can be seen in the following juxtapostion of Comestor's narration and the biblical original:

AND IT RAINED *OVER THE EARTH FOR FORTY DAYS AND FORTY NIGHTS*, AND THE ARK, HAVING BEEN RAISED *UP, WAS BORNE INTO THE HEIGHTS. THE WATER ROSE OVER ALL OF THE MOUNTAIN RANGES. HIGHER THAN THEM ALL BY FIFTEEN CUBITS* ... .[122]

This pithy account of the flood is taken from a patchwork of phrases, excerpted from reorganized Scripture:

Genesis 7.12: And it rained **over the earth for forty days and** for forty **nights**.[123] Genesis 7.17: And there was a flood for forty days over the earth, and the waters multiplied and raised the Ark **on high** above the earth.[124]

---

119 GI, Gen. 7.9 *ad loc.*, 1: 37, col. b: "divino nutu."
120 G, Gen. 7.11 *ad loc.*, 1: 37, col. b: "mense secundo septimodecimo die mensis rupti sunt omnes fontes abyssi magne et catharactae caeli apertae sunt."
121 G, Gen. 7.13–16 *ad loc.*, 1: 38, col. a.
122 V, fol. 17rb: "ET PLUIT *SUPER TERRAM QUADRAGINTA DIEBUS ET NOCTIBUS*, ET ELEVATA ARCHA *IN SUBLIME DEFEREBATUR SUPER OMNES MONTES* EXCREVIT *AQUA ALTIOR CUBITIS QUINDECIM* ... ."
123 G, Gen. 7.12 *ad loc.*, 1: 38, col. a: "Et facta est pluvia super terram quadraginta diebus et quadraginta noctibus."
124 G, Gen. 7.17 *ad loc.*, 1: 38, col. a: "Factumque est diluvium quadraginta diebus super terram et multiplicatae sunt aquae et elevaverunt arcam in sublime a terra."

Genesis 7.18: They poured down violently and filled everything on the earth's surface. In turn, the Ark **was borne** above the waters.[125]
Genesis 7.19: And the waters swelled greatly over the earth and covered **all the mountain ranges,** the highest under all the heavens.[126]
Genesis 7.20: **The water was higher by fifteen cubits over the mountain ranges,** which it covered.[127]

As in the previous example, Comestor can be seen here cutting and pasting, taking a word here and a phrase there while omitting redundant material.

Comestor then summarizes in one line God's closing the Ark's door and the subsequent rising of the waters that killed every living creature on the earth:

AND AFTER NOAH HAD ENTERED, GOD *SHUT* THE DOOR AND COVERED IT ON THE OUTSIDE. *AND EVERY* LIVING *THING ON EARTH DIED, AND THE WATERS* raised up on high *COVERED THE EARTH FOR ONE HUNDRED AND FIFTY DAYS,* from that day namely when Noah want onto the Ark.[128]

In this one-sentence summary, Comestor excerpted parts of various lines from the sixth and seventh chapters of Genesis 7.16, 21–24 (emphasis supplied):

Genesis 6.14: and you shall line it **with pitch** within and **without.** [129]
Genesis 7.16: **And the Lord closed it** from outside.[130]

125 G, Gen. 7.18 *ad loc.,* 1: 38, col. a: "Vehementer enim inundaverunt et omnia repleverunt in superficie terrae. Porro ferebatur arca super aquas."
126 G, Gen. 7.19 *ad loc.,* 1: 38, col. a: "Et aquae praevaluerunt super terram nimis oper tique sunt omnes montes excelsi sub universo caelo."
127 G, Gen. 7.19 *ad loc.,* 1: 38, col. a: "Quindecim cubitis altior fuit aqua super montes, quos operuerat."
128 V, fol. 17va: "ET CUM INTRASSET NOE *CLAUSIT* DEUS OSTIUM ET BITU-MINAVIT EXTERIUS. *ET MORTUA EST OMNIS* ANIMA VIVENS *SUPER TERRAM, ET OBTINUERUNT AQUE TERRAS* exaltate *CENTUM QUIN-QUAGINTA DIEBUS* ab illa scilicet die qua ingressus est Noe."
129 G, Gen. 6.14 *ad loc.,* 1: 35, col. b – 1:36, col. a: "et bitumine linies intrinsecus et extrinsecus."
130 G, Gen. 7.16 *ad loc.,* 1: 38, col. a: "Et inclusit eum Dominus deforis."

Genesis 7.21: And there was destroyed **all** flesh that moved **over the earth**, all the birds, all the beasts, and all the reptiles, which crawl over the earth, all mankind.[131]

Genesis 7.22: And everything in which there was the breath of life on the earth **died**.[132]

Genesis 7.23: And God destroyed every living thing that was on the earth, from humankind to all grazing animals, reptiles as well as the birds of the air; they were all wiped from the earth. And there remained only Noah and those that were with him on the Ark.[133]

Genesis 7.24: **And the waters covered the earth for one hundred and fifty days.**[134]

In comparison with the narrative in Genesis, which repeatedly returns to the destruction of the earth's inhabitants, Comestor's account is circumspect: "every living thing on the earth died." He skips speadily over the entire episode, choosing a word here and a word there until Genesis 7.24, which he takes over in its entirety.

Comestor then moves the narrative speedily along to the recession of the waters, settling an age-old dispute by quoting the *Gloss* for the key words of Genesis 8.7: "THE RAVEN *DID NOT RETURN*."[135] Comestor concludes by streamlining the account of Noah's departure from the Ark and the rainbow.

---

131 G, Gen. 7.21 *ad loc.*, 1: 38, col. a-b: "Consumptaque est omnis caro quae movebatur super terram volucrum animantium bestiarum omniumque reptilium, quae reptant super terram, universi homines."

132 G, Gen. 7.22 *ad loc.*, 1: 38, col. b: "Et cuncta in quibus spiraculum vitae est in terra mortua sunt."

133 G, Gen. 7.23 *ad loc.*, 1: 38, col. b: "Et delevit omnem substantiam quae erat super terram ab homine usque ad pecus tam reptile quam volucres caeli et deleta sunt de terra. Remansit autem solus Noe et qui cum eo erant in arca."

134 G, Gen. 7.24 *ad loc.*, 1: 38, col. b: "Obtinueruntque aquae terras centum quinquaginta diebus."

135 V, fol. 17vb: "QUI *NON REVERTEBATUR*." Cf. G, Gen. 8.7 *ad loc.*, 1: 39, col. a. The text of the Vulgate for Genesis 8.7 reads: "qui egrediebatur et revertebatur donec siccarentur aquae super terram." This particular text had generated controversy for almost a millennium owing to a discrepancy between the LXX, according to which the raven did not return, and the Hebrew, according to which it went out and came back. See Jerome, *Hebraicae Quaestiones in Genesim*, Gen. 8.6–7 (CCSL 72: 10). On Bede's role in passing on the *Vetus latina* reading to the later Middle Ages, see Richard Marsden, *The Text of the Old Testament in Anglo-Saxon England*, Cambridge Studies in Anglo-Saxon England 15 (Cambridge: Cambridge University Press, 1995), 118.

He narrates concisely God's command to Noah to leave the Ark with all of the animals and Noah's construction of an altar and sacrifice to God of clean animals on it.[136] In his chapter on the rainbow, Comestor abridges greatly the scriptural account, reducing for example all of Genesis 9.5–6 to a one-line paraphrase, "AND GOD MADE CLEAR TO HIM THAT HOMICIDE WAS FORBIDDEN."[137] He captures with a one-line mixture of Scripture and paraphrase the main points of the scriptural conclusion, recounted at length in Genesis 9.8–17: "GOD PROMISED THEM THAT THERE WOULD NEVER AGAIN BE *A FLOOD*, AND AS *A SIGN* OF THIS *PACT* HE PLACED HIS OWN *RAINBOW IN THE CLOUDS*."[138]

Considered as a whole, this account of Noah and the Ark constitutes a radical reorganization and reduction of the scriptural account. Even while adding colorful details from outside sources (Josephus et al.), Comestor eliminates redundancy and streamlines the whole story, in large part by abridging Scripture and organizing topics in such a way as to carry the narrative forward without repetition. The result was a textbook that, unlike the biblical *Gloss*, offered to students a fast-paced story combining Scripture, gloss, and extra-scriptural sources in a cogent narrative.

b. *History Alone*

Comestor also created a manageable scale by focusing exclusively on the literal/historical sense of Scripture. In this section, by means of a few examples typical of the *History* as a whole, I show how Comestor's *History* not only communicated in interesting fashion the Christian tradition of historical/literal glosses on the Bible but also presented that tradition in the form of a narrative history of salvation.

History as Literal Interpretation

We have already seen that Comestor used glosses, the historical/literal interpretation of Scripture, in a variety of ways. In contrast to the biblical *Gloss*, in

---

136 See V, 17vb–18ra. In doing so, Comestor uses less than half of the text of Genesis 8.14–20, taking for example just three words – "crescite et multiplicamini" – from the lengthy verse, Genesis 8.17. Comestor accomplishes this reduction principally by omitting the lists of animals.

137 V, fol. 18ra: "ET PROHIBUIT EI DEUS HOMICIDIUM FIERI."

138 V, fol. 18ra–b: "PEPIGIT EIS FEDUS, NE ULTRA FIERET *DILUVIUM*, ET IN *SIGNUM FEDERIS* HUIUS POSUIT *ARCUM* SUUM *IN NUBIBUS*."

which the glosses, literal as well as figurative, were distinct from the biblical text, Comestor frequently integrated Scripture and gloss into a single whole. In so doing, he put the interpretation of Scripture front and center. A typical example, taken in this case from the *Historia evangelica*, which Comestor forged from all four Gospels, will serve to illustrate the extent to which he unified Scripture and historical gloss into a single story.

In the second chapter of the *Historia evangelica*, Comestor interposes a single gloss into the middle of his long, paraphrased version of Luke's account of the conception of Jesus:

AND IN THE SIXTH MONTH THE ANGEL GABRIEL WAS SENT TO NAZARETH TO MARY, WHO WAS BETROTHED TO JOSEPH. AND HAVING GREETED MARY AND AFTER HE HAD SAID THAT SHE WOULD GIVE BIRTH TO JESUS, THE SON OF THE MOST HIGH, AND AFTER SHE HAD SOUGHT TO KNOW HOW THIS WOULD COME ABOUT, since she had vowed in her soul that she would not know man, THE ANGEL ADDED THAT SHE WOULD CONCEIVE NOT FROM MAN BUT BY THE OPERATION OF THE HOLY SPIRIT, AND HE MADE KNOWN TO HER THAT HER RELATIVE, ELIZABETH, HAD ALSO CONCEIVED.[139]

Luke 1.26–35:

And in the sixth month the angel Gabriel was sent by God to a city of Galilee, whose name was Nazareth, to a virgin betrothed to a man, whose name was Joseph, of the house of David. And the virgin's name was Mary. And having come into her presence, the angel said to her: "hail, oh full of grace, the Lord is with you. Blessed are you among women." Mary, when she had seen the angel, was disturbed by his words and pondered over what kind of greeting this was. And the angel said to her: "do not fear, Mary.

---

139 *Historia evangelica Petri Comestoris*, 2 (ed. Clark, Textual Appendix B.1 below, 17–22): "*MENSE AUTEM SEXTO MISSUS EST ANGELUS GABRIEL IN NAZARETH* AD MARIAM DESPONSATAM IOSEPH. CUMQUE EA SALUTATA DIXISSET EAM PARITURAM IESUM FILIUM ALTISSIMI QUESISSETQUE QUOMODO HOC FIERET, cum se non cognituram virum in animo vovisset, nisi aliter Deus disponeret, ADDIDIT ANGELUS NON DE VIRO SED OPERE SPIRITUS SANCTI CONCEPTURAM, ET ETIAM CONCEPISSE COGNATAM SUAM HELISABETH SIBI INDICAVIT."

For you have found favor with God. Behold, you will conceive in your womb and will bear a Son. And you will give him the name, Jesus. He will be great and will be called Son of the Most High and the Lord God will give to him the seat of David, his father, and he will reign in the House of Jacob for ever. And his kingdom will have no end. But Mary said to the angel: "how can this come about, since I do not know man?" And the angel, responding, said to her: "The Holy Spirit will come over you and the strength of the Most High will overshadow you ... ."[140]

According to Langton, the gloss interposed by Comestor, namely Mary's vow in her heart that, God permitting, she would not know man, had been handed down by the *sancti* as an explication.[141] Here, however, it serves as part of the historical narrative; a traditional literal interpretation becomes in Comestor's narrative a unified part of that history. We have seen throughout this chapter how Comestor blurred the lines between text and interpretation. The result, as in the present example, is a cogent blend of Scripture (or other extra-scriptural sources that Comestor privileges as authoritative) and interpretation. As a consequence, students using Comestor's work as a textbook had the tradition of the historical/literal sense of Scripture at their fingertips.

History as Narrative

While the *History*'s account of Noah and the Ark shows how (and how much) Comestor abridged the Scriptures, his version of the story of Abraham and Isaac exemplifies Comestor's arrangement of his sources into a unified historical narrative. In retelling the story of Abraham, Comestor was going over

---

140 G, Lucas 1.26–31 *ad loc.*, 4: 141, col. a–b: "In mense autem sexto missus est Gabriel angelus a Deo in civitatem Galylee, cui nomen Nazareth, ad virginem desponsatam viro, cui nomen erat Ioseph de domo David. Et nomen virginis Maria. Et ingressus angelus ad eam dixit: "Ave, gratia plena, Dominus tecum; benedicta tu in mulieribus. Que, cum audisset, turbata est in sermone eius et cogitabat qualis esset ista salutatio. Et ait angelus ei: "ne timeas, Maria. Invenisti enim gratiam apud Deum. Ecce concipies in utero et paries filium et vocabis nomen eius Ihesum."

141 *Prima Stephani glosa scilicet lectiones a Stephano viva voce ante 1176 datae in Historiam evangelicam*, 2 (ed. Clark, Textual Appendix B.2 below, lines 12–14): "Capitulum. MENSE AUTEM ETC. QUESISSETQUE Beata Virgo scilicet CUM SE NON COGNITURAM Sic enim exponunt sancti: *quoniam virum non cognosco* id est me non cognituram propositum habeo."

some of the most well-known narrative ground in Genesis: Hagar's flight from her mistress, Sarah, and the birth of Ismael; the changing of Abram's name to Abraham and the covenant witnessed by circumcision; the visit by three divine beings and the foretelling of Isaac's birth; the destruction of Sodom and Gomorrah; and other equally familiar episodes. Even though the scriptural account was already a stirring account of salvation history, Comestor placed his own distinctive stamp on each episode, and the unity between text and gloss so central to his method in the *History* is especially evident in these chapters on Abraham.

Comestor's chapter recounting the visitation of three divine beings to Abraham ("De tribus angelis susceptis ab Abraham") provides perhaps the best example of the striking unity inherent in Comestor's method in retelling Abraham's story. Comestor opens the chapter with an abbreviated and much revised version of Genesis 18.1–2:

> And the Lord appeared to him in the Valley of Mambre, as he was sitting in the entrance to his tent during the hottest part of the day. And when he had raised his eyes, there appeared to him three men standing before him. After he had seen them, he ran up to them from the entrance to his tent and adored on the ground.[142]

Historia Genesis:

> THE LORD APPEARED TO ABRAHAM IN THE VALLEY OF MAM-BRE. AND WHEN HE HAD RAISED HIS EYES, HE SAW THREE MEN AND, RUNNING UP TO THEM, HE ADORED ONE OF THESE.[143]

Scripture does not specify whom Abraham adored in falling to the ground. Comestor does, making the interpretation of the *Gloss* (both marginal and interlinear), namely that Abraham adored only one of the three, part of his

---

142 Gen. 18.1–2: "Apparuit autem ei Dominus in convalle Mambre sedenti in ostio tabernaculi sui in fervore diei. Cumque elevasset oculos apparuerunt ei tres viri stantes propter eum. Quos cum vidisset cucurrit in occursum eorum de ostio tabernaculi et adoravit in terra."

143 V, fol. 22va: "*Apparuit Dominus* Abrahe *in convalle Mambre. Cumque elevasset oculos* vidit tres viros et occurrens unum ex eis adoravit."

introduction to this chapter.[144] His version unifies text and commentary by blurring the lines between them.

After conflating Genesis 18.3–5 and Josephus, who provides more comprehensive information about the initial exchange between Abraham and the divine visitors, Comestor reorganizes one of the most famous scenes in Scripture:[145]

Gen. 18.8–11:

Abraham stood next to them under a tree. And when they had eaten, they said to him: where is your wife, Sarah? He answered: She's over there in the tent. And one said to him: I shall come to you on my way back at this time next year and your wife, Sarah, will have a son. Having overheard this, Sarah laughed behind the flap of the tent. For they were both old and far along in years. And Sarah no longer had her menstrual cycle.[146]

Historia Genesis:

ABRAHAM *STOOD NEXT TO* THEM. SARAH HOWEVER WAS STANDING *BEHIND THE DOOR OF THE TENT*. AND THE ANGEL *SAID: I SHALL COME TO YOU ON MY WAY BACK AT THIS TIME* that is on the same day a year from now *AND SARAH WILL HAVE A SON. HAVING OVERHEARD THIS, SARAH LAUGHED.* FOR *THEY WERE BOTH OLD AND SARAH NO LONGER HAD HER PERIOD*, that is, the menstrual flow without which the power of bearing children fails. If one of them were young, it would not be impos-

---

144 See GI, Gen. 18.2 *ad loc.*, 1: 52, col. a, and GM, Gen. 18.2 *ad loc.*, 1: 52, col. a, marginal gloss 4.

145 V, fol. 22va: "QUOS ET ROGAVIT ABRAHAM UT DIVERTERENT AD EUM ET PAULULUM COMEDENDO CONFORTARENTUR. QUI ASSENSERUNT." Cf. Gen. 18.3–5 and Jos., *Antiquitates Judaicae* 1.196–197 (ed. Blatt, 149: 5–6).

146 "Ipse vero stabat iuxta eos sub arbore. Cumque comedissent dixerunt ad eum: ubi est Sarra uxor tua? Ille respondit: ecce in tabernaculo est. Cui dixit: revertens veniam ad te tempore isto vita comite et habebit filium Sarra uxor tua. Quo audito Sarra risit post ostium tabernaculi. Erant autem ambo senes provectaeque aetatis et desierant Sarrae fieri muliebria."

sible to produce offspring out of an old man and a young woman. But *THEY WERE BOTH ADVANCED IN YEARS.*[147]

Comestor here takes a detail from Genesis 18.10, namely where Sarah was standing when she laughed, and juxtaposes it with a related detail from Genesis 18.8, namely where Abraham was standing. Having excised the middle portion of Genesis 18.11 ("erant autem ambo senes provectaeque aetatis"), he uses it to punctuate the glosses that he had attached to the rest of Genesis 18.11.

Comestor's version integrates the scriptural account with historical interpretation into a passage not much longer than Sacred Scripture by itself. This was something new, at least for Christian commentators on the Bible.[148] Masters and students alike now had a convenient presentation of Scripture and historical interpretation alike. It is no wonder that Comestor's *History* was taken up into the schools immediately as a handy introduction to the Bible. As a textbook, it was vastly superior to the biblical *Gloss*, and had Comestor followed through with his plan to collect the entire figurative tradition in one volume as well – Langton tells us that he intended to do so but never did – he would have bequeathed to the schools a two-part abridgement and reorganization of the *Gloss*.[149]

Even though Comestor did not follow through with his intent to create a figurative counterpart to the *History*, he did entrust his student, Langton, with the task of carrying on with that project, and thus Langton too had a role in the making of the *History*. This is the subject of Chapters 5–7 of this monograph.

---

147 V, fol. 22vb: "ABRAHAM AUTEM *STABAT IUXTA* EOS. SARA VERO ERAT *POST OSTIUM TABERNACULI.* ET DIXIT ANGELUS: *REVERTENS VENIAM AD TE TEMPORE ISTO* id est eodem die revoluto anno *ET HABEBIT SARA FILIUM. QUO AUDITO RISIT SARA. ERANT* ENIM *AMBO SENES ET DESIERANT SARE FIERI MULIEBRIA* id est menstrua quibus deficientibus deficit vis pariendi. Si alter iuvenis esset, non erat impossibile ex sene et iuvene proles fieri. Sed *AMBO PROVECTE ETATIS ... ."*

148 Josephus, one of Comestor's principal sources, had done the same thing, and in many ways Comestor can be seen as the Christian Josephus.

149 In 1193, revising his course on the *History* for the second time, Langton added the following gloss, which was clearly based on personal knowledge: "PRINCIPIUM LOQUENDI. Proposuerat enim forsitan componere allegorias. Quod tamen non invenimus fecisse Magistrum." *Tertia Stephani glosa scilicet magistralis anno 1193 recensa supra Historiam Genesis,* 2 (ed. Clark, Textual Appendix A.4 below, lines 59–60).

CHAPTER FIVE

The Case for a "Langton" Edition of the *History*

I suggested in Chapter One that a principal reason why the *Historia scholastica* has not been carefully studied by scholars is the lack of a reliable edition. Here it is instructive to compare the respective *fortunae* of the *Sentences* and the *History*. Scholars have produced three critical editions of the *Sentences* since 1882.[1] These editions, and in particular Brady's magisterial edition, have made it possible for anyone seriously interested in studying the *Sentences* to do so. By contrast, those who wanted to read and study Comestor's *History* until recently had only the edition reprinted in Migne's *Patrology*.[2] There are, however, several reasons to mistrust that edition. Chief among these is the fact that the editors did not themselves understand the structure of Comestor's work.[3] Moreover, the *Patrology* edition preserves a later version of the *History*. Although we cannot yet say how late, it is clear that it postdates Langton's commentary on the *History*, since it routinely incorporates parts of his commentary on the *History*.[4]

---

1 See Ignatius Brady, "The Three Editions of the 'Liber Sententiarum' of Master Peter Lombard (1882–1977)," *Archivum Franciscanum Historicum* 70 (1977): 400–411. For the most recent, see Peter Lombard, *Sententie in IV libris distinctae*, ed. Ignatius Brady, 3rd rev. ed., vol. 1, pt. 2: Liber I et II, Spicilegium Bonaventurianum 4 (Grottaferrata, 1971); and vol. 2: Liber III et IV, Spicilegium Bonaventurianum 5 (Grottaferrata, 1981).

2 PL 198: 1053–1644.

3 They formatted the *History* as they would a conventional biblical commentary, italicizing all scriptural quotations, but as we have seen Comestor used Scripture in all sorts of ways: for lemmata as well as glosses. Moreover, he paraphrased Scripture more than he quoted it verbatim. There is no indication in the *Patrology* edition that the editors of the *Historia scholastica* recognized its basic structure.

4 A typical example is the passage lifted from Langton's preface to his lectures on the *History* and interpolated into Comestor's preface in the *Patrology* edition of the *History* extends from "sumitur allegoria quandoque a persona ..." through "... anagoge ad triumphantem et ad Domini trinitatem." Cf. *Prima Stephani glosa scilicet lectiones a Stephano viva voce ante 1176 datae in Historiam scholasticam, In magistri prologum* (ed. Clark, Textual Appendix A.2 below, lines 21–32) with Peter Comestor, *Historia scholastica*, Prologue (PL 198: 1053–1056). Langton's fourfold division of scriptural senses is patently at variance with Comestor's use of the threefold division in composing his preface to the *History*.

There is also Agneta Sylwan's edition of the first book of that work, the *Historia Genesis*.[5] In this chapter, after setting forth the principal assumptions underlying Sylwan's edition, I shall show those assumptions to be false in the light of Stephen Langton's witness to the early textual history of the *Historia scholastica*. I then propose a solution to the salient problems facing any would-be editor of Comestor's *History*, namely a modern edition founded principally on the textual information provided by Langton's course on the *History*, which would reproduce to the greatest extent possible the text of the *History* that was used in the schools of Paris from the time of its first appearance in the late 1160s through the close of the twelfth century and into the thirteenth.[6] Because of Langton's role in adapting this version of the *History* for the schools, I propose to call this the "Langton" or "University" edition of the *History*.

I. The Quest for a Pre-Scholastic Edition of the Comestor's History

The difficulties facing any scholar attempting a modern, critical edition of Comestor's *Historia scholastica* are well illustrated by Sylwan's edition of his *Historia Genesis*. Chief among these is the sheer number of manuscripts spread across the globe. Stegmüller's *Repertorium biblicum* lists two hundred and thirty-four manuscript copies of the *History*, most of them complete.[7] Sylwan, however, uncovered more than 800 extant manuscripts.[8] She not only produced a list of the extant manuscripts, organized by the country where they are now located, but also provided descriptions of and estimated dates of origin for each manuscript.[9] In undertaking the Herculean task of sorting through so many

---

5   Peter Comestor, *Scolastica historia Liber Genesis* (CCCM 191).
6   The question of how far into the thirteenth century will not be known until the commentary put together by the Dominicans under the leadership of Hugh of St. Cher in the 1230s has been edited. My research thus far suggests that the Dominicans relied extensively on Langton's commentary on the *History* for their own commentary on the same. Mark J. Clark, "The Commentaries on Peter Comestor's *Historia scholastica* of Stephen Langton, Pseudo-Langton, and Hugh of St. Cher," *Sacris erudiri* 44 (2005): 301–446.
7   Friedrich Stegmüller, *Repertorium Biblicum Medii Aevi*, 9 vols. (Madrid: Instituto Francisco Súarez, 1950–1976), vols. 4 and 9, sections 6543–6565.
8   Peter Comestor, *Scolastica historia* (ed. Sylwan, xxxi–xxxii).
9   Unfortunately, this tremendous work of scholarship remains unpublished. I am grateful to Ms. Sylwan for granting me permission to look at the copy of her work, now contained at the IHRT in Paris.

manuscripts, Sylwan pursued what was manifestly a reasonable course of action. Acknowledging the impossibility of one scholar's examining all extant manuscripts, Sylwan prudently decided to restrict her efforts to early (pre-1200 or soon thereafter) copies of the *History*, basing her edition of the *Historia Genesis* on what she concluded were four families of manuscripts, represented by two manuscripts apiece.[10] Based upon these manuscript families, she published a provisional *stemma codicum*.[11] But when difficulties arose that led her subsequently to rethink her positions, she decided not to include a *stemma codicum* in her published edition.[12]

In spite of her laudable industry, Sylwan's edition proved deficient in several crucial respects. First, neither her text nor her apparatus is trustworthy.[13] The second problem, in part the consequence of inaccurate transcriptions of the manuscripts, is that her division of the eight manuscripts into four basic families is faulty. I have discovered from my own research, for example, that one alleged family, which Sylwan calls the beta family and which contains two manuscripts (Vienna, Östereichische Nationalbibliothek, MS 363 and Troyes, Bibliothèque municipal, MS 290) does not exist.[14] Most importantly, however, Sylwan excludes from her edition eight other manuscripts, because they preserve what she considers to be the scholastic adaptation of Comestor's *History*, accomplished in her view before 1190, that served as the text used in the University of Paris.[15]

---

10   Peter Comestor, *Scolastica historia* (ed. Sylwan, xxxvi–xxxix and lxv–lxxxiv).

11   Agneta Sylwan, "Petrus Comestor, *Historia Scholastica*: Une nouvelle edition," *Sacris erudiri* 39 (2000): 345–382.

12   Peter Comestor, *Scolastica historia* (ed. Sylwan, xxxvi–xxxix).

13   Significant transcription errors abound. I document briefly the extent and seriousness of the problem and elucidate the other principal difficulties with her edition in Mark J. Clark, "How to Edit the *Historia scholastica* of Peter Comestor," *Revue Bénédictine* 116, Fascicle 1 (2006): 83–91. The sheer number of mistakes renders impractical any attempt to account for or reproduce them all here. The reader will be able to compare the transcriptions of Paris, BnF, MS lat. 16943 and Vienna, Östereichische Nationalbibliothek 363, in my edition from those in Sylwan's text and apparatus.

14   Nevertheless, Troyes, Bibliothèque municipale, MS 290, even though it is not part of the same family with Vienna, Östereichische Nationalbibliothek 363, is important as a manuscript witness to an intermediate stage between Paris, BnF, MS lat. 16943 and Vienna, Östereichische Nationalbibliothek 363.

15   Speaking of these eight manuscripts, Sylwan writes: "J'ai exclu les manuscripts ... qui transmettent une adaptation réalisée avant 1190 ... probablement à Sens ... . Cette adaptation du texte a eu une grande influence par la suite, puisqu'elle a servi de modèle au texte de l'Université et à des traductions vernaculaires en néerlandais, français et allemande." Peter Comestor, *Scolastica historia* (ed. Sylwan, xxxviii).

For Sylwan, this scholastic version of the *History* has little relevance to establishing the text of Comestor's original.[16]

Sylwan's views regarding the origins of the *History* and its early textual history could not be more different from my own, for a principal thesis of this book is that Comestor's *History* was emphatically scholastic from the very beginning. I set forth in this chapter incontrovertible evidence that the version of the *History* that would serve as the university text entered the schools of Paris before 1176 at the latest and in all probability well before then, that it underwent numerous changes predating our earliest extant manuscripts (1180–1183) at the hands of masters in the schools of Paris, including Comestor himself, and that this same version was subsequently edited systematically by Langton, in all likelihood before 1176. Nevertheless, Sylwan's edition provides an ideal starting point for my discussion in this chapter of the early textual history of the *History* owing to the assumptions that Sylwan makes.

Her edition presupposes two early versions of the *History*: a pristine, pre-scholastic original, and a second version, taken up into the schools.[17] Of the two earliest extant manuscripts (Paris, BnF, MS lat. 16943, which was copied in 1183 and which I call P, and Vienna, ÖNB, MS lat. 363, which was copied in 1180–1183 and which I call V), Sylwan assigns P to the family descended from Comestor's pristine original, which she denominates as X, and V (which Sylwan denominates "w") to a later, scholastic version; her edition constitutes an attempt to get back to what she believes to be Comestor's original, pre-scholastic version of the *History*.[18]

Underlying Sylwan's edition are three, related assumptions, all of which are questionable. Sylwan first assumes that Comestor's "original" text was not meant for the schools; it was in other words a *Historia* but not a *Historia scholastica*.[19] She also assumes that we have access to that pre-scholastic, original version through manuscript P and the tradition that it represents.[20] Finally, she

---

16 "Pour l'établissement du texte original, toutefois, ces manuscrits n'ont que peu d'importance et peuvent donc être éliminés." Ibid., xxxix.

17 Ibid., xxxvi–xxxix and lxv–lxxxiv.

18 Ibid., lxxxv–lxxxvi. Although I have in my articles routinely referred to Paris, BnF, MS lat. 16943 as C (for Corbie), I adopt herein Sylwan's *siglum*, namely P. But, although Sylwan uses "w" for Vienna, ÖNB, lat. 363, I shall refer to it as V (for Vienna). My reason for doing so is that it will serve as the manuscript of first resort for my "Langton" edition of the *History*.

19 Peter Comestor, *Scolastica historia* (ed. Sylwan, xxxix–xl).

20 Ibid., lxxxiv–lxxxvi.

assumes that Comestor himself composed a primary group of additional "notes" to the *History*, which were part of the original, pre-scholastic version of the *History*.[21]

I shall first address this last assumption, for it provides us a bridge between Langton's testimony and Sylwan's assumption that we can get behind the "notes" to Comestor's original *History* through manuscript P. I shall then be able to show, based on Langton's intimate knowledge both of Comestor's original text and of the many additional "notes" that were constantly being added to that original text, that each of Sylwan's first two assumptions are false as well.

a. *The Problem of the "Notes" to the* History

In undertaking to edit the *History*, Sylwan faced a problem that I would consider more formidable even than the daunting number of manuscripts: namely the problem of the so-called "notes" to the *History*.[22] Anyone who looks at the *History* comes across them constantly. In the Patrology edition, they are appended to the end of chapters with signs indicating which texts in the chapter they are supplementing.[23] Sylwan too chose to include them as additional "notes" following individual chapters, indicating by signs the texts to which each corresponded.[24] There are, however, numerous difficulties with this approach, which assumes certain answers to important questions raised by the presence of these texts in the manuscripts of the *History*: Are all such texts additions to an already finished ur-text? If they are in fact additional, who added them, when, and why? How were they added? To which texts in the *History* are they related? Most importantly, can we get behind these "additional texts" such that we can recover the "ur-text" of the *History*?

Even a superficial glance at the manuscripts reveals how seemingly intractable these questions are. For one thing, different notes appear in different manuscripts, even in contemporary manuscripts and even, as I show below, in the earliest that we have. For another, these texts are to be found in different locations in the manuscripts themselves. Some are written into the margins. Others are written above lines of the main text. Others are set off by

---

21 Ibid., lxxvi–lxxvii.
22 Smalley called them notes, recognizing their additional character. Beryl Smalley, *The Study of the Bible in the Middle Ages*, 3rd rev. ed. (1941; Oxford: Basil Blackwell, 1984), 214–215.
23 PL 198: 1053–1644.
24 Peter Comestor, *Scolastica historia* (ed. Sylwan, lxxvi–lxxxi).

boundaries within the principal columns of the main text. The only constant seems to be that over time an increasing quantity of such texts attached themselves to the text of the *History*.

Sylwan's solution to the problem of such notes in the earliest manuscripts, namely the supposition of an original set added by Comestor himself to the *History*, preserves her notion of a definitive ur-text, because of her further assumptions that this set of "notes" was private, that it was added by Comestor before "publication," and that it predated any scholastic additions to the *History*.[25] Like most scholars, Sylwan assumes that Comestor finished and "published" the *History* between 1169 and 1173.[26] Based on these many assumptions, therefore, Sylwan presents her edition, which is founded upon P and the textual tradition that it represents, as a return to Comestor's original, pre-scholastic version of the *History*.

Sylwan is right that P, although copied later (1183), represents a more primitive textual tradition than V (1180–1183). Nevertheless, both manuscripts represent early textual traditions of the *Historia scholastica*, and since the version in V is closely related to that which Stephen Langton and his students were using in the 1170s, I pay careful attention to its text.[27]

In the next section, I document Langton's irreplaceable value as the key to understanding the *History*'s early textual tradition, making use of evidence provided by Langton to show the falsehood of Sylwan's many assumptions about the origins of the *Historia scholastica* and to support my view that Comestor's *History* was scholastic from the beginning. Since a reliable chronology is a necessary condition to doing so, I first set forth the fact-based chronology both for the early history of the *History* and for the first part of Langton's lengthy tenure in Paris, which I have established in recent years.[28]

---

25 Ibid., lxxvi–lxxvii.

26 Ibid., xi. For pertinent literature, see Chapter One at nn15–16.

27 For this reason, V is in fact the principal manuscript upon which I found my "University" edition of the *History*.

28 See Clark, "Commentaries on Peter Comestor's *Historia scholastica*," and more recently: "The Commentaries of Stephen Langton on the *Historia Scholastica* of Peter Comestor," in *Étienne Langton: Prédicateur, bibliste, théologien*, ed. Louis-Jacques Bataillon, Nicole Bériou, Gilbert Dahan, and Riccardo Quinto (Turnhout: Brepols, 2010): 373–393; "Peter Comestor and Stephen Langton: Master and Student, and Co-Makers of the *Historia scholastica*," *Medioevo* 35 (2010): 123–149; and "Le cours d'Étienne Langton sur *l'Histoire scolastique* de Pierre le Mangeur: Le fruit d'une tradition unifiée," in *Pierre de Troyes, dit Pierre le Mangeur, maître du XIIe siècle*, éd. G. Dahan, Bibliothèque d'histoire culturelle du moyen âge (Turnhout: Brepols, 2013), 243–266.

II. *Langton as a Witness to the Early Textual History of the* Historia scholastica

Until quite recently, very little was known for sure about the early history of the *Historia scholastica*. According to the standard account, adopted and repeated by scholars from Lacombe in 1930, Comestor wrote the *History* at the end of his career, in all likelihood during a supposed retirement at the Abbey of St. Victor.[29] In this view, the *History* stands outside of Comestor's lengthy and distinguished teaching career as a sort of post-scholastic crowning achievement. Sylwan's view, therefore, that Comestor did not in fact intend the *History* for the schools is but a logical extension of this historiographical best guess: the *History* as quasi-private magnum opus. In support of her view Sylwan cites Comestor's statement in his dedicatory letter to Archbishop William ("Causa suscepti laboris fuit instans peticio sociorum"), interpreting Comestor's reference to his "socii" narrowly to mean his friends at the Abbey of St. Victor.[30]

This whole idea is problematic. For one thing, Sylwan's understanding of Comestor's "socii" is unreasonably narrow. Comestor spent most of his adult life in the schools of Paris, and he counted among his "socii" some of the most famous names in the history of scholastic theology: Peter Lombard, Stephen Langton, and Peter of Poitiers, to name just a few. His circle of friends and colleagues doubtless encompassed the schools as well as the Abbey of St. Victor. Moreover, as I showed in Chapters Two through Four of this study, Comestor's experience, and in particular his frustrations, in using the biblical *Gloss* to teach the Bible led him to compose the *History*. There is, in short, no justification for imagining that the *History* was a private work, not intended for circulation. It was clearly meant for the schools.

More broadly still, Sylwan's use of the word "scholastic" is too narrow. It can be argued that a work is scholastic if its author was or had been a scholastic, that is, a master in the schools, whenever in his career he wrote it. It can be argued that a work is scholastic if it was written for pedagogy in the schools – for students in

29 George Lacombe, "Studies on the Commentaries of Cardinal Stephen Langton, Part I," *Archives d'histoire doctrinale et littéraire du moyen âge* 5 (1930): 52–152, at 22.

30 "*Historia Scolastica* ou *Scolastica Historia* ne peut pas être le titre originel de l'ouvrage. Comestor ne pouvait pas savoir dès le début que son livre serait utilize dans les écoles. Il explique dans son prologue qu'il a composé son livre en réponse aux demandes renouvelées de ses socii, c'est à dire les members de la communauté religieuse de l'abbaye de Saint-Victor ou, peut-être, de l'église Notre Dame." Peter Comestor, *Scolastica historia* (ed. Sylwan, xxxix–xl).

training as professional theologians and pastors. It can be argued that a work is scholastic if its methodology and genre were those used by professional school-men of the day. All of these conditions apply to the *Historia scholastica* and are non-debatable and legitimate reasons for calling it a scholastic work.

But the question of Comestor's doings during the 1170s remains. We have seen that he dedicated the *History* to William of the White Hands sometime between 1169 and 1173. Scholars have assumed that Comestor was finished with the *History* at this time, but is this true? Several questions naturally arise about a long-time master, holder of the Chair of Theology at the Cathedral School of Notre Dame: Did Comestor himself teach using the *History*? Did he continue to work on it? What was Comestor doing between that so-called publication and his death, estimated by scholars to have occurred in 1178 or 1179?[31] Until now, no one has been able to provide a satisfactory answer to these questions, but Langton's knowledge of Comestor's doings gives us a solid basis for doing so.

Until quite recently the standard chronology of the beginnings of Stephen Langton's long and distinguished career as a teacher of theology in Paris was that of Maurice Powicke; writing in 1928, he first estimated that Langton began his studies in Paris around 1180.[32] Soon thereafter, however, in an article pub-lished in 1930, George Lacombe, citing a passage in Langton's initial lecture course on the *Historia scholastica* that indicated Langton's ignorance of the fall of Jerusalem in 1187, concluded that Langton had lectured on the *History* some-time before 1187.[33] Powicke, relying upon Lacombe's research and also upon Beryl Smalley's findings that a number of Langton's Old Testament commen-taries predated 1190, revised his original estimate accordingly. Noting that Langton had first taught on the arts faculty before becoming the leader of the theology faculty, Powicke wrote of Langton: "If he taught theology after 1180 he must have come to Paris about 1170. ... On the whole, I am disposed to push back the date of Langton's birth and to add ten or twelve years to his life in Paris. ... Stephen, if he went to Paris about 1170 or a little earlier, could not have been born before 1155."[34] Powicke, therefore, assuming ten years or so

---

31 As I noted in Chapter One (5–6 and relevant footnotes), these dates are quite specula-tive. No one knows for sure when Comestor retired or when he died.

32 F.M. Powicke, *Stephen Langton: Being the Ford Lectures Delivered in the University of Oxford in Hilary Term 1927* (London: Merlin Press, 1928), 10.

33 Lacombe, "Cardinal Stephen Langton," 21–23.

34 F.M. Powicke, "Bibliographical Note on Recent Work upon Stephen Langton," *The English Historical Review* 48, no. 192 (1933): 554–555.

for Langton's studies in arts as well as for his teaching on the arts faculty at Paris, placed the beginning of Langton's tenure as Master of Theology "about 1180 or soon afterwards."[35] This account of Langton's career at Paris has been repeated by scholars ever since, for Powicke's account, buttressed by Lacombe's review of available internal evidence, has seemed until recently dispositive.[36]

Scholars have taken 1180 ever since as the starting point of Langton's illustrious teaching career at Paris, believing that it was then that he delivered his inception sermon, thereby inaugurating his career as a theologian.[37] Moreover, historians of early scholastic theology continue to build their chronologies around this starting point. Marcia Colish, for example, in a recent survey of the state of scholastic theology in the later twelfth century, writes as a matter of fact: "In theology, our one datum from that period is Stephen Langton's inception sermon as master in 1180."[38] Yet as Quinto has pointed out, this date was only a guess, hazarded on the basis of Lacombe's preliminary researches into Langton's career and morphing gradually from the status of a guess to a supposed fact.[39]

35 Ibid., 554.

36 For an influential example, see John Baldwin, *Masters, Princes, and Merchants: The Social Views of Peter the Chanter and His Circle*, 2 vols. (Princeton University Press, Princeton 1970), 2: 26–30.

37 For a frequently cited example, see Nancy K. Spatz, "Evidence of Inception Ceremonies in the Twelfth-Century Schools of Paris," *History of Universities* 13 (1994): 3–19, at 4, 6–7 and 10–13. For the text of the sermon, see *Selected Sermons of Stephen Langton*, ed. Phyllis B. Roberts (Toronto: Pontifical Institute of Mediaeval Studies, 1980), 17–34.

38 Marcia Colish, "Scholastic Theology at Paris around 1200," in *Crossing Boundaries at the Medieval Universities: Intellectual Movements, Academic Disciplines, and Societal Conflict*, ed. Spencer A. Young, Education and Society in the Middle Ages and Renaissance (Leiden: Brill, 2011), 31–50, at 29, noting the importance of this date in the work of Nancy Spatz.

39 "Nous avons déjà rappelé la demonstration donnée par Mark Clark que la première version du commentaire de Langton sur *l'Histoire Scolastique* de Pierre le Mangeur ne peut pas être postérieure à 1176 ... . Langton doit donc avoir commenté cette œuvre quand il était encore un étudiant. Quant au moment où il devint maître, nous n'avons aucune certitude: l'année 1180 comme date de sa leçon inaugurale – hypothèse qui a acquis petit à petit un status de quasi-évidence – est simplement le fruit d'une série de conjectures avancées par Maurice Powicke et reprises par Phyllis B. Roberts (voir *'Stephanus de Lingua-Tonante'. Studies in the Sermons of Stephen Langton*, Toronto, 1968, p. 1, note 6 et p. 224; la leçon inaugurale est datée de 1180 avec moins de nuances dans l'édition: Ph. B. Roberts, *Selected Sermons of Stephen Langton*, Toronto, 1980, p. 15)." Riccardo Quinto, "La constitution du texte des *Quaestiones theologiae* d'Étienne Langton," in *Étienne Langton*, 525–562, at 554 and n84.

Given these twin guesses, namely that Comestor died at the close of the 1170s around the time that Langton is supposed to have commenced his theological studies, it is no surprise that, even though historians of the Bible and theology in the later twelfth century have consistently recognized that the work of Langton and Comestor should somehow be treated together, no historian could posit their collaboration. Instead, Langton was viewed as Comestor's successor in the schools.[40] Scholars assumed that their careers did not intersect.[41] This explains why even Lacombe, who long ago came across some of the evidence suggesting Langton's firsthand acquaintance with Comestor's work and work habits on the *History* and was tempted to consider the possibility that Langton had actually been Comestor's student, rejected this as impossible.[42]

It turns out, however, that Lacombe, ordinarily a careful scholar, inexplicably overlooked crucial internal evidence relating to William's change of sees when he dated Langton's first commentary on the *History* to sometime before 1187. Although Langton begins what Lacombe considered to be both of his two commentaries on the *History* with a reference to Comestor's dedication to Archbishop William, in the first Langton addresses William at Sens, whereas in the second he addresses him at Reims.[43] In fact, therefore, Langton first lectured on Peter Comestor's *Historia scholastica* sometime before 1176, when Archbishop William changed sees from Sens to Reims. He also revised these lectures before 1176.[44]

The early date of Langton's lecture course on the *History* and of his revision of the same is doubly significant. First, it pushes back the starting point of

40 See, for example, Smalley's chapter on Comestor, Peter the Chanter, and Stephen Langton as "Masters of the Sacred Page." Smalley, *Study of the Bible*, 196–263. She wrote: "It would be pleasant to arrange them neatly in order as masters and pupils; but this is not possible." Ibid., 197.

41 Henri de Lubac, speaking of Langton, wrote of "son aîné Pierre le Mangeur," an apt image for two scholars thought to be separated by too much space and time to be imagined as actual family relations. Henry de Lubac, *Exégèse médiévale: Les quatre sens de l'écriture*, 2 parts, each in 2 vols. (Paris: Aubier, 1961–1964), 3: 385.

42 Lacombe, "Cardinal Stephen Langton," 19.

43 Cf. *Prima Stephani glosa scilicet lectiones a Stephano viva voce ante 1176 datae in Historiam Genesis*, Prologus epistolaris (ed. Clark, Textual Appendix A.2 below, lines 1–2: "Premittit Magister prologum epistolarem id est epistolam loco prologi, quam dirigit ad Dominum Senonensem"); cf. *Tertia Stephani glosa scilicet magistralis ante 1193 recensa supra Historiam Genesis* (ed. Clark, Textual Appendix A.4 below, lines 25–26: "Premittit autem epistolam, quam dirigit archiepiscopo Remensi quondam Senonensi ..."). See also: Clark, "Commentaries on Peter Comestor's *Historia scholastica*," 315–317.

44 I provide the evidence for dating the first revision to before 1176 in the next five pages.

Langton's teaching career at Paris by a good bit, for we now know that Langton was already lecturing on theology in Paris before 1176. Second, the new chronology means that Comestor and Langton were in Paris together for a long time. Langton must have been in Paris for the Arts course during the 1160s, when Comestor was lecturing on the four glossed Gospels.[45] Moreover, they were contemporaries teaching theology in Paris during the 1170s. That makes it certain that Langton lectured in Paris on Comestor's *History* while Comestor himself was still alive and working in Paris.

This revision of the chronology of the early portion of Langton's career in Paris has important consequences for our consideration of his course on the *History* itself. Lacombe mistakenly thought that Langton had left two discrete commentaries on the *History*, one literal and the other moral.[46] In fact, however, Langton did not leave two separate commentaries or courses but rather three versions of the same course on the *History*: an initial lecture course, comprehensive in scope, and two subsequent revisions.[47] Three manuscripts preserve copies of Langton's pre-1176 series of lectures, two partial and one complete: Paris, Arsenal 177, fol. 100ra–111vb (A in my edition); Paris, BnF, MS nat. lat. 14417, fol. 129ra–158rb (P¹ in my edition); and Tarragona, Biblioteca Publica 130, fol. 37ra–52rb (T in my edition).[48] These copies are themselves in all likelihood copies of student reports.[49] The second revision, which Lacombe cor-

---

45 If one were to use Powicke's method of ascribing to Langton ten years or so in the arts curriculum, then it would appear that Langton came to Paris in 1160, the year when the Lombard became bishop and died, and the year when Comestor took over the Lombard's theological responsibilities. See Powicke, *Stephen Langton: Being the Ford Lectures*, 10, and also his "Bibliographical Note on Recent Work upon Stephen Langton," *The English Historical Review* 48, no. 192 (1933): 554–557, at 554–555.

46 For an explanation why Lacombe and others mistakenly supposed the first commentary to be literal and the second to be moral, see Clark, "Commentaries on Peter Comestor's *Historia scholastica*," 321–322.

47 Part of Lacombe's confusion arose from his thinking that both were student reports. Lacombe, "Cardinal Stephen Langton," 20. He was mistaken about this, for although the first is a *reportatio*, the second is not. See Clark, "Commentaries on Peter Comestor's *Historia scholastica*," 322–324.

48 Of the three, P¹ has the only complete copy of Langton's course. A's copy reproduces only part of Langton's first course on the Old and New Testament portions of the *History*, while T has only part of Langton's treatment of the former.

49 None of the three has a colophon that would permit us to conclude that we had the original copy of the student reporter. Nevertheless, there are good reasons, based on material evidence, to believe that these contain copies of a course given by Langton before 1176. Clark, "Commentaries on Peter Comestor's *Historia scholastica*," 392–396.

rectly dated to 1193, also survives in three manuscripts: Avranches, Bibliothèque Municipale, MS 36, fol. 176ra–201ra (hereinafter Av); Paris, BnF, lat. 14414 (hereinafter P²), fol. 115ra–142rb; and Naples, Biblioteca Nazionale Vittorio Emanuele III, MS VII.C.14, fol. 122ra–149va (hereinafter N).[50] It is, however, the first revision, a copy of which survives in the Heidelberg manuscript, Salem, IX 62, at folios 89ra–122vb (hereinafter H), that is the key to a full understanding not only of Langton's course but also of the early development of the text of the *History* itself.

Following Lacombe, I thought for a time that H also contained a copy of Langton's first lecture course on the *History*.[51] Several things misled me. Like P¹, the only extant manuscript containing a complete copy of Langton's pre-1176 lectures on the *History*, H retains the reference to Comestor's dedication of the *History* to Archbishop William when he was still at Sens.[52] Moreover, H retains some of the *inquits* found in P¹, thus signaling what I formerly believed to be the presence of a reporter.[53]

Three observations, however, led me to see that H contains a first revision of Langton's first lecture course on the *History*. The first is the consistent character of the changes throughout H, which vary (additions, deletions, alterations, etc.) but which nevertheless bear the mark of an editor seeking to turn a lecture course into something more permanent.[54] It became clear to me that someone had taken the trouble to work through and revise the entire lecture course in a systematic way. The second is the unmistakable evidence linking the revision in H to a revision of the text of the *History* itself.[55] The third is the

---

50 For the date, see Lacombe, "Cardinal Stephen Langton," 21–23. For descriptions of the three extant manuscripts containing copies of Langton's second commentary on the *History* that I rely on for this study, see Clark, "Commentaries on Peter Comestor's *Historia scholastica*," 392–396.

51 For descriptions of H as well as the three manuscripts that do in fact contain whole or partial copies of Langton's lecture course on the *History*, namely A, P¹, and T, see Clark, "Commentaries on Peter Comestor's *Historia scholastica*," 387–392.

52 *Secunda Stephani glosa supra Historiam Genesis scilicet prima lectionum recensio datarum viva voce ante 1176, effecta a Stephano ipso traditaque in codice H* (ed. Clark, Textual Appendix A.3 below, lines 2–3: "Premittit Magister prologum epistolarem id est epistolam loco prologi, quam dirigit ad Dominum Senonensem … .").

53 See, for example, *Secunda Stephani glosa supra Historiam Genesis scilicet prima lectionum recensio datarum viva voce ante 1176, effecta a Stephano ipso traditaque in codice H* (ed. Clark, Textual Appendix A.3 below, lines 7, 24, 73, 91, 108, 116, etc.).

54 For the evidence, see the three studies cited above at n28.

55 I set forth the evidence for this, below, in this chapter.

first revision's impeccable correspondence with the final revision, dated by Lacombe to 1193, when Langton was a master at the height of his powers. Once I looked at H not as containing a patently defective and unusual copy of the lecture course but as a first revision of that lecture course, I immediately saw that it was the starting point for the second revision, accomplished in 1193. It became obvious to me that whoever revised the first course also revised it again, making careful use of the first revision.

The question must be asked whether it was Langton himself who effected the revision, for in light of the findings of Quinto and Bieniak that Langton's *Quaestiones* were revised not by him but by others, we cannot simply assume that Langton undertook to revise his own course on the *History*.[56] Nevertheless, for several reasons I am convinced that Langton was responsible both for the first revision of the original student reports, sometime before 1176, and the second, final revision in 1193.

My first reason for believing that Langton, rather than one of his students, did so is that both the first and second revisions reveal firsthand knowledge of Comestor, his personal history, his teaching, and his ongoing work on the *History*. Whoever effected these two revisions had intimate, firsthand knowledge of Comestor's teaching and his life outside of the classroom. Lacombe concluded that this evidence supported well the attribution to Langton of what he mistakenly thought to be two separate commentaries on the *History*.[57] I agree, especially since the revised chronology of Langton's theological studies at Paris makes this not only plausible but likely.

My second reason for believing that Langton was himself responsible for both is the nature of the revisions, which are careful and complete and which form a unity, as will be seen below in Chapter Seven. It is clear that the same person accomplished both revisions. We do not yet know whether Langton's *Quaestiones* were less or more magisterial than the original student reports; Magdalena Bieniak believes that the *fortuna* of individual questions may prove different in this respect. Here, however, the first and second revisions of Langton's lecture course on the *History* reveal a clear magisterial aim, namely a course on the *History* that could be given again, either by Langton or by other masters

---

56   I am grateful to Professors Quinto and Bieniak for sharing this fruit of their research on Langton's *Quaestiones*. See also: Stephen Langton, *Quaestiones theologiae*, Liber I, ed. Riccardo Quinto and Magdalena Bieniak, Auctores Britannici Medii Aevi (Oxford: Oxford University Press for The British Academy, 2014).

57   Lacombe, "Cardinal Stephen Langton," 20–23.

of theology. The evidence shows that the modifications made, additions, subtractions, and alterations, all tend towards preserving a course on the *History*
that would rise above the occasional and ascend to the permanent.

Langton, therefore, turns out to be the key figure in understanding the
early textual history of the *History*. In particular, we are fortunate to have the
first two versions of his course on the *Historia scholastica*, the pre-1176 lecture
course on the entire *History* and the careful, pre-1176 revision of the same.

a. *Comestor and Langton at Paris, ca. 1160 to ca. 1180*

The revised chronology makes it clear how important Langton is to a proper
understanding of Comestor's *Historia scholastica* and also how important
Comestor is to a proper understanding of Langton's career. As a preliminary
overview and preview of evidence that I shall present in this and the next two
chapters, I list here dates, facts, and deductions from evidence that I shall present, which taken together give a foretaste of how interwoven were the contributions of each theologian to the making of the *Historia scholastica*:[58]

1. Sometime between 1167–1173: Peter Comestor made public what
   Langton recognized as the original text of the *History* ("textus
   intrinsecus"), that is, the text itself in contradistinction to any notes
   added to it, whether by Comestor or someone else;[59]

2. During the 1160s: Comestor lectured on the four Glossed Gospels;
   these lectures predate the *Historia evangelica*, Comestor's unified
   account of Gospel history in the *History*;[60]

3. It is possible and perhaps even likely that Langton attended some or all
   of these lectures. He was already in Paris, and I show below that
   Comestor's lectures on all four Glossed Gospels were a primary source
   for Langton's own treatment of the Gospels in his course on the
   History;

58 I here considerably expand a list first set forth in Clark, "Le cours d'Étienne
   Langton."

59 This estimate of when Comestor finished and made public the original text of the
   History, although established long ago on the basis of the dates of Comestor's
   dedication to Archbishop William of Champagne and the notice taken of Comestor
   and the *History* in Robert of Auxerre's *Chronicon*, is of great importance here because,
   as I show in the next section, Langton knew the boundaries of that original text well
   enough to recognize any additions to it.

60 Chapters Two and Three document the extent to which Comestor made use of those
   lectures in composing the *History*.

4. During the 1160s or early 1170s, Comestor lectured on the *History* at Paris; we know this from Langton's extensive knowledge of Comestor's classroom teaching, which I document below;

5. It is likely, therefore, that Langton attended Comestor's lectures on the *History*;

6. Before 1176 (and without any doubt continuing up to the time of his death): Peter Comestor continued to revise his work, adding what Langton calls extrinsic glosses ("glosas extrinsecas") to the *History*;[61]

7. Well before 1176 and long afterwards as well: other theologians lecturing on the *History*, beginners and masters alike, themselves added notes to its text;[62]

8. Before 1176: Langton gave a comprehensive series of lectures on the *History* at Paris; I call this SL[1];

9. Also before 1176: Langton carefully edited his lectures on the *History* for the first time; I call this revision SL[2];

10. Also before 1176: Langton revised the text of the *History* itself to make it correspond with the text of his own revised course on the *History*. Because this would have taken a substantial amount of time owing to the size of the *History*, I am inclined to place Langton's initial lectures on the *History* during the early 1170s;[63]

11. 1193: Langton revises his course on the *History* for the second time; I call this, the magisterial version of his course, SL[3].

If I am right about everything on the list – and there is ample evidence to support each assertion – then the making of the *Historia scholastica* and its reception into the developing curriculum of the nascent university resulted from one of the greatest collaborations in the history of early scholastic theology. Comestor, Peter Lombard's student and disciple, paid his master the great compliment of imitation when he undertook himself to compose the *History*, a Bible-based *summa* that I have argued was a theological *via media*.[64] Langton, Comestor's student and disciple, paid his master the compliment of not only

---

61 I document this assertion in the next section, where I review Langton's firsthand knowledge of and testimony to Comestor's addition of notes to the *History*.

62 I shall present ample evidence, below, that Langton and other masters also added notes to the *History*'s text before 1176.

63 I shall make the case that Langton was also to a certain extent a co-maker of the *History*.

64 Mark J. Clark, "Peter Comestor and Peter Lombard: Brothers in Deed," *Traditio* 60 (2005): 85–142.

working with the *History* but adding to it. Langton's reverence for his master, which shows itself in many ways in Langton's course on the *History*, allows us to see into the early history of that text, well before our earliest extant manuscripts.

Moreover, all scholarly discussions of the theological map in the second half of the twelfth century that rely on Powicke's mistaken chronology about Langton's life and the guess based on that chronology that Langton incepted in 1180 must now be discarded in favor of the revised chronology presented above. Langton came to Paris far earlier than has been supposed, and his theological education started far earlier than has been supposed. It is possible that he was studying the Bible with Comestor in the 1160s; it is certain that by the mid-1170s he was not only teaching the *Historia scholastica* but revising it as well, as I shall show. The fact that he revised the text of the *History* itself, a magisterial responsibility if ever there was one, especially given that Comestor himself was still alive and continuing to work on the *History*, raises the distinct possibility that Langton incepted as a master closer to 1170 than to 1180. One key to understanding what that theological map actually looks like will be a serious search for Langton's sources, which will evidently have to be radically different owing to the revised chronology of his life.

b. *Langton and the "Notes" to the* History

Langton is our best witness to the early history of the *Historia scholastica*, because he is by far our earliest witness to the text of the *History*. His work predates our earliest extant manuscripts (P and V) by a minimum of five to six years, a gap that is all the more remarkable when we consider that Langton produced a complete lecture course on the *History* and revised the same within a few years of the dates (1168–1173) during which scholars have assumed that the *History* first appeared. What Langton has to say in his first commentary (and his revision thereof) about the *History*'s text, therefore, carries great weight. Happily, Langton has a lot to say, for he routinely remarks upon the state of the *History*'s text.[65] His testimony provides us with a clear picture of how rapidly Comestor's text was changing as it entered the schools.

Langton's testimony can be divided conveniently into two categories: explicit and implicit. By the former I mean Langton's own comments about the

---

65 I report in detail much of what Langton has to say about Comestor's teaching and about the text of the *History* in Chapter Eight, below, where I treat the institutionalization of that work.

state of the *History*'s text. By the latter I mean what we can infer about the state of the *History*'s text by comparing Comestor's text with the various stages of Langton's own course on the *History*. Langton's witness gives us a picture of the development of Comestor's text from two intimately related processes. His explicit remarks tell us about glosses added to the *History*, by Comestor and others. We learn that many such glosses made their way into the *History*'s text – and quickly. At the same time, close comparison of the *History*'s text with the various stages of Langton's course on that work also affords clear insight into the evolution of Comestor's text and its *fortuna* in the schools, for we see clearly that among such glosses added to the *History* were many that originated with teachers of the *History*, including Langton himself. Langton thus provides us a window through which we can gaze upon what was a multifaceted and dynamic development of a quintessentially scholastic text.

Langton's Witness to the "Notes": Comestor's Continuing Work on the *History*
Arguably the most important evidence provided by Langton about the early history of the *History*'s text is his testimony to the fact that Comestor himself continued to revise the *History*. I present here two texts that make this fact clear. Both are found in Langton's initial lecture course, which has come down to us in the form of student reports.

The evidence given by Langton that Comestor continued to work on the *History* is unequivocal. Langton remarks briefly in the third chapter of his initial lecture course on the *Historia evangelica* that Comestor had added a gloss explaining why the Gospel canticles of Mary and Zachary, namely the Magnificat and the Benedictus, are not sung in the daily offices of the Church in the order in which they were uttered: "PUER ENIM super hoc ponit Magister glosam extrinsecam, ubi reddit causam de preposteratione horum canticorum."[66] Both extant manuscripts that contain this portion of Langton's first commentary on the *Historia evangelica* have this text: A at fol. 109va; and P¹ at fol. 153ra.[67]

---

66 *Prima Stephani glosa scilicet lectiones a Stephano viva voce ante 1176 datae in Historiam evangelicam*, 3 (ed. Clark, Textual Appendix B.2 below, lines 25–26).

67 Only A has the same lemma, at fol. 109va ("PUER AUTEM" as P and V). Langton, however, deletes this gloss in his revised version of the lecture course. *Secunda Stephani glosa supra Historiam Genesis scilicet prima lectionum recensio datarum viva voce ante 1176, effecta a Stephano ipso traditaque in codice H*, 3 (ed. Clark, Textual Appendix B.3 below, lines 32–34).

Langton calls the gloss in question extrinsic, which I understand as a gloss copied outside of (that is, extrinsic to) the principal text, itself set forth in regular columns in a manuscript.[68] This could mean that an extrinsic gloss is copied either in the margins or between the lines of the principal text as an interlinear gloss; this latter option represents an intermediate stage in the process by which extrinsic glosses entered the *History*'s principal text: from the margins to between the lines to part of the principal text. We also find glosses that are written into the principal columns of the earliest manuscripts of the *History* but are set off from the surrounding text by a line of some sort. I call these glosses intrinsic, since they are added within the regular columns of the principal text. These too represent an intermediate stage of incorporation within the main text.

In this particular case, we find the whole of the extrinsic gloss ascribed to Comestor by Langton as an undifferentiated part of the principal text in V (at fol. 169rb), our earliest extant manuscript, while we find the greater portion of it as an intrinsic gloss in P (at fol. 142vb-143ra), our next earliest.[69] This means that in V the added gloss had already moved through the various intermediate stages into the main text, whereas in P it was still in an intermediate stage of incorporation.

The gloss in question, added by Comestor above the lemma, PUER etc., reads as follows:[70]

AND ZACHARY'S *TONGUE WAS LOOSENED*, AND PROPHESY-ING HE MADE UP A SONG FOR THE LORD: *BLESSED BE THE LORD, THE GOD OF ISRAEL* ETC. [These two canticles are not sung in church in the order in which they were originally uttered. For the one is sung first that was uttered second. For since we read in the Canticle of Zacharia, *and he raised up for us a horn of salvation*, which took place in the resurrection of our Lord, as if he were speaking to the child at the break of dawn, this canticle is therefore sung in Lauds. And since we read in the Canticle of the Virgin, *he has looked with favor on the humility of his handmaid*,

---

68   Clark, "Commentaries of Stephen Langton."
69   *Petri Comestoris Historia evangelica*, 3 (ed. Clark, Textual Appendix B.1 below, lines 46–55).
70   To make it easier to understand the discussion that follows and in particular to understand the layers of gloss that were added, I bracket the entire block of text added to Comestor's original lemma.

that is, of the Church and of Mary herself, which indeed took place in the sixth age, and since this canticle treats of the Incarnation in this passage, *he has raised up Israel as his own son*, therefore also it is sung in the sixth daily office. The third canticle, of Simeon, that follows, is sung in the seventh office, that is, in Compline, since he prays that he be dismissed in peace, which happens in the seventh of those who rest. And since these are Gospel canticles, therefore we sing them standing.] AND THE BOY etc.[71]:

Thanks to Langton, we know that Comestor added a gloss explaining the reverse order ("preposteratio") of the Canticles. The entire bracketed text fits this description nicely, and we could assume without difficulty that Comestor had added this entire text as an explanatory gloss, especially since it works so well as a unity.

But careful attention to the manuscripts reveals a more complex story. We know in fact that the text that I have bracketed was not one gloss but rather a conglomeration of added glosses, because P omits what must have been two separate and additional glosses: the first from "Domini" to "solis" ("... Domini, quasi loquitur ad puerum dum fuit in aurora solis ..."); the second specifying exactly where in the *Benedictus* Zachary refers to the Incarnation ("... et agit de incarnatione ibi: *suscepit Israel puerum suum*, et ...").[72] Yet in V, both of these glosses appear (at fol. 169rb) as part of the main text. This tells us that already by 1180–1183 in at least one early textual tradition these particular glosses had been thoroughly integrated together with the gloss added by Comestor into the *History*'s text.

---

71   *Petri Comestoris Historia evangelica*, 3 (ed. Clark, Textual Appendix B.1 below, lines 44–55): " ET *APERTUM EST OS* ZACHARIE, ET PROPHETANS CANTICUM FECIT DOMINO: *BENEDICTUS DOMINUS DEUS ISRAEL* ETC. [Hec duo cantica non cantantur in ecclesia eo ordine quo sunt edita. Prius enim cantatur, quod secundo est editum. Quia enim in cantico Zacarie legitur, *et erexit cornu salutis nobis*, quod est factum in resurrectione Domini, quasi loquitur ad puerum dum fuit in aurora solis, ideo canitur in Laudibus.* Et quia legitur in cantico Virginis, *respexit humilitatem ancille sue*, Ecclesie scilicet et ipsius Marie, quod quidem factum est in sexta etate, et agit de incarnatione ibi: *suscepit Israel puerum suum*, et ideo canitur ad Vesperas in sexto scilicet officio diurno. Tercium canticum Simeonis, quod sequitur, canitur in septimo officio, id est Completorio, quia orat se dimitti in pace, quod fit in septima quiescentium. Et quia hec evangelica cantica sunt, ideo stando cantamus ea.] PUER AUTEM etc."
72   *Petri Comestoris Historia evangelica*, 3 (ed. Clark, Textual Appendix B.1 below, lines 48–49, 51–52).

But the textual story is still more complex: in P (at. fol. 142vb) the last sentence of the bracketed text added above the lemma, PUER etc. ("Et quia hec duo evangelica cantica sunt, ideo stando cantamus ea") is already, in contradistinction to the rest of its text, part of the *History*'s principal text. This suggests that it too was a separate gloss added at a different time. It is, of course, possible that Comestor was responsible for adding all of the above: a principal gloss explaining the order of the canticles and then the three complementary glosses just noted. On the other hand, someone else may have added to Comestor's original gloss.

The presentation of this gloss in P and V reveals almost by itself the story of how fast the *History*'s text was changing from the beginning of its first appearance in public sometime in the late 1160's and throughout the 1170s. What is impressive is the extent to which this entire conglomeration of glosses coheres with the original text. The seams do not show, and without the clue about authorship and extrinsic provenance afforded by Langton together with the witness of P and V we would have no reason to suspect multiple layers of text in either manuscript.

There is still more evidence, however, of rapid textual change and dynamism, for of the three additional glosses in this chapter found in V, one intrinsic and the other two extrinsic, two attached themselves to the augmented version of Comestor's gloss preserved in that manuscript. The first of these ("Morning lauds take place in memory of our Lord's resurrection. Whence it is that the "'iubilus'" that is sung at the end of the antiphons also notes our ardent desire for the future resurrection. In certain churches silence is observed in morning lauds. For the resurrection having taken place we expect nothing more."), which provides us a glimpse into what was at that time local custom in the singing of Lauds, was added in V (at fol. 169rb) to the first of the glosses omitted in P.[73] Nevertheless, it appears in V as an intrinsic gloss, that is, as a gloss written into the principal columns but clearly demarcated as an additional text. It was, in other words, a third layer of text that was already far along in the process of becoming part of the *History*'s principal text, at least in that particular textual tradition. We find a second additional text attached to

---

73 "Laudes matutine in memoriam Dominice resurrectionis fiunt. Inde est quod iubilus ille, qui in fine antiphonarum cantatur et ardens desiderium future resurrectionis notat. In aliquibus ecclesiis tacetur in matutinis laudibus. Habita enim resurrectione nil amplius expectamus." *Petri Comestoris Historia evangelica*, 3 (ed. Clark, Textual Appendix B.1 below, lines 68–71).

Comestor's gloss as extrinsic in V (also at fol. 169rb) but attached to the final sentence of Comestor's gloss, which as we saw was itself an additional gloss that had already become part of the principal text of the *History* in both manuscript traditions.[74] Here too we see a snapshot of another layer of text added to what was already a many-layered conglomeration.

We can see in Comestor's gloss, therefore, a microcosm of the text of the *History*, for Comestor's gloss was itself a dynamic center of textual activity and change. How much Langton knew of the complicated textual history of the conglomeration of texts surrounding what I have here called Comestor's gloss is debatable. Langton's typically pithy gloss tells us only that Comestor added a gloss to the *History* explaining why the evangelical canticles were not sung in the same order in which the Gospels introduced them. Even if we suppose that Langton's reference excluded the two additional glosses omitted in P, the gloss that he attributes to Comestor is substantial. But we do not require additional information, for the crucial point is that Langton not only had firsthand knowledge of Comestor's continuing work on the *History* but also that this knowledge was very precise. Langton had access, either as a student or as a colleague and collaborator, to the details of Comestor's ongoing revision of the *History*'s text.

In the same lecture course, Langton points out another extrinsic gloss added by Comestor, in this case to his treatment in the *Historia evangelica* of the parable of the vineyard owner who continues to engage workers throughout the day but who pays each of them the same wage, whether they began to work early or late.[75] Comestor focuses mainly on explaining what is meant by the grumbling of those laborers who started working early and worked more than the others, all the while earning the same "denarius diurnus." He first gives a positive interpretation of the murmuring referred to by Jesus in the parable, which is in reality admiration and wonder, expressed in questioning why it is that everyone will receive the same share in future glory.[76] Then, having

---

74   *Petri Comestoris Historia evangelica*, 3 (ed. Clark, Textual Appendix B.1 below, lines 72–75).

75   This chapter, which is entitled "De denario diurno," is found in V at folio 186va, in P at folios 157vb–158ra, and in Tr at folio 29ra–b.

76   "De murmure autem recipientium dici potest quia non erit murmur invidentium sed admirantium de magnitudine premii. Solet enim murmur quandoque accipi pro confusione vocum. Vel potest ad statum presentem murmur retrahi, interrogatio autem cur pares fecisset in gloria ad futurum. Causam enim dilationis a gloria pro qua antiqui murmurare potuerunt tum demum scient quam numquam sciverant scilicet ne sine nobis glorificarentur. Admiratione autem eorum de causa cognita expressit Dominus sub interrogatione." V, fol. 186va. See also: P, fol. 157vb–158ra, and Tr, fol. 29ra–b.

reminded his listeners what Jesus had said in concluding this parable, namely that the last would be first, and the first last, Comestor explained that both the Jews and the Gentiles would enter Paradise on an equal footing.[77] Indeed, in the general Resurrection, all will be on an equal footing, although a privileged few may have already entered Paradise.[78] Comestor does acknowledge, however, that many commentators have interpreted the parable to mean that among the laborers in the vineyard, who stand for the faithful of every age, there are both the bad, namely the murmurers, and the good.[79] He concludes by citing a rule of Ticonius in support of his multi-layered interpretations.[80]

Commenting on Comestor's treatment of this parable in his own lecture course on the *History*, Langton first tells his students that in explaining this parable, the most difficult in the Gospels, Comestor had alleviated the difficulty as much as possible.[81] Langton himself concentrates on explaining to his own students the application of the rule of Ticonius.[82] He also notes that Comestor had added another possible solution in an extrinsic gloss: "In an extrinsic gloss the Master provides another solution. And this <gloss> is: OR

---

77 "Post, concludens parabolam, ait: sic erunt novissimi primi et primi novissimi. Multi enim sunt vocati, pauci vero electi id est Iudei et Gentiles equabuntur in ingressu regni celorum ... ." V, fol. 186va. See also: P, fol. 157vb–158ra, and Tr, fol. 29ra–b.

78 "In resurrectione quoque corporum electi cuiusquam etatis vel temporis vel hominis equabuntur, nisi forte pauci ante resurrexerunt quasi privilegiati." V, fol. 186va. See also: P, fol. 157vb–158ra, and Tr, fol. 29ra–b.

79 "Quidam tamen – quia in parabola legitur, an oculus tuus nequam est, et in fine: multi enim sunt vocati, pauci vero electi – dicunt laborantes in vinea omnes fideles cuiusque temporis vel etatis, quorum quidam boni, alii vero mali. Et vocant accipientes cum murmure malos putantes se accepturos, quia priores fuerunt in ecclesia vel tempore vel dignitate, etiam plus accepturos aliis, de quibus dicit propheta: cadent a latere tuo mille et decem milia a dextris tuis. Et Dominus in Evangelio dicit se dicturum talibus: nescio vos." V, fol. 186va. See also: P, fol. 157vb–158ra, and Tr, fol. 29ra–b.

80 "Quamvis ergo de eisdem videatur sermo fieri scilicet de accipientibus denarium, tamen secundum regulam Ticonii de diversis ibi agitur scilicet de accipientibus et non accipientibus sed putantibus se accepturos, sed tunc nec putabant nec accipient. V, fol. 186va. See also: P, fol. 157vb–158ra, and Tr, fol. 29ra–b. Comestor would have had access to Augustine's version of the seven rules of Tyconius, used here by Comestor to support a diversity of interpretation, in the *De doctrina christiana*, 3.30.42–43.37.56, ed. Joseph Martin (Turnhout: Brepols, 1972), 102–116.

81 "Capitulum. TUNC PROPOSUIT EIS ETC. Maxima est huius parabole difficultas in libro Evangelii, sed Magister hic quantum potest alleviat ... ." P¹, fol. 155vb.

82 "... secundum regulam Ticonii ut est illud, cum occiderent eos querebant eum, et alibi, et eduxit eos de Egipto et induxit eos in terram sanctificationis, quod non fuit verum nisi de duobus scilicet Caleph et Iosue." P, fol. 156ra.

IT CAN BE SYNCRESIS, that is, a spontaneous concession."[83] This gloss referred to by Langton is not found in P.[84] It is, however, in V, added in the margin in an expanded form: "Or it could be sincresis, that is, spontaneous concession, since if the first wanted to grumble, their grumbling could be reasonably understood. But if the first grumbled, nevertheless, our Lord acted justly with the latecomers, whom he first pays."[85] We cannot know whether Comestor was responsible for the whole gloss found in the margins of V or just the first part, which Langton quotes, but here again the importance of his testimony to the fact that Comestor continued to work on the *History* is manifest. Evidently, Langton knew well not only the text of the *History* that was being changed but also the changes Comestor was himself responsible for.

In both of the examples just considered, Langton's knowledge helps us make sense of the dynamic state of the text handed down both in V, which though contemporary with P and perhaps even earlier nevertheless represents a later tradition of the *History*'s text, and in P and other early manuscripts.[86] The first example cited, which gives us a snapshot of a later stage of the process of incorporation of notes added to the *History*, shows that Comestor's extrinsic gloss had already become an undifferentiated part of the text in V, while in P it was included as an intrinsic gloss together with other glosses, whose history I have shown above to be quite complicated, to yet another gloss that had already become an undifferentiated part of the *History*'s principal text. Moreover, Langton's testimony about this particular extrinsic gloss added by Comestor also makes clear that he and his students had in front of them a manuscript or manuscripts

---

83   P, fol. 156ra: "In glosa extrinseca ponit Magister aliam solutionem. Et hoc est VEL POTEST ESSE SYNCRESIS id est spontanea concessio." Langton kept this same text in the two revised versions of his lecture course on the *History*. See H, fol. 119va, and N, fol. 144rb.

84   See P, fol. 157vb–158ra.

85   V, fol. 186va: "Vel potest esse sincresis, id est spontanea petitio, quia si vellent primi murmurare, posset rationabiliter murmur eorum conprimi. Quod si murmuraverunt primi, nihilominus tamen Dominus iuste agit cum novissimis, quos primo remunerat." There is a briefer version of the same gloss in the margins of Tr, at fol. 29ra–b.: "Vel potest esse sineresis (*sic*), quia si vellent primi murmurare, posset rationabiliter murmur eorum conprimi."

86   As in the previous footnote, I sometimes include information about the state of the notes in the text of Troyes, MS 290 (Tr), one of the eight pre-1200 manuscripts relied on by Sylwan, in order to provide a basis of comparison with P and V. For Sylwan's misclassification of this manuscript as part of a family including V, see n14 above.

containing a version of the *History*'s text in which Comestor's gloss was already integrated into the text, for Langton tells them that it had been placed above a certain lemma: "*PUER AUTEM* super hoc ...," and he would have been no reason to point out the note's extrinsic origin had the students been able to see this themselves. We know, therefore, that his students had in front of them a text of the *History* more akin to the tradition handed down by V than the older one in P.

The second example, while not as complicated, tells much the same story, albeit at an earlier stage, for the gloss added by Comestor is not found in P but is found in both V and Tr in the margins, that is, as marginal glosses one level removed from the so-called intrinsic glosses, which were written into the main columns of the principal text but set off by borders from it. Moreover, we see clearly the same process of layering of glosses.

I have focused here on Langton's identifying for his auditors extrinsic glosses added by Comestor, but the fact is that he routinely identifies such extrinsic glosses throughout his initial lecture course on the *History*. A typical example is his comment regarding the fifth chapter of the *Historia evangelica*: "ALIUS LOCUS istud 'alius' glosa est; hic leges glosam extrinsecam: DICITUR QUIA ETC. ... QUIESCUNT NON LONGE A PRESEPIO."[87] Here too, Langton's comment enables us to see the same process of rapid absorption of such "extrinsic" texts into the *History* itself, for we find this particular gloss, altered to fit the context, as part of the principal text in both V and P.[88] Langton does not here name the source of the extrinsic gloss in question, referring to that source impersonally. An argument from silence is always of questionable worth, but given Langton's explicit reference just a few chapters earlier (in the third chapter of the *Historia evangelica*) to Comestor's having added an extrinsic gloss, it is probably safe to assume that, even if Comestor himself had added this text, Langton did not know about it. Nevertheless, whoever added this particular extrinsic gloss, by 1180 it too had become part of the principal text in several different yet early textual traditions of the *History*.

There is no need to multiply examples here. Those adduced suffice to show that very early on, and long before our earliest extant manuscripts allow us to see, the *History* was a dynamic text subject to change. Already before 1176, just several years after scholars have commonly supposed that the *History* first

---

87 *Prima Stephani glosa scilicet lectiones a Stephano viva voce ante 1176 datae in Historiam evangelicam* (ed. Clark, Textual Appendix B.2 below, lines 53–54).

88 *Petri Comestoris Historia evangelica*, 5 (ed. Clark, Textual Appendix B.1 below, lines 114–117).

entered the public sphere, the extrinsic glosses in question, known to Langton as such, had become an undifferentiated part of the *History*'s text in versions available in the schools. This should not surprise us for, as I showed in Chapters 2–4, Comestor's experience and frustrations in using the biblical *Gloss* to teach introductory courses on the four Gospels led him to make a new textbook, whose form, method, and structure were such that teachers could adapt it as they chose.

Comestor himself made use of this flexibility of format in composing and revising the *History*. We are fortunate that Langton knew the original version well enough to recognize additions and also knew Comestor himself and his ongoing work on the *History* well enough to be personally familiar with changes that he made to the original. It is of course possible and perhaps even likely that Comestor, as did so many of his distinguished twelfth-century predecessors, left an autograph copy of the *History*. It may be too that we shall be fortunate enough to find it. But even if we do, it would not alter the fact that the *History* was a dynamic text, one whose structure was amenable to ongoing revision and adaptation.

It should be abundantly clear by now that all such testimony Langton provides about the *History*'s text is invaluable, for it furnishes us with insight that we could not otherwise have had. Indeed, the light shed by Langton's remarks about the extrinsic glosses added by Comestor shows that the *History*'s text was changing, and even at Comestor's hands, extremely rapidly even before the mid-1170s. Moreover, even apart from Langton's testimony, the manuscripts themselves tell the tale of a rapidly evolving text. We can see extrinsic glosses becoming intrinsic, and already by the time we see versions of the *History* in P and in V an indeterminate number of such glosses are already beyond our seeing. Thanks to Langton, we can spot some, but it would be a mistake to assume that these are anything more than the tip of a scholastic iceberg. Many glosses of other, unnamed masters who were teaching the *History* also made their way into its text. Even when they did not, magisterial positions found their way into the living tradition of teaching the *History*.

A good example is the first gloss added to the fourth chapter of the *Historia evangelica*, which is found as an extrinsic gloss in V but omitted in P.[89] The

---

89   "Sunt qui dicunt censi capite esse unam dictionem tercie declinationis et ablativi casus, et tunc sic exponitur quia numerus eorum qui ferebantur id est referebantur censi capite id est numeratione capitis. Alii item dicunt qualis sit una dictio prime declinationis." *Petri Comestoris Historia evangelica*, 4 (ed. Clark, Textual Appendix B.1 below, lines 103–106).

gloss refers to various magisterial positions about whether *censicapite* is one word or two. Langton glosses this very passage in his lecture course on the *History*, telling his students that it is in fact one word.[90] But the marginal gloss recorded in V refers to various teachers. The question at issue is a simple one, but it is valuable precisely because it is typical. It was evidently the subject of an ongoing classroom discussion in the 1170s. Masters teaching the *History* would naturally argue with Comestor and with each other, and such debates would frequently be recorded in the margins of manuscripts, as here.

It seems clear, therefore, that Comestor was not the only one who "made" the *History*'s text, for his text evidently became public property of a sort that would be difficult for us to comprehend today.[91] Langton seems to have enjoyed a privileged status as approved editor, but the *History*'s text changed at the hands of numerous, anonymous contributors as well. From the standpoint of one seeking to produce a modern edition, this is a real difficulty, for our earliest and best textual witness is a teacher and editor whose testimony reveals the startling rapidity with which the text of the *History* was changing. Nevertheless, even if we cannot hope to recover Comestor's "original" *History* without discovering the autograph itself, we have thanks to Langton a much better understanding of the text of the *History* that entered the schools. That *Historia*, dating to the early 1170s and probably even to the later 1160s, was emphatically *scholastica*, and it is Langton who makes it a realistic possibility to re-present that dynamic text in a modern edition.

Sylwan's Assumptions

Absent Langton's textual witness, Sylwan's many assumptions ordered to supporting the view that the *History* was originally a private, static text might plausibly be maintained. In view of his testimony, however, such a view is evidently untenable, for Langton puts beyond doubt that our earliest extant manuscripts of the *History* are late witnesses to rapidly evolving textual traditions. Langton's testimony settles decisively the three fundamental and related questions raised by Sylwan's assumptions about the early history of the *Historia scholastica*:

---

90   "CENSICAPITE una dictio, cuius nominativus censicaput id est tali censu capitis." *Prima Stephani glossa scilicet lectiones a Stephano viva voce ante 1176 datae in Historiam evangelicam* (ed. Clark, Textual Appendix B.2 below, lines 37–38).

91   Perhaps web sites such as Wikipedia provide a modern basis for comparison.

the problem of the so-called "notes" to the *History*; whether or not it is possible to get back to Comestor's original text based upon the manuscripts that are extant; and whether Comestor's *History* was scholastic from the first.

Langton's testimony about the extrinsic glosses added by Comestor and others to the *History*'s intrinsic text, coupled with the dynamic, rapidly evolving state of the textual traditions found in our earliest manuscripts, V and P, shows that Sylwan's idea of a private, self-contained set of notes added by Comestor to the *History* before publication and predating any scholastic additions to the *History* is pure fiction. The reality, as we have just seen, is far more complex. By the time Langton lectured on the *History* and revised those lectures, which must have been a short time after the so-called publication of the *History*, the scholastic evolution of Comestor's text is plain for all to see, even in P.

Sylwan's second assumption, therefore, that we can get back to that original, pre-scholastic version of the *History* through P is also patently false. Sylwan is right that P contains a more primitive version of the *History*'s text than V and other extant early manuscripts. She is, however, demonstrably wrong in thinking that the version of the *History* preserved in P is any less scholastic. Langton's testimony alone suffices to show that P, like V, preserves an already late textual tradition that was subject to the same inexorable scholastic additions and changes.

Finally, her principal assumption that the *History* was not originally meant for the schools, the foundation and framework for her edition of the *Historia Genesis*, has no basis in fact. Indeed, all available evidence supports the opposite conclusion, that the *History* was scholastic from the first. Even were we fortunate enough to find Comestor's autograph, the very framework that Comestor developed for the *History* would still be concrete evidence for its essentially scholastic character.[92] In short, in the light of all available evidence, there is every reason to suppose that the *History*, in its conception, design, composition, and use, was emphatically a *Historia scholastica*.

---

92   There were of course many different scholastic approaches to the Bible in the twelfth century. For teachers less interested in showing students how to resolve conflicts among authorities and to extract doctrine from the Bible than in how to apply semantic theories to knotty readings, there were the works of Peter of Poitiers, Prepositinus, Peter of Capua, Alan of Lille, and Peter the Chanter. These were parallel contemporary approaches to the Bible, all equally "scholastic."

It is for this reason that any modern edition of the *History* must reflect to the greatest extent possible the dynamic reality of its transmission. We have seen that the *History* was a highly unstable text from the start. By the time that we see versions of its text in our earliest extant manuscripts, namely in V (1180–1183) and in P (1183), there are multiple textual traditions, all of which have undergone extensive changes. Langton's testimony shows us that the *History* was a public text, taught by many *magistri*, to a degree that we can hardly imagine. In reality, what we have even in our earliest manuscripts are snapshots of a text that is changing rapidly as it is used in the schools.

Nevertheless, owing to the privileged role that Langton played in its early history and to the information provided by his course, we are in the fortunate position of being able to reconstruct to a great, if not perfect extent the text of the *History* that was used in Paris during the last four decades of the twelfth century.

III. *Towards a "Langton" or "University" Edition of the* Historia scholastica

In light of the foregoing, the case for a "Langton" edition of the *History* is quite strong. Langton is not only our earliest but also our best witness to the early textual development and history of the *Historia scholastica*. His observations together with his own glosses that became part of the *History* add up to an impressive and compelling body of evidence. Indeed, the evidence that he provides about the state of the *History*'s text reveals that P and V transmit copies of late rather than early, and dynamic rather than static, textual traditions.[93] Langton's course on the *History* thus enables us to document many changes that . we would not otherwise see.

The many glosses added to the *History*, by Comestor, by Langton, and by others, turn out to be a key to interpretation, for they reveal to us the rapidity with which Comestor's text was changing as it entered the schools.[94] Sylwan's

---

93   The text in P is older to be sure than that in V, but we learn from Langton that both are late. In this respect, Sylwan deserves much credit for her groundbreaking researches into the early state of Comestor's text. She was right in thinking that V belonged to a later, scholastic tradition, although that tradition is much earlier than she supposed.

94   Smalley was prescient in writing that "[t]he best way to get an insight into the historical study of the Bible at about the year 1200 would be to examine glosses on the *Histories* and the notes written in the margins of early copies." Smalley, *Study of the Bible*, 214–215.

hypothesis of an original and discrete "set" of notes compiled by Comestor and added to the *History* privately is far removed from the reality we encounter of various and multiple glosses crashing into each other and forcing their way into the principal text of the *History* itself.[95] In fact, thanks to Langton we see the very process by which these texts moved from the margins to notes added above lines to part of the main text in the manuscripts. The picture that we get is not one of order and stability but rather one of flux and dynamism.

Several years ago, in reviewing Sylwan's edition of the *Historia Genesis*, I concluded that she had taken a wrong turn in attempting to get back to a pre-scholastic, ur-text of the *History*.[96] As an alternative, I suggested that scholars would be well served if we could get back to the text of the *History* that Langton was teaching.[97] I am now confident that we can do so, precisely because the glosses, together with the evidence of Langton's lectures and subsequent revisions of his course on the *History*, make it possible to approximate the text of the *Historia scholastica* used in the schools of Paris from the late 1160s/early 1170s through the end of the twelfth century.[98]

Langton's lecture course on the *History* and his two subsequent revisions of the same, especially the pre-1176 revision, thus afford us a blueprint of lemmata, which we can compare to the readings in manuscripts of the *History*.[99]

---

95 In maintaining that Comestor's work was not initially meant for the schools, Sylwan assumes a static text to which a certain number of fixed notes had been added. Peter Comestor, *Scolastica historia* (ed. Sylwan, lxxvi–lxxvii).

96 Clark, "How to Edit the *Historia Scholastica* of Peter Comestor?"

97 Ibid.

98 The obvious way to carry my study forward another forty years would be to examine the text or texts of the *History* that served the Dominican *équipe* working for Hugh of St. Cher in the 1230s, when the massive and encyclopedic Dominican commentary on that work was put together. My preliminary researches suggest that the Dominicans made copious use of the various versions of Langton's course on the *History*. Clark, "Commentaries on Peter Comestor's *Historia scholastica*," 340–342, 431–436 (Textual Appendix E). See also Mark J. Clark, "Stephen Langton and Hugh of St. Cher on Peter Comestor's *Historia scholastica*: the Lombard's *Sentences* and the Problem of Sources used by Comestor and his Commentators," *Recherches de Théologie et Philosophie médiévales* 74 (2007): 63–117. Anyone editing the Dominican commentary on the *History* would be able to compare at a glance the manuscripts used by the Dominicans with the scholastic textual tradition begun by Comestor and continued by Langton.

99 The fact that the readings in Langton's first revision frequently match those in V shows us that we can make use of the textual data provided by Langton to get as close as we can to the text of the *History* used by him and his students in the Parisian classrooms of the 1170s and beyond.

Langton's course also gives us precious information on the early text of the *Historia scholastica*, on the rapid change and development it underwent, and on how it became established in the schools of Paris as a pedagogical classic by the second half of the twelfth century. To Stephen Langton's work on the *Scholastic History* we now turn.

Stephen Langton

Comestor's Student, Collaborator, Colleague

Like most twelfth-century writers, Langton reveals little about himself and his past in his writings. There is the occasional exception, when he provides his students with bits of information about his past life, as for example when, discussing the story of Martha's ministrations in the context of Jewish practices current in the time of Jesus, Langton told his students that he himself had seen similar practices as a young man living in England: "BUT MARTHA WAS SERVING This very thing, he says, I saw in my own country, that youths would serve at the tables of the rich."[1] The student reporter here quotes Langton's own words, noting Langton's eye-witness account of practices in England. From Langton's report, we can surmise either that his was one of the rich families spoken of or that he himself had served at the tables of the rich. Langton here provides a rare glimpse into his own past.

Happily, Langton was less reticent about the doings and teaching of his own Master, Peter Comestor. The many details provided by Langton about Comestor and especially about the *History*'s text, either directly through his own remarks or indirectly through his own course on the *History*, enables us to piece together what happened, when, and by whom. We learn, for example, that Comestor not only composed the *History* but also taught it, that Langton not only probably attended Comestor's lectures on the *History* but may also have attended his lectures on the Glossed Gospels. We learn furthermore that Langton became one of Comestor's most privileged collaborators, working so closely with his Master that the *History*'s place in the developing curriculum of the University of Paris owes at least as much to Langton as to Comestor.

In fact, Langton's course on the *History* enables us to reconstruct with great accuracy the story of the *History*'s institutionalization between 1170 and 1200: as a text; as a textbook; and as a key component of the scholastic curriculum

---

1 Paris, BnF, lat. 14417, fol. 156rb: "SED MARTHA MINISTRABAT Sic, inquit, vidi in terra mea, quod iuvencule ministrabant mensis divitum."

of the developing University of Paris. Indeed, if Comestor's role was that of a master teacher and creative genius who saw and met a pressing need occasioned by the rapidly evolving schools of Paris, we learn from Langton's course on the *History* that his own role evolved quickly from that of graduate student to that of collaborator, colleague, and ultimately caretaker of his Master's legacy.

This story can be divided into three parts. In the first stage (before 1176) Langton began to teach the *History* as a young theologian, perhaps as Comestor's student. In the second (still before 1176) he became Comestor's colleague and collaborator, revising his own lectures and editing the text of the *History* itself. In the third he revised his course once more as an established Paris master in the 1190s.

In this chapter, I focus mainly on the first two, presenting evidence that links Langton to Comestor personally as well as institutionally and which draws a portrait of a relationship that started as master and student, developed into a collegial collaboration, and resulted in a true passing of the educational torch. We shall see that Langton was inextricably linked to Comestor and the *Historia scholastica*, for he became Comestor's heir in the schools of Paris, the caretaker of his Master's legacy.

I. The Formation of the University Text: The Pre-1176 Series of Lectures

Relying on details that Langton provides his students about texts that are extrinsic to the *History*'s original text, we can see the university edition of the *History* taking shape. Langton also tells his students about the author of the *History*. This and other evidence makes a strong case that Langton was himself in Comestor's classroom.

a. Langton as Textual Witness

Although there are exceptions, as a general rule Langton gives us most of this textual information in his lecture course on the *History*. Moreover, he provides such information so routinely that a reader of this first version of his course comes to expect Langton's references to extrinsic glosses. For this reason and to avoid repetition, I shall here provide only a typical example, in this case taken from the sixth chapter of the *Historia evangelica* ("De natu Domini").

The sixth chapter of the *Historia evangelica* ("De natu Domini") reveals in many ways the dynamism of that evolving university text, not only the extent to which Comestor's text was changing but also just how valuable is Langton's witness to those changes.[2] To make it easier to see the extent of those changes and also to understand the process by which they occurred, I provide a translation of the full chapter; all bracketed texts are additions to Comestor's text:[3]

Chapter 6: On the Birth of our Lord

And the Savior was born in the forty-second year of the reign of Augustus Caesar. For we reckon with the twelve years that had gone by from the death of Iulius to the battle at Actium during the reign of Augustus. But in the thirtieth year of the reign of Herod, when the whole world was at peace, the Lord was born [in the third year of the hundred and eighty-third Olympiad, in the seven hundred and fifty second year from the founding of Rome.] And he was born at night on the Lord's Day, [since if you work backwards through the table for computing dates, you will find for this year a regular group of five and a group of three for January, running together, which when these have been joined and then seven taken away, one remains. And so you will find that the kalends of January falls on a Sunday, which suggests itself] [from this, that the kalends of April fell on the Friday following the death of Jesus. In the same year <you have> the following: the day of his birth was on the Lord's Day, and this same thing happened in the year of his conception and birth.] For on the day on which *God said let there be light and there was light, he visited us arising from on high.* But according to some the sixth age began from the birth of Christ, as according to Saint Paul, who says: *when the fullness of time comes etc.,* according to others from the day on which he was baptized on account of the regenerative power given to the waters, according to others from his passion, since then the gate <of heaven> was opened wide, and the seventh age of those at rest began. Indeed five thousand one hundred and ninety-six years had gone by from the time of Adam, from that of Abraham two thousand and twelve according to the Seventy, but according to the Hebrews fewer years by far.

[Olympus was next to the city of Elidom, where after every four years they held the games, and therefore they are read to have taken place sometimes every fourth year and sometimes every fifth.]

2   In what follows, I again cite Troyes, Bibliothèque municipale, MS 290, as I did in Chapter Five, since not only does it bear witness to the early textual tradition available to Langton but not found in either V or P, it also provides additional evidence of the *History's* rapidly changing text during the closing dates of the twelfth century.

3   I treat this as a separate chapter, as in V (at fol. 169vb), even though neither in P (at 143rb) nor in Tr (starting at the bottom of fol. 7rb) is it a separate chapter.

[At Rome the temple of peace collapsed, the fountain of oil erupted. Caesar had ordained that no-one should call him lord. While one day Caesar was entering the city in triumph the sun seemed to encircle the earth like a rainbow.][4]

As is evident these additions constitute just about half of the chapter.

We know that the first bracketed text, namely "[Olympiadis – secundo]," is a note, even though it is part of the principal text in V (at fol. 169vb), because it is omitted in P (at fol. 143rb).[5] Likewise, the last few words of the first full paragraph – "[secundum septuaginta, secundum Hebreos vero longe pauciores.]" – are omitted in P (at fol. 143va, top), though found in V (at fol. 169vb) and in Tr (at fol. 7va).[6] Presumably, this too is an added gloss. Langton says nothing about either text; he neither calls the attention of his students to them nor glosses any part of either. But we can make no inference from his silence, for we do not know whether these two texts were in the text or texts of the *History* used by him and

4 *Petri Comestoris Historia evangelica*, 6 (ed. Clark, Textual Appendix B.1 below, lines 127–152): "**Capitulum VI. De natu domini.** Natus est autem Salvator anno regni Augusti Cesaris quadragesimo secundo. Annos enim duodecim qui a morte Iulii fluxerant usque ad Actium bellum regno Augusti communeramus. Anno vero regni Herodis trigesimo universo orbe paccato natus est Dominus, [Olympiadis centesime octogesime tertie anno tertio, ab urbe condita septingentesimo quinquagesimo secundo]. Natus est autem nocte dominice diei, [quia si tabulam compoti retro percurras, invenies huius anni concurrentem quinarium regularem ianuarii ternarium quibus iunctis et sublatis septem unum remanet. Itaque kalendis ianuarii in Dominica invenies, quod occurrit] [ad hoc, quia kalende Aprilis fuerunt sexta feria post mortem Iesu. In anno eodem sequens dies nativitatis eius fuit in dominica et idem fuit in anno conceptionis et nativitatis.] Nam eadem die qua *dixit fiat lux et facta est lux, visitavit nos oriens ex alto*. Incoata est vero secundum quosdam sexta etas a nativitate Christi, ut secundum Apostolum qui ait: *cum venerit plenitudo temporis etc.*, secundum alios a die qua baptizatus est propter vim regenerativam datam aquis, secundum alios a passione, quia tunc aperta est porta et inchoata est septima etas quiescentium. Fluxerant quidem ab Adam anni quinque milia centum nonaginta sex, ab Abraham bis mille duodecim [secundum septuaginta, secundum Hebreos vero longe pauciores.]

[[Olympus fuit mons iuxta Elidom civitatem ubi quattuor annis transpositis ludos exercebant, et ideo aliquando quarto aliquando quinto anno leguntur facti.]]

[Rome templum pacis corruit, fons olei erupit. Cesar preceperat, ne quis eum dominum vocaret. Dum quadam die Cesar ovans urbem ingrederetur hora tertia instar arcus celestis orbem sol ambire visus est.]"

5 *Petri Comestoris Historia evangelica*, 6 (ed. Clark, Textual Appendix B.1 below, lines 147–149). It is, however, found in Tr (at fol. 7va) as part of the principal text.

6 *Petri Comestoris Historia evangelica*, 6 (ed. Clark, Textual Appendix B.1 below, lines 145–146 and apparatus).

his students.[7] Since I argue below in this chapter that Langton himself had privileged access to a version of the *History* closely approximating Comestor's ur-
text, the absence of notes such as these in Langton's text would come as no surprise. In any case, we can recognize in their presence in V and absence from P
another sign of the dynamism of the *History*'s early textual history.

Fortunately, we do learn from Langton that the rest are definitely notes
added to the text of the *History*. After explaining and corroborating Comestor's
mathematically based argument that our Lord was born on a Sunday evening,
Langton provides his student listeners with the following textual gloss:[8]

And this is an extrinsic gloss, from that place: SINCE IF A TABLE ETC.
FOR ON THE SAME DAY This is about the literal understanding that is
said about the Sunday on which God created, after the empyreum heaven
and the angels and the matter of all bodies, simultaneously and immediately on the same day he created light, that is, a certain light-filled cloud.
And all these are called the work of the first day.[9]

Owing to the apparent unity of the text that follows – there are no seams
in the argument of *Historia evangelica* 6, which is cogent and clear – we would
have no idea where the note ends that starts from "quia si tabulam," had not
Langton also provided his students with a second textual key: "Item alia glosa,
que est: *AB HOC ETC.*"[10]

7   There are three possibilities: he recognized them as notes but said nothing; he saw
     these texts, either or both, but did not recognize them as notes; he did not have them
     in the text before him.
8   Langton's text, which repeats the word "created," shows clearly the character of a lecture.
9   *Prima Stephani glosa scilicet lectiones a Stephano viva voce ante 1176 datae in Historiam
     evangelicam*, 6 (ed. Clark, Textual Appendix B.2 below, lines 72–76): "Et hec est glosa
     extrinseca ab eo loco: QUIA SI TABULAM ETC. NAM EADEM DIE Hoc de littera quod de
     dominica dicitur, qua Deus creavit post celum empireum et angelos et materiam
     omnium corporum simul et statim eadem die creavit lucem id est nubem quandam
     lucidam et hec omnia dicuntur opus prime diei."
10   *Prima Stephani glosa scilicet lectiones a Stephano viva voce ante 1176 datae in Historiam evan-
     gelicam*, 6 (ed. Clark, Textual Appendix B.2 below, lines 76–77). Cf. *Petri Comestoris
     Historia evangelica*, 6 (ed. Clark, Textual Appendix B.1 below, lines 133–136). This note,
     which is found in V (at fol. 169vb) as an undifferentiated part of the principal text, is
     formatted as an intrinsic note, that is, as a note formatted as such but placed within the
     boundaries of the principal columns of the manuscript, in P (at fol. 143rb, bottom)
     and in Tr (at fol. 7va).

This second and consecutive gloss – "[from this, that the kalends of April fell on the Friday following the death of Jesus. In the same year <you have> the following: the day of his birth was on the Lord's Day, and this same thing happened in the year of his conception and birth.]" – completes the note just discussed. Indeed, it literally picks up in mid-sentence the thought expressed by the preceding note – "... quod occurrit] [ab hoc ...]," and the two together form a unity following and explicating Comestor's concise statement about the time of Jesus's birth: "He was born on a Sunday night."[11] Absent Langton's testimony, we would have no idea that either text was an added note, much less that there were two such notes added to Comestor's text.

Langton also attends to a fifth additional text in this chapter, namely "Rome templum pacis ... ambire visus est."[12] This particular note, which is found neither in P (at fol. 143) nor in V (at fol. 169vb), is found in Tr (at fol. 7va), where it is set off as an intrinsic note that follows the note ("Ad hoc etc.") just discussed. Langton explicates this text at some length in his first revision of his lecture course on the *History*:

The temple of Roman peace etc. At the time of the Roman Emperor, Augustus, since there was continual peace for almost twelve years, they built a temple of peace, since this was very beautiful and wondrous in the eyes of men. And when they consulted the oracle at Delphi how long this would last, they received the response: until such time as a virgin should give birth. Hearing this, they said: therefore, it will stand forever, since it seemed impossible to them according to the ordinary course of nature that a virgin should give birth. Whence on the doors of this temple they wrote: the eternal temple of peace. But on the night when the Blessed Virgin gave birth <to our Savior> the whole thing was destroyed to such an extent, that not one stone remained there on another. And on the same night on which our Lord was born a fountain of oil erupted and flowed all the way into the Tiber, but how long that lasted I do not know.[13]

---

11   *Petri Comestoris Historia evangelica*, 6 (ed. Clark, Textual Appendix B.1 below, line 133). On Comestor's use of the *tabula compoti* to establish the chronology of the birth of Jesus, see David Luscombe, "Peter Comestor and Biblical Chronology," *Irish Theological Quarterly* 80 (2015): 136–148, at 141. I am grateful to Professor Luscombe for sharing this recently published article with me.

12   *Petri Comestoris Historia evangelica*, 6 (ed. Clark, Textual Appendix B.1 below, lines 150–152).

13   *Secunda Stephani glosa supra Historiam evangelicam scilicet prima lectionum recensio datarum viva voce ante 1176, effecta a Stephano ipso traditaque in codice H*, 6 (ed. Clark, Textual Appen-

Langton's explication of the note shows that he was an excellent story-teller, for he brings the legend to life. The interesting point here, however, is not the substance of the explication, but rather the fact that this text must have entered the *Historia scholastica* during the early 1170s, possibly before Langton's lectures on that work and certainly before his revision of those lectures. The *History's* text was changing, and Langton's taking notice of this particular text in the revised version of his lecture course doubtless served to strengthen its place in the *History's* text. A sign of this is that Langton retained these lemmata and his gloss on the same in the second revision of his course on the *History*.[14]

Chapter Six of the *Historia evangelica* is one example of many that could be cited showing that Langton provided copious information about the *History's* text to his students while lecturing. He makes constant reference to notes added to the *History*, and even where he does not do so, he frequently glosses lemmata taken from such texts, as in the example just considered, which reveal the presence of such notes in the versions of the *History* used by Langton's students. Owing to the information provided by Langton's lecture course and his revision of the same, we see the emergence of the version of the *History* used in the nascent University of Paris, and Langton's role in that process.

b. *Langton as Student*

At the end of his lecture on Chapter Six of the *Historia evangelica*, following his own pellucid explanation of the dating of the conception and birth of Jesus, Langton makes the following observation about Comestor to his hearers: "Likewise, the Master provides additionally ("*extra*") certain signs for a Sunday birth, which happened on the same night on which Jesus was born."[15] In search-

---

dix B.3 below, lines 110–119): "ROME TEMPLUM PACIS ETC. Romani tempore Augusti Cesaris, quia pax fuit continua fere per duodecim annos, templum pacis edificaverunt, quia pulcerrimum erat et mirabile in oculis hominum. Qui consulantes Apollinem quantum duraret, receperunt responsum: quousque virgo pareret. Hoc audientes dixerunt: ergo in eternum stabit, quia impossibile eis videbatur secundum cursum solitum nature quod virgo pareret. Unde in foribus illius templi titulum scripserunt: templum pacis eternum. Nocte vero qua Beata Virgo peperit totum ita destructum est, quod non remansit ibi lapis super lapidem. Et eadem nocte qua natus est Dominus FONS OLEI ERUPIT et fluxit usque in Tiberim, sed quantum duraverit nescio."

14 *Tertia Stephani glosa scilicet magistralis ante 1193 recensa supra Historiam evangelicam*, 6 (ed. Clark, Textual Appendix B.4 below, lines 107–116).

15 *Prima Stephani glosa scilicet lectiones a Stephano viva voce ante 1176 datae in Historiam evangelicam*, 6 (ed. Clark, Textual Appendix B.2 below, lines 87–88): "Item ponit extra Magister quedam signa dominice nativitatis que in eadem nocte qua natus est contigerunt."

ing for the text in the *History* to which Langton is here referring, one finds only one possibility, namely the note added to the end of the chapter: "At Rome the temple of peace collapsed, the fountain of oil erupted. Caesar had ordained that no-one should call him lord. While one day Caesar was entering the city in triumph the sun seemed to encircle the earth like a rainbow."[16] It is certain that Langton was pointing out to his students that Comestor had provided "*extra*" certain signs for a Sunday birth, and in the light of the signs listed in this note, it is possible and perhaps even likely that Comestor himself had added this note.

This particular text is fascinating because, in contrast to his practice elsewhere, Langton does not tell his students that this is an extrinsic gloss. Why not? We cannot know for sure, but one obvious possibility is that it was not an extrinsic gloss but something else. Moreover, there is a clue. Langton uses the word *extra*, and there is no doubt, given its position in the sentence and the syntax of the sentence, that it is an adverb. According to Langton, therefore, Comestor set forth *extra* – that is, besides, additionally, a common meaning in its extended signification – certain signs that support the position that Jesus was born on a Sunday night. It may be that *extra* just means extrinsic, but it may also mean something else. Perhaps Comestor gave these examples in class first and it was written down subsequently, by him or by a student. Perhaps there was a private list of such "extras" to which Langton had access. Perhaps Langton got it straight from Comestor, inside or outside of class. Whatever the truth of the matter – and it is unlikely that we shall ever find out for sure – Langton's knowledge of Comestor's teaching was firsthand.

It is obvious that such firsthand knowledge could have come from the classroom. There is more evidence in Langton's lecture course to support the idea that Langton was Comestor's student. Several examples will suffice here. Comestor devotes a long chapter in the *Historia evangelica* to explaining the meaning of the jar filled with precious ointment that an unknown woman used to anoint the feet of Jesus. He writes about the ointment: "For <there are>

---

16   *Petri Comestoris Historia evangelica*, 6 (ed. Clark, Textual Appendix B.1 below, lines 150–152): "[Rome templum pacis corruit, fons olei erupit. Cesar preceperat, ne quis eum dominum vocaret. Dum quadam die Cesar ovans urbem ingrederetur hora tertia instar arcus celestis orbem sol ambire visus est.]"

other kinds of pure nard, that is, genuine and not corrupted."[17] Langton, glossing this passage in his lecture course, tells his students how Comestor had learned the meaning of this Greek word, *pisteuo*: "PISTEUO: I believe, which the Master used to say that he had heard at Rome about a certain Greek archbishop making his profession of faith to the Pope."[18]

For our purposes, however, it is the incidental that is more important, for in relating this anecdote to his students, Langton lets us know that Comestor had gone to Rome, where he heard about the archbishop's meeting with the pope. Comestor must have gone to Rome before writing these words, in all probability before 1170 and perhaps even quite a bit before. How and when did Langton hear this story from Comestor? Chances are very good that Langton heard Comestor when he was a student, and that he heard the story from Comestor in class.

We find an interesting anecdote in connection with the fourth chapter of the *Historia Genesis*, in which Comestor treats, as part of his treatment of the hexameron, that is, the six days of creation, God's arrangement of the higher parts of creation. Referring first to heaven in its most proper sense, the *empyreum*, where the angels worship God, Comestor goes on to discuss two more parts of the universe that are also called heaven: the firmament, in which the stars are fixed, which is called heaven ("celum") because it covers ("celat") everything else; and the aerial heaven, where the birds fly.[19] The chapter ends with a reference to a fourth possible heaven: "Certain thinkers suspect that there is a fourth heaven above the *empyreum*, since we read that Lucifer, when he was in the empyreum, said: I shall go up into heaven etc. And in the same way they say that Christ is a man above the angels, who are in the *empyreum*."[20] This text is found in both P (at fol. 3rb) and V (at fol. 8rb) as part of the principal

17 V, fol. 188va, and P, fol. 159vb: "Alia enim genera nardi pistici id est fidelis et non adulterini. Pisteuo enim credo et pistis fides dicitur nulla scilicet adulterina commixtione corrupti."

18 SL[1] = Paris, BNF, lat. 14417, fol. 156rb: "PISTEUO CREDO quod Magister dicebat se audisse Rome de quodam archiepiscopo Greco faciente professionem Domino Pape." Langton's gloss is impressively accurate, for *pisteuo* does literally mean "I entrust myself to someone," and this is precisely what the Greek archbishop was saying to the Pope.

19 *Petri Comestoris Historia Genesis*, 4 (ed. Clark, Textual Appendix A.1 below, lines 134–145).

20 Ibid., lines 145–148: "[Quidam quartum suspicantur celum esse super empireum, quia Lucifer, cum esset in empireo, legitur dixisse: *ascendam in celum etc*. Et in eo modo dicunt esse Christum hominem super angelos, qui sunt in empireo.]"

text; there is no indication whatsoever in these, our earliest manuscripts, that it was ever a note added to the *History*.[21] Nonetheless, we learn from Langton that this too is a note added to the *History*.[22]

What is interesting, however, is not that it is another note identified as such by Langton – by this point we should come to expect that – but rather his own glossing of the note in the lecture course, which places him in Comestor's hometown:

CERTAIN THINKERS A FOURTH ETC. And this, he says, is an opinion I have heard from certain others, and I saw it written down and even depicted in a church in Troyes, where in a certain stain-glassed window Christ is being born up on carrying-clouds to the empyreum. And that heaven is sapphire-colored and filled with angels, above which is a certain sphere somewhat reddish in hue.[23]

The *inquit* signals the presence of a student reporter, who is recording Langton's words, which in this instance are personal. Langton, speaking before 1176 while Comestor was still alive, tells his students what he saw in Troyes, Comestor's hometown, a fact that would not have been lost on any of his listeners.

I provide conclusive evidence for Langton's firsthand knowledge of Comestor's teaching in the next section when I consider Langton's first revision of his course on the *History*.[24] For now, the evidence set forth for Langton's

---

21 It is also part of the principal text in Tr (at fol. 3rb).

22 *Tertia Stephani glosa scilicet magistralis ante 1193 recensa supra Historiam Genesis*, 4 (ed. Clark, Textual Appendix A.4 below, lines 207–208). Curiously, all three manuscripts containing copies of Langton's second revision of the *History* have "querunt" for "quartum"; Pseudo-Langton, who reproduces substantial portions of all three versions of Langton's course on the *History*, repeats the same mistake. That it is a mistake is clear from a comparison of the texts in SL³ and SL⁴ (Pseudo-Langton's course) with SL¹ and SL², both of which have the reading as it appears in the *History*.

23 *Prima Stephani glosa scilicet lectiones a Stephano viva voce ante 1176 datae in Historiam Genesi*, 4 (ed. Clark, Textual Appendix A.2 below, lines 107–111): "QUIDAM QUARTUM ETC. Et hanc, inquit, opinionem audivi a quibusdam, et vidi scriptam et etiam pictam in Trecensi Ecclesia, ubi ad celum empireum in quadam vitrea baiulis nubibus fertur Christus. Et illud saphirium est et angelis repletum, supra quod est sperula quedam admodum rubicunda." The same gloss is repeated with one small change in Langton's first revision of that lecture course. *Secunda Stephani glosa supra Historiam Genesis scilicet prima lectionum recensio datarum viva voce ante 1176, effecta a Stephano ipso traditaque in codice H*, 4 (ed. Clark, Textual Appendix A.3 below, lines 107–111).

24 See, in particular, the three examples at 198–205, below.

firsthand knowledge of Comestor's teaching, coupled with the timing of his lecture course and first revision of the same, both of which took place while Comestor was still active and working on the *History*, suffices to show that they were colleagues working closely together on Comestor's *magnum opus*.

There is one other type of evidence worth mentioning in connection with the case for Langton as Comestor's student. Thus far, I have considered evidence that could place Langton in Comestor's classroom as the latter lectured on the *History*. It is also possible that Langton may have heard Comestor's lectures on the Glossed Gospels. In lecturing upon the *Historia evangelica* Langton frequently makes use of material lifted straight out of those lectures. A typical example can be seen in his treatment of Chapter Five of the *Historia evangelica*. Glossing Luke's statement that Jesus was Mary's firstborn ("primogenitus") child, Comestor explains that this could mean either "before whom no one" or "after whom another."[25] Langton explicates this for his students, including a grammatical distinction made by Priscian as a way to support his gloss.[26] His source, however, was undoubtedly Comestor's lecture on the Glossed Luke; Langton himself added only a little, chiefly the identification of Priscian as the source of the grammatical distinction.[27] The revised chronology makes it possible that Langton attended Comestor's lectures. But it is also clear that he could have had access to Comestor's class notes on the Glossed Gospels by other means as well.

In either case, the evidence thus far presented shows that Langton the young theologian was devoting ample time to Comestor's works. I show

25   "*FACTUM EST AUTEM CUM ESSENT IBI PEPERIT* VIRGO *PRIMOGENITUM FILIUM SUUM*, non post quem alius sed ante quem nullus ... ." *Petri Comestoris Historia evangelica*, 5 (ed. Clark, Textual Appendix B.1 below, lines 112–113).

26   *Prima Stephani glosa scilicet lectiones a Stephano viva voce ante 1176 datae in Historiam evangelicam*, 5 (ed. Clark, Textual Appendix B.2 below, lines 46–53): "NON POST QUEM ALIUS ut mentitus est Eliodius hereticus dicens Beatam Virginem et peperisse fratres Christo de Ioseph. Christum tamen de Virgine natum non negabat. Cum ergo hoc nomen primogenitum quasi duplicem habebat difinitionem scilicet ante quem nullus et post quem alius. Hic tamen in prima accipitur, sicut finalem sillabam post quam nulla in eadem dictione et ante quam alia, tamen Priscianus dicit plus finalem sillabam et o principalem vocalem in mons non quod eam sequatur alia in eadem sillaba."

27   Troyes, Bibliothèque municipale, MS 1024, fol. 148va, middle: "*PRIMOGENITUM* Ecce ex hoc videtur esse verum quod ait Eliudius et alii heretici scilicet quod Ioseph genuerit alios filios post Christum de alia uxore. Ideo determinat glosa: NON POST QUEM ALII, quod non dicitur primogenitus quod alii post eum sint geniti, sed quia nullus ante eum, sicut monosillabas dictiones dicimus esse primas sillabas, non quia post eas sequuntur alie sed quia ante eas nulle."

in the next section that Langton was more than just another lecturer on the *History*. In fact, he played a starring role in the the evolution of this textbook.

II. *The Formation of the University Text: Revising the Pre-1176 Lectures and the* History

The very fact that Langton revised his lecture course on the *History* is a sign of the institutionalization not only of Comestor's text but of Langton's as well.[28] Langton's revision of his own course was extensive. He went through the whole thing, adding, subtracting, and modifying. The sum total of such changes reveals a commitment on Langton's part to turn his lectures into something more permanent: a companion to the *History* for his own students. There is also clear and substantial evidence that Langton revised the text of the *History* itself at the same time and in conjunction with the revision of his own course on that work.[29]

The timing of these revisions – both were accomplished before 1176, when Comestor was still alive and shortly after Langton as Comestor's student had first lectured on the *History* – together with the character of certain changes made to the *History*, which serve to tie Langton more closely to Comestor, suggest strongly that Langton undertook these twin projects at the least with Comestor's blessing but more likely at his master's suggestion. Indeed, some of these changes make plain that Langton was taking care as well to institutionalize Comestor's oral teaching.

a. *Langton as Colleague*
One of the great puzzles still to be solved in editing Langton's course on the *History* is the occasional presence of the word, *inquit*, side-by-side with the elimination of other instances, in Langton's revised treatment of his commentary on the *Historia Genesis*.[30] As I noted in Chapter Five, it was the repeated pres-

---

28 I presented the material evidence for Langton's pre-1176 revision of his lecture course in Chapter Five. Both versions, the lecture course and the revision, pre-date 1176, but the lecture course, which covers the entire *Historia scholastica*, must have lasted for an entire year owing to the huge amount of material covered. It may even have taken place over several years.

29 I set forth this evidence, below, in subsection c.

30 See, for example, *Secunda Stephani glosa supra Historiam Genesis scilicet prima lectionum recensio datarum viva voce ante 1176, effecta a Stephano ipso traditaque in codice H* (ed. Clark,

ence of such terms, signaling the presence of the student reporter, that led me for a long time to think, with Lacombe, that the version of Langton's course found in the Heidelberg manuscript, Salem, IX 62, at folios 89ra–122vb was another copy of his first, pre-1176 lecture course.[31] Nonetheless, progressing through the version in H, one finds that the majority of such *inquits* are eliminated. This suggests that their elimination was an editorial choice and not an accident. It may be that, as he went through the first revision, Langton decided to eliminate all such *inquits* but that he never went back to the beginning of the course to get rid of those that he had left in. What is certain is that in revising his course for a second time (in 1193), Langton eliminated all references to his own oral teaching.

The simplest explanation for why Langton decided to get rid of such references to his own speaking is that by eliminating any traces of a *reportatio*, he changed a lecture course into a magisterial text of his own. This interpretation accords well with Langton's treatment of his many references to the notes added to the *History*. As I have shown, Langton consistently pointed out to his auditors the presence of notes added to Comestor's text. In revising his lecture course, however, Langton eliminated all such references to notes.[32] Both the elimination of the *inquits*, inserted by the student reporters, and the elimination of his own remarks about notes added to the *History*'s text made his course on the *History* more polished.

A good example, showing this effect, is Langton's deletion, in his first revision, of his two references to added notes in his lecture on Chapter Six of the *Historia evangelica*:

~~Et hec est glosa extrinseca ab eo loco:~~ QUIA SI TABULAM ETC. NAM EADEM DIE ~~Hoc de littera quod de dominica dicitur~~ qua Deus creavit post celum empireum et angelos et materiam omnium corporum simul et statim eadem die creavit lucem id est nubem quandam lucidam et hec omnia

---

Textual Appendix A.3 below), lines 7, 24, 73, 91, 108, 116, etc. where *inquit* is retained, and line 34, where it is not.

31   See Chapter Five, 168-170 and n53.

32   A typical example is Langton's elimination of his own reference to the note added by Comestor on the order of the singing of the Canticles. *Secunda Stephani glosa supra Historiam evangelicam scilicet prima lectionum recensio datarum viva voce ante 1176, effecta a Stephano ipso traditaque in codice H, 3* (ed. Clark, Textual Appendix B.2 below, lines 25–26): "~~PVER ENIM super hoc ponit Magister glosam extrinsecam ubi reddit causam de prepostera-tione horum canticorum.~~"

dicuntur opus prime diei. Item alia ~~glosa, que est: AB HOC ETC~~. +probatio,
sed hic continuatur: IN DOMINICA INVENIES.+[33]

In the passage just quoted, Langton was able to excise these references in such
a way that no one would notice, simply cutting one gloss (in the second line of
the quoted passage) and adding another at the end. The revised passage shows
that Langton was a terrific editor, and he often combined these types of cuts
with others that rendered his commentary both cogent and concise.[34]

Both such changes, namely the systematic excision of the references of student reporters to Langton's speaking and of Langton's own references to texts
added to the *History*, rendered more permanent Langton's course on the *History*. Whereas the reader of the lecture course is constantly reminded of the
many changes that have accrued to the text of the *History*, the reader of Langton's first revision of that course is unaware of such changes, especially when
he gets past the initial, surviving references to Langton's voice. Indeed, Langton the editor is after textual stability, and the elimination of his own voice
supports this impression, since the reader no longer has classroom notes but
rather a polished commentary on the *History* in his hands.

What is fascinating about this is that the *History*'s text was itself still undergoing great change.[35] Langton must have revised his lecture course soon after
he gave the course.[36] Compared with both the *Historia scholastica* and his first lecture course, Langton's first revision carries with it the impression of permanence and stability. It is hard to believe that this was not by design, especially
when one sees that Langton employed systematically all kinds of editorial

33 *Secunda Stephani glosa supra Historiam evangelicam scilicet prima lectionum recensio datarum
viva voce ante 1176, effecta a Stephano ipso traditaque in codice H*, 6 (ed. Clark, Textual Appendix B.3 below, lines 93–98).

34 Another very good example can be seen in his exposition of the fifth chapter of the
Historia evangelica, where Langton eliminates a lengthy grammatical explanation as well
as a reference to an external gloss, cutting out half of his original commentary. *Secunda
Stephani glosa supra Historiam evangelicam scilicet prima lectionum recensio datarum viva voce ante
1176, effecta a Stephano ipso traditaque in codice H*, 5 (ed. Clark, Textual Appendix B.3
below, lines 65–71).

35 See subsection c, below, where I show that Langton himself was tailoring its text to
fit his revised lecture course.

36 The revision, which is careful and comprehensive, must have taken a significant amount
of time to accomplish. Coupled with the pre-1176 date of the lecture course, this suggests that Langton began his work on the *History* shortly after Comestor's dedication of
a copy of that work to Archbishop William of Champagne between 1167 and 1173.

changes – additions, subtractions, revisions – to revise the initial lecture course. In the next section, we shall see that Langton also made changes that feature and highlight Comestor's magisterial stature.

b. *Langton as Disciple*
One of the most striking things about Langton's first revision of his course on the *History* is that, while he systematically eliminates references to himself and also to the addition of notes to the *History*'s text, by Comestor and by others, Langton also identifies previously anonymous glosses and teachings as Comestor's. Even as he was taking out any *inquit* that referred to his own oral teaching, he was simultaneously adding others that were the product of Comestor's oral teaching.

I will give here three examples, which show clearly that Langton took special care to render permanent a tradition handed down first from Comestor to Langton and to other students, and then by Langton to his own students. As a consequence, Langton's revision of his lecture course memorialized Comestor's classroom teaching.

The first example occurs in the sixth chapter of the *Historia evangelica*, in which as we have seen Comestor treats the timing of the Lord's birth. In contrast to most chapters of the *History*, which Comestor begins either with verbatim scriptural quotations or with a paraphrase of Scripture, Comestor begins the sixth chapter with a simple declarative sentence: "Our Savior was born in the forty-second year of the reign of Augustus Caesar."[37] In his lecture course on the *History*, Langton gives us some interesting information about local custom, glossing Comestor's beginning as follows: "HE WAS BORN ETC. which in this same fashion, he says, is pronounced on the same day in our chapter meetings."[38] Comestor must have started this chapter on the birth of the Lord ("De natu Domini") with the same words used in the chapter meeting referred to by Langton. The student reporter, who inserts *inquit* in the middle of Langton's gloss, seems to us to be reporting Langton's voice.

It turns out, however, that he is not, for in his revised version of that lecture course, Langton adds one word: "*NATUS EST ETC.* quod sic, inquit +Magister+,

---

37 *Petri Comestoris Historia evangelica*, 6 (ed. Clark, Textual Appendix B.1 below, lines 128–129): "Natus est autem Salvator anno regni Augusti Cesaris quadragesimo secundo."

38 *Prima Stephani glosa scilicet lectiones a Stephano viva voce ante 1176 datae in Historiam evangelicam*, 6 (ed. Clark, Textual Appendix B.2 below, lines 57–58): "NATUS EST ETC. quod sic, inquit, pronunciatur eadem die in capitulo nostro."

pronunciatur eadem die in capitulo nostro."[39] There are two possible explanations for the change: either the student reporter at Langton's initial lecture did not realize that he was actually recording for posterity Comestor's words and not Langton's, in which case the reporter chose to insert an *inquit* in this very spot to signal Langton's words, or he heard Langton himself say, "he says," and simply recorded the reference that he recognized as referring to Comestor. Whichever of the two was the case, however, Langton made sure in revising his initial lecture that posterity would know the truth of the matter.[40]

A second instance occurs in connection with the chapter Comestor devoted to the question posed by John the Baptist through his disciples about Jesus's identity. Comestor's treatment reads in relevant part:

> But John, after he had heard in prison about the works of Christ, sent to him two of his disciples asking: *are you he who is to come, or shall we wait for another?* John, who had said, behold the Lamb of God, behold him who takes away the sins of the world, was not himself in doubt, but since his disciples still doubted, he sent them to Jesus to say as it were, go to him and find out from him whether he is the Christ, or whether the Christ is still to come. Gregory the Great, however, in his commentary on Ezekiel seems to interpret this passage to say that John did not himself know whether Jesus was going to open the gates of hell by himself or through another, as if to say: the time is near for me to descend to my people. Since therefore I was your herald here on earth, do you want me to announce you to those below as well? But Jesus removed their doubts by showing to them true signs of his coming.[41]

---

39   *Secunda Stephani glosa supra Historiam evangelicam scilicet prima lectionum recensio datarum viva voce ante 1176, effecta a Stephano ipso traditaque in codice H, 6* (ed. Clark, Textual Appendix B.3 below, lines 77–78).

40   Langton also retained the revised wording in his second revision, effected in 1193. *Tertia Stephani glosa scilicet magistralis ante 1193 recensa supra Historiam evangelicam, 6* (ed. Clark, Textual Appendix B.4 below, lines 74–75).

41   P, fol. 152rb; and V, fol. 179vb: "Iohannes autem cum audisset in vinculis opera Christi misit ad eum duos ex discipulis suis dicens: *tu es qui venturus es, an alium expectamus?* Non dubitabat Iohannes qui dixerat, *ecce agnus Dei, ecce qui tollit peccata mundi,* sed cum adhuc discipuli eius dubitarent, misit eos ad Iesum quasi diceret, ite ad eum et ab ipso querite utrum ipse sit Christus, an adhuc venturus sit. Tamen Gregorius super Ezechielem videtur velle quod Iohannes nesciebat utrum per se an per alium spoliaret infernum quasi dicat, prope est ut descendam ad populum meum. Quia ergo te nuntiavi superis, vis ut inferis te nuntiem? Iesus autem amovit dubitacionem eorum ostendendo eis vera signa sui adventus."

Comestor's exposition centers on the question attributed to John in the Gospels of Matthew and Luke.[42] He sets forth clearly the position that John the Baptist had no doubt about Christ's divinity but adds that Gregory the Great differed in thinking that John was posing for himself a real question.

In his lecture course on the *History*, Langton focuses on this disagreement, explaining to his students that Comestor, even though he points out that Jesus had removed the doubts of John's disciples, had not himself adopted Gregory's interpretation: "BUT JOHN ETC ... . *ARE YOU HE WHO IS TO COME*, that is, whom the prophets foretold was going to come? BUT JESUS REMOVED To the prior opinion, he says, we return, retreating from Gregory's exposition."[43] Here once more we find an *inquit* that seems to refer to Langton's words, yet Langton again clarifies in revising this lecture course that he is repeating Comestor's words, not his own: "To the prior opinion, the Master says, we return, retreating from Gregory's exposition."[44] Langton, making explicit that this gloss came straight from Comestor's mouth, made sure that readers of his course understood which of the two positions his Master had taken.[45]

A third example leaves no doubt that Langton habitually repeated Comestor's oral teaching in his own lecture course. In his chapter on the famous request of the sons of Zebedee, Comestor repeats the list of sufferings that Jesus foretold to the future Apostles: "On the Request of the sons of Zebedee. And Jesus, taking the twelve aside again, said: we are going up to Jerusalem, and there will be fulfilled the prophecies about the Son of Man: for he will be handed over to the gentiles, mocked and whipped, spit upon, crucified, and on the third day he will rise from the dead."[46] Glossing this account in his lecture

---

42 Mathew 11.2–3; Luke 7.18–20.

43 Paris, Bibliothèque de l'Arsenal, MS 177, fol. 111rb, and Paris, BnF, lat. 14417, fol. 154va: "IOHANNES AUTEM ETC ... . *TU ES QUI VENTURUS ES* id est quem prophete predixerunt venturum? IHESUS AUTEM AMMOVIT Ad priorem, inquit, opinionem redimus et ab expositione Gregorii recedimus."

44 Heidelberg, Universitätsbibliothek, MS Salem IX, 62, fol. 118ra: "Ad priorem, inquit +Magister+, opinionem redimus et ab expositione Gregorii." See also Mark 10.32–34.

45 As with the first example, cited above, Langton kept the revised form in his second revision of his course on the *History*: "IOHANNES AUTEM ... *TU ES QUI VENISTI* ... IESUS AUTEM ETC. Ad priorem, inquit Magister, opinionem redimus et ab expositione Gregorii recedimus ... ." Naples, Biblioteca Nazionale Vittorio Emanuele III, MS VII.C.14, fol. 143va.

46 V, fol. 188ra, and P, fol. 159ra: "De peticione filiorum Zebedee. Et assumens Ihesus iterum seorsum duodecim ait: ascendimus Ierosolimam, et consummabuntur prophetie de filio hominis: tradetur enim gentibus, illudetur et flagellabitur, conspuetur, crucifigetur et tercia die resurget."

course, Langton cites to his student listeners a similar example of suffering foretold, namely the very recent and celebrated example of Thomas of Canterbury, who spent five years of exile in France (1165–1170): "AND TAKING ETC. While he was on route. WE ARE GOING UP present tense. In this same fashion, as they say (*ut aiunt*), Blessed Thomas foretold his own passion to the praiseworthy King Louis when, once a compromise had been made, he would cross over into England."[47] Langton's use of *ut aiunt* could not have been more general; common knowledge was his source, or so it seemed.

Once again, however, revising his lecture course, Langton revealed that his source for this fascinating gloss was Comestor himself, who must have recounted the anecdote in class as he taught this very chapter to Langton and to other students: "AND TAKING ETC. While he was on route. WE ARE GOING UP present tense. In this same fashion, the Master says, Blessed Thomas foretold his own passion to the praiseworthy King Louis when, once a compromise had been made, he would go over to England."[48] Langton retained the attribution to his Master in his second revision of his course two decades or so later.[49]

This last example is especially interesting, since the story was common knowledge. Langton could have gotten the anecdote from anyone, and indeed he doubtless heard it over time from a number of sources. Nonetheless, he handed it down to posterity as something he heard from Comestor himself. Langton retained his piety towards his revered master over his whole career; he made sure to give all credit due to Comestor.

The preceding three examples show that Langton habitually passed on to his own students the oral teachings of his Master. They also show that in his lecture course, he did so without attribution, at least in some cases, since it is not always entirely clear, when *inquit* appears, if the passage reports what Langton

---

47 Paris, BnF, lat. 14417, fol. 156ra: "ET ASSUMENS ETC. Dum esset in via. ASCENDIMUS presens. Sic, ut aiunt, predixit Beatus Thomas passionem suam laudabili regi Ludovico dum facta pace transiret in Angliam." See Louis Halphen, "Les entrevues des rois Louis VII et Henry II durant l'exil de Thomas Becket en France," in *Mélanges d'histoire offerts à M. Charles Bémont* (Paris: F. Alcan, 1913), 151–162, still an excellent source for the efforts of the French King, Louis VII, to reconcile Becket with the English King, Henry II.

48 Heidelberg, Universitätsbibliothek, Salem IX, 62, fol. 119vb: "ET ASSUMENS ETC. Dum esset in via. ASCENDIMUS *presentis temporis*. Sic, inquit +Magister+, predixit Beatus Thomas +Cantuariensis+ passionem suam laudabili +et catholico+ regi Ludovico dum facta pace ... transiret in Angliam."

49 Naples, Biblioteca Nazionale Vittorio Emanuele III, MS VII.C.14, fol. 145va.

said in class or Langton's report of what Comestor said. What is certain is that Langton incorporated references to Comestor's oral teaching into his own lecture course, sometimes but not always with a named attribution. In this way he sought to keep alive the personal authority of his master, as well as his master's text.

Langton's revision of his lecture course gave him a forum for rendering permanent that firsthand knowledge. The examples just cited make clear that he used that forum to create a testament to a living tradition passed on from master to student. Moreover, Langton, in remaking the lectures that he had given on the *History*, made the transition from talented student to trusted colleague, in spite of the fact that he was still at the beginning of his theological career.[50] The extent of Comestor's trust in Langton can be seen in the latter's concomitant revision of the *History* itself.

c. *Langton as Collaborator*

Langton's first revision of his course on the *History* corresponds so closely to revisions made to the text of the *History* itself, both before 1176, that I am persuaded that Langton also revised the *History*'s text at the same time, while Comestor was still alive. It is hard to believe that Langton did so without Comestor's blessing, especially given his intimate knowledge of Comestor's ongoing work on the *History*. This makes the case for Langton as a co-maker of the *Historia scholastica* even stronger.

Langton himself added many glosses to the *History* from his course on that work, which explains the presence in the *Patrology* edition of the *History* of numerous "Langton" glosses.[51] The glosses from his own course that Langton added to the *History* provide the key to seeing that he revised the *History* itself. Two manuscripts above all are essential to seeing what happened. The first is H, which as we have seen transmits Langton's careful and extensive revision of his initial series of lectures on the *History*. The second is V, whose copy of the

---

50   I agree with Lacombe's long-ago assessment that Langton's lecture course on the *History* was a first step towards becoming a Master of Theology. George Lacombe, "Studies on the Commentaries of Cardinal Stephen Langton, Part 1," *Archives d'histoire et littéraire du môyen age* 5 (1930): 5–151, at 19–23. It seems equally evident that Langton's pre-1176 revision of that lecture course also took place at the beginning of his theological career.

51   One example is the passage, noted above in Chapter 5 at n4, lifted from Langton's preface to his lecture course on the *History* and interpolated into Comestor's preface in the Patrology edition of the *History*.

History most closely approximates the copies with which Langton and his students were working. Of our two earliest extant manuscripts containing copies of the *History*, therefore, V – and not P – is the key manuscript for understanding Langton's role in revising the *History*'s text.

Langton's routine omission from the revision in H of remarks that he made in his original lecture course about the *History*'s text resulted in a more permanent version of his course, one less ordered to the moment. The changes made to the *History*'s text in coordination with Langton's revision of his own course on that work achieved the same result, since they tied the two works more closely together.

We see one such "Langton" gloss working its way into the *Historia evangelica* in the first line of the very first chapter, where Comestor, quoting and paraphrasing St. Luke's Gospel, begins his Gospel account as follows: "FUIT AUTEM IN DIEBUS HERODIS REGIS IUDEE fluxis annis regni eius undetriginta [id est xxviiii, et est una dictio] SACERDOS NOMINE ZACHARIAS DE VICE ABIA ET UXOR EIUS AARONITA NOMINE ELISABETH."[52] We discover that the text in brackets was not initially part of the *History* because, lecturing on that work for the first time, Langton himself glossed the lemma "UNDETRIGINTA" as follows: "UNDETRIGINTA una dictio, id est viginti novem."[53] We know, therefore, that when Langton lectured on the *History*, this gloss, namely "una dictio, id est viginti novem," was not in it; he was its author. Langton retained this gloss in the pre-1176 revision of his course on the *History*.[54] The same gloss found in H, modified again slightly, is retained in Langton's second and final revision of his course on the *History*.[55]

Of our two earliest extant manuscripts of the *History*, P (at fol. 142va) omits the gloss in question.[56] It is, however, present in V (at fol. 168vb) as an interlin-

---

52 *Petri Comestoris Historia evangelica*, 1 (ed. Clark, Textual Appendix B.1 below, lines 2–4).

53 *Prima Stephani glosa scilicet lectiones a Stephano viva voce ante 1176 datae in Historiam evangelicam*, 1 (ed. Clark, Textual Appendix B.2 below, lines 3–4). Both manuscripts containing this portion of Langton's lecture course on the *History*, A and P[1], have the same gloss. I discuss these manuscripts in Chapter Five at 167–168.

54 *Secunda Stephani glosa supra Historiam evangelicam scilicet prima lectionum recensio datarum viva voce ante 1176, effecta a Stephano ipso traditaque in codice H*, 1 (ed. Clark, Textual Appendix B.3 below, line 3). The lemma, "UNDETRIGINTA," is missing in H, presumably owing to a copyist's error.

55 *Tertia Stephani glosa scilicet magistralis ante 1193 recensa supra Historiam evangelicam*, 1 (ed. Clark, Textual Appendix B.4 below, lines 6–7): "UNDETRIGINTA una dictio est: ~~id est~~ viginti novem."

56 Tr (at Vol. II, fol. 6rb) also omits the gloss in question.

ear, intrinsic gloss written in above the line. The version written in above the line in V matches that preserved in H, although the order is reversed. In light of the chronology of the texts involved – Langton's initial lecture course and his revision of the same pre-date 1176, while V was copied sometime between 1180 and 1183, it is possible that Langton added the gloss to the text of the *History*.

We find a second example of a gloss from Langton's course making its way into the *History* in the same first chapter of the *Historia evangelica*. The text in question is found in V (at fol. 168vb) as an undifferentiated part of the principal text, that is to say, without any indication whatsoever that it was a gloss added to the original text: "Statuit autem sedecim viros de Eleazar et octo de Ithamar, et *SECUNDUM* SORTES dedit unicuique ebdomadam vicis sue, [ne forte inter eos esset contentio de septimanis, quia una erat melior altera id est lucrosior"].[57] We know that the bracketed portion of this passage was not initially part of the *History*, since we do not find it in P (at fol. 142va). The process of integration for this text is farther along than for the first example, where the gloss was added in V as an interlinear gloss above the line. In the present case, the gloss in question had already been absorbed into the principal text in the textual tradition preserved in V.

As in the first example, we find a striking correspondence between the gloss added to the *History*'s text in V and the gloss we find in Langton's first revision in H. In his initial lecture course on the *History*, Langton glossed the lemma "*SECUNDUM* SORTES" as follows: "*SECUNDUM* SORTES, ne litigarent de melioribus vel minus bonis ebdomadis. Prestat enim quandoque una septimana in redditibus altaris."[58] We find in H a slightly different version, in which the key descriptive word in the first sentence is modified as follows: "*SECUNDUM* SORTES, ne contentio fieret de melioribus vel minus bonis ebdomadis. Prestat enim quandoque una septimana in redditibus altaris."[59] The revised version of this same gloss, namely the one recorded in H, is preserved verbatim in the final, magisterial version of Langton's commentary on the *His-*

---

57 *Petri Comestoris Historia evangelica*, 1 (ed. Clark, Textual Appendix B.1 below, lines 6–9).

58 *Prima Stephani glosa scilicet lectiones a Stephano viva voce ante 1176 datae in Historiam evangelicam*, 1 (ed. Clark, Textual Appendix B.2 below, lines 6–8). I here present the reading in A (where *litigarent* appears instead at fol. 109va) rather than P[1] (*possent* is the reading at fol. 152vb), since the latter is unintelligible.

59 *Secunda Stephani glosa supra Historiam evangelicam scilicet prima lectionum recensio datarum viva voce ante 1176, effecta a Stephano ipso traditaque in codice H*, 1 (ed. Clark, Textual Appendix B.3 below, lines 9–11).

tory: "*SECUNDUM* SORTES, ne contentio fieret de melioribus vel minus bonis ebdomadibus. Prestat enim quandoque una septimana in redditibus altaris."[60]

The presence of the key word, *contentio*, used by Langton in his revision and added to the *History*, coupled with that of another key word, *septimana*, used by Langton in all three versions of his course and incorporated into the gloss added to the *History*, suggests that we have here another example of Langton's influence on the text of the *History*. The texts in V ("ne forte inter eos esset contentio de septimanis, quia una erat melior altera id est lucrosior") and in H ("ne contentio fieret de melioribus vel minus bonis ebdomadis. Prestat enim quandoque una septimana in redditibus altaris") are clearly related – they are different ways of saying the same thing – but the question arises whether they are immediately connected, and, if so, which is prior.

The absence of this gloss from P and its incorporation as part of the principal text in V is consistent with what we know about the versions of the *History* preserved in these two manuscripts, since P, although possibly copied later (1183), nevertheless preserves an earlier textual tradition than V (1180–1183). Neither P nor V, however, is a perfect match for the text of the *History* presupposed by the first or second version of Langton's course on the *History*, although V is closer.

Nonetheless, we know for a fact that Langton recognized in both the P and V traditions numerous glosses that were extrinsic to Comestor's original text, not just to the older version preserved in P. In other words, Langton was thoroughly familiar with the ur-text of the *History*. Moreover, Langton's *History* predates the traditions found in P and V. My guess is that Langton actually had a copy of the *History* that closely approximated Comestor's original in front of him as he lectured. Comestor doubtless made available to his prized student a copy of the same version of the text redacted for dedication to William of the White Hands. In any case, Langton clearly knew of a version that predated the one on which he lectured.

This makes it unlikely that either the paraphrased version of this gloss found in V or some unknown and independent source influenced Langton, for he would likely have recognized the text in question as a gloss. He does not, however, identify it as a gloss. Why not? Although he routinely identifies for his students glosses added by others, Comestor included, he does not call atten-

---

60   *Tertia Stephani glosa scilicet magistralis ante 1193 recensa supra Historiam evangelicam*, 1 (ed. Clark, Textual Appendix B.4 below, lines 12–14).

tion to his own glosses in the *History*. A possible explanation for his silence is modesty. A more likely explanation is that such glosses were not in the text in front of his students when he was lecturing to them and glossing the *History* sometime before 1176. My guess, therefore, is that he added these glosses to the *History* at the time that he revised his lectures, also sometime before 1176.

Available evidence supports this explanation. The text found in V, a paraphrased version of the gloss found in Langton's commentaries, matches that in H rather than that in his first lectures, which supports the view that the correspondence between the *History*'s text in V and Langton's first revision of his lecture course in H is not accidental. Moreover, we know that H predates P and V and indeed all extant manuscripts containing the *History*. We also know that where Langton's lecture course has *litigarent*, H has *contentio fieret*. Did Langton himself make this change? Again, it is possible that someone copying Langton's revision of his lecture course made such a change, but not likely. It is not a copyist's change but rather that of an editor.

The most reasonable explanation, therefore, is that Langton, revising both his lecture course and the *History* at the same time, insinuated a paraphrased version of his own gloss, built around the key word "contentio," into the text of the *History*. The groundbreaking work of Quinto and Bieniak in establishing relationships between and among oral versions of Langton's *Quaestiones* supports my theory, for it turns out that finding key words that link superficially dissimilar versions is the single most important factor in determining what those relationships are.[61]

We find a third example of the same process in the fourth chapter of the *Historia evangelica*. Speaking of the census that led Joseph and Mary to travel to Bethlehem, Comestor infers, based on a passage in St. Matthew's Gospel, that such registrations were not a one-time event but rather took place yearly: "Hec descriptio fieri quot, [id est singulis], annis videtur, quia in Evangelio legitur: magister vester non solvit hoc anno tributum."[62] As in the two examples already adduced, the bracketed, additional gloss is part of the principal text in

---

61 According to Quinto and Bieniak, the editors of Langton's *Quaestiones*, such key words are crucial for establishing the sequence of the revisions. I am grateful for their sharing with me the fruits of their research into the complicated tradition of Langton's theological questions. In this connection, see Stephen Langton, *Quaestiones theologiae, Liber I*, ed. Riccardo Quinto and Magdalena Bieniak, Auctores Britannici Medii Aevi (Oxford: Oxford University Press for The British Academy, 2014).

62 *Petri Comestoris Historia evangelica*, 4 (ed. Clark, Textual Appendix B.1 below, lines 96–98).

V (at fol. 168va) but not in P (at fol. 143ra) or Tr (at fol. 7rb), which shows that this particular addition had already, like the others just discussed, been absorbed into one of several early manuscript traditions into the *History*'s text.

We discover again from Langton that it is a note added to the *History*. In his lecture course, Langton glossed this passage as follows: "QUOT ANNIS per singulos annos."[63] In the revised version contained in H, however, Langton modified slightly his original gloss: "QUOT ANNIS id est singulis annis."[64] Langton preserved this latter version verbatim in his final revision of his course.[65] If we compare Langton's pithy glosses with Comestor's text, both in the more primitive textual tradition preserved in P and the later one preserved in V, it is obvious that Langton's gloss was interpolated into the *History*, for had the phrase "id est singulis" been in Comestor's narrative in the first place, there would have been no reason for Langton to gloss the lemma "QUOT ANNIS." We have here another of Langton's glosses that early on became part of the *History*. Moreover, for the third time in four chapters we see evidence that Langton changed the *History*'s text in connection with the revision of his lecture course.

One last example is worth considering, for it shows that Langton added notes to the *History* in certain chapters, even though in his course they were part of his exposition of other chapters. In the second chapter of the *Historia evangelica*, Comestor treats the conception of Jesus.[66] After first providing a concise but comprehensive account of the Annunciation, he focuses on the conception itself, noting among other things that Christ was at the moment of conception fully human in both body and soul, in spite of the fact that his body had not yet formed.[67] In the final sentence of the chapter, Comestor speaks to

---

63 *Prima Stephani glosa scilicet lectiones a Stephano viva voce ante 1176 datae in Historiam evangelicam,* 4 (ed. Clark, Textual Appendix B.2 below, line 43).

64 *Secunda Stephani glosa supra Historiam evangelicam scilicet prima lectionum recensio datarum viva voce ante 1176, effecta a Stephano ipso traditaque in codice H,* 4 (ed. Clark, Textual Appendix B.3 below, line 59).

65 *Tertia Stephani glosa scilicet magistralis ante 1193 recensa supra Historiam evangelicam,* 4 (ed. Clark, Textual Appendix B.4 below, lines 61–62).

66 "De conceptione Salvatoris." *Petri Comestoris Historia evangelica,* 2 (ed. Clark, Textual Appendix B.1 below, lines 16–30).

67 Ibid., lines 25–27: "et statim conceptus est Christus de virgine plenus homo in anima et carne, ita tamen quod liniamenta corporis et membrorum visibus discerni non possent."

the timing of Jesus's conception in Mary's womb: "It is believed that he was conceived a week before the Kalends of April, and that after thirty-three years had passed he died on the same day."[68]

We find in V (at fol. 169ra), however, a line added as part of the principal text: "[Whence the Jews transgressed that precept: thou shalt not cook a kid in its mother's milk.]"[69] We can be sure that this was an added text, which I have bracketed to show that it was a note added to the *History*, because we find no trace of it either in P (at fol. 142vb) or in Tr (at fol. 6va). Comestor had glossed this same text in his lectures on the Glossed Luke as a mystical or allegorical prohibition, which warned the Jewish people against cooking, that is, killing by the fire of his Passion, the kid, that is, Christ, in his mother's milk, that is, on the day of his conception.[70] We can be quite sure, therefore, that Comestor himself did not add this note to the *History*.

Who added it then? Most likely it was Langton, who in lecturing on Chapter Six of the *Historia evangelica* made use of this very text in defending and explicating at great length both Comestor's treatment of and the Church's position on the dates of Jesus's conception, birth, and death.[71] Langton's source was evidently Comestor's lecture on the Glossed Luke, and when sometime before 1176 he revised the *History* concomitantly with his own lecture course, he added this gloss to the end of the second chapter of the *Historia evangelica*.

There is no need to multiply examples, since the four just adduced shed adequate light on the process by which Comestor's own additions as well as those of others like Langton made their way into the *History*. This process was part of a scholastic *modus operandi* that preceded and succeeded the *History*. More important for my purposes here, however, is the timing of these particular glosses, which found their way from Langton's commentaries into the text of

---

68   Ibid., lines 27–28: "Creditur autem conceptus octavo Kalendas Apriles, et revolutis triginta tribus annis eadem die mortuus est."

69   Ibid., lines 28–30: "[Unde Iudei transgressi sunt illud: *non coques hedum in lacte matris sue*, id est non occides Christum in die conceptionis sue.]"

70   Troyes, MS 1024, fol. 144vb, top-middle: "Unde mistice in lege prohibitum est: *ne coques edum in lacte matris sue*, ac si diceretur: cave o Iudee, ne hedum, id est Christum, qui significatur per hedum, decoques – igne passionis – in lacte matris sue, id est in die conceptionis sue."

71   *Prima Stephani glosa scilicet lectiones a Stephano viva voce ante 1176 datae in Historiam evangelicam*, 4 (ed. Clark, Textual Appendix B.2 below, lines 77–87).

the *Historia evangelica*. All four are found in V (1180–1183), which preserves an early textual tradition but which also bears the influence of Langton's course on the *History*. None is found in P (1183), which among extant manuscripts of the *History* seems to preserve the most primitive textual tradition. But we can see all four making their way into the *History*'s text, just as Langton was carefully revising his course on the same.

Whatever version or versions of the *History* Langton had at his disposal – and we have seen that he was able routinely to point out to his students additions to the versions available to them – we know that they predated those in both P and V. The most likely explanation, therefore, for the introduction of these glosses from Langton's first revision into the *History*'s text is that Langton, who doubtless had Comestor's original in front of him, was intentionally remaking that pristine original in conjunction with his revision of his own course on the *History*.

Langton did what any other teacher using a new textbook would do: he undertook to improve the *History*, just as he undertook to improve his lecture course on that work. Comestor had devised a format and structure for the *History* that was well suited to classroom instruction and to ready use of the treasury of glosses at the Church's disposal. Glosses could be and were extracted from and implanted into the *History* with the greatest of ease, for it was designed precisely for this. To teach in the classrooms of the twelfth century was to gloss, and Langton, who was teaching the *History*, glossed it, as did the many others who lectured on Comestor's work.

We are fortunate that Langton's course survives, and doubtless the reason that all three versions of his course have come down to us is that they were known and valued. That Langton took the time to revise comprehensively and carefully his lecture course on the *History*, while Comestor was still alive and working on the *History*, gives some indication of the value that he attached to his master's project. The evidence just presented suggests that Langton revised at the same time the text of the *History* itself, doubtless with his master's blessing.

III. *The Final, Magisterial Revision*

The evidence presented in this study makes a strong case for supposing that Comestor himself taught the *History* and that Langton was one of his students. We can now be confident that Langton was referring to Comestor, when in his second revision he wrote: "Aliter a magistro nostro et a magistro Beleth audivimus."[72]

Langton was not only Comestor's student but his collaborator and colleague as well. The transition from student to colleague must have taken place early on, for Langton's revision of his lecture course and his concomitant revision of the *History* predate 1176. Comestor must right away have recognized in Langton a kindred spirit, a student talented enough and serious enough to carry on his legacy.

In fact, Langton justified Comestor's confidence in him, for he went on to an illustrious career as a theological Master at Paris, and to an even more illustrious career as Archbishop of Canterbury. In 1193, when Langton revised his course on the *History* for the second time, he was approaching the peak of his theological career. His decision to revise his course on the *History* was seemingly unique in the context of that career. In the more than three decades that Langton taught theology at Paris, he produced an enormous theological corpus ranging from commentaries on every book of the Bible to collections of theological *quaestiones*. So far as we know, he revised none of this.[73] Langton's atypical decision to revise his course on the *History*, and to do so more than once, attests vividly to his sense of the importance of Comestor's work and the need for its continuing pedagogical refinement.

In the next chapter, I turn my attention to Langton's course on the *History*, considered as a whole.

---

72   The text quoted is from P² (Paris, BnF, lat. 14414, fol. 117va); I discuss this manuscript in Chapter 5 at n51. Lacombe, who also quoted this passage, was unwilling to hazard a firm guess as to the identity of Langton's unnamed master owing to what he considered to be chronological impossibility. Lacombe, "Cardinal Stephen Langton," 19.

73   None of those who have studied Langton's corpus in some depth – and the list is impressive: Lacombe, Smalley, Quinto – have thought that Langton took the time and trouble to revise the long list of works that he produced over his teaching career. He was probably too busy to do so, since he was always moving on to the next teaching project.

CHAPTER SEVEN

Langton's Course on the *Historia scholastica*

The Making of a University Textbook

Having described in the last chapter Langton's role in the institutionalization of the *Historia scholastica*, I now turn my attention to a consideration of Langton's course on the *History*, which as we have seen he developed over the course of several decades, starting with a lecture course on the entire *History* and a revision of the same when he was a beginning theologian, and ending with a second revision in 1193, when he was a mature master, one of the jewels on the crown of the theology faculty at Paris.

That Langton revised the *History* not once but twice is remarkable, for he did not otherwise revise or polish his massive corpus of courses. For example, Magdalena Bieniak and Riccardo Quinto, the editors of Langton's *Quaestiones*, have found that, while they underwent several redactions, it was not Langton himself who did the revising.[1] Other commentaries and lectures on the Bible produced by Langton do not appear to have been polished or revised.[2] Evidently, Langton, a busy teacher and scholar, did not as a rule have the time necessary to edit and perfect his work. So the fact that Langton did return to his course on the *Historia scholastica* twice suggests a high degree of commitment on Langton's part to the project that he had taken over from his master as a young theologian. Moreover, the fact that a leading theological master saw fit to perfect what was already a highly polished course on the *Historia scholastica* suggests a high estimate of the *History*'s importance within the developing theological curriculum at Paris.

In this chapter I shall focus on the organic development of Langton's course, paying special attention to what Langton did to perfect it. I shall also show what Langton did to put his own impress on the *History* for, although he

---

1 Quinto and Bieniak, in personal communications with the author.
2 George Lacombe, "Studies on the Commentaries of Cardinal Stephen Langton, Part 1," *Archives d'histoire et littéraire du môyen age* 5 (1930): 5–151, at 52–151; and Beryl Smalley and Alys L. Gregory, "Studies on the Commentaries of Cardinal Stephen Langton, Part 2," *Archives d'histoire doctrinale et littéraire du Moyen Âge* 5 (1930): 152–266.

inherited the legacy of Comestor's *History*, he did not always agree with Comestor's individual judgments. In polishing his initial lecture series on the *History* twice, Langton had ample chance to exercise his own influence.

I. *The Series of Lectures*

When Langton first lectured on the *History* sometime during the first half of the 1170s, he was doubtless taking, as Lacombe conjectured long ago, the "first step towards the mastership of theology."[3] He was, in other words, the twelfth-century equivalent of a graduate teaching assistant. Like all graduate students, Langton was dealing with the pressures of the moment, starting at the foundation of the curriculum with the historical sense of Scripture. For the most part, the tools that he had at his disposal were those of the arts curriculum that he had just completed, and we see his application of those in his lecture course on the *History*.

Lacombe aptly described Langton's glossing of the *History* in this initial series of lectures as something more than *cursorie*.[4] Reading through the lecture course, one can almost hear the young Langton working through the text quickly, glossing it for his hearers in staccato fashion for the most part but pausing from time to time to go more deeply into a question. All the same, he stuck very close to the text and frequently even to Comestor's organization. Comestor, for example, had provided a concisely paraphrased account of the appearance of dry land on the third day of creation:

> Or the earth subsided a bit, in order that it might enclose the waters in a womb as it were, and thus THE DRY LAND APPEARED, which hidden under the waters was properly called *humus*. But after THE DRY LAND APPEARED, IT WAS CALLED TERRA, since it was being worn down by the feet of living things. Or surrounded by the other three elements it is called *solum*, since it is solid. It is called *tellus*, since it suffers the working of men.[5]

3 Lacombe, "Cardinal Stephen Langton," 19.
4 Lacombe, "Cardinal Stephen Langton," 19.
5 *Petri Comestoris Historia Genesis*, 5 (ed. Clark, Textual Appendix A.1 below, lines 176–180): "Vel terra subsedit paululum, ut eas tanquam in matrice concluderet, et sic APPARUIT ARIDA, quia latens sub aquis humus proprie dicta est. Sed cum APPARUIT ARIDA, EADEM DICITUR TERRA, quia teritur pedibus animantium. Vel tribus circumpositis elementis dicitur solum, quia solida. Dicitur tellus, quia tolerat labores hominum."

Langton, following closely Comestor's explication, succinctly explained each of the earth's names to his listeners:

> And see, he says, that for different outcomes and times the earth was able to be called by various names. For it was called HUMUS properly speaking, when it was covered with the waters, *ARIDA*, however, after the gathering together of those waters INTO ONE PLACE, *TERRA* after it was rendered walkable by whose feet it began to be worn down, TELLUS at the time of Cain when it began to be worked upon, suffering primitive tillers and rakes, SOLUM, however, as if it were substantial, because it is solid.[6]

Like his master, Langton here grounded each explanation etymologically, adding only little details to Comestor's account.

Even where Langton's glosses do not track closely Comestor's, they tend to be concise and to the point. A good example comes at the end of his lecture on the eighth chapter of the *Historia evangelica*, in which Comestor treats expansively Herod's dealings with the Magi and the latter's resourceful escape. The chapter ends with a large intrinsic gloss, that is, a note making its way into the main text, dealing with questions concerning the origins and fate of the star that guided the Magi:[7] The note, which I bracket to indicate its status as a gloss added at an early stage to Comestor's text, follows Comestor's paraphrase of Scripture:

> AND THE KING SAID TO THE MAGI THAT THEY SHOULD LET HIM KNOW ABOUT THE CHILD, WHEN HE HAD BEEN FOUND, SO THAT COMING HIMSELF HE COULD ADORE HIM. For already he had decided to destroy the child. AND AS THEY WERE LEAVING JERUSALEM THE STAR WENT BEFORE THEM UNTIL

---

6   *Prima Stephani glosa scilicet lectiones a Stephano viva voce ante 1176 datae in Historiam Genesis,* 5 (ed. Clark, Textual Appendix A.2 below, lines 131–136): "Et vide, inquit, quod pro diversis eventibus et temporibus terra potuit variis censeri nominibus. HUMUS enim PROPRIE DICTA EST cum operiretur aquis, *ARIDA* vero post congregationem aquarum IN UNUM LOCUM, *TERRA* postquam facta sunt gressibilia pedibus quorum cepit teri, TELLUS tempore Cahin quo exerceri cepit ligones tolerando et rastra, SOLUM vero quasi substantiale sit, eo quod solida sit."

7   We know that this text is a *notula*, because it is formatted as such in P (at fol. 143vb, bottom to fol. 144ra), where it is included in the columns containing the principal text but clearly demarcated by enclosing lines.

THE TIME WHEN COMING TO THE PLACE WHERE THE CHILD WAS IT RESTED OVER THE HOUSE. [Fulgentius says that the star, which had been created at that time, was noteworthy and separated from the others, in its brilliance, which the light of day did not obscure, and in its location, since it was neither in the firmament with the other lesser stars, nor was it in the aether with the planets, but it held its course close to the atmosphere of the earth, and in its movement, since first immobile over Judea it gave to the Magi the signal for coming into Judea, because in consulting it they went to Jerusalem, the head as it were of Judea. Only after they had departed from Judea did the star with a marked motion go before them. And as soon as its duty was fulfilled it ceased to exist, reverting back into the preexistent matter whence it had been formed.][8]

Langton lectured pithily in class on this whole text, moving rapidly from lemma to lemma:

AND THE KING SAID with intention to deceive ABOVE THE HOUSE that is, a certain structure between houses for travelers WHICH THE DAILY LIGHT DID NOT OBSCURE as a star does FIRST IMMOBILE while they came THEY WENT TO JERUSALEM thinking that they had found the place WHENCE IT HAD BEEN FORMED like the dove in which the Holy Spirit appeared and occasionally at other times.[9]

---

8   *Petri Comestoris Historia evangelica*, 8 (ed. Clark, Textual Appendix B.1 below, lines 209–224): "DIXIT AUTEM REX MAGIS, UT INVENTUM PUERUM SIBI INDICARENT, UT *VENIENS ADORARET EUM.* Iam enim animum direxerat ad perdendum puerum. QUOS EGREDIENTES DE IERUSALEM STELLA *ANTECEDEBAT USQUE DUM VENIENS STARET* SUPER DOMUM *UBI ERAT PUER.* [Dicit Fulgentius stellam tunc creatam notabilem et discretam a ceteris et in splendore, quam lux diurna non impedit, et in loco, quia neque in firmamento cum stellis minoribus erat, nec in ethere cum planetis, sed in aëre vicinas terre tenebat vias, et in motu, quia prius immobilis super Iudeam Magis dedit signum veniendi in Iudeam, quia ex deliberatione sua Ierusalem tamquam caput Iudee adierunt. Quibus egressis tunc primum motu notabili precessit eos. Que peracto officio mox esse desiit, revertens in preiacentem materiam unde sumpta fuerat.]"

9   *Prima Stephani glosa scilicet lectiones a Stephano viva voce ante 1176 datae in Historiam evangelicam*, 8 (ed. Clark, Textual Appendix B.2 below, lines 110–114): "DIXIT AUTEM REX in dolo SUPRA DOMUM id est diversorium QUAM LUX DIURNA NON IMPEDIVIT sicut stella facit PRIUS IMMOBILIS dum venirent IERUSALEM ADIERUNT putantes se ibi invenire illum UNDE SUMPTA FUERAT ut columba in qua Spiritus Sanctus apparuit quandoque per aliud tempus."

Since Langton was lecturing aloud, his students must have had to be alert to follow him, since he moved rapidly through the text.

In his lectures, following Comestor's lead, Langton makes sure that his student listeners know their way around the Bible. In those places where Comestor is content to leave the biblical text implicit, Langton makes it explicit for his students. Towards the end of the first chapter of the *Historia evangelica*, for example, Comestor had paraphrased succinctly a large chunk of Luke's first chapter, from verses eleven through twenty-three in the modern system of versification. Comestor paraphrased these verses without using a single biblical word. Speaking of Zacharias, he wrote:

AN ANGEL FORETOLD TO HIM THAT A SON WOULD BE BORN TO HIM FROM HIS WIFE. ZACHARIAS, WHO PONDERED THE STERILITY OF HIS WIFE AND THE OLD AGE BOTH OF HIMSELF AND HIS WIFE, DID NOT BELIEVE THE ANGEL, AND FOR THIS REASON HE BECAME DUMB RIGHT UP TO THE DAY OF THE BIRTH. THE ANGEL ALSO MADE KNOWN TO ZACHARIAS THE BOY'S NAME AND HIS GREATNESS TOGETHER WITH THE ABSTINENCE THAT THE CHILD WAS TO OBSERVE.[10]

Langton, whose mode of commenting on the *History* in these lectures here as elsewhere is typically cogent, nevertheless adds to the *History*'s text several of the scriptural phrases omitted by Comestor. Glossing the words 'magnificentiam' and 'cum abstinentia', Langton reintegrates Gabriel's well-known prophecy about the Baptist: "MAGNIFICENTIAM cum ait: *hic erit magnus coram Domino.* CUM ABSTINENTIA ubi ait: *vinum et siceram non bibet.*"[11] There are many such examples, for Langton consistently unpacks Comestor's narrative of biblical text, scriptural paraphrases, and interwoven glosses.[12]

Langton also pays careful attention to the words used in Sacred Scripture quoted by Comestor, a preview of the close attention to semantic distinctions

10 *Petri Comestoris Historia evangelica*, 1 (ed. Clark, Textual Appendix B.1 below, lines 11–14): "PREDIXIT EI ANGELUS NASCITURUM SIBI FILIUM DE UXORE. QUI CONSIDERANS STERILITATEM UXORIS SUE ET UTRIUSQUE SENECTUTEM NON CREDIDIT, ET OB HOC OBMUTUIT USQUE AD DIEM PARTUS. NOMEN QUOQUE PUERI ET MAGNIFICENTIAM CUM ABSTINENTIA EI INDICAVIT."

11 *Prima Stephani glosa scilicet lectiones a Stephano viva voce ante 1176 datae in Historiam evangelicam*, 1 (ed. Clark, Textual Appendix B.2 below, lines 9–11).

12 They abound in the opening chapters of Langton's lecture course on the *Historia evangelica*. See, for example, *Prima Stephani glosa scilicet lectiones a Stephano viva voce ante 1176 datae in Historiam evangelicam*, 2 (ed. Clark, Textual Appendix B.2 below, lines 14–16,

that will characterize his work as a mature theological master.[13] In the third chapter of the *Historia evangelica*, Comestor treats the various scriptural events that relate to the coming of John the Baptist: Mary's visit to Elizabeth; Elizabeth's exclaiming the *Magnificat*; the mystery surrounding the naming of the child; Zachariah's recovery of his voice and his *Benedictus*.[14] Addressing the confusion of those present when Elizabeth and Zachary, rejecting the child's taking of his father's name, called him instead John, Comestor provides a verbatim scriptural quotation: "*IOHANNES EST NOMEN EIUS*."[15] Glossing this passage, Langton tells his students that the scriptural text does not say "he will be John" but rather "he is John," since he already had this name.[16] Another typical example occurs in the same chapter, where Comestor mixed Scripture, this time from St. Matthew, and scriptural paraphrase in his treatment of Mary's return from Elizabeth's house and Joseph's discovery that she was visibly pregnant: "*REVERTENS AUTEM MARIA NAZARETH INVENTA EST A SPONSO IN UTERO HABENS DE SPIRITU SANCTO*."[17] Glossing the verbatim scriptural quotation, Langton says: "*IN UTERO HABENS* — ibi pausa — id est gravida, postea supple quod erat *DE SPIRITU SANCTO*."[18] The pause is necessary for a proper understanding of this passage, Langton explains, for if you were to say that Joseph knew already that Mary was pregnant, you would have no explanation for why he hesitated over the fact that she was pregnant.[19]

22–23): "DE OPERE SPIRITUS SANCTI cum ait: *Spiritus Sanctus superveniet in te etc.* COG-NATAM SUAM de regio semine ex parte matris ... MATREM DOMINI SUI ... PROPHETARET dicens: *unde hoc mihi ut veniat mater Domini mei ad me?* ET BEATAM ut *et beata que credidisti etc.*"

13   On Langton's originality and depth as a theologian, see Riccardo Quinto, "Divine Goodness, Divine Omnipotence and the Existence of Evil: A Discussion of Augustine's *Enchiridion*, 24–26, from Anselm of Laon to Stephen Langton," *Przegląd Tomisty-czny* 17 (2011): 1–23.

14   *Petri Comestoris Historia evangelica*, 3 (ed. Clark, Textual Appendix B.1 below, lines 31–37).

15   Ibid., line 42, quoting Luke 1.63.

16   *Prima Stephani glosa scilicet lectiones a Stephano viva voce ante 1176 datae in Historiam evan-gelicam*, 3 (ed. Clark, Textual Appendix B.2 below, line 24): "*IOHANNES EST* Non ait erit quasi dicens iam habet nomen."

17   *Petri Comestoris Historia evangelica*, 3(ed. Clark, Textual Appendix B.1 below, lines 58–59), quoting Matthew 1.18.

18   *Prima Stephani glosa scilicet lectiones a Stephano viva voce ante 1176 datae in Historiam evangelicam*, 3 (ed. Clark, Textual Appendix B.2 below, lines 28–29).

19   "Si enim diceres Ioseph hoc totum nosse, non hesitaret unde gravida esset." Ibid., lines 29–30.

Several other salient interests of the young Langton reveal themselves in his lectures on the *History*. His training as a *grammaticus* in the Arts course shines through, as for example when he glosses Luke's description of Jesus as Mary's firstborn, which opens Comestor's treatment of the birth of the Christ in the fifth chapter of the *Historia evangelica*.[20] Langton, explicating the distinction that Comestor makes between "ante quem nullus" and "post quem alius," brings Priscian into the discussion as a way of making plain the distinction.[21] Langton's love for numbers and their use in establishing dates for key events in sacred history is also conspicuously on display in the lecture course.[22] Indeed, his enthusiasm for the subject probably accounts for the length of his glosses in dealing with this subject. Thus Langton, glossing Comestor's statement that our Lord was born on a Sunday night, lectures at length in support of his master's statement and the Church's tradition.[23]

The most charming part of the lecture course is Langton's matter-of-fact familiarity with his master, Comestor. As we have seen, his firsthand knowledge of Comestor's oral teaching, of his ongoing work on the *History*, and of his life indicate that Langton was close enough to Comestor as a student and young colleague that they must have shared a great deal, personally and professionally. To some extent, Langton must have been in the shadow of the esteemed and already famous *Magister Historiarum*. Nevertheless, already in his lecture course on the *History*, Langton displays the characteristic keenness and clarity of thought that would distinguish his own work as a mature theological master.

---

20 *Petri Comestoris Historia evangelica*, 5 (ed. Clark, Textual Appendix B.1 below, lines 112–113), quoting Luke 2.6–7.

21 *Prima Stephani glosa scilicet lectiones a Stephano viva voce ante 1176 datae in Historiam evangelicam*, 3 (ed. Clark, Textual Appendix B.2 below, lines 46–53): "NON POST QUEM ALIUS ut mentitus est Eliodius hereticus dicens Beatam Virginem et peperisse fratres Christo de Ioseph. Christum tamen de Virgine natum non negabat. Cum ergo hoc nomen primogenitum quasi duplicem habebat difinitionem scilicet ante quem nullus et post quem alius. Hic tamen in prima accipitur, sicut finalem sillabam post quam nulla in eadem dictione et ante quam alia, tamen Priscianus dicit plus finalem sillabam et o principalem vocalem in mons non quod eam sequatur alia in eadem sillaba."

22 Lacombe makes reference to a treatise on numbers composed by Langton but now lost. Lacombe, "Cardinal Stephen Langton," 10.

23 *Prima Stephani glosa scilicet lectiones a Stephano viva voce ante 1176 datae in Historiam evangelicam*, 6 (ed. Clark, Textual Appendix B.2 below, lines 57–88). See my discussion of this passage in Chapter Six, 188–193.

A good example, which centers on the sixth chapter of the *Historia evangelica*, features two of the glosses that, as we saw in Chapter Six, were added to Comestor's original.[24] The *Magister historiarum* originally wrote simply: "For he was born on a Sunday night."[25] Interestingly enough, the two glosses added to the *History* only make sense if you put them together, juxtaposing the last line of the first with the whole of the second:

[And so you will find that the Kalends of January falls on a Sunday, which suggests itself] [from this, that the Kalends of April fell on the Friday following the death of Jesus. In the same year <you have> the following: the day of his birth was on the Lord's Day, and this same thing <namely, that the Kalends of April fell on a Friday and the Kalends of January fell on a Friday> happened in the year of his conception and birth.][26]

Even when these notes are read together, however, the version in the *History* is cryptic and awkward syntactically. It is difficult to make sense of the Latin *sequens*, which could only modify *dies* but clearly does not. Moreover, the antecedent in Latin of *idem* is not immediately clear, although the juxtaposition of the two glosses makes plain what it has to refer to, namely the synchronicity of the Kalends of April and January, respectively.

After telling his students that these were notes, Langton lectures on the augmented passage, emphasizing that the Church's tradition on this matter — Christ was born on a Sunday, conceived following the Annunciation on March 25 and born on December 25 — is unassailable ("Hoc irrefragibiliter tenet Ecclesia").[27] In both the *History* and in Langton's lecture course, the essential point

---

24 See Chapter Six, 191–192.
25 "Natus est autem nocte dominice diei ... ." *Petri Comestoris Historia evangelica*, 6 (ed. Clark, Textual Appendix B.1, below, line 133).
26 Ibid., 133–138: "[quia si tabulam compoti retro percurras, invenies eius anni concurrentem quinarium regularem ianuarii ternarium quibus iunctis et sublatis septem unum remanet. Itaque kalendis ianuarii in Dominica invenies, quod occurrit] [ab hoc, quia kalende Aprilis fuerunt sexta feria post mortem Iesu. In anno eodem sequens dies nativitatis eius fuit in dominica et idem fuit in anno conceptionis et nativitatis.]"
27 *Prima Stephani glosa scilicet lectiones a Stephano viva voce ante 1176 datae in Historiam evangelicam*, 6 (ed. Clark, Textual Appendix B.2 below, lines 72–84): "Et hec est glosa extrinseca ab eo loco: QUIA SI TABULAM ETC. NAM EADEM DIE Hoc de littera quod de dominica dicitur, qua Deus creavit post celum empireum et angelos et materiam omnium corporum simul et statim eadem die creavit lucem id est nubem quandam

was to make clear that the Kalends of April, namely April 1, fell on a Friday ("feria sexta"), one week after Jesus died and also one week after he was conceived, while the Kalends of January fell on a Sunday ("feria prima"), one week after Jesus's birth. The consequences of this chronological argument were plain to see: Jesus was conceived on March 25 and born on December 25.[28]

Langton's explication was superior in clarity to the text that he was glossing. Moreover, near the end of his lecture, Langton summarized for his students the whole discussion in just a few words: "The Kalends of April fell on a Friday and the Kalends of January on a Sunday, and the same thing happened in the year in which Jesus was conceived and born. Therefore, he was conceived on a Friday, the sixth day of the week and born on the first, and so on a Sunday."[29] Even lecturing, Langton as a young theologian could get right to the heart of a matter.

Nevertheless, Langton revised his lecture course, making many changes that in effect turned a series of lectures into a textbook that could be used by students of the *History* at any time. That first revision of his lecture course is the subject of the next section.

II. *From Lecture Course to Textbook*

Not surprisingly, we find many of the young Langton's characteristic tendencies in his first revision of the lecture course. He continues to add or to restore verbatim biblical quotations, paying close attention, as in the lecture course, to the meaning of words. One example that illustrates both can be seen in Lang-

---

lucidam et hec omnia dicuntur opus prime diei. *Item alia glosa, que est: AB HOC ETC. Idem* probat quod premissa scilicet Christum natum in dominica die. Octavo siquidem kalendas Aprilis conceptus est et octavo kalendas Ianuarii natus. Hoc irrefragibiliter tenet Ecclesia, in utroque illorum dierum sollempnizans: in altero de conceptione seu annunciatione Beate Virginis, que duo eadem die facta sunt, et de Christi nativitate in altero, sed iterum constat quod eadem die mortuus est qua conceptus iuxta expositionem illius prophetie: *ne coquas edum in lacte matris,* id est ne interficias Christum in die conceptionis sue, quod transgressi sunt sed in anno illo quo mortuus est, scilicet in sexta feria."

28 Ibid., lines 78–79: "Octavo siquidem kalendas Aprilis conceptus est et octavo kalendas Ianuarii natus."

29 Ibid., lines 85–87: "Fuerunt kalende Aprilis sexta feria et kalende Ianuarii in prima, et eodem modo fuit in anno illo quo conceptus est et natus. Ergo sexta feria conceptus et in prima natus et sic in dominica."

ton's glossing of Comestor's exposition of the Annunciation in the second chapter of the *Historia evangelica*. Comestor had quoted Mary's famously beautiful words of assent, stating that Christ's conception followed *statim*: "ET AIT MARIA: FIAT MIHI SECUNDUM VERBUM TUUM, et statim conceptus est Christus de virgine ... ."[30] Langton, who had omitted Mary's words in his lecture course, restored them in his revision, making explicit that Jesus's conception had followed immediately upon Mary's assent.[31]

The salient theme of the revision, however, is, as one would expect, refinement, clarification, and enhancement. One interesting way in which Langton accomplished this was by tailoring his course to accord more closely with the *History*. I showed in the last chapter that Langton revised the *History* to accord with his course, but it is also clear that at the same time he brought his own course more into line with Comestor's exposition.

We see this in the very first chapter of the *Historia evangelica*, in which Comestor treats the conception of the precursor to the Lord, John the Baptist. Comestor there devotes considerable attention to a discussion of the priesthood, explaining why Zachary was in the temple at the time that the angel appeared to him:

> AND THERE WAS IN THE DAYS OF KING HEROD OF JUDEA, IN THE TWENTY-NINTH YEAR OF HIS REIGN [that is 29, and it is one word] A PRIEST BY THE NAME OF ZACHARIAS, DESCENDED FROM THE PRIESTLY FAMILY OF ABIAS, AND HIS WIFE, ELIZABETH BY NAME, DESCENDED FROM THE TRIBE OF AARON. For David, who wished to augment the liturgical worship of God, appointed twenty-four high priests, only one of which was greater. This one was called the chief priest. And David appointed sixteen men from the family of Eleazar and eight from that of Ithamar, AND BY LOT he assigned to each man a week for his turn, [lest by chance there should be dispute about the weeks, since one was better than another, that is, more lucrative]. And the priest Abias had the eighth week, from whose line was ZACHARIAS. And when on the day of Atonement Zacharias WAS PLACING THE INCENSE, AN

---

30 *Petri Comestoris Historia evangelica*, 2 (ed. Clark, Textual Appendix B.1 below, lines 24–25).

31 *Secunda Stephani glosa supra Historiam evangelicam scilicet prima lectionum recensio datarum viva voce ante 1176, effecta a Stephano ipso traditaque in codice H*, 2 (ed. Clark, Textual Appendix B.3 below, lines 21–22): "+FIAT MIHI SECUNDUM VERBUM TUUM ET STATIM ad concessionem ipsius Virginis+."

ANGEL FORETOLD TO HIM THAT A SON WOULD BE BORN TO HIM FROM HIS WIFE.[32]

Langton, as we saw in the last chapter, added two notes to this passage at the time that he revised his lecture course.[33] In his lecture course, Langton treated cursorily the heart of Comestor's exposition, namely his explication of Zacharias's priestly background and schedule: "AN AARONITE from the tribe of Aaron. FOR DAVID This is a response to that which he had said about the turn of the Abia section. ABOUT ELEAZAR the firstborn of Aaron. ITHAMAR born afterwards ... THE EIGHTH WEEK in the month of September."[34]

In revising that lecture course, Langton added two glosses, each of which addressed the heart of Comestor's commentary:[35]

AN AARONITE from the tribe of Aaron. FOR DAVID This is a response to that which he had said about the turn of the Abia section. +HE SET UP TWENTY-FOUR SECTIONS, so that each of the twenty-four might serve its own week according to the casting of lots. ABIAS HAD THE EIGHTH, from whom Zachary is descended.+ ABOUT ELEAZAR the firstborn of Aaron. ITHAMAR born afterwards ... THE EIGHTH WEEK in the month of September.[36]

---

32 "*FUIT AUTEM IN DIEBUS HERODIS REGIS IUDEE* fluxis annis regni eius undetriginta [id est xxviiii, et est una dictio] *SACERDOS NOMINE ZACHARIAS DE VICE ABIA ET UXOR EIUS AARONITA NOMINE ELISABETH.* David enim ampliare volens cultum Dei viginti quattuor instituit summos sacerdotes, quorum unus tantum maior erat. Qui princeps sacerdotum dicebatur. Statuit autem sedecim viros de Eleazar et octo de Ithamar, et *SECUNDUM* SORTES dedit unicuique ebdomadam *VICIS SUE,* [ne forte inter eos esset contentio de septimanis, quia una erat melior altera, id est lucrosior]. Habuit autem Abias octavam ebdomadam, de cuius genere *ZACHARIAS.* Cum in die propitiacionis *INCENSUM PONERET,* PREDIXIT EI ANGELUS NASCITURUM SIBI FILIUM DE UXORE." *Petri Comestoris Historia evangelica,* 1 (ed. Clark, Textual Appendix B.1 below, lines 2–11).

33 I discuss these two notes in Chapter Six, 206–208.

34 *Prima Stephani glosa scilicet lectiones a Stephano viva voce ante 1176 datae in Historiam evangelicam,* 1 (ed. Clark, Textual Appendix B.2 below, lines 4–8): "AARONITA de tribu Aaron. DAVID ENIM Responsio est ad hoc quod dixerat de vice Abia. DE ELYAZAR primogenito Aaron. YTHAMAR post genitus ... OCTAVAM et in mense Septembri."

35 To make it easier to spot the added glosses, I bracket them with plus signs.

36 *Secunda Stephani glosa supra Historiam evangelicam scilicet prima lectionum recensio datarum viva voce ante 1176, effecta a Stephano ipso traditaque in codice H,* 1(ed. Clark, Textual Appendix B.3 below, lines 4–11): "AARONITA de tribu Aaron. DAVID ENIM Responsio

The first added gloss, in which Langton explains that each of the twenty-four high priests had his own week, which was determined by lot, restates somewhat more concisely what is in the *History*. Nonetheless, it fills in an obvious gap in the lecture course, summarizing pithily Comestor's treatment. The second added gloss is another restatement: from Comestor's "de cuius genere Zacharias" to Langton's "a quo descendit iste Zacharias." Together with the first gloss, however, it forms a cogent, substantive addition to Langton's revised course, the first chapter of which now aligns more smoothly, in both directions, with Comestor's account of the same.

More typical, however, are the additions that add something new to Comestor's exposition, clarifying and enhancing the *History*. Examples abound; one or more can be found in every chapter, but a few will suffice here to show what is typical in the revision. We find one at the end of Langton's revised treatment of the same chapter. Comestor had ended that first chapter of the *Historia evangelica* with a three-sentence scriptural paraphrase followed by a verbatim scriptural quotation. The paraphrase, which included only a few words from Scripture, nevertheless restated and condensed the story of the naming of John the Baptist, recounted in various places in Luke's Gospel: Luke 1.1–17 (the first sentence), Luke 18, 25, and 62–65 (the second sentence), and Luke 1.15 (the third sentence):

> When on the day of propitiation he *WAS PLACING THE INCENSE,* AN ANGEL FORETOLD TO HIM THAT A SON WOULD BE BORN TO HIM FROM HIS WIFE. ZACHARIAS, WHO PONDERED THE STERILITY OF HIS WIFE AND THE OLD AGE BOTH OF HIMSELF AND HIS WIFE, DID NOT BELIEVE THE ANGEL, AND FOR THIS REASON HE BECAME DUMB RIGHT UP TO THE DAY OF THE BIRTH. THE ANGEL ALSO MADE KNOWN TO ZACHARIAS THE BOY'S NAME AND HIS GREATNESS TOGETHER WITH THE ABSTINENCE THAT THE CHILD WAS TO OBSERVE.[37]

---

est ad hoc quod dixerat de vice Abia. +VIGINTI QUATTUOR INSTITUIT, ut quisque illorum viginti quattuor ebdomadam suam facerent et secundum proiectionem sortium. ABIAS HABUIT OCTAVAM, a quo descendit iste Zacarias+. DE ELEAZAR primogenito Aaron. UTAMAR post genitus ... OCTAVAM et in mense Septembri."

37 "Cum in die propitiacionis *INCENSUM PONERET,* PREDIXIT EI ANGELUS NASCITURUM SIBI FILIUM DE UXORE. QUI CONSIDERANS STERILITATEM UXORIS SUE ET UTRIUSQUE SENECTUTEM NON CREDIDIT, ET OB HOC OBMUTUIT USQUE AD DIEM PARTUS." *Petri Comestoris Historia evangelica,* 1 (ed. Clark, Textual Appendix B.1 below, lines 10–14).

Comestor quoted verbatim Luke 1.24 to end the chapter: "*AND ELIZABETH CONCEIVED AND HID HERSELF FOR FIVE MONTHS.*"[38] Glossing the final line in his lecture course, Langton gave a characteristically pithy explanation why Elizabeth hid herself: "SHE HID HERSELF owing to her embarrassment about the birth."[39] He expanded this in his revision: "SHE HID HERSELF owing to her embarrassment about the birth, +lest perhaps it be said that she somehow began to lust and to indulge in such activities."+[40] One wonders what Langton's students thought of the addition – the idea of Elizabeth in her old age giving herself over to pleasure seems a bit far-fetched – but Comestor's straightforward ending now had a gloss.

Not infrequently, Langton's revisions build on and clarify Comestor's own account, as for instance in his re-working of his commentary on the fourth chapter of the *Historia evangelica* ("De descriptione orbis"), in which Comestor treats the census spoken of in the second chapter of Luke's Gospel.[41] The *Magister historiarum*, after beginning this chapter with a verbatim quotation from Luke's Gospel ("*IN DIEBUS ILLIS EXIIT EDICTUM A CAESARE AUGUSTO UT DESCRIBERETUR UNIVERSUS ORBIS*"), provides a straightforward and comprehensive guide to understanding that census:

> Caesar, who wished to know the number of the regions in the world that were subject to Roman dominion, as well as the number of states in each such region, and also the number of individuals in each state, had ordered that people from all suburban towns, villages, and districts should return en masse to their own state, and especially that, no matter where they were living, all should return to the state where they had come from originally, and that each person registering, after handing to the chief of the province

---

38   Ibid., lines 14–15: "*CONCEPIT AUTEM HELISABETH ET OCCULTABAT SE MENSIBUS QUINQUE.*"

39   *Prima Stephani glosa scilicet lectiones a Stephano viva voce ante 1176 datae in Historiam evangelicam*, 1 (ed. Clark, Textual Appendix B.2 below, line 11): "*OCCULTABAT SE pre verecundia partus.*"

40   *Secunda Stephani glosa supra Historiam evangelicam scilicet prima lectionum recensio datarum viva voce ante 1176, effecta a Stephano ipso traditaque in codice H*, 1 (ed. Clark, Textual Appendix B.3 below, lines 13–15): "*OCCULTABAT SE pre verecundia partus, +ne forte diceretur quod modo inciperet lascivire et talibus operam dare.*"+

41   G, Luc. 2.1 *et seq., ad loc.*; *Biblia Latina com Glossa Ordinaria*, intro. Karlfried Froehlich and Margaret T. Gibson (Turnhout: Brepols, 1992), 4: 145. I here cite the biblical *Gloss*, since that is what Comestor and his students were using.

a silver denarius – a charge worth ten of the usual coins, whence it was called a "denarius" – should declare his subjection to the Roman Empire. For this coin not only bore the image of Caesar but also his name written above the image, and since the number of those who bore the designation "subject to Roman taxation" ("censicapites") was being established down to a specific number and was being recorded in writing, therefore a declaration of this type was called an enrollment.[42]

In his lecture course, Langton gave to his student listeners a typically pithy restatement of Comestor's exposition, punctuating this with a series of brief, staccato-like glosses: .

IN THOSE DAYS ETC ... THERE WAS ENROLLED that is, it was put down in writing how many regions there were in the Roman Empire, how many citizens there were in each region, how many persons there were in individual communities, such that everyone besides the citizens of each community were counted as citizens of that community. HE PUT FORTH in a sculpture BY A COUNTING OF HEADS one word, whose nominative, *censicaput*, that is, by such a counting of the head.[43]

In revising the lecture course, having made a few small adjustments to what he had originally said, Langton added a fascinating gloss that explained clearly the

---

42 *Petri Comestoris Historia evangelica*, 4 (ed. Clark, Textual Appendix B.1 below, lines 80–89): "Volens Caesar scire numerum regionum in orbe que Romane suberant ditioni, numerum civitatum in qualibet regione, numerum quoque capitum in qualibet civitate, preceperat ut de suburbanis oppidis et vicis et pagis ad suam confluerent homines civitatem, et maxime ubicumque habitarent ad civitatem convenirent unde trahebant originem, et quisque denarium argenteum – pretii nummorum decem usualium, unde et denarius dicebatur – presidi provincie tradens, se subditum Romano imperio profiteretur. Nam et nummus** imaginem preferebat Cesaris et superscriptionem nominis, et quia numerus eorum qui censicapites* ferebantur certo determinabantur numero et redigebatur in scriptis, ideo professio huiusmodi descriptio est vocata."

43 *Prima Stephani glosa scilicet lectiones a Stephano viva voce ante 1176 datae in Historiam evangelicam*, 1 (ed. Clark, Textual Appendix B.2 below, lines 33–38): "*IN DIEBUS ETC ... DESCRIBERETUR* id est in scriptum redigeretur quot regiones in Imperio Romano, quot civitates in singulis regionibus, quot capita hominum in civitatibus singulis, ita ut omnes de appendiciis cuiusque civitatis pro civibus illius civitatis numerarentur. PREFEREBAT in sculptura FEREBANTUR id est tenebantur CENSICAPITE una dictio, cuius nominativus censicaput id est tali censu capitis."

meaning of "censicaput": "For that denarius was called a *censicaput*, since each and every person, when he was rendering his denarius to the presiding official of the province, placed it on his own head and with his own mouth professed that he was subject to the Roman Empire, and owing to this custom the whole thing was called a profession, that is, an acknowledgement of his own mouth, and this was done with every subject people."[44]

Occasionally, Langton felt the need in revising his lecture course to clarify things that he himself had said previously. We find a good example in the same chapter, in which Comestor had also devoted considerable attention to explaining Luke's statement that this was the first census and in particular what was meant by the word "first": the first census taken by Cyrinus, governor of Syria; or the first universal census, whereas others had been particular in nature, affecting only certain regions; and finally, the first of those included in the census.[45] He also explained that "[h]ere for the first time Judea was made a *stipendiaria* for the Romans."[46]

In his lecture course, Langton gave two examples of so-called particular censuses that had been taken before the census spoken of in Luke's Gospel, one at the time of King David and the other by Pompey, and explained the meaning of *stipendiaria*, saying that these were payments from individuals, in contradistinction to *tributaria*, sums of money taken from entire communities.[47] In revising this lecture, Langton expanded upon that distinction, making sure that

---

44 *Secunda Stephani glosa supra Historiam evangelicam scilicet prima lectionum recensio datarum viva voce ante 1176, effecta a Stephano ipso traditaque in codice H,* 4 (ed. Clark, Textual Appendix B.3 below, lines 41–50): "*IN DIEBUS +ILLIS EXIIT+ ETC ... DESCRIBERETUR* id est in *scriptis* redigeretur quot regiones in Imperio Romano, quot civitates in regionibus singulis, quot capita hominum in civitatibus singulis, ita ut omnes de appendiciis cuiusque civitatis pro civibus illius civitatis numerarentur. PREFEREBAT in sculptura FEREBANTUR id est tenebantur CENSICAPITE una dictio +est+, cuius nominativus censicaput id est tali censu capitis. +Dicebatur enim denarius ille censicaput, quia unusquisque quando reddebat presidi provincie ponebat illum super caput suum et proprio ore profitebatur se esse subditum Romano Imperio, et inde dicebatur professio id est proprii oris fassio, et hoc fiebat coram omni populo+."

45 *Petri Comestoris Historia evangelica,* 4 (ed. Clark, Textual Appendix B.1 below, lines 90–96).

46 Ibid., line 96: "Hic primum Iudea facta est stipendiaria Romanis."

47 *Prima Stephani glosa scilicet lectiones a Stephano viva voce ante 1176 datae in Historiam evangelicam,* 1 (ed. Clark, Textual Appendix B.2 below, lines 51–58): "PARTICULARES ut sub Pompeio et tempore David, qui populum numeravit. STIPENDIARIA non dico tributaria, quia tributum summam pecunie notat a communi datam, a quibusdam plus, a quibusdam minus. Stipendia singulorum dona intelliguntur hic et omnium paria."

his readers would not think that he had contradicted himself in giving as an example Pompey's making of Judea a tributary.[48]

In some cases, Langton abandoned his original exposition entirely, replacing it with new glosses. A good example can be seen in his evolving approach to the seventh chapter of the *Historia evangelica*, where Comestor situates the generation of Christ into two contexts: the ordered generation of all creatures and the corresponding history of salvation that attended such generations:

> And the generation of Christ was thus: first indeed the creation of man from the earth; second from the side of a man; third from a man and a woman; fourth was such, that without a man this particular man was born a man from a woman. Whence, having adopted a circumlocution for his name, Christ was also called the son of man. The first and second generations fell into ruin. In the third, we are descended from that ruin. In the fourth, we are raised up out of that ruin.[49]

In his lecture course, Langton had been content to point out that Comestor's exposition was satisfactory.[50] Revising his course, however, Langton erased this gloss and added several of his own:

> FOR THE BIRTH OF CHRIST WAS SUCH THAT And right away he explains how. +For Joseph was his supposed father, BUT IT WAS SUCH about the Virgin alone WITHOUT A HUSBAND which subsequently+ he explains +ABOUT A HUSBAND AND WIFE, just as we see today

48 *Secunda Stephani glosa supra Historiam evangelicam scilicet prima lectionum recensio datarum viva voce ante 1176, effecta a Stephano ipso traditaque in codice H*, 4 (ed. Clark, Textual Appendix B.3 below, lines 51–55): "PARTICULARES ut sub Pompeio et tempore David *quo* populum numeravit, +et forte alii suas fecerunt descriptiones+. STIPENDIARIA non dico tributaria, +nec vos turbet quod supradictum est scilicet quod Pompeius fecit tributariam Iudeam et hic dicitur quod facta est stipendiaria. Aliud est enim hoc et aliud illud+."

49 *Petri Comestoris Historia evangelica*, 7 (ed. Clark, Textual Appendix B.1 below, lines 171–176): "Christi enim generatio sic erat: prima quidem hominis creatio vel condicio de terra; secunda de latere viri; tercio de viro et femina; quarta sic erat, ut sine viro hic nasceretur homo de femina. Unde et adpropriata circumlocutione pro nomine Christus filius hominis dictus est. Prima et secunda generatio ruerunt; in tercia de ruina generamur; in quarta de ruina resuscitamur."

50 *Prima Stephani glosa scilicet lectiones a Stephano viva voce ante 1176 datae in Historiam evangelicam*, 7 (ed. Clark, Textual Appendix B.2 below, line 95): "CHRISTI ENIM GENERATIO SIC ERAT Et statim exponit quomodo."

THE SON OF MAN of one, that is, of the Virgin THE FIRST AND
THE SECOND but Adam and Eve.[51]

Finally, Langton clarified glosses in the *History* that readers might find ambiguous. In the same seventh chapter of the *Historia Evangelia*, Comestor glosses "Glory to God in the highest ... good will" by affirming that, thanks to the birth of Christ, God the Father had been glorified and peace had been established, not only between angels and men but also between Jews and gentiles.[52] A note following Comestor's affirmation reports that the words of the *Gloria* following those from the Gospel were added by Pope Thelesphorus.[53] In his lecture course Langton had skipped over this passage entirely.[54] In his first revision of that course, however, Langton pointed out that Hilary of Poitiers was the one responsible for adding that part of the *Gloria*'s text which followed the initial quotation taken from Luke's Gospel.[55] Interestingly enough, Langton's probable source was Comestor himself, who in lecturing on the Glossed Luke had pointed out to his students that Hilary of Poitiers had added the remaining words of the *Gloria*, while Pope Thelesphorus had instructed that it not be sung except by bishops and on great feasts.[56]

---

51 *Secunda Stephani glosa supra Historiam evangelicam scilicet prima lectionum recensio datarum viva voce ante 1176, effecta a Stephano ipso traditaque in codice H, 7* (ed. Clark, Textual Appendix B.3 below, lines 131–134): "~~CHRISTI ENIM GENERATIO SIC ERAT Et statim exponit quomodo.~~+Ioseph enim fuit pater eius putativus, sed SIC ERAT de sola virgine SINE VIRO quod consequenter+ exponit +DE VIRO ET FEMINA, sicut cotidie videmus.+ +FILIUS HOMINIS unius id est virginis. PRIMA ET SECUNDA sed Adam et Eva.+"

52 *Petri Comestoris Historia evangelica, 7* (ed. Clark, Textual Appendix B.1 below, lines 159–162): "ET *FACTA EST CUM ANGELO MULTITUDO* ANGELORUM *DICENTIUM: GLORIA IN EXCELSIS DEO ET IN TERRA PAX HOMINIBUS BONE VOLUNTATIS*, quia per Christum glorificatus est Pater. Et facta est pax inter Deum et hominem, inter angelum et hominem, inter Iudeum et gentilem."

53 Ibid., lines 162–164: "[In gestis pontificum legitur quod ea que sequuntur evangelica verba Thelesphorus Papa adiecit.]"

54 See *Prima Stephani glosa scilicet lectiones a Stephano viva voce ante 1176 datae in Historiam evangelicam, 1* (ed. Clark, Textual Appendix B.2 below, lines 89–96).

55 *Secunda Stephani glosa supra Historiam evangelicam scilicet prima lectionum recensio datarum viva voce ante 1176, effecta a Stephano ipso traditaque in codice H, 7* (ed. Clark, Textual Appendix B.3 below, lines 124–126): "+*GLORIA IN EXCELSIS ET IN TERRA PAX HOMINIBUS BONE VOLUNTATIS* Hucusque dixerunt angeli, sed quod prosequimur ad finem – "laudamus te, benedicimus etc." – additum est a Beato Hylario Pictaviensis episcopo."+

56 *Glose Comestoris in Lucam glosatam* (Troyes, Bibliothèque municipale, MS 1024, fol. 149ra, top; *est glosa intrinseca*): "Nota quod superadditur huic cantico apposuit Hilarius, et statuit Telephorus Pappa ut non diceretur nisi ab episcopo et in magnis sollempnitatibus ... ."

The examples just cited suffice to show that Langton's revision of his lectures was by no means superficial. On the contrary, he revised carefully the entire series of lectures, refining, clarifying, and enhancing both the *History* itself and his own course on the same. Nevertheless, Langton was still a beginning theologian, who relied in great part on what he had learned from Comestor. Indeed, the example just cited, in which Langton drew on material from Comestor's lectures on the Glossed Gospels for his own purposes, is typical, for Langton made ample use of those lectures in revising his course on the *History* for the first time.[57]

I show in the next section, however, that although Langton would continue to refine his course on the *History* two decades later, when he again returned as a Master of Theology to this subject so dear to his heart, he would also show in that course his considerable growth as a theologian.

III. *The Second, Revised Edition*

The prologue that Langton composed to his course on the *History*, when he revised it for the second time in 1193, gives a picture in miniature not only of the care that Langton put into the entire work but even more of its magisterial quality.[58] Carefully crafted, it is a self-contained piece of literature; not a word

---

57 Another example is found in his treatment of the fifth chapter of the *Historia evangelica*, where Langton adds a gloss to his treatment of Comestor's discussion of the famous ass and ox taken by Joseph and Mary to Bethlehem: "+ET BOVI ad vendendum vel aliud faciendum ASINO asinum forte duxerat super quem venerat Beata Virgo. Unde et quando fugit in Egyptum super asinam legitur sedisse.+" *Secunda Stephani glosa supra Historiam evangelicam scilicet prima lectionum recensio datarum viva voce ante 1176, effecta a Stephano ipso traditaque in codice H,* 5 (ed. Clark, Textual Appendix B.3 below, lines 72–74). *Cf. Glose Comestoris in Lucam glosatam* (Troyes, MS 1024, fol. 148va, top): "Et de asino quidem probabile est quod adduxerit eum Ioseph super quem sederet sponsa pregnans. Et paraverit ei presepe in aliqua parte diversorii. De bove autem improbabile est, nisi forte habuit venalem." Comestor's original lecture on the Glossed Luke had clearly served as the basis for an assertion in his own treatment in the *History*: "Forte ibi Ioseph presepium fecerat et bovi et asino quos secum duxerat, in quo repositus est Iesus." *Petri Comestoris Historia evangelica,* 5 (ed. Clark, Textual Appendix B.1 below, lines 122–123). But it was also undoubtedly Langton's source for the gloss that he added to his revised version of the *History*.

58 It will be interesting to revisit this prologue, after Langton's biblical corpus has been studied. He composed it after two decades of lecturing on the Bible.

is out of place.[59] Only after providing a comprehensive introduction to the four senses of Sacred Scripture, elaborating each one in turn, does Langton introduce the *History*: "Tribus omissis agit Magister de sola historia."[60]

Langton's prologue, therefore, serves as a magisterial introduction to the study of Sacred Scripture in general. At the same time, while it serves as a fitting introduction of Comestor and the *History* to the reader, it also introduces Langton himself as a new master of history and biblical interpretation and his own course as a masterpiece.

a. *Refining the Course*

As in the first revision of his course on the *History*, we find Langton continuing to polish and to perfect his course to a high degree throughout his second revision, altering phrasing, removing superfluous words, and adding new glosses. The impression of careful editorial work in general is strengthened by the fact that Langton edits again what he had already edited in his first revision. This second, magisterial revision, therefore, can be seen first of all as another refinement of his course on the *History*.

A typical example can be seen in Langton's commentary on the fourth chapter of the *Historia evangelica*, where Comestor treated the census spoken of in Luke's Gospel.[61] As we have seen, in the first revision of his course on the *History*, Langton added a sizeable gloss – "... nor should what was said above disturb you, namely that Pompey made Judea a tributary <of Rome> and here it is said that a *stipendiaria* was put into place. For that was one thing and this is something else" – in order to alert his students to a possible ambiguity in what he himself had said in lecturing on this topic.[62] So too, we saw that Langton also added other glosses to make sure that his students understood the difference between a tribute and a stipend exacted by the Romans.[63]

---

59 *Tertia Stephani glosa scilicet magistralis ante 1193 recensa supra Historiam Genesis*, Prologus (ed. Clark, Textual Appendix A.4 below, lines 1–24).

60 Ibid., lines 23–24.

61 *Petri Comestoris Historia evangelica*, 4 (ed. Clark, Textual Appendix B.1 below, lines 79–98).

62 *Secunda Stephani glosa supra Historiam evangelicam scilicet prima lectionum recensio datarum viva voce ante 1176, effecta a Stephano ipso traditaque in codice H*, 4 (ed. Clark, Textual Appendix B.3 below, lines 53–55): "+ ... nec vos turbet quod supradictum est scilicet quod Pompeius fecit tributariam Iudeam et hic dicitur quod facta est stipendiaria. Aliud est enim hoc et aliud illud.+"

63 Ibid., lines 55–59: "Tributum +enim+ summam pecunie notat a communi datam, a quibusdam plus, *ab aliis* minus, +sicut centum vel mille talenta+. Stipendia singulorum dona intelliguntur hic et omnium paria. +Denarii enim qui in tali descriptione colligebantur militibus dabantur pro stipendiis."+

In his second revision, however, Langton re-edited his already substan-tially revised commentary. A comparison of the two revisions is revealing:

First revision = SL²:

PARTICULARS as under Pompey and at the time of David when he made a census of his people, +and perhaps he made other such enrollments as well.+ IMPOSTS I do not say tributes, +nor should it disturb you what was said above, namely that Pompey made Judea a tributary, and here it is said that an impost was made. For this is one thing and that another.+ For a tribute denotes a sum of money given from the commonwealth, from certain persons more, from others less, +such as a hundred or thousand tal-ents.+ Imposts are understood here as payments of individuals, all of which are equal. +For the coins that were collected in such an enrollment of cit-izens were given to soldiers as imposts.⁶⁴

Second revision = SL³:

PARTICULARS as under Pompey and at the time of David when he made a census of his people, and perhaps he made other such enrollments as well. IMPOSTS I do not say tributes, since Pompey did this. For a tribute denotes a sum of money given from the commonwealth, from certain per-sons more, from others less, such as a hundred or thousand talents. Imposts are understood here as payments of individuals, all of which are equal. For the coins that were collected in such an enrollment of citizens were given to soldiers as imposts, since they were fighting to defend Rome.+⁶⁵

---

64 Ibid., lines 51–59: "PARTICULARES ut sub Pompeio et tempore David *quo* pop-ulum numeravit, +et forte alii suas fecerunt descriptiones+. STIPENDIARIA non dico tributaria, +nec vos turbet quod supradictum est scilicet quod Pompeius fecit tribu-tariam Iudeam et hic dicitur quod facta est stipendiaria. Aliud est enim hoc et aliud illud+. Tributum +enim+ summam pecunie notat a communi datam, a quibusdam plus, *ab aliis* minus, +sicut centum vel mille talenta+. Stipendia singulorum dona intelli-guntur hic et omnium paria. +Denarii enim qui in tali descriptione colligebantur mil-itibus dabantur pro stipendiis+."

65 *Tertia Stephani glosa scilicet magistralis ante 1193 recensa supra Historiam evangelicam,* 4 (ed. Clark, Textual Appendix B.4 below, lines 55–61): "PARTICULARES ut sub Pom-peio et tempore David quo populum numeravit, et forte alii suas fecerunt descrip-tiones. STIPENDIARIA Non dico tributaria, *quia hoc fecit Pompeius*. Tributum enim summam pecunie notat a communi datam, a quibusdam plus, a quibusdam minus, sicut centum vel mille talenta. Stipendia singulorum dona intelleguntur et

Langton made two changes. The first was cutting out the sizeable gloss that he had added in the first revision, substituting instead four words: "since Pompey did this." The second was another addition, a gloss explaining why stipends were exacted and given to soldiers "who were fighting to defend Rome." The first change rendered Langton's commentary clearer and more concise. The second filled it out. Together, they rendered the final version clear and complete.

We see another typical example at the end of Langton's treatment of the fifth chapter of the *Historia evangelica* where Comestor, after speculating that perhaps Joseph built the stable for the ox and ass, cited two Old Testament passages that anticipated prophetically this very event.[66] Comestor ended the chapter by remarking that pictures in churches, the books of the laity, commonly depict this scene: "Et in picturis ecclesiarum, que sunt quasi libri laicorum, hoc representatur nobis."[67] Langton glossed this differently in all three versions of his course. Lecturing, he simply restated in different words what Comestor had written: "THE BOOKS OF THE LAITY, because they read on the wall what we read in a manuscript."[68] Revising his lecture, he added a bit more: "THE BOOKS OF THE LAITY, +since the laity are instructed in them, as we are in books,+ because they read on the wall what we read in a manuscript."[69] In his final revision, however, Langton edited this passage once more: "THE BOOKS OF THE LAITY, since the laity are instructed in them."[70] The final result was a concise gloss, which did not repeat or restate what was already in the *History*.

---

omnium paria. Denarii enim qui in tali descriptione colligebantur militibus dabantur pro stipendiis, +qui pro orbe defendendo pugnabant+."

66 *Petri Comestoris Historia evangelica*, 5 (ed. Clark, lines 122–125): "Forte ibi Ioseph presepium fecerat et bovi et asino quos secum duxerat, in quo repositus est Iesus. Ad quod quidam referunt illud Isaie: *cognovit bos possessorem suum et asinus presepe domini sui*, et illud Abaccuch: *in medio duorum animalium cognosceris*."

67 Ibid., lines 125–126.

68 *Prima Stephani glosa scilicet lectiones a Stephano viva voce ante 1176 datae in Historiam evangelicam*, 5 (ed. Clark, Textual Appendix B.2 below, lines 55–56): "LIBRI LAICORUM quod legunt in pariete quod nos in codice."

69 *Secunda Stephani glosa supra Historiam evangelicam scilicet prima lectionum recensio datarum viva voce ante 1176, effecta a Stephano ipso traditaque in codice H*, 5 (ed. Clark, Textual Appendix B.3 below, lines 74–76): "LIBRI LAICORUM +ut in eis instruantur laici, sicut nos in libris+ quod +qui+ legunt in pariete quod nos in codice."

70 *Tertia Stephani glosa scilicet magistralis ante 1193 recensa supra Historiam evangelicam*, 5 (ed. Clark, Textual Appendix B.4 below, lines 72–74): "LIBRI LAICORUM ut in eis instruantur laici, ~~sicut nos in libris quod qui legunt in pariete quod nos in codice~~."

Examples such as these and many others found in almost every chapter of the final version of his course on the *History* show that Langton took special care to refine and polish what he had already written. As in his first revision, however, Langton in the second also added breadth and depth to his explication of the *History* as part of refining that course. A good example occurs right at the beginning of Langton's commentary on the *Historia evangelica*. In his lecture course, glossing the opening words of Luke's Gospel, "FUIT IN DIEBUS," which Comestor used to demarcate the opening of his *Historia evangelica*, properly speaking, Langton had told his students just this, namely that Luke had thus begun his Gospel and that Comestor's *Historia evangelica* began here and not, as others supposed, with the lemma "MORTUO SYMONE."[71] In his first revision, Langton made one small change to this text.[72] In his second revision, by contrast, Langton added a lengthy gloss making clear that all of the material in the *History* from the end of the Books of Maccabees up to Comestor's quotation from the Gospel of Luke ("fuit in diebus"), which Langton took to be the start of the *Historia evangelica* properly speaking, was not from the Old Testament but was material from Josephus and Hegesippus, which Comestor had inserted to provide a fitting transition between the Old and the New Testaments.[73]

He also continued to add zest to his course with local details that would resonate with his students. Thus, for example, in revising for the second time his commentary on the third chapter of the *Historia evangelica*, Langton addressed himself to Comestor's closing gloss, a tripartite explanation of why it was that the Virgin Mary had need of a husband: lest being found pregnant she be disgraced; that she enjoy the solace and service of a husband; that the birth of

---

71 *Prima Stephani glosa scilicet lectiones a Stephano' viva voce ante 1176 datae in Historiam evangelicam*, 1(ed. Clark, Textual Appendix B.2 below, lines 1–3): "Capitulum. FUIT IN DIEBUS ETC. Sic incipit Lucas evangelium suum, et incipit hic Hystoria evangelica secundum distinctiones huius voluminis. Alii distinguunt aliter, ibi scilicet MORTUO SYMONE ETC."

72 He changed "distinguunt aliter" to "aliter incipient." *Secunda Stephani glosa supra Historiam evangelicam scilicet prima lectionum recensio datarum viva voce ante 1176, effecta a Stephano ipso traditaque in codice H*, 1 (ed. Clark, Textual Appendix B.3 below, lines 1–3).

73 *Tertia Stephani glosa scilicet magistralis ante 1193 recensa supra Historiam evangelicam*, 1 (ed. Clark, Textual Appendix B.4 below, lines 1–6): "*FUIT IN DIEBUS ETC*. Sic incipit Lucas evangelium suum, et hic incipit Historia evangelica secundum distinctiones huius voluminis. Alii *altius* incipiunt, ibi scilicet MORTUO SIMONE ETC. +Et notandum quod quicquid dictum est a fine libri Machabeorum usque ad hunc locum scriptum est de Iosepho et Egessipo historiographo, et non continetur in Veteri Testamento, sed ideo interseruit Magister ut Vetus Testamentum congrue continuaretur Novo+."

God be hidden from the Devil.[74] Langton had said nothing about this either in his lecture course or in his first revision of the same. Glossing Comestor's account for the first time in his final revision, however, Langton revised the lemma slightly and provided a fascinating insight into contemporary liturgical practices: "IN ORDER THAT MARY <SHOULD HAVE THE CONSO-LATION> OF A HUSBAND Whence it is that older men in certain churches, as in the Parisian Church, minister to the altar in the vigil of the birth of our Lord, as for example in carrying candles and incense and in all the other liturgical tasks that Parisians are accustomed to perform on other days."[75] It is worth noting that other masters who were teaching the *History* followed Langton's lead, adding notes to the *History* that shed light on Comestor's account by means of contemporary liturgical practices.[76]

b. *Correcting the Magister Historiarum*

I have thus far addressed the similarities between Langton's first and second revisions of his course on the *History*, but there is a salient difference as well – one which renders the final version a pleasure to read. Owing to his growth as a theological Master over two decades, Langton had not only grown tremendously in theological acumen but had also arguably outpaced his revered Magister in this respect as well. This is not to say that Langton was anything but reverent to his former master. Quite the contrary, his affection and reverence for Peter Comestor are, as we have seen, manifest throughout every version of his

---

74   *Petri Comestoris Historia evangelica*, 3 (ed. Clark, Textual Appendix B.1 below, lines 65–67): "Habuit autem Virgo virum, ne gravida infamaretur, et ut viri solatio ministerioque frueretur, et ut Diabolo occultaretur Dei partus."

75   *Tertia Stephani glosa scilicet magistralis ante 1193 recensa supra Historiam evangelicam*, 3 (ed. Clark, Textual Appendix B.4 below, lines 41–44): "+UT MARIA VIRI Inde est quod maiores in quibusdam ecclesiis sicut in ecclesia Parisiensi ministrant altari in vigilia natalis Domini scilicet in ferendo candelabra turibula et in omnibus aliis in quibus Parisii solent ministrare aliis diebus+."

76   There are three such examples in the same third chapter of the *Historia evangelica*, all found in the margins of V as extrinsic notes. *Petri Comestoris Historia evangelica*, 3 (ed. Clark, Textual Appendix B.1 below, lines 68–77). The last of these (Ibid., 76–77: "Ad representandum ministerium Ioseph in quibusdam ecclesiis quam provecte persone ministrant in natum Domini.") is close enough to the gloss that Langton added to the second and final revision of his course on the *History* to raise the possibility of some relationship between the two texts. Indeed, its place in the text – I have used asterisks inserted into the text, to indicate where the last of these three notes was intended to go – also supports the idea that it was somehow related to Langton's own gloss.

course on the *History*. Nevertheless, a comparison of Langton's lecture course and first revision with his second reveals a striking difference between the young Langton and the mature Master of Theology. The former looks very much like Comestor. Indeed, it is sometimes difficult to distinguish between them. The latter often displays Langton's considerable theological ability in the final revision of his course on the *History*.

We see this principally in two ways. The first is that Langton frequently corrects Comestor. Some of these corrections are minor, as for example Langton's objection to an image used by Comestor in his prologue to the *History*. Comestor there likens the three senses of Scripture to the majesty of an emperor who has three rooms in his palace: an auditorium, where he gives the law; a dining hall, where he feeds his guests; a bedroom, where he takes his rest.[77] Throughout his prologue, as he explicates this theme, Comestor makes frequent use of Scripture to punctuate his images:

> In this way our Emperor, who *commands the winds and the sea*, has the universe for his auditorium, where at his nod all things are arranged. Whence that [passage of Sacred Scripture]: *I fill heaven and earth*. According to this, he is called Lord. Whence: *for the earth and its fullness belong to the Lord*. [He has] the soul of the just for his bed-chamber, since *his delight is to be with the sons of men*. According to this, he is called a spouse. For his dining hall, [he has] Sacred Scripture, in which he so inebriates his own that he renders them sober. Whence: *we have walked in the house of God harmoniously,* that is, tasting that very thing in Sacred Scripture. According to this, he is called the Head of the Household.[78]

Neither in his lecture course nor in his first revision of those lectures did Langton comment on Comestor's choice of scriptural texts in this prologue. In his second

77 *Petri Comestoris Historia Genesis*, Prologus (ed. Clark, Textual Appendix A.1 below, lines 19–21): "Imperatorie maiestatis est tres in palatio habere mansiones: auditorium vel consistorium in quo iura decernit; cenaculum in quo cibaria distribuit; thalamum in quo quiescit."

78 Ibid., lines 21–28: "Ad hunc modum Imperator noster, qui *imperat ventis et mari,* mundum habet pro auditorio, ubi ad eius nutum omnia disponuntur; unde: *celum et terram ego adimplebo*. Secundum hanc dicitur Dominus; unde: *Domini est terra et plenitudo eius*. Animam iusti pro thalamo, quia *delicie* sunt ei *esse cum filiis hominum*. Secundum hanc sponsus dicitur. Sacram Scripturam pro cenaculo, in qua suos sic inebriat, ut sobrios reddat; unde: *in domo Dei ambulavimus cum consensu* id est in Sacra Scriptura id ipsum sapientes. Secundum hanc dicitur paterfamilias."

revision, however, addressing for the first time Comestor's metaphor, Langton altered the substance of his own commentary by questioning his master's choice of imagery.[79] He also provided what he thought would be a better choice:

> Note that about the dining hall of the Lord he puts forth this example: *we have walked in the house of the Lord with permission*. But since in this example the name 'dining hall' is not used but rather 'house' the example does not seem altogether fitting. It would have been better, therefore, as it seems to us, had he said in place of the image of a dining hall that stands for Sacred Scripture: *in a place of pasturage there he placed me*. For *pasturage* signifies Sacred Scripture.[80]

Here Langton displays once again his characteristic sensitivity to the meaning of words. There are many such examples throughout the final version of his course on the *History*. In most of these, Langton simply adds a level of precision missing from Comestor's exposition.

Another excellent example where Langton corrects Comestor is found at the beginning of his exposition of the fourth chapter of the *Historia Genesis*, in which Comestor treats the works of the second day, starting with God's disposition of the higher parts of the sensible world: "On the second day God arranged the higher parts of the sensible world. For the *empireum* heaven, as quickly as it was created, was at once arranged and adorned, that is, filled with

---

79 *Tertia Stephani glosa scilicet magistralis ante 1193 recensa supra Historiam Genesis*. In prologum magistri (ed. Clark, Textual Appendix A.4 below, lines 34–37): "Sic ergo incipit: IMPERATORIE MAIESTATIS. In hoc prohemio quandam similitudinem assignat inter aliquem mundanum imperatorem et summum Deum, quorum uterque tres habet mansiones et ab eis diversa divinorum vocabula sortiuntur.*'" For the discussion that follows, for purposes of comparison, see the following: *Prima Stephani glosa scilicet lectiones a Stephano viva voce ante 1176 datae in Historiam Genesis*, in prologum magistri (ed. Clark, Textual Appendix A.2 below, lines 12–13); and *Secunda Stephani glosa supra Historiam Genesis scilicet prima lectionum recensio datarum viva voce ante 1176, effecta a Stephano ipso traditaque in codice H*, in prologum magistri (ed. Clark, Textual Appendix A.3 below, line 9).

80 *Tertia Stephani glosa scilicet magistralis ante 1193 recensa supra Historiam Genesis*, in prologum magistri (ed. Clark, Textual Appendix A.4 below, lines 37–42): "+Nota quod de cenaculo Domini ponit hoc exemplum: *ambulavimus in domo Domini cum consensu*. Sed cum in hoc exemplo non ponatur nomen cenaculi sed nomen domus, non videtur exemplum circumquaque conveniens. Melius ergo ut nobis videtur pro exemplo cenaculi quod pro Sacra Scriptura ponitur diceret: *in loco pascue ibi me collocavit*. Pascua enim Sacram significat Scripturam.+"

holy angels."[81] Langton skipped over the opening lines of Chapter Four of the *Historia Genesis* both in his lecture course and his first revision of the same.[82] In his second revision, however, Langton again took issue with Comestor's choice of words: "ON THE SECOND DAY HE ARRANGED ... FILLED WITH HOLY ANGELS. But what can be filled with simple beings? 'Filled', therefore, is maintained here inappropriately. Nevertheless, he wants to note their abundance."[83] Langton, now himself a Master of Theology, had become more sensitive to theological distinctions and was now able to point out such theological errors, however minor, to his students. Angels are immaterial beings and cannot therefore fill anything. As always, though, Langton corrected his master gently, noting what he had meant to convey.

Langton, however, also saw fit to make corrections of a more substantial character. One of the best examples comes at the very beginning of the *History* proper. Comestor began the *History* with a paraphrased conflation of the opening lines of Genesis and of John's Gospel: "*IN PRINCIPIO ERAT VERBUM ET VERBUM ERAT PRINCIPII PRINCIPIUM, IN QUO ET PER QUOD PATER CREAVIT MUNDUM.*"[84] Because this was itself theologically innovative – Comestor's paraphrase inverted the precedent tradition of Christian commentary by setting forth the key interpretations of that tradition in his paraphrase of Scripture; he also made the Word a principal literal meaning of "in the beginning" for the first time – it will be worthwhile to summarize here Comestor's explication of his opening paraphrase.[85]

---

81 *Petri Comestoris Historia Genesis*, 4 (ed. Clark, Textual Appendix A.1 below, lines 129–131): "Secunda die disposuit Deus superiora mundi sensilis. Empireum enim quam cito factum statim dispositum est et ornatum id est sanctis angelis repletum."

82 *Prima Stephani glosa scilicet lectiones a Stephano viva voce ante 1176 datae in Historiam Genesis*, 4 (ed. Clark, Textual Appendix A.2 below, lines 101–122); and *Secunda Stephani glosa supra Historiam Genesis scilicet prima lectionum recensio datarum viva voce ante 1176, effecta a Stephano ipso traditaque in codice H*, 4 (ed. Clark, Textual Appendix A.3 below, lines 102–122).

83 *Tertia Stephani glosa scilicet magistralis ante 1193 recensa supra Historiam Genesis*, 4 (ed. Clark, Textual Appendix A.4 below, lines 180–182): "*SECUNDA DIE* +DISPOSUIT ... REPLETUM SANCTIS ANGELIS Sed quid potest repleri rebus simplicibus? Tenetur ergo improprie repletum. Habundantiam tamen vult notare."

84 *Petri Comestoris Historia Genesis*, 1 (ed. Clark, Textual Appendix A.1 below, lines 40–42).

85 I document the unique character of Comestor's opening paraphrase, reviewing the precedent theological and commentarial tradition and situating Comestor's treatment both in the context of that whole tradition and of twelfth-century developments to that tradition in Mark J. Clark, "The Commentaries on Peter Comestor's *Historia scholastica* of Stephen Langton, Pseudo-Langton, and Hugh of St. Cher," *Sacris erudiri* 44 (2005): 301–446, at 342–364.

Comestor actually works backwards through this text, providing first a fourfold explication of "mundum": the world has been taken to refer variously to the angelic heaven, the sensible world, the sublunar world, and to man himself.[86] He then distinguishes the fourth of these possible interpretations of "mundum" from the previous three since man, unlike the other three, was not created from nothing.[87] Having distinguished the proper object of "creavit," Comestor quotes verbatim the opening line of Genesis ("in principio creavit Deus caelum et mundum"), explicating in turn "caelum" and then "terram."[88] Comestor then comments on "Deus," making no reference to the wording of his paraphrase in which he stated that the Father ("pater") created the world.[89] Comestor's failure to explicate this part of his paraphrase provided ample material for his commentators to explain complexities regarding agency in creation.[90] Still proceeding backwards through the text, Comestor concludes his

86   *Petri Comestoris Historia Genesis*, 1 (ed. Clark, Textual Appendix A.1 below, lines 42–48): "MUNDUS quatuor modis dicitur: quandoque empireum celum mundus dicitur propter sui mundiciam; quandoque sensibilis mundus, qui a Grecis pan, a Latinis omne dicitur, quia philosophus empireum non cognovit; quandoque sola regio sublunaris dicitur mundus, quia hec sola animantia nobis nota habet, de qua: *princeps mundi huius eicietur foras*; quandoque homo mundus dicitur, quia in se totius mundi ymaginem representat. Unde a Domino omnis creatura dictus est, et Grecus ipsum microcosmum id est minorem mundum vocat."

87   Ibid., lines 49–50: "Empireum autem et sensibilem mundum et sublunarem regionem CREAVIT Deus id est de nichilo fecit. Hominem vero CREAVIT id est plasmavit."

88   Ibid., lines 50–55: "De creatione ergo illorum trium inquid legis lator – *in principio creavit Deus celum et terram – celum*, id est continens et contentum, id est celum empireum et angelicam naturam, *terram* materiam omnium corporalium, id est quatuor elementa, id est mundum sensilem ex his constantem. Quidam celum superiores partes mundi sensibilis intelligunt, terram inferiores et palpabiles."

89   Ibid., lines 41 and 55–57. Cf. GI, Gen. 1.1 *et seq., ad loc.* (Froehlich and Gibson, ed., vol. 1, p. 9, col. a):"Hebreus tantum habet eloim quod tam singulare quam plurale est, id est deus vel dii, quia tres persone unus Deus creator est." Comestor's substitution of "pater" for "Deus" came straight from the *Glossa interlinearis*, where *pater* was listed as one of the traditional glosses for *Deus*: "In the beginning God – that is, the Father – created heaven and earth."

90   Clark, "Commentaries on Peter Comestor's *Historia scholastica*," 363–364: "Comestor simply substituted the sense for the letter without any explication. Unlike his confident and comprehensive exposition of *caelum et terram, creavit*, and *in principio*, Comestor glossed *Pater* with one single-sentence comment: "the Hebrew has 'eloim' which is as singular as it is plural, that is, [God] or gods, since one God in three persons is the creator." This particular comment is somewhat cryptic. It is the only instance in the first chapter in which Comestor did not recall specifically the word or phrase of the paraphrase upon which he was commenting. Moreover, it is not immediately evident how

lengthy explication of his opening paraphrase by providing traditional Christian interpretations for "creavit" and also for "in principio."[91]

In his lectures on the *History* , Langton treated Comestor's innovative paraphrase and explication summarily, quoting the opening of the paraphrase and restating concisely, albeit erroneously, his master's account:

IN THE BEGINNING that is, in the Son, that is through etc. This title begins the *Scholastic History*. The Book of Genesis begins the same way. And in this chapter the Master expounds nothing beyond this sentence: *in the beginning God created heaven and earth*. Since this book has been expounded many times, the Master sets forth diverse meanings of this noun 'beginning,' namely for the beginning of time, and for the Son, and for the Holy Spirit. And since by heaven and earth the entire universe is understood, he posits various meanings of the noun 'universe.' Finally, he drives out the opinion of the philosophers through this word 'he created.' For to create is to make something from nothing. Indeed, the philosophers said that the universe had been made from preexisting matter.[92]

Comestor's citation of the Hebrew *eloim* and the Trinitarian doctrine of three persons in one God was consistent with his substitution of *Pater* for *Deus*. Taken together with his predicating *principium* of *Verbum* in the opening paraphrase, Comestor's substitution of *Pater* for *Deus* left much for his commentators to explain surrounding the thorny issue of agency in creation."

91   *Petri Comestoris Historia Genesis*, 1 (ed. Clark, Textual Appendix A.1 below, lines 57–71): "Cum vero dixit Moyses CREAVIT trium errores elidit: Platonis, Aristotilis, Epicuri. Plato dixit tria fuisse ab eterno: deum, ydeas, ylem, et in principio temporis mundum de yle fuisse factum. Aristotiles vero mundum et opificem, qui de duobus principiis scilicet materia et forma operatus est sine principio et operatur sine fine. Epicurus duo: inane et athomos, et in principio natura quosdam athomos solidavit in terram, alios in aquam, alios in ignem, alios in aërem. Moyses vero solum Deum eternum prophetavit et sine preiacenti materia mundum creatum. Creatus est autem IN PRINCIPIO, id est in Filio, et iterandum est IN PRINCIPIO sic: *in principio creavit Deus celum et terram*, IN PRINCIPIO scilicet temporis. Coeva enim sunt mundus et tempus. Sicut autem solus Deus eternus, sic mundus sempiternus, id est semper eternus, id est temporaliter eternus; angeli quoque sempiterni. Vel IN PRINCIPIO omnium creaturarum *creavit celum et terram*, id est has creaturas primordiales fecit et simul, sed quod simul factum est simul dici non potuit."

92   *Prima Stephani glosa scilicet lectiones a Stephano viva voce ante 1176 datae in Historiam Genesis*, 1 (ed. Clark, Textual Appendix A.2 below, lines 36–44): "*IN PRINCIPIO* id est in Filio, id est per etc. Hic titulus incipit <scolasticam historiam>. Sic incipit Geneseos liber. In hoc autem capitulo nichil ultra hanc clausulam exponit Magister: *in principio creavit Deus celum et terram*. Quod quia super librum multipliciter exponitur, ostendit Magis-

Although the first and last parts of Langton's restatement of his master's treatment are accurate, the middle portion is not, for Comestor gives three understandings of the phrase "in the beginning": of time, of the Son, of all things. Nowhere does he mention the Holy Spirit. Apart from this apparent misreading, Langton's restatement is a straightforward summary of his master's account. Moreover, the young Langton was apparently satisfied with it, for he made only one, minor change to it when he revised his lectures.[93]

When Langton returned to this material in 1193, however, he redid not only his own treatment of Comestor's opening paraphrase but that very paraphrase as well:

IN THE BEGINNING WAS THE WORD. Fittingly two cherubim are noted in this *BEGINNING* gazing at each other, that is, the Old and the New Testaments. For Moses begins the Old Testament thus: *In the beginning God created heaven and earth.* John, though, <begins> his Gospel, which we take here as if for the beginning of the New Testament, thus: *In the beginning was the Word.* The Magister joins together these two beginnings of the Testaments, saying: *IN THE BEGINNING WAS THE WORD AND THE WORD WAS IN THE BEGINNING,* in which word and through which God created the world, IN THE BEGINNING therefore, that is, in the Son *GOD CREATED THE WORLD,* and this restatement, *IN THE BEGINNING* OF TIME. Indeed, God is said to create in the Son or through the Son, since the Son is of the same essence with the Father and their operation is indivisible. This noun beginning, therefore, placed one

---

ter diversas acceptiones huius nominis principii, scilicet pro inchoatione temporis et pro Filio et pro Patre et Spiritu Sancto. Et quia per celum et terram mundus intelligitur, ponit varias acceptiones huius nominis mundus. Ad ultimum opinionem philosophorum elidit per hoc verbum creavit. Est enim creare de nichilo aliquem facere. Philosophi autem dicebant mundum ex preiacenti materia factum."

93 *Secunda Stephani glosa supra Historiam Genesis scilicet prima lectionum recensio datarum viva voce ante 1176, effecta a Stephano ipso traditaque in codice H, 1* (ed. Clark, Textual Appendix A.3 below, lines 38–46): "*IN PRINCIPIO* id est in Filio, id est PER +et est+ hic titulus: <incipit *scolastica ystoria. Sed non* ultra hanc clausulam exponit Magister: *in principio creavit Deus celum et terram.* Quod quia super librum multipliciter exponitur, ostendit quoque diversas acceptiones huius nominis principii, scilicet vel inicio temporis, pro Filio et Patre et Spiritu Sancto. Et quia per celum et terram mundus intelligitur, ponit varias acceptiones huius nominis mundus. Ad ultimum opiniones philosophorum elidit per hoc verbum creavit. *Cum enim creare est de nichilo aliud facere, philosophi* dicebant mundum ex preiacenti materia factum."

time in the beginning of Genesis, is understood equivocally, namely for the Son of God, and for the beginning of time.[94]

Langton changed virtually everything about his treatment of this material; his new treatment reads more like a polished and independent restatement of the traditionally equivocal understandings of the word "beginning," common to the beginning of both the Old and the New Testament, than a commentary. Indeed, the whole passage bears the same literary quality of Langton's magisterial prologue to the second and final revision of his course on the *History*. For one thing, there is the symmetry of the twofold opening lines of John's Gospel and Genesis, which center around the word "beginning" and which Langton uses at the beginning of the passage to frame his discussion here, and the twofold symmetry of the gloss, namely the equivocal understanding of "beginning," which Langton uses to conclude his discussion. For another, there is the constant playing off of the word "beginning" itself, which Langton repeats in almost every line as if a cadence around which he winds Scripture and gloss.

Substantively too, Langton makes several obvious improvements. Whereas in his lecture course and his first revision of that course Langton had spoken only of the Book of Genesis, he here writes beautifully about the balance between the two Testaments in Comestor's opening paraphrase. He also makes explicit for the first time that Comestor is taking the opening words of John's Gospel for the beginning of the New Testament. Moreover, Langton not only makes his own treatment clearer but also clarifies that in which Comestor's own treatment was conspicuously lacking, namely the issue of agency in creation, when he makes explicit how God is said to create in and through the Son.

---

94 *Tertia Stephani glosa scilicet magistralis ante 1193 recensa supra Historiam Genesis*, 1(ed. Clark, Textual Appendix A.4 below, lines 62–73): "*IN PRINCIPIO ERAT VERBUM*. Convenienter notantur in hoc *PRINCIPIO* duo Cherubyn sese respicere id est Vetus et Novum Testamentum. Vetus enim Testamentum sic inchoat Moyses: *In principio creavit Deus celum et terram*. Iohannes vero Evangelium suum, quod hic sumimus quasi pro initio Novi Testamenti, sic: *In principio erat Verbum*. Hec duo Testamentorum initia coniungit Magister dicens: *IN PRINCIPIO ERAT VERBUM ET VERBUM ERAT IN PRINCIPIO*, IN QUO VERBO ET PER QUOD *CREAVIT* MUNDUM, *IN PRINCIPIO* itaque id est in Filio *CREAVIT DEUS* MUNDUM, et hoc resume, *IN PRINCIPIO* TEMPORIS. Dicitur autem Deus creare in Filio vel per Filium, quia Filius est eiusdem essentie cum Patre et eorum operatio est indivisa. Sumitur ergo hoc nomen principio semel positum equivoce in initio Geneseos, scilicet pro Filio Dei et pro temporis initio."

Significantly, however, Langton also changed the words of Comestor's opening prologue. Comestor had written: "*IN PRINCIPIO ERAT VERBUM ET VERBUM ERAT PRINCIPII PRINCIPIUM, IN QUO ET PER QUOD PATER CREAVIT* MUNDUM."[95] Other manuscripts, such as P, omit the genitive "principii" that precedes the substantive "principium."[96] The important point, however, is that Comestor had altered the opening words of John's prologue – "In principio erat Verbum et Verbum erat apud Deum, et Deus erat Verbum. Hoc erat in principio ..." – in predicating "principium" of "verbum." Langton, quoting his Magister verbatim, actually misquotes him: "*IN PRINCIPIO ERAT VERBUM ET VERBUM ERAT IN PRINCIPIO,* IN QUO VERBO ET PER QUOD *CREAVIT* MUNDUM."[97]

Langton made two key changes. First, he changed Comestor's paraphrase to accord more clearly with the text of John's Gospel. Second, he added the word "verbo" to make explicit what was implicit in Comestor's treatment. Both changes accord with the substantive changes that, as we saw above, Langton had added to the second revision of his course. There is, therefore, no reason to believe that Langton's misquotation of the *Magister historiarum* was anything other than intentional.

We see in this final revision an intentional reworking of the *History*. Even as a beginner working under Comestor's supervision Langton started to revise both the text of the *History* and his initial lectures on it. The changes he made in the 1190s are quite different. He did not merely refine his commentary but also changed some of the text's substance, its literary character, the comprehensiveness of its overview, and the clarity of its explanation of God's creative agency. This was the work of a mature, self-confident exegete who did not hesitate to overrule his master.

A second example from the same opening chapter also shows in a striking way the extent of the change between Langton's first and second revisions. Once more, Langton seems to misrepresent Comestor's position. Treating creation and its four primal elements in the first chapter of the *Historia Genesis*, Comestor had first listed four possible meanings of the world or universe that had been created, understood broadly: the angelic heaven, the sensible uni-

---

95 *Petri Comestoris Historia Genesis*, 1 (ed. Clark, Textual Appendix A.1 below, lines 40–42).

96 P, fol. 2rb.

97 *Tertia Stephani glosa scilicet magistralis ante 1193 recensa supra Historiam Genesis*, 1(ed. Clark, Textual Appendix A.4 below, lines 67–69).

verse, the sublunar regions, and mankind.⁹⁸ Man, after all, "who represents the image of the whole universe in himself," has been traditionally referred to in this way both by the Lord and by the Greeks.⁹⁹ Comestor then explicated at some length the various possible meanings of the scriptural assertion that God "created" everything:

> The fiery heaven, however, and the sensible world and the sub-lunar region God CREATED, that is, he made them from nothing. Man, however, God CREATED, that is, formed. It is, therefore, about the creation of the former three that the bearer of the law says – *in the beginning God created heaven and earth* – *heaven*, that is, that which contains and is contained, that is, the fiery heaven and angelic nature, *earth* the matter of all bodies, that is, the four elements, that is, the sensible world consisting of these. Certain thinkers understand *heaven* as the higher parts of the sensible world, *earth* as the lower and tangible parts. The Hebrew has *eloim*, which is both singular and plural, that is, God or gods, since the creator is three persons, one God. When, however, Moses said CREATED, he smashed the errors of three thinkers: Plato, Aristotle, and Epicurus. Plato said that there were three things from eternity: god, the ideas, and matter, and that in the beginning of time the world was made from matter. Aristotle, however, <said that there was> the universe and a fabricator, who from two principles, namely matter and form, worked without beginning and works without end. Epicurus <posited> two: the void and atoms, and in the beginning nature solidified certain atoms into earth, others into water, others into fire, and others into air. Moses, however, prophesied that God alone was eternal and that the world had been created without pre-existing matter.¹⁰⁰

---

98 *Petri Comestoris Historia Genesis*, 1 (ed. Clark, Textual Appendix A.1 below, lines 42–46): "MUNDUS quatuor modis dicitur: quandoque empireum celum mundus dicitur propter sui mundiciam; quandoque sensibilis mundus, qui a Grecis pan, a Latinis omne dicitur, quia philosophus empireum non cognovit; quandoque sola regio sublunaris dicitur mundus, quia hec sola animantia nobis nota habet, de qua: *princeps mundi huius eicietur foras*; quandoque homo mundus dicitur ... ."

99 Ibid., lines 46–48: "... quandoque homo mundus dicitur, quia in se totius mundi ymaginem representat. Unde a Domino omnis creatura dictus est, et Grecus ipsum microcosmum id est minorem mundum vocat."

100 Ibid., lines 49–64: "Empireum autem et sensibilem mundum et sublunarem regionem CREAVIT Deus id est de nichilo fecit. Hominem vero CREAVIT id est plasmavit. De creatione ergo illorum trium inquid legis lator – *in principio creavit Deus celum et terram* – *celum*, id est continens et contentum, id est celum empireum et angelicam naturam,

This part of Comestor's account of creation was a straightforward re-presentation of the medieval Christian understanding of the tradition. One might reasonably argue about the details of the cosmology presented even on the basis of the limited works of Plato and of Aristotle then available to medieval thinkers, such as Plato's *Timaeus*, but it must be admitted that here Comestor stands in the Victorine and Lombardian tradition.

In his initial series of lectures on the *History*, Langton's comments on this – as on other aspects of Comestor's account of the initial creation – were cursory: "Finally, he dashes to bits the opinion of the philosophers with respect to this word 'he created.' For to create is to make something from nothing. The philosophers, however, used to say that the world had been made from preexistent matter."[101] Langton, revising his lectures for the first time, made only a minor, editorial change.[102] Langton's early glosses, therefore, clearly agreed with the crux of Comestor's argument.

In revising those lectures for the second time, however, Langton altered fundamentally his own commentary:

Fittingly and truly it is said "he created." For to be created is to come into existence from nothing. If you take "the world" for "man," who is called *microcosmus* by the Greeks, that is, a small world, then it is not properly said

---

terram materiam omnium corporalium, id est quatuor elementa, id est mundum sensilem ex his constantem. Quidam celum superiores partes mundi sensibilis intelligunt, terram inferiores et palpabiles. Hebreus tantum habet eloim quod tam singulare quam plurale est, id est deus vel dii, quia tres persone unus Deus creator est. Cum vero dixit Moyses CREAVIT trium errores elidit: Platonis, Aristotilis, Epicuri. Plato dixit tria fuisse ab eterno: deum, ydeas, ylem, et in principio temporis mundum de yle fuisse factum. Aristotiles vero mundum et opificem, qui de duobus principiis scilicet materia et forma operatus est sine principio et operatur sine fine. Epicurus duo: inane et athomos, et in principio natura quosdam athomos solidavit in terram, alios in aquam, alios in ignem, alios in aërem. Moyses vero solum Deum eternum prophetavit et sine preiacenti materia mundum creatum."

101 *Prima Stephani glosa scilicet lectiones a Stephano viva voce ante 1176 datae in Historiam Genesis*, 1 (ed. Clark, Textual Appendix A.2 below, lines 42–44): "Ad ultimum opinionem philosophorum elidit per hoc verbum creavit. Est enim creare de nichilo aliquem facere. Philosophi autem dicebant mundum ex preiacenti materia factum."

102 *Secunda Stephani glosa supra Historiam Genesis scilicet prima lectionum recensio datarum viva voce ante 1176, effecta a Stephano ipso traditaque in codice H*, 1 (ed. Clark, Textual Appendix A.3 below, lines 43–46): "Ad ultimum opiniones philosophorum elidit per hoc verbum creavit. *Cum enim creare est de nichilo aliud facere, philosophi* dicebant mundum ex preiacenti materia factum."

"he created the world," that is, man, unless you take the word for creating as the word for forming. On the contrary, God made man from preexisting matter that had already been created. Between the opinions of Plato and Aristotle this was the area of agreement, that each insisted that there were three principles from eternity. This was the difference, namely that Plato said that God had worked on preexistent matter through the ideas, that is, the forms. Aristotle, however, said that the world had been formed and separated from the ideas from eternity, as it now is. Therefore, although the Master states that Plato had said that there were two from eternity, namely God and the world, nevertheless we understand by the world two things, namely matter and form.[103]

Several things stand out from Langton's explication. First, he seems once again to misrepresent what Comestor had said, since Comestor had clearly attributed to Plato three rather than two eternal principles. Langton seems not to acknowledge Comestor's discussion of the ideas. Moreover, Comestor seemed to have attributed four eternal principles to Aristotle: the universe and an artisan, God, who worked from the beginning with matter and form. Indeed, it is hard to recognize in Langton's account Comestor's original. The second is that Langton also remade Comestor's discussion about mankind as the world, weaving the two parts of Comestor's discussion into a single whole and rendering that whole briefer and more cogent.

What are we to make of such a commentarial passage that artfully combines faithful repetition with glosses based on seeming ignorance of what was plainly written in Comestor's text? I would suggest that Langton, knowing full well what Comestor had written and taught, nevertheless presented his own way of reading Plato and Aristotle and of accounting for the similarities

---

103 *Tertia Stephani glosa scilicet magistralis ante 1193 recensa supra Historiam Genesis*, 1 (ed. Clark, Textual Appendix A.4 below, lines 76–86): "Convenienter et vere dicitur CREAVIT. Creari enim est ex nichilo fieri. Si mundum accipias pro homine, qui microcosmos dicitur a Grecis, id est minor mundus, non dicitur proprie CREAVIT MUNDUM, id est hominem, nisi verbum creandi sumas pro verbo plasmandi. Immo fecit hominem ex materia preiacenti iam creata. Inter opinionem Platonis et Aristotelis hec erat convenientia, quod uterque voluit tria esse ab eterno. Hec erat differentia, quod Plato dixit Deum esse operatum in ylem per ydeas, id est formas. Aristoteles vero dixit mundum esse formatum et ydeis distinctum ab eterno sicut modo est. Licet ergo dicat Magister Platonem dixisse duo fuisse ab eterno, scilicet Deum et mundum, per mundum tamen duo intelligimus scilicet materiam et formam.*"

and disparities in their systems of thought. We cannot of course know for sure what Langton had in mind in stating that Comestor had attributed to Plato two eternally existing principles. But we can see that Langton moved a good distance both from Comestor's presentation of the cosmology of the ancient philosophers and from his own early commentary on that presentation. One might argue over whose account was more accurate, but to a great extent that would be to miss the essential point that Langton and not Comestor had the last word owing to the former's decision – and there can be no doubt that it was Langton himself who made the decision to revise his course on the *History* a second time – to revisit this foundational material. What is patent is that he preferred his own account to that of his master. Revising his course on the *History* provided Langton with a convenient forum for substituting his own views.

It is clear, therefore, that by the time he revised his course on the *History* for the second time in 1193, Langton had not only arrived at his own, mature opinions about various matters treated in the *History* but also that he had found his own voice. It remains to consider briefly that voice, which was always respectful, if not always faithful or accurate, in reporting his master's positions.

c. *A Magisterial Voice*

It is no surprise to find that Langton frequently speaks in the first person throughout the final revision of his course on the *History*, nor to discover that such references are almost always framed in such a way as to be dispositive of whatever issue is at stake. A good example is Langton's glossing of the third chapter of the *Historia Genesis*, where Comestor provided the conventional Augustinian explanation of God's creation of light: "*GOD ALSO SAID 'LET THERE BE LIGHT' AND THE LIGHT WAS MADE*, that is, he begat the Word in whom it was that light should come into being, that is, as easily as anyone names light by a word, so easily did he create light."[104] In both of the first two versions of his course on the *History* Langton addressed himself cursorily to the metaphor of a person speaking a word: "*AS ANYONE BY A WORD*, that is, by speaking, and thus by this word '*HE SAID*' the ease is

---

104 *Petri Comestoris Historia Genesis*, 3 (ed. Clark, Textual Appendix A.1 below, lines 104–106): "*DIXIT QUOQUE DEUS FIAT LUX ET FACTA EST LUX* id est Verbum genuit in quo erat ut fieret lux, id est tam facile ut quis verbo vocat lucem, tam facile fecit lucem."

thereby indicated."[105] In his second revision, however, Langton added a gloss that was not only longer but more authoritative:

+*AND GOD SAID 'LET THERE BE LIGHT'* that is, a mental word or a thought of the mind, which is God's son. HE BEGAT THE WORD IN WHOM and through whom he made light and all things. Note that whenever someone utters a word, it can be said that he begets a word that he conceives in his mind, but a spirit, who neither speaks nor has any tools for speaking, how does it beget a word? We maintain that for the soul or that spirit to beget a word is for it to think or to have something conceived in its mind from eternity. In this way God is said to have begotten the Word, that is, to have had a conception of his mind from eternity, in whom and through whom he created all things. For that mental word is the Son of God.+[106]

Langton's theological acumen is on display here for all to see.[107] He writes confidently, as befits a Master of philosophy and theology. Most importantly for

---

105 *Prima Stephani glosa scilicet lectiones a Stephano viva voce ante 1176 datae in Historiam Genesis,* 3 (ed. Clark, Textual Appendix A.2 below, lines 96–97): "UT QUIS VERBO id est loquendo, et ita per hoc verbum *DIXIT* innuitur ibi facultas." Langton made only a slight change in wording in his first revision: "UT QUIS VERBO id est loquendo, et ita per hoc verbum *DIXIT* innuitur ibi *facilitas*." *Secunda Stephani glosa supra Historiam Genesis scilicet prima lectionum recensio datarum viva voce ante 1176, effecta a Stephano ipso traditaque in codice H,* 1 (ed. Clark, Textual Appendix A.3 below, lines 97–98).

106 *Tertia Stephani glosa scilicet magistralis ante 1193 recensa supra Historiam Genesis,* 3 (ed. Clark, Textual Appendix A.4 below, lines 159–167): "+*DIXIT AUTEM DEUS FIAT LUX* id est verbum mentale sive mentis conceptum, qui est ipsius Filius. GENUIT IN QUO et per quem operatus est lucem et omnia. Nota quod quando aliquis profert verbum, potest dici gignere verbum quod in mente concipit, sed Spiritus, qui non loquitur nec instrumenta loquendi habet, quomodo gignit verbum? Asserimus quod a<nimam> vel illum spiritum gignere verbum est ipsum cogitare vel habere aliquid mente conceptum ab eterno. Hoc modo dicitur Deus genuisse Verbum, id est habuisse mentis conceptum ab eterno, in quo et per quem omnia creavit. Illud enim verbum mentale est Filius Dei.+"

107 Langton was clearly more informed on and interested in doctrinal questions than Comestor was. He here appropriates without attribution Augustine's doctrine on the Word eternally generated as the *logos endiathetos* and the Word revealed as the *logos prophorikos* of God the Father, concepts which Augustine got from Stoicism. See, most fully, his *De trinitate* and also *De quantitate animae* and *Sermo* 288. For a thorough treatment of these texts and doctrines, see Marcia L. Colish, *The Stoic Tradition from Antiquity to the Early Middle Ages,* 2 vols. (Leiden: Brill, 1985; repr. 1990), 2: 181–82, 197–98, with references.

our purposes, he speaks in his own voice, using the royal 'we'; even his word choice ("asserimus"), a declaration, is authoritative.

There are, however, other ways in which Langton's magisterial voice shines through. We saw above that Langton, in revising his lecture course, systematically eliminated the references by student reporters ("inquit") to his own words; in his final revision, he got rid of those that remained. Nevertheless, the reader of Langton's second revision of his course on the *History* sees quickly that this had more to do with the appearance of permanence than with any reticence, for Langton does not hesitate to interject his own opinions into the discussion. Quite the contrary, Langton routinely provides his own authoritative judgments, speaking frequently in his own voice and continuing to mold both the *History* and the tradition of Comestor's teaching.

IV. *The Creation of a Lasting Tradition*

In this chapter I have treated separately the three versions of Langton's course on the *History*, in order to give a sense of how Langton developed that course over two decades. To some extent, however, my tripartite organization gives a false impression, since in reality it was a single course that Langton refined over time. It would be worthwhile, therefore, however briefly, to convey some sense of the continuity of the tradition that Langton created in his course. To do so, I shall provide one example of many that could be adduced, where Langton's lasting influence is seen from first to last.

To Comestor's chapter in the *Historia evangelica* on Jesus's choice of the twelve apostles ("De electione duorum discipulorum") some unnamed master added very early on the following gloss. Indeed, since Langton presented this text and gloss to his students in his first lectures on the *History*, he may have added the gloss himself:

> The *Ecclesiastical History* says that he (Thaddeus, one of the seventy) was sent by the Lord to Abaragus, King of Edessa, but note that Thomas sent him after the Lord was taken up to heaven. This king was sick and, having heard about the miracles that had been wrought by Jesus, sent a letter asking that Jesus come and cure him, taking care of all things necessary for him and his subjects, even though his kingdom was small. The Lord, once he had heard the king's humility, wrote back that he would visit him after his resurrection. And this happened, when Thomas sent Thaddeus to

preach <to the king and his followers>, and King Abaragus was healed both in mind and body.[108]

This passage recounts the famous and apocryphal story, initially told by Eusebius and subsequently retold by the Fathers and their many successors throughout the Middle Ages, of King Abgar, who wrote to Jesus asking him to come heal his own illness and that of his subjects; what made the story altogether compelling was that Jesus wrote back, promising to come.[109]

The young Langton, lecturing on this chapter, dwelt mainly on Abaragdus:

TO ABARAGUS This Abaragus, king of Edessa, which is across from Antioch, quite a small kingdom but rich. The king was sick with a serious and incurable disease and, hearing the report of the miracles of Christ and the envy of the Jews towards Jesus, asked him through messengers to come and heal him and all that belonged to him and his kingdom. In the letter he also make known to Jesus that, although his kingdom was small, it was nevertheless sufficient for them. And the Lord, attentive to his devotion, wrote back to him a letter, which begins thus: Blessed are you Abaragus etc., and promised that he would come to him, saying that when I shall have been taken up to heaven, I will come to you and cure you, that is, after my ascension. We do not read, however, that he did this in person but rather through his apostle, for after Jesus's ascension, when Blessed Thomas, sent by the Lord, was traveling into India, he sent Jude the apostle, who was also called Thaddeus, to the aforementioned Abaragus, and he healed him and converted the king's whole kingdom to the faith. And in this way the promise of Christ was fulfilled.[110]

---

108 V, fol. 177ra: "Dicit ecclesiastica historia a Domino missum ad Abagarum regem Edisse, sed nota quod Thomas misit eum, postquam assumptus est Dominus. Rex iste infirmabatur auditis miraculis ab eo factis et misit litteras deprecativas ut iret et curaret eum et omnia sibi et suis necessaria ministraret, et si parvum esset regnum eius. Audita humilitate eius rescripsit Dominus quod post resurrectionem visitaret eum. Et hoc factum est cum Thomas misit Thatheum ibi ad predicandum, et sanatus est mente et corpore." It is not found in the same chapter in P, fol. 150ra.

109 Eusebius, *The Ecclesiastical History of Eusebius Pamphilus*, 1.13, trans. Christian Frederic Cruse (Grand Rapids, MI: Baker Book House, 1989), 43–47.

110 Paris, Bibliothèque de l'Arsenal, MS 177, fol. 110vb, and Paris, BnF, lat. 14417, fol. 154rb – fol. 154va: "AD ABAGARUM Abagarus iste rex fuit Edisse civitatis illius parve quidem sed opulente, que est contra Antiochiam. Hic infirmabatur morbo gravi et incurabili, et audiens famam miraculorum Christi et invidiam Iudeorum in ipsum rogavit

Langton here adds numerous details, some from the original story, which were omitted in the gloss added to the *History*: the description of Abgar's kingdom and its proximity to Antioch; the incurability of the king's illness; the envy of Jesus on the part of the Jews; the *incipit* of the letter; the reaction of Jesus when he received the letter; and so on. But the main difference between the story as recounted in the gloss added to the *History* and Langton's version in his lecture is that his students understood clearly that Jesus fulfilled his promise. Jesus affirms that this will occur after his Ascension, and Langton makes clear that Jesus did so through his apostles. A beautiful letter was written and responded to; a promise was made and kept. Indeed, not only was King Abgar cured but his whole kingdom converted to Christianity.

In focusing on the story of Abgar, added via gloss to the *History*, Langton even as a graduate student lecturing on the *History* placed his own stamp on that work, for the students who attended Langton's lectures heard a different version of the *History*, at least for that lecture. Langton made only minor changes in the first revision and even fewer in the second. Still, in polishing his own mature course on the *History* he effected a notable and permanent shift in Comestor's emphasis.[111]

Any master teaching the *History* was able to add his own perspective, depending on what material he attended to, but Langton was in a unique position to influence the *History*'s text and tradition owing to his privileged status as student, colleague, and ultimately successor to Comestor. He did not have to change Comestor's words to remake the *History*; he could do so in many different ways, merely by what he emphasized or did not.

---

per nuncios quatenus veniret et sanaret eum et omnia que habebat et civitatem. Communicaret ei, que licet parva esset, illis tamen sufficere posset. Dominus autem illius attendens devotionem rescripsit ei epistulam, que sic incipit: *Beatus es Abagare etc.* et promittit se ad illum venire dicens cum assumptus fuero veniam ad te et curabo te id est post ascensionem meam. Quod tamen non legitur fecisse corporaliter sed per apostolum suum, nam post ascensionem, cum beatus Thomas missus a Domino ageret iter in Indiam, misit Iudam apostolum, qui et dicebatur Thaddeus, ad Abaragum predictum, qui in nomine Christi sanavit eum et totam civitatem illam ad fidem convertit. Et ita completa Christi promissio fuit."

111 Langton retained most of this lecture, changing only small details in the first, pre-1176 revision of his course on the *History*. See Heidelberg, Universitätsbibliothek, Salem IX, 62, fol. 118ra. He made even fewer changes for his final, magisterial revision in 1193. See: Naples, Biblioteca Nazionale Vittorio Emanuele III, MS VII.C.14, fol. 142vb, et Paris, BnF, lat. 14414, fol. 137ra.

Thus, considered as a whole, Langton's course constituted an influential part of the shaping and transmission of the *Historia scholastica*. Together with the *History* itself, it was taken into the curriculum of the nascent University of Paris. Later, through the encyclopedic Dominican commentary put together under the leadership of Hugh of St. Cher in the 1230s, it became an integral part of the curriculum of the friars as well. Entrusted by Comestor with preserving and passing on his *magnum opus*, Langton exercised considerable influence over that tradition, which he himself helped to create. We are fortunate, almost eight and a half centuries later, that Langton was charged with this commission and that he was so diligent about it, for without the testimony of the course that he so painstakingly developed, and the survival of the manuscripts that preserve it, we could know very little about the early history of the *Historia scholastica*.

CHAPTER EIGHT

Conclusions

This study makes the case for a "Langton" or "University" edition of the *Historia scholastica*, which will reproduce to the greatest extent possible the text of the *History* that Comestor, Langton, and many other *magistri* were using to teach at Paris in the decades between the 1160s and the 1190s. This was, as we have seen, a living, prototypically scholastic text, which changed constantly at the hands of the *magistri* who were at the same time teaching with it and adding to it.

That the *History* proved so malleable is a testament to Comestor's genius, for he invented a novel method for introducing the Bible to students. Unlike the *Gloss*, the *History* presented just the historical/literal tradition and did so in a format that offered students both the scriptural text and the tradition of literal glosses in a single, unified historical narrative.[1] Additionally, Comestor chose a felicitous narrative structure for the *History*, organizing its chapters into discrete topics that lent themselves readily to individual lesson plans. In the *History* Comestor established the narrative coherence of the salvific events related in the Old and New Testaments. Reorganizing biblical history in cogent fashion, Comestor thus charted a course in scholastic biblical education that was as fresh as it was durable.

Comestor's *History* proved adaptable in the classroom owing to its versatile substructure. He wove together lemmata – these were mostly biblical (either verbatim quotations or paraphrases) but also taken from other key historical sources – with glosses. Both the lemmata and the glosses could be added or subtracted as a master saw fit without damaging the core text or its general

---

1   We know from Langton that Comestor intended to do the same for the allegorical senses but never got around to it, since Langton tells us precisely this in the magisterial revision of his course on the *History*: "Proposuerat enim forsitan componere allegorias. Quod tamen non invenimus fecisse Magistrum." *Tertia Stephani glosa scilicet magistralis ante 1193 recensa supra Historiam Genesis, in praefationem magistri* (ed. Clark, Textual Appendix A.4 below, lines 59–60).

approach, a process which began with Comestor himself. Thus individual masters readily and anonymously placed their stamp on Comestor's masterwork even as they used it to teach. The result was a textbook both sturdy and flexible enough to meet the needs of introductory biblical instruction in the theological faculties of the universities and in mendicant houses of study. Serving as a platform for the interpretations of diverse masters, it was incorporated into the curriculum of both institutions.

Another key figure in that development was Stephen Langton. Comestor's prized student, collaborator, colleague, editor, and most prominent successor in the schools and nascent University of Paris, Langton first lectured on the *Scholastic History* as Comestor's teaching assistant. Comestor had such confidence in Langton that, while still a working master and holder of the Chair of Theology at the Cathedral School of Notre Dame, he entrusted to his assistant the task of revising the *History* itself. At the same time, Langton revised his own lecture course on the *History*. This whole collaboration occurred before 1176, when Langton was a young theologian at the start of his career.

Langton again returned to his course on the *History* as a mature master in 1193, before he left Paris to become a cardinal and Archbishop of Canterbury. Langton's *Historia scholastica* project was so important to him that it may be unique within his *oeuvre*, the only one of the works in his massive output that he ever revised. The teaching tradition that this book uncovers opens a window onto Langton's approach to biblical pedagogy over a long teaching career and cements his role in establishing the text of the *Scholastic History* on the eve of the thirteenth century.

Langton's work on the *History* is also vitally important for another reason: we could not now reconstruct the changing contents and contours of Comestor's work in the decades before the redaction of the first extant manuscripts of that work without Langton's extensive testimony about Comestor, the *History*, and its text. The invaluable evidence from Langton's course on the *History* is a by-product of his teaching style and ongoing commitment to his master's project. Among other things, we would not otherwise know that Comestor himself taught the *History*, that he continued to work on it and strengthen it, and added glosses to it like any other *magister*. Nor would we know of Comestor's life and work habits, and that his fruitful association with Langton, as master and student, as mentor and guide, as colleague and collaborator, began so early.

In this connection, Langton's presence in Paris far earlier than scholars have supposed revises considerably what is known about the theological map of the second half of the twelfth century. Peter Lombard studied with Hugh of St. Victor in the 1130s and taught Peter Comestor in the 1150s. Hugh's pedagogical program, which accented both the foundational role of a literal/historical reading of Scripture and the application of the liberal arts to that task, was thus passed on to Comestor and to Langton. Both masters, therefore, carried the Victorine program of Bible-centered education into the heart of the university.[2]

The revised chronology of Langton's early career in Paris also reveals a direct pedagogical line between Peter Lombard, who taught Peter Comestor in the 1150s, and Stephen Langton, whom Comestor taught and mentored. Chapters Two and Three showed that Comestor and his students had in front of them a Great *Gloss* for Luke.[3] Comestor and his students also had the Lombard's prologue to John.[4] Brady, aided by Smalley's research, was certain that the Lombard had glossed not only the Gospels but many more biblical books besides the Pauline Epistles and the Psalms.[5] In speculating about what could possibly have happened to the many glossed books of the Bible (besides the Psalms and the Pauline epistles) glossed again by the Lombard, Brady naturally considered the possibility that the Lombard simply turned these over to his students.[6] This possibility should be taken seriously.

But here again Comestor and Langton must be considered together. Brady, although he knew that Langton was a prime witness to the Lombard's glossed Bible, nevertheless puzzled over the fact that Langton was several generations

---

2   This confirms Smalley's insight that Langton himself, like Comestor, was inspired by the Victorine program of education: "Langton actually glossed the Bible according to the order of books which Hugh had recommended to students .... It looks like a carefully thought-out programme, based on a study of the *Didascalicon*." Beryl Smalley, *The Study of the Bible in the Middle Ages*, 3rd rev. ed. (1941; Oxford: Basil Blackwell, 1984), 198.

3   Chapter Two, 56–57, and Chapter Three, 102 and n39.

4   Mark J. Clark, "The Biblical *Gloss*, the Search for the Lombard's Glossed Bible, and the School of Paris," *Mediaeval Studies* 76 (2014): 57–113.

5   See Peter Lombard, *Sententiae in IV Libris Distinctae*, ed. Ignatius Brady (Grottaferrata: Collegii S. Bonaventurae ad Claras Aquas, 1971–1981), 2: 7*–52*. Brady relied especially on two of Smalley's studies: "Some Gospel Commentaries of the Early Twelfth Century," *Recherches de théologie ancienne et médiévale* 45 (1978): 147–180; and "Peter Comestor on the Gospels and his Sources," *Recherches de théologie ancienne et médiévale* 46 (1979): 84–129. These articles, which Smalley updated slightly, are reprinted in reverse order as the first two chapters in Beryl Smalley, *The Gospels in the Schools c.1100 – c.1280* (London: The Hambledon Press, 1985), 1–83.

6   See Lombard, *Sententiae in IV Libris Distinctae*, ed. Brady, 2: 23*.

removed from the fact.[7] He could not understand how Langton had such intimate knowledge of the Lombard's glossed Bible. In the light of the new chronology for Langton's early career in Paris, however, Langton's evidence must be revisited and reconsidered, for together with his master, Peter Comestor, Langton must now be deemed the likeliest candidate for having privileged access to copies of the Lombard's glosses on the Bible.[8]

The revised chronology also means that Langton, together with Comestor, will be a key to unlocking the story of the biblical *Gloss*, which was nearing completion in the mid-twelfth century. The story of what changes the *Gloss* underwent in Paris must now be re-thought in the light of the discovery of the potential survival of the Lombard's glosses on much of the Bible and in the light of the close connections of Comestor and Langton to each other and of both masters to the Lombard.

In short, the theological map of the second half of the twelfth century will have to be redrawn. Grabmann mistakenly placed Comestor in the school of Peter the Chanter and put Langton in a separate category.[9] Henceforth, instead of looking to Peter the Chanter's influence on Langton, to cite the most obvious example, we shall be obliged to investigate Langton's influence on the Chanter.[10] This study, which shows the central importance of Comestor's lectures on the Glossed Gospels and of Langton's course on the *History* to a proper

---

7   In his introduction to the second volume, which was published in 1981 and which contained his edition of the third and fourth books of the *Sentences*, Brady carefully examined the testimony of Langton in connection with his investigation of which biblical books besides the Psalms and the Pauline Epistles the Lombard had glossed. See Lombard, *Sententiae in IV Libris Distinctae*, ed. Brady, 2: 44*–52*.

8   If we recover in the works of Comestor and Langton the Lombard's long-lost glosses on the Gospels, we will then have to revise the conventional idea that the Lombard was responsible for the "systematic/doctrinal" side of that curriculum. The words are those of Rorem, one among literally hundreds of scholars repeating the conventional view that Peter Lombard represented the speculative rather than the biblical side of theological interest in the twelfth century. Paul Rorem, *Hugh of St. Victor*, Great Medieval Thinkers (Oxford: Oxford University Press, 2009), 12.

9   Martin Grabmann, *Die Geschichte der scholastischen Methode*, 2 vols. (Freiburg in Breisgau: Herder, 1911), 2: 476–485 (for Peter Comestor and Peter the Chanter) and 497–501 (for Langton).

10 Ignatius Brady provides a typical example of a scholar whose investigation of Langton's sources was ruined by the mistaken chronology, since he mistakenly supposed that the Chanter preceded Langton at Paris: "Immo, quaeri potest quomodo et quantum dependeat a simili opera Petri Cantoris." See Lombard, *Sententiae in IV Libris Distinctae*, ed. Brady, 2: 45*.

understanding of the creation and development of the *Historia scholastica*, makes a good start. But we need editions of the former, and Langton's massive corpus of biblical lectures itself will need to be studied and edited.[11]

Yet as this book itself shows, even before these editorial desiderata have seen the light of day, research in this area can be conducted on the basis of the manuscripts. Several topics come to mind as natural sequels to the findings on Comestor and Langton here presented. More can be done to document the long-term influence of the Victorine tradition in the later twelfth century. Whether Langton carried over the same techniques to books of the Bible not in the *Scholastic History* project is a question well worth investigating, as is the Dominican interest in the *History* and in Langton's course on it. More could be done to uncover the Franciscan reception of that tradition as well.

In the high Middle Ages mendicant houses of study were far more numerous than university faculties of theology. Most of the mendicant *studia* were not located in university towns and most mendicants did not teach or study at universities but ministered to the laity. How the project of Comestor and Langton factored into the biblical studies that prepared friars for their preaching mission, and how it may emerge in their actual sermons, Latin and vernacular, are additional avenues which readers of this book might traverse. It remains the case that pursuit of the editorial and substantive studies of the kinds suggested here will enhance our understanding of the intellectual history of the high Middle Ages, and, in so doing, will reinforce the significance of the place that the *Historia scholastica* of Peter Comestor and Stephen Langton hold in that history.

Finally, this study sheds needed light on the emergence of the *Historia scholastica* during the final three decades of the twelfth century. Until now the least well understood of the three great textbooks produced during the twelfth century, the *History* should henceforth be as accessible as Gratian's *Decretum* and the Lombard's *Sentences* to scholars and students interested in the masterworks produced during that innovative time. Chenu had ample reason to see in the medieval legend of the three brothers a "symbol full of truth."[12] Indeed

---

11 The sole edition to my knowledge is Saltmann's edition of Langton's commentary on the Book of Chronicles: Stephen Langton, *Commentary on the Book of Chronicles*, ed. Avrom Saltmann (Ramat-Gan: Bar-Ilan University Press, 1978).

12 "... la légende de la fraternité charnelle de Comestor et du Lombard est un symbole plein de vérité." Marie-Dominique Chenu, *Introduction à l'étude de saint Thomas d'Aquin*, 2nd ed. (Montreal: Institut d'études médiévales; Paris: Vrin, 1954), 205.

this study, which has made clear Peter Comestor's creative debt to the Victorines, the biblical *Gloss*, and to his master, Peter Lombard, provides a basis for understanding why the *Historia scholastica* was formerly so famous. In doing so it fills a large lacuna in our understanding of the theological landscape of the second half of the twelfth century.

Textual Appendices

Editorial Conventions

I here present eight selections from a series of working editions: the first group of four texts (Appendices A.1–4) consists of the opening chapters of the *Historia Genesis*, the first of Comestor's "Histories," and the three versions of Langton's course on those chapters; the second set of four (Appendices B.1–4) consists of the opening chapters of the *Historia evangelica*, Comestor's unified treatment of the four Gospels and the last of the "Histories" he wrote, together with the three corresponding versions of Langton's course.

To attempt a modern critical edition of Comestor's *Historia scholastica*, copies of which are preserved in more than 800 extant manuscripts, is out of the question at this time. Agneta Sylwan, who hazarded and then rejected a provisional *stemma codicum* based upon extant pre-1200 manuscripts, posited four families, but this division is not borne out by the evidence. What seems certain is that of the two earliest extant manuscripts containing the *History*, Paris Bibliothèque nationale de France, MS lat. 16943 ("P"), copied in 1183 at the Monastery of Saint-Pierre de Corbie in Amiens, France, and Vienna, Östereichische Nationalbibliothek, MS lat. 363 ("V"), copied at Mondsee between 1180 and 1183, the former preserves an earlier tradition. Ordinarily, any scholar would prefer this more primitive tradition, since it is closer to the author's text. But the *History* is no ordinary text, and Comestor no ordinary author. We know from Langton's course on the *History* – both his initial lecture course and his first revision of it predate 1176 – that Comestor himself continued to revise the *History* long after its initial "publication," when he dedicated the work to William of the White Hands sometime before 1173. The notion of getting back to Comestor's text, therefore, is problematic, since he himself continued to change and perfect it. It is made even more problematic, by the fact that he turned it over to Langton, who himself altered it to accord with his own course on it, before he died and in all likelihood before he himself stopped working on it. The historical reality thus points to a mobile and flexible text that changed rapidly as it was being taught, by Comestor, by Langton, as well as by other masters.

My first goal in editing the *Historia scholastica* is to adhere to this complex historical reality by getting as close as possible to the text that Langton and his students were using during the first half of the 1170s, while acknowledging and taking account of the changes the text was undergoing at the same time. The pre-1176 versions of Langton's course on the *History* make this possible, not only because of the many citations of the *History* that he glosses but also owing to his many observations about the development of its text. Neither P nor V fits these criteria perfectly, but because V is much closer to the version with which Langton and his students were working, I start with V. The resulting text is by no means a diplomatic edition, however, since I treat the two pre-1176 versions of Langton's course as authoritative witnesses and base my text of the *History* as much on Langton's authority as I do on V. Moreover, because P preserves in some places a text more closely approximating that used by Langton, I also make use of the readings in P. My editions, therefore, are of necessity eclectic.

My second goal is to record to the fullest extent possible changes to the text of the *History* from its first appearance sometime around 1170 up to 1193, when Langton revised his course on it for the second time. In my edition of the *History* proper I have tried to accomplish this by recording the various levels of "notes" added to the *History*, and by documenting in the apparatus points of significant correspondence between Langton's course and the oldest extant manuscripts, P and V. This is exceedingly complex, because these "notes" are found in the manuscripts in various stages of being assimilated into the main text. Moreover, they are often found in different stages in different manuscripts, even in P and V. To document this fluidity, I adopt of the following conventions:

1. I enclose all notes that worked their way into the main text of the *History* by the time that Langton lectured on the *History* in square brackets [ ] within the main text. The reader will see at a glance the proliferation of such notes within the text, many added by Comestor himself, which had already, at a very early date, become part of the text of the *History*. It is crucial to realize that some of these notes, already an undifferentiated part of the main text in V, are found in P as notes bracketed by lines but positioned within the main text itself. In keeping with my goal

of getting as close to the text used by Langton and his students in the early 1170s, I almost always represent the state of the text in its later form, i.e. as part of the main text; however, these notes are bracketed to indicate their status as subsequent additions.

2. I enclose notes that are set off by lines within the margins of the main text within brace brackets {}; these texts are one stage away from becoming part of the main text.

3. I enclose notes found in the margins of the manuscripts in double square brackets [[]] to show that they are still two stages away from entering the main text. I identify the place in the text these notes are meant to gloss with a numeral. Thus a chapter with three such notes will have three double-bracketed passages, each differentiated by a prefatory 1, 2, or 3.

These notes or additions also complicate the task of editing the three versions of Langton's course on the *History*. Before discussing that course, therefore, it is worth emphasizing that the text of the *History* that Langton chose to use for his own course – and I say chose to use, since the fact that he knew which texts had been added shows that he was acquainted with the original state of the text – is a complicated tapestry of originals and additions and accretions. He makes ample use of texts from all three of the levels just described. We do not have the manuscripts that he and his students used, and for that reason we cannot say for certain which notes were in what stage at any one time. All we can do is record the stages of such additions in the manuscripts still extant. In the light of Langton's extensive testimony about the state of the text before 1176, such a record can serve to show just how malleable a scholastic text the *History* was.

My working editions of the three versions of Langton's course on the *History* themselves remain works in progress. There is only one manuscript for the pre-1176 revision, but there are several for the initial lecture course and for the final revision from 1193. Because the quality of readings in these manuscripts varies, I present an eclectic text in the selections that follow, although I will, of course, establish a *stemma codicum* for these versions when I publish a critical edition of Langton's tri-partite course on the *History*.

For now, however, a more pressing issue is to establish typographical conventions to show the changes that Langton made to his own course. After considering the possibilities, I have decided to use the following: (i) additions appear between +plus signs+; (ii) revisions to the original text are placed between *asterisks*; (iii) ~~strikethrough~~ is used to show deletions in the original text; and (iv) editorial emendations are enclosed in <angle brackets>. These sigla allow me to show the many careful editorial changes Langton made to his course over time.

Comestor was especially creative in forging the lemmata of the *History*, using not only verbatim scriptural quotations but also paraphrasing Scripture and other sources he deemed authoritative for history, such as Peter Lombard, Josephus, and Pseudo-Methodius. I have sought to reflect these distinctions by using SMALL CAPS to delimit all lemmata in the *History*. I follow conventional practice in setting off in *italics* all scriptural quotation, whether in lemmata or part of glosses or narrative.

A.1: The prefaces and opening chapters of Comestor's *Historia Genesis*.

Incipit liber scolastice historie.

Reverendo patri et domino suo Guillelmo Dei gratia Senonensi archiepiscopo Petrus presbyter Trecensis servus Christi vitam bonam et exitum beatum. Causa suscepti laboris fuit instans petitio sociorum. Qui cum historiam Sacre
5 Scripture in serie et glosis diffusam lectitarent brevem nimis et inexpositam opus aggredi me compulerunt ad quod pro veritate historie consequenda recurrerent. In quo sic animus stilo imperavit, ut a dictis patrum non recederem, licet novitas favorabilis sit et mulcens aures. Porro a cosmographia Moysi incipiens rivulum historicum deduxi usque ad ascensionem Domini Salvatoris, pelagus
10 mysteriorum peritioribus relinquens, in quibus et vetera prosequi et nova cudere licet. De historiis quoque ethnicorum quedam incidentia pro ratione temporum inserui, instar rivuli qui secus alveum diverticula que invenerit replens, preterfluere tamen non cessat. Verumtamen quia stilo rudi opus est lima vobis pater inclite limam reservavi, ut huic operi Deo volente et correctio vestra
15 splendorem et auctoritas prebeat perennitatem. Per omnia benedictus Deus. Amen.

Item prefatio Magistri Petri Manducatoris in historia Veteris et Novi Testamenti.

Imperatorie maiestatis est tres in palatio habere mansiones: auditorium vel
20 consistorium in quo iura decernit; cenaculum in quo cibaria distribuit; thalamum in quo quiescit. Ad hunc modum Imperator noster, qui *imperat ventis et mari*, mundum habet pro auditorio, ubi ad eius nutum omnia disponuntur; unde: *celum et terram ego adimplebo*. Secundum hanc dicitur Dominus; unde: *Domini est terra et plenitudo eius*. Animam iusti pro thalamo, quia *delicie* sunt ei
25 *esse cum filiis hominum*. Secundum hanc sponsus dicitur. Sacram Scripturam pro cenaculo, in qua suos sic inebriat, ut sobrios reddat; unde: *in domo Dei ambulavimus cum consensu* id est in Sacra Scriptura id ipsum sapientes. Secundum hanc dicitur paterfamilias. Cenaculi tres sunt partes: fundamentum, paries, tectum. Historia fundamentum est, cuius tres sunt species: annalis, kalendaria,

ephemera. [Annalis historia factum quod per annum factum est; kalendaria que 30
in uno mense facta est, id est factum aliquod insigne quod in uno mense factum
est; ephemera quod repente factum est, id est in uno die vel in parte mensis, id
est hac similitudine ephemera est piscis qui eo die quo nascitur moritur.] Allegoria paries superinnitens, quae per factum aliud figurat. Tropologia doma culminis superpositum, que per factum quid nobis sit faciendum insinuat. Prima 35
planior, secunda acutior, tertia suavior.[1] A fundamento loquendi sumamus
principium, immo ab ipsius fundamenti principio eo iuvante qui omnium princeps est et principium.

    Cap. I – De creatione celi et quattuor elementorum.

    IN PRINCIPIO ERAT VERBUM ET VERBUM ERAT PRINCIPII 40
PRINCIPIUM, IN QUO ET PER QUOD PATER *CREAVIT* MUNDUM.
MUNDUS quattuor modis dicitur: quandoque empyreum celum mundus dicitur propter sui munditiam; quandoque sensibilis mundus, qui a Grecis pan, a
Latinis omne dicitur, quia philosophus empyreum non cognovit; quandoque
sola regio sublunaris dicitur mundus, quia hec sola animantia nobis nota habet, 45
de qua: *princeps mundi huius eicietur foras*; quandoque homo mundus dicitur, quia
in se totius mundi imaginem representat. Unde a Domino omnis creatura dictus est, et Grecus ipsum microcosmum id est minorem mundum vocat.
Empyreum autem et sensibilem mundum et sublunarem regionem *CREAVIT*
Deus id est de nihilo fecit. Hominem vero *CREAVIT* id est plasmavit. De cre- 50
atione ergo illorum trium inquit legis lator – *in principio creavit Deus celum et terram* – *celum*, id est continens et contentum, id est celum empyreum et angelicam naturam, *terram* materiam omnium corporalium, id est quattuor elementa,
id est mundum sensilem ex his constantem. Quidam celum superiores partes
mundi sensibilis intelligunt, terram inferiores et palpabiles. Hebreus tantum 55
habet eloim quod tam singulare quam plurale est, id est deus vel dii, quia tres
persone unus Deus creator est. Cum vero dixit Moyses *CREAVIT* trium
errores elidit: Platonis, Aristotilis, Epicuri. Plato dixit tria fuisse ab eterno:
deum, ydeas, ylem, et in principio temporis mundum de yle fuisse factum. Aristotiles vero mundum et opificem, qui de duobus principiis scilicet materia et 60
forma operatus est sine principio et operatur sine fine. Epicurus duo: inane et
atomos, et in principio natura quosdam atomos solidavit in terram, alios in
aquam, alios in ignem, alios in aërem. Moyses vero solum Deum eternum
prophetavit et sine preiacenti materia mundum creatum. Creatus est autem *IN*

---

  1 Eadem glosula (id est "Historia annalis…moritur") modo suprascripta hoc in loco
     recordatur in codice V.

65 *PRINCIPIO,* id est in Filio, et iterandum est *IN PRINCIPIO* sic: *in principio creavit Deus celum et terram, IN PRINCIPIO* scilicet temporis. Coeva enim sunt mundus et tempus. Sicut autem solus Deus eternus, sic mundus sempiternus, id est semper eternus, id est temporaliter eternus; angeli quoque sempiterni. Vel *IN PRINCIPIO* omnium creaturarum *creavit celum et terram,* id est has crea-
70 turas primordiales fecit et simul, sed quod simul factum est simul dici non potuit. [Sicut quam cito oculos aperio, statim acies mea solem icit in oriente, quod non faceret nisi multa aëris spatia que sunt inter me et solem transvolaret. Quam momentaneam transvolationem, si velim explicare, sepe addam prius et post sic: prius transit acies mea aërem vicinum, post aërem qui est super Alpes,
75 post aërem qui est super alias terras usque ad oceanum, post aërem qui est super oceanum, et tandem tangit solem.] Licet enim hic prius nominetur *celum* quam *terra,* tamen scriptum est: *in initio tu Domine terram fundasti et opera manuum tuarum sunt celi.* Hanc creationem mundi prelibatam sub operibus sex dierum explicat Scriptura insinuans tria: creationem, dispositionem, ornatum. In primo die cre-
80 ationem et quandam dispositionem; in secundo et tertio dispositionem; in tribus reliquis ornatum.

Cap. II – De primaria mundi confusione.

TERRA AUTEM ERAT INANIS ET VACUA id est mundialis erat machina adhuc inutilis et infructuosa et vacua ornatu suo. *ET TENEBRE*
85 *ERANT SUPER FACIEM ABYSSI.* Eandem machinam quam terram dixerat abyssum vocat pro sui confusione et obscuritate. Unde et Grecus chaos eam vocat. Quod vero dictum est *TENEBRE ERANT,* quidam dogmatizaverunt tenebras fuisse eternas, quae iam scilicet cum mundus fieret erant. Alii irridentes Deum Veteris Testamenti dicunt eum prius creasse tenebras quam lucem. Sed
90 tenebre nihil aliud sunt nisi lucis absentia. Obscuritas autem quedam aëris a Deo creata est et dicta tenebre. Unde et in catalogo creaturarum dicitur: *benedicite lux et tenebre Domino. ET SPIRITUS DEI FEREBATUR SUPER AQUAS* vel Dominus vel Dei voluntas *FEREBATUR SUPER AQUAS* sicut voluntas artificis habentis pre oculis omnem materiam domus faciende super
95 illam fertur, dum quid de quo facturus sit disponit. Predictam machinam *AQUAS* vocat quasi ductilem materiam ad operandum ex ea. Ideo vero sic vari-antur nomina eius, ne si unius elementi nomine tantum censeretur illi magis putaretur accomoda. Hebreus habet pro *SUPERFEREBATUR* incubabat vel Syra lingua fovebat sicut avis ova. In quo etiam cum regimine nascentis mundi
100 notatur initium. Hunc locum male intellexit Plato dictum hoc putans de anima mundi, sed dictum est de Spiritu Sancto creante, de quo dicitur: *emitte spiritum tuum et creabuntur.*

Cap. III – De opere prime diei.

DIXIT QUOQUE DEUS FIAT LUX ET FACTA EST LUX id est Verbum genuit in quo erat ut fieret lux, id est tam facile ut quis verbo vocat lucem,   105
tam facile fecit lucem, et itera sic quam lucem vocat: nubem candidam quandam illuminantem superiores mundi partes, claritate tamen tenui ut diluculo
fieri solet, et hec ad modum solis circumagitata. Presentia sui superius emisperium et inferius uicissim illuminabat. Per *FIAT* intelligitur essentia lucis in
Deo priusquam fieret; per *FACTA EST* essentia eiusdem in actu scilicet cum   110
prodiit ad esse. *ET VIDIT DEUS LUCEM QUOD ESSET BONA* id est que
placuerat in prescientia ut fieret placuit in essentia ut maneret. Vel tropice,
VIDIT, id est videri fecit. *ET DIVISIT LUCEM AC TENEBRAS*. Hic incipit
dispositio, et tamen aliquid dicitur de creatione quasi diceret cum luce tenebras
creavit id est umbram ex obiectione corporum luci. Et creatas divisit locorum   115
distantia et qualitate, ut scilicet numquam simul sed semper e regione diversa
emisperia vicissim sibi vendicarent. Intelligitur etiam hic angelorum facta divisio: stantes *lux,* cadentes *tenebre* dicti sunt. ET *APPELLAVIT LUCEM DIEM*
a *dian* greco, quod est claritas, sicut lux dicitur quia luit id est purgat tenebras.
TENEBRAS DIXIT *NOCTEM* a nocendo, quia nocent oculis ne videant.   120
Sicut tamen dies exortum est a *dian* greco, ita nox a *nictin. ET FACTUM EST*
VESPERE ET post *FACTUM EST MANE* et sic completus est *DIES UNUS*
naturalis. Primo enim cum celo et terra lux est creata, qua paulatim occidente
FACTUM EST VESPERE prime diei usualis, et eadem sub terras migrante et
ad ortum redeunte *FACTUM EST MANE* id est terminata est nox, et inchoavit   125
dies secunda. Itaque precedente luce diei et sequente nocte terminata exstitit
DIES UNUS.

Cap. IV – De opere secunde diei.

Secunda die disposuit Deus superiora mundi sensilis. Empyreum enim
quam cito factum statim dispositum est et ornatum id est sanctis angelis reple-   130
tum. *FECIT* ERGO EA DIE *DEUS FIRMAMENTUM IN MEDIO*
AQUARUM id est quandam exteriorem mundi superficiem ex aquis congelatis ad instar crystalli solidatam et perlucidam intra se cetera sensibilia continentem ad imaginem teste que in ovo est. Et in eo fixa sunt sidera. ET DICITUR *FIRMAMENTUM* non tantum propter sui soliditatem, sed quia   135
terminus est aquarum que super ipsum sunt, firmus et intransgressibilis. DICITUR *CELUM* ETIAM, quia celat id est tegit omnia sensibilia, et cum legitur
FIRMAMENTUM CELI endiadis est id est firmamentum quod est celum, ut
cum dicitur creatura salis. Unde et pro sui concameratione grece dicitur uranon
id est palatum vel palatus. Vel DICITUR *CELUM* quasi casa helios, quia sol sub   140

ipso positus illum illustrat. Hanc tamen circumvolutam concamerationem philosophus summitatem intellexit ignis. Cum enim ignis non habet quo ascendat, circumvolvitur ut in clibano patet, ita et circa mundi exteriora ignis volvitur. Et hoc est ethereum vel sidereum celum. Est etiam tertium celum infra,

145 quod aërium dicitur, de quo: *aves celi comederunt illud.* [Quidam quartum suspicantur celum esse super empyreum, quia Lucifer, cum esset in empyreo, legitur dixisse: *ascendam in celum etc.* Et in eo modo dicunt esse Christum hominem super angelos qui sunt in empyreo.]

Sane firmamentum DIVIDIT *AQUAS QUE SUB* IPSO SUNT *AB*
150 *AQUIS QUE* SUPER IPSUM SUNT, de quibus dicitur: *qui tegis aquis superiora eius.* Et sunt sicut et ipsum congelate ut cristallus, nec igne solvi possunt, vel in modum nebule vaporabiles. Cur vero ibi sint Deus novit, nisi quod quidam autumant inde rorem in estate descendere. Quod autem dictum est, *FIAT FIRMAMENTUM,* et post dicitur, *FECIT DEUS FIRMAMENTUM,* et tertio,
155 *FACTUM* EST FIRMAMENTUM, non superfluit, quia sicut in domo facienda prius domus fit in scientia artificis, fit etiam materialiter cum levigantur ligna et lapides, fit etiam essentialiter cum levigata in structuram domus disponuntur, ita cum dicitur *FIAT* ad prescientiam Dei refertur, *FECIT* ad opus in materia, *FACTUM EST* ad opus in essentia. Illud primo die, istud
160 secundo factum est, et cum huius diei opus bonum fuerit ut ceterorum, tamen non legitur de eo: *vidit Deus quod esset bonum.* Tradunt enim Hebrei, quod hoc die angelus factus est Diabolus [id est *Sathanel, Lucifer: Sathan,* adversarius; *El, Deus,* et invenitur hoc nomen in epistula Clementis tantum.], quibus consentire videntur qui in secunda feria missam de angelis cantare consueverunt quasi
165 in laudem stantium angelorum. Sed tradunt sancti quia in signum factum est hoc, quia binarius infamis numerus est in theologia, quia primus ab unitate recedit. Deus autem unitas est et sectionem et discordiam detestatur. Possumus autem dicere, quia opus tertie diei quasi adhuc est de opere secunde diei, quod post patebit. Unde non commendatur, nisi in tertio die quasi post sui consum-
170 mationem.

Cap. V – De opere tercie diei.

Tercia die *SUB FIRMAMENTO DEUS* CONGREGAVIT *AQUAS IN UNUM LOCUM.* Que licet plurima obtineant loca, tamen quia omnes continuantur in visceribus terre *IN UNUM LOCUM* dicte sunt CONGRE-
175 GATAE. Et potuit esse ut aque, que totum spatium aëris occupabant vaporabiles, solidate modicum obtineant locum. Vel terra subsedit paululum, ut eas tanquam in matrice concluderet, et sic APPARUIT *ARIDA,* quia latens sub aquis humus proprie dicta est. Sed cum APPARUIT *ARIDA,* EADEM DICI-

TUR *TERRA*, quia teritur pedibus animantium. Vel a tribus circumpositis elementis dicitur solum quia solida. Dicitur tellus, quia tolerat labores hominum. 180 *CONGREGATIONES AQUARUM APPELLANTUR MARIA* hebreo idiomate, quod quaslibet aquarum congregationes vocat maria. Completo ergo aquarum opere subditur: *ET VIDIT DEUS QUOD ESSET BONUM.* Et addidit illi opus aliud, cum *DIXIT, GERMINET TERRA,* nec de opere germinandi intelligendum est tantum, sed de potentia quasi diceret potens sit ger- 185 minare. *EDUXITQUE TERRA HERBAM VIRENTEM ET FACIENTEM SEMEN ET LIGNUM POMIFERUM FACIENS FRUCTUM SECUNDUM GENERA SUA.* Patet quia non per moras temporum, ut modo, produxit terra plantas suas, sed statim in maturitate viridi, in qua et herbe seminibus et arbores pomis onuste sunt. Notandumque quod dictum est *VIRENTEM.* Quidam 190 dicunt mundum factum in vere, quia viror illius temporis est et fructificatio. Alii quia legunt, *LIGNUM…FACIENS FRUCTUM,* et additum, *HERBAM HABENTEM SEMEN,* factum esse dicunt in Augusto sub leone, sed in Martio factum dogmatizat Ecclesia. Nota cum primo ait, *FACIENTEM SEMEN,* et addit, *UNUMQUODQUE HABENS SEMENTEM,* quia sementis proprie 195 dicitur dum adhuc est in sementino vel sementum; semen vero cum seminatur; seminium vero cum seminatum est. Distinguitur tamen aliter: sementis frugum et arborum; semen animalium; seminium cuiuslibet rei exordium. Nec nos moveat quia in dispositione elementorum videtur aër non dispositus, quia non est nominatus, sed dispositus est cum, liber ab aquis, notam nobis accepit for- 200 mam. [Vel ideo non dicitur dispositus, quia nullum ornatum ex substantia sui factum in se habuit.]

A.2: The prefaces and opening chapters of the first version, namely the classroom lectures, of Stephen Langton's course on the *Historia Genesis*.

REVERENDO PATRI ETC. Premittit Magister prologum epistolarem id est epistolam loco prologi, quam dirigit ad Dominum Senonensem, ut manum correctionis huic operi apponat et favorem suum eidem exhibeat. NOVA CUDERE id est novas expositiones facere, dumtaxat ad edificationem sit.
5 QUEDAM INCIDENTIA ut de incendio Troiano et similibus. Legitur enim, inquit, super Esdram quod rex proprium scriptorem Persarum cronicorum id est gesta sui temporis et proprium incidentium eorum scilicet que temporibus suis finitimis regionibus emenserant. INSTAR RIVULI quia sicut rivulus non dimittit cursum suum propter incidentia, sic nec ego propositum id est historie
10 cursum. ETHNICORUM id est gentilium. Ennos enim grece, gens latine. STILO RUDI scripture nove. LIMA correctione.
   IMPERATORIE. Prefatio est in qua fit <descensus> ad litteram per quoddam simile. VEL CONSISTORIUM quod idem est. KALENDARIA id est menstrua vel mensurna. EFFIMERA id est diurna a pisce vel verme, qui
15 hoc nomine censetur et eodem die quo nascitur moritur vel paulo post. Et est ANNUALIS HYSTORIA de gestis unius anni et supra ut Troiana, quamvis et decennalis dicatur, mensurna de gestis unius mensis et supra, ita quod infra annum ut de Hester, diurna de gestis unius diei et supra ita quod infra mensem est ut de Iudith vel de opere sex dierum, quod alio nomine dicitur cosmo-
20 graphia id est descriptio mundi – cosmos enim mundus – alio exameron ab Augustino, ab exa quod est sex, quia de operibus sex dierum ibi agitur. QUE PER FACTUM ALIUD FIGURAT. Exemplum est, inquid, non diffinitio. Sumitur enim quandoque allegoria a persona ut Isaac significat Christum; quandoque a re que non est persona ut vervex occisus humanitatem passam
25 (persona est individua rationalis nature substantia); quandoque a numero ut – *apprehendent septem mulieres virum unum* etc – id est septem dona gratiarum; quandoque a loco ut per montem in quo docebat Christus eminenciam virtutum; quandoque a tempore ut – *non sit fuga uestra in hieme* – id est in refrigeratione caritatis; quandoque a facto ut interfectio Golie, interfectio

Diaboli a Christo. Tropologia est sermo conversivus pertinens ad mores animi 30
et magis movet quam allegoria, que pertinet ad ecclesiam militantem, anagoge
ad triumphantem et ad Deum Trinitatem. Et nota, inquit, quod sicut voces
significant historiam, sic historia allegoriam et alia vocabula. DOMA tectum
domus. AB IPSIUS FUNDAMENTI PRINCIPIO id est a libro Genesis, qui
est principium historie. 35

IN PRINCIPIO id est in Filio, id est per etc. Hic titulus incipit <scolasticam
historiam>. Sic incipit Geneseos liber. In hoc autem capitulo nichil ultra hanc
clausulam exponit Magister: *in principio creavit Deus celum et terram.* Quod quia
super librum multipliciter exponitur, ostendit Magister diversas acceptiones
huius nominis principii, scilicet pro inchoatione temporis et pro Filio et pro 40
Patre et Spiritu Sancto. Et quia per celum et terram mundus intelligitur, ponit
varias acceptiones huius nominis mundus. Ad ultimum opinionem philosophorum elidit per hoc verbum creavit. Est enim creare de nichilo aliquem
facere. Philosophi autem dicebant mundum ex preiacenti materia factum. PAN
eo quod omnia contineret, sicut ait philosophus, sed mentitus est QUIA 45
ETC...OMNIS CREATURA quia convenientiam habet cum omni. Et vide
quod creare dupliciter dicitur, altero improprie. SUPERIORES a luna sursum.
INANE vocavit locum in quo nunc est mundus. ITERANDUM EST ut scilicet
dicatur: *in principio* id est in Filio *creavit Deus celum et terram*, in principio id est
in inicio temporis. SEMPER ETERNUS id est cum tempore. LICET ENIM 50
Probatio est quod simul omnia facta sint, alioquin contrarie essent auctoritates
quas ponit; sed utraque vera est, quia quodlibet eorum factum est in inicio. IN
PRIMO DIE. Hoc in sequentibus apparebit.

Capitulum sive distinctio, *TERRA AUTEM*, cui premittitur rubrica hec:
De primaria mundi confusione, quam aliter attendit philosophus, aliter 55
theologus. Dicebat philosophus elementa omnia permixta, sicut fex permiscetur vino in musto, ubi est confusio donec paulatim fex residat, sed postea
sortita sunt loca propria: ignis et aër superiorem, terra et aqua inferiorem. In hac
opinione erat qui dicebat: "et corpore in uno frigida pugnabant calidis et
humentia siccis." Theologus dicit quod ab inicio creationis sue singula sunt 60
sortita loca propria. In hoc tamen solo erat confusio, quod aque vaporabiles
erant usque ad sublunarem regionem tenues ad modum nebule. Et vide quod
tribus nominibus appellat materiam illam primordialem quattuor elementorum,
scilicet mundum istum sensibilem, primo nomine terre, secundo nomine abissi,
tertio nomine aquarum, et in fine capituli subdit causam quare. INUTILIS ET 65
INFRUCTUOSA. Glossa est eius quod dixerat inanis. ORNATU SUO quem
postea recepit, ut celum sidera, aër aves, et huiusmodi. Abissus proprie est

profunditas obscura – a sine, byssus genus lini candidissimi – et nascitur in Egypto. SED *TENEBRE.* Respondit ad utramque obiectionem hereticorum,

70 quia tunc nichil erat quod appellaretur hoc nomine tenebre, sicut modo silentium nichil est nisi absencia vocis, nuditas nichil est nisi absencia vestis. Sed modo, inquit, fateor creaturas esse tenebras postquam lux creata est, nam ex obiectu corporis ad lucem habent creari. Unde subdit, OBSCURITAS AUTEM, et tu intellige postea. CATALOGO enumeratione. MATERIAM

75 DOMUS ligna scilicet et lapides strata coram se in area. QUID DE QUO scilicet columpnam, basem vel epistilium. DUCTILEM tamquam ceram mollem in manu artifices. PRO *SUPERFEREBATUR* quod est in littera nostra. SIRA LINGUA que in plerisque consona est Hebreo. IN QUO scilicet in fovendo attenduntur duo scilicet inicium et regimen sive dispositio, quia tunc

80 incipit esse animal in ovo et <disponi> secundum membra, dum illud fovet avicula. MALE quia Spiritum Sanctum nichil aliud intellexit esse quam animam mundi. Descenderat enim in Egyptum, ut annales legeret Egyptiorum, inter quos repperit hoc opus Moysi et quedam apposuit libris suis.

　　Capitulum. *DIXIT QUOQUE DEUS* Dicere Dei tripliciter: pro gignere,

85 ut hic; et disponere, ut: *dixit Dominus Domino meo;* et pro manifestare in effectis: *Quid est facilius dicere, dimittantur tibi peccata tua?* Rubrica: De opere prime diei. Quamvis tamen precedencia fuerunt opus prime diei, id est spacii viginti quattuor horarum, creatio vero lucis proprie dicta est opus prime diei secundum qualitatem scilicet diei illuminate per illam lucem creatam. Veritas enim, inquid,

90 est post creationem premissorum quantulamcumque morulam temporis defluxisse – alioquin nichil esset ad hystoriam, *et tenebre erant super* – et tunc lucem creatam esse in oriente, id est nubem quandam lucidam, que ad modum solis peregit cursum suum usque ad occidentem, et ita *FACTUM EST VESPERE.* Revoluta vero eadem luce per subterius emisperium usque ad

95 ortum, *FACTUM EST MANE,* et ita factus est *DIES UNUS.* TAM FACILE operatus est in creando UT QUIS VERBO id est loquendo, et ita per hoc verbum *DIXIT* innuitur ibi facultas. UT NUMQUAM SIMUL quantum ad distantiam SED SEMPER quantum ad qualitatem. INTELLIGITUR ETIAM HIC id est ex verbo *FIAT LUX,* ac si diceret ad creaturam angelicam. SICUT

100 TAMEN quasi quamvis dixerim noctem dici a nocendo.

　　Capitulum. SECUNDA DIE. Rubrica: De opere secunde diei. *IN MEDIO AQUARUM* superiorum scilicet et inferiorum. ET DICITUR *FIRMA-MENTUM.* Duas assignat inde causas: tum quia firmum et solidum quantum ad materiam, tum quia TERMINUS FIRMUS EST AQUARUM.

105 CONCAMERATIONE id est concavatione. URANON ID EST PALATUM,

eo quod sic concavum, vocant Greci sic celum, ut – *"Pater noster qui es in uranis"* – hoc est in celis. QUIDAM QUARTUM ETC. Et hanc, inquit, opinionem audivi a quibusdam, et vidi scriptam et etiam pictam in Trecensi Ecclesia, ubi ad celum empireum in quadam vitrea baiulis nubibus fertur Christus. Et illud saphirium est et angelis repletum, supra quod est sperula quedam admodum 110 rubicunda. ET POST Repete dictum est; similiter cum dices ET TERCIO. Et notat hic tres modos operandi, scilicet mentaliter, materialiter, essentialiter; illud, quod factum est in materia, istud, quod factum est in essentia. ET CUM HUIUS ETC. Triplicem reddet solutionem huius questionis, unam Iudeorum, aliam a sanctis, tertiam a se, et forsan aliunde. ANGELUS FACTUS EST 115 DIABOLUS a se ipso, et solet, inquit, extra esse glosula: id est Sathael, Lucifer: Sathan, adversarius; El, deus, et invenitur hoc nomen in epistola Clementis tantum. CANTARE CONSUEVERUNT Et hoc, inquit, maxime persequabatur Magister G<uillelmus>, eo quod de dominica cantandum est per totam ebdomadam. ADHUC EST DE OPERE SECUNDE DIEI Adhuc enim 120 dicturus est de aquis. Unde supra mentionem fecerat cum ait: *fecit Deus firmamentum in medio aquarum;* et alibi: *ut divideret aquas ab aquis.*

Capitulum. TERCIA DIE ETC. Rubrica: De opere tercie diei, quod fuit distinctio elementorum scilicet terre et aëris, remotis aquis illis vaporalibus et locatis *IN UNUM* id est in oceanum, quod sicut habes super Ecclesiasten: 125 *protensum est ab oriente in occidentem, et circulares faciens reflexiones, labens per subterraneos meatus, et plerisque locis emergens, creat ex se fontes et flumina.* Rubrica: quantum etiam ad terram; ornatus quidam arborum et herbarum fuit huius diei opus. SOLIDATE Postea sicut, inquit, est videre in panno humectato, quem si applices igni, totam domum obnubilabit, aqua inde evaporans. SUBSEDIT Per 130 concavationem iuxta opinionem Bede. Et vide, inquit, quod pro diversis eventibus et temporibus terra potuit variis censeri nominibus. HUMUS enim PROPRIE DICTA EST cum operiretur aquis, *ARIDA* vero post congregationem aquarum IN UNUM LOCUM, *TERRA* postquam facta sunt gressibilia pedibus quorum cepit teri, TELLUS tempore Cahin quo exerceri cepit ligones 135 tolerando et rastra, SOLUM vero quasi substantiale sit, eo quod solida sit. COMPLETO ERGO OPERE secunde diei et tertie. *GERMINET TERRA* Actualiter et potentialiter, quod factum est sic. PLANTAS SUAS Generale nomen est planta arboris et herbe. FRUCTIFICATIO quia tunc incipiunt frugescere spice campis. 140

A.3: The prefaces and opening chapters of the second version, namely the first revision (accomplished before 1176), of Stephen Langton's course on the *Historia Genesis*.

+Incipit prologus epistolaris+.

REVERENDO PATRI ETC. Premittit Magister prologum epistolarem id est epistolam loco prologi, quam dirigit ad Dominum Senonensem, ut manum correctionis huic operi apponat et favorem suum eidem exhibeat.
5 NOVA CUDERE id est novas expositiones facere, dumtaxat ad edificationem *sint*. QUEDAM INCIDENTIA ut de incendio Troiano et similibus. Legitur enim, inquit, super Esdram quod rex *Persarum proprium scriptorem* cronicorum id est gesta sui temporis et proprium incidentium eorum scilicet que temporibus suis finitimis regionibus emenserant. INSTAR RIVULI
10 quia sicut rivulus non dimittit cursum suum propter incidentia, sic nec ego propositum id est historie cursum. ENNICORUM id est gentilium. Ennos enim grece, gens latine. STILO RUDI scripture nove. LIMA correctione.

IMPERATORIE Prefatio est in qua *est* *descensus* ad litteram per
15 quoddam simile. VEL CONSISTORIUM quod idem est. KALENDARIA id est menstrua vel mensurna. EFFIMERA id est diurna a pisce vel verme, qui hoc nomine censetur et eodem die quo nascitur moritur vel paulo post. Et est *ANNALIS* HYSTORIA de gestis unius anni et supra ut Troiana, quamvis et decennalis dicatur, mensurna de gestis unius mensis et supra, ita quod infra
20 annum ut de Hester, diurna de gestis unius diei *vel* supra ita quod infra mensem est ut de Iudith vel de opere sex dierum, quod alio nomine dicitur cosmographia id est descriptio mundi – cosmos enim mundus – alio exameron ab Augustino, ab exa quod est sex, quia de *opere* sex dierum ibi agitur. QUE PER FACTUM ALIUD FIGURAT. Exemplum est, inquit, non diffinitio.
25 Sumitur enim *allegoria quandoque* a persona ut Isaac significat Christum; quandoque a re que non est persona ut vervex occisus humanitatem passam (persona +enim+ est individua rationalis nature substantia); quandoque a numero ut – *apprehendent septem mulieres virum unum* etc. – id est septem dona gratiarum; quandoque a loco ut per montem in quo docebat Christus

eminentiam virtutum; quandoque a tempore ut – *non sit fuga uestra in hieme* – id 30
est in refrigeratione caritatis; quandoque a facto ut interfectio Golie +a David+,
interfectio Diaboli a Christo. Tropologia est sermo conversivus pertinens ad
mores animi et magis movet quam allegoria, <que> pertinet ad ecclesiam
militantem, anagoge ad triumphantem et ad Deum Trinitatem. Et nota, ~~inquit~~,
quod sicut voces significant historiam, sic historia allegoriam et alia vocabula. 35
DOMA tectum domus. AB IPSIUS FUNDAMENTI PRINCIPIO id est a
libro Genesis, qui est principium historie.

    IN PRINCIPIO id est ~~in~~ Filio, id est PER +et est+ hic titulus: <incipit
scolastica ystoria. Sed non ultra hanc clausulam exponit Magister: *in principio
creavit Deus celum et terram*. Quod quia super librum multipliciter exponitur, 40
ostendit quoque diversas acceptiones huius nominis principii, scilicet vel inicio
temporis, pro Filio et Patre et Spiritu Sancto. Et quia per celum et terram
mundus intelligitur, ponit varias acceptiones huius nominis mundus. Ad
ultimum opiniones philosophorum elidit per hoc verbum creavit. *Cum enim
creare est de nichilo aliud facere, philosophi* dicebant mundum ex preiacenti 45
materia factum. PAN eo quod omnia contineret, sicut ait philosophus>, sed
mentitus est QUIA ETC...OMNIS CREATURA quia convenientiam habet cum omni.
Et vide quod creare dupliciter dicitur, altero improprie. SUPERIORES a luna
sursum. INANE vocavit locum in quo nunc est mundus. ITERANDUM EST ut
scilicet dicatur: *in principio* id est in Filio *creavit Deus celum et terram*, in principio 50
id est in inicio temporis. SEMPER ETERNUS id est cum tempore. LICET ENIM
Probatio est quod simul omnia facta sint, alioquin contrarie essent auctoritates
quas ponit; sed utraque vera est, quia quodlibet eorum factum est in inicio. IN
PRIMO DIE. Hoc in sequentibus apparebit.

    Capitulum sive distinctio, TERRA AUTEM, cui premittitur rubrica hec: De 55
primaria mundi confusione, quam aliter attendit philosophus, aliter theologus.
Dicebat philosophus elementa omnia permixta, sicut fex permiscetur vino in
musto, ubi est confusio donec paulatim fex residat, sed postea sortita sunt
propria loca: ignis et aër superiorem, <terra> et aqua inferiorem. In hac
opinione erat qui dicebat: "et corpore in uno frigida pugnabant calidis et 60
humentia siccis." Theologus dicit quod ab inicio creationis sue singula sunt
sortita loca propria. In hoc tamen solo erat confusio, quod aque vaporabiles
erant usque ad sublunarem regionem tenues ad modum nebule. Et vide quod
tribus nominibus *appellant* materiam illam primordialem quattuor
elementorum, scilicet mundum *illum* sensilem, primo nomine terre, secundo 65
nomine abissi, tertio nomine aquarum, et in fine capituli subdit causam quare.
INUTILIS ET INFRUCTUOSA. Glosa est eius quod dixerat inanis. ORNATU SUO

quem postea recepit, ut celum sidera, aër aves, et huiusmodi. Abissus proprie est profunditas obscura — a sine, byssus genus lini candidissimi — et nascitur in
70 Egypto. SED TENEBRE. Respondit ad utramque obiectionem hereticorum, quia tunc nichil erat quod appellaretur hoc nomine tenebre, **89ra/89rb** sicut <modo> silentium nichil est nisi absencia vocis, +et+ nuditas nichil est nisi absentia vestis. Sed *postmodo*, inquit, fateor creaturas esse tenebras postquam lux creata est, nam ex obiectu corporis ad lucem habent creari. Unde subdit,
75 OBSCURITAS AUTEM, et tu intellige postea. CATALOGO enumeratione. MATERIAM DOMUS ligna scilicet et lapides strata coram se in area. QUID DE QUO scilicet columpnam, basem vel epistilium. DUCTILEM tamquam ceram mollem in manu artifices. PRO SUPERFEREBATUR quod est in littera nostra. SIRA LINGUA que in plerisque consona est Hebreo. IN QUO scilicet in fovendo attenduntur duo
80 scilicet inicium et regimen sive dispositio, quia tunc incipit esse animal in ovo et disponi secundum membra, dum illud fovet avicula. MALE quia Spiritum Sanctum nil aliud intellexit esse quam <animam> mundi. Descenderat enim in Egyptum ut *legeret annales* Egyptiorum, inter quos repperit hoc opus Moysi et *quoddam* apposuit libris suis.
85 Capitulum. DIXIT QUOQUE DEUS ~~Dicere Dei tripliciter: pro gignere, ut hic; et disponere, ut: *dixit Dominus Domino meo;* et pro manifestare in effectis: *Quid est facilius dicere, dimittantur tibi peccata tua?*~~ Rubrica: De opere prime diei. Quamvis tamen precedentia *fuerint* opus prime diei, id est spatii viginti quattuor horarum, creatio vero lucis proprie *dicitur* opus prime diei
90 secundum qualitatem scilicet diei illuminate per *ipsam* lucem creatam. Veritas enim, inquit, est post creationem premissorum quantulamcumque morulam temporis defluxisse — alioquin nichil esset ad historiam, *et tenebre erant super* — et tunc lucem creatam esse in oriente, id est nubem quandam lucidam, que ad modum solis peregit cursum suum usque ad occidentem, et ita FACTUM EST
95 VESPERE. Revoluta vero eadem luce per subterius emisperium usque ad ortum, FACTUM EST MANE, et ita factus est DIES UNUS. TAM FACILE operatus est in creando UT QUIS VERBO id est loquendo, et ita per hoc verbum DIXIT innuitur ibi *facilitas*. UT NUMQUAM SIMUL quantum ad distantiam SED SEMPER quantum ad qualitatem. INTELLIGITUR ETIAM HIC id est ex verbo FIAT LUX, ac si diceret ad
100 creaturam angelicam. SICUT TAMEN quasi quamvis dixerim noctem dici a nocendo.
  Capitulum. SECUNDA DIE. *Et* de opere secunde diei. IN MEDIO AQUARUM superiorum scilicet et inferiorum. ET DICITUR FIRMAMENTUM. Duas assignat inde causas: tum quia firmum et solidum quantum ad materiam, tum quia
105 TERMINUS FIRMUS ~~EST~~ AQUARUM. CONCAMERATIONE id est concavatione.

URANON ID EST PALATUM, eo quod sic concavum, vocant Greci sic celum, ut −
"Pater noster qui es in uranis" − hoc est in celis. QUIDAM QUARTUM ETC. Et hanc,
inquit, opinionem audivi a quibusdam, et vidi scriptam et etiam pictam in
Trecensi Ecclesia, ubi ad celum empireum in quadam vitrea baiulis nubibus
fertur Christus. Et illud saphirium est et angelis repletum, supra quod est   110
sperula ~~quedam~~ admodum rubicunda. ET POST Repete +ut+ dictum est; similiter
cum dices ET TERCIO. Et notat hic tres modos operandi, scilicet mentaliter,
materialiter, +et+ essentialiter; illud, quod factum est in materia, istud, quod
factum est in essentia. ET CUM HUIUS ETC. Triplicem reddet solutionem huius
questionis, unam Iudeorum, aliam a sanctis, tertiam a se, et forsan aliunde.   115
ANGELUS FACTUS EST DIABOLUS a se ipso, et solet, inquit, extra esse glosula: id
est Sathael, Lucifer: *Satan*, adversarius; *Hel*, deus, et invenitur hoc nomen
in epistola Clementis tantum. CANTARE CONSUEVERUNT Et hoc, inquit, maxime
persequabatur Magister G<uillelmus>, eo quod de dominica cantandum est per
totam ebdomadam. ADHUC EST DE OPERE SECUNDE DIEI Adhuc enim dicturus est   120
de aquis. Unde supra mentionem fecerat cum ait: *fecit Deus firmamentum in medio
aquarum;* et alibi: *ut divideret aquas ab aquis.*
   ~~Capitulum~~. TERCIA DIE ETC. Rubrica: De opere tercie diei, quod fuit
distinctio elementorum scilicet terre et aëris, remotis aquis illis vaporalibus et
locatis *IN UNUM* id est ~~in~~ oceanum, quod sicut habes super Ecclesiasten: *protensum*   125
est ab orientem in occidentem, et circularens faciens reflexiones, labens per subterraneos
meatus, et plerisque locis emergens, creat ex se fontes et flumina. Rubrica: quantum
etiam ad terram; ornatus quidam arborum et herbarum fuit opus huius diei.
SOLIDATE Postea sicut, inquit, est videre in panno humectato, quem si applices
igni, totam domum obnubilabit, aqua inde evaporans. SUBSEDIT Per   130
cavationem iuxta opinionem Bede. Et vide, inquit, quod pro diversis
eventibus et temporibus terra potuit variis censeri nominibus. HUMUS enim
PROPRIE DICTA EST cum operiretur aquis, *ARIDA* vero post congregationem
aquarum IN UNUM LOCUM, *TERRA* postquam facta sunt gressibilia pedibus
quorum cepit teri, TELLUS tempore Chaim quo exerceri cepit tollerando ligones   135
et rastra, SOLUM vero quasi substantiale *est ei*, eo quod solida sit.
COMPLETO ~~ERGO~~ secunde diei OPERE et tertie. *GERMINET TERRA*
Actualiter et potentialiter, quod sic factum est. PLANTAS SUAS Generale nomen
est planta arboris et herbe. FRUCTIFICATIO quia tunc incipiunt frugescere spice
~~campis~~.   140

A.4: The prefaces and opening chapters of the third version, namely the second revision (accomplished before 1193), of Stephen Langton's course on the *Historia Genesis*.

+*Fluvius egrediebatur de loco voluptatis qui dividebatur in quattuor capita*: uni est nomen Gion, alii Physon, tertio Tigris, quarto Eufrates. Locus voluptatis est Spiritus Sanctus, in quo est vera et summa plenitudo voluptatis. Fluvius inde egrediens est Sacra Scriptura a Spiritu Sancto edita et eodem summi Dei digito
5 depunctata. Dividitur autem fluvius ille in quattuor flumina id est Sacra Scriptura in quattuor species scilicet historiam, allegoriam, anagogem, tropologiam. Prima istarum scilicet hystoria significatur per Gion et convenienter. Gion enim interpretatur terre hiatus. Qui vero solam historiam sequebantur, scilicet antiqui veteris synagoge, sola terrena expectabant. Historia
10 dicitur ab ystoron, quod est videre vel gesticulari. Narrat enim de eis tantum que gesta sunt et visa. Secunda scilicet allegoria significatur per Physon. Phison interpretatur oris mutatio. Mutatur quodammodo os in allegoria, quia aliud dicitur et aliud significatur. Unde dicitur allegoria ab alleon, quod est alienum. Tercia scilicet anagoge significatur per Tygrim. Tygris interpretatur velox.
15 Veloci autem opus est ingenio et acuto ut intelligantur ea de quibus est anagoge scilicet unitatem in Trinitate et Trinitatem in unitate et ordines angelorum. Dicitur autem anagoge ab ana, quod est sursum, et goge, quod est ductio; unde anagoge quasi sursum ductio, unde ysagoga id est introductio. Quarta scilicet tropologia significatur per Eufraten. Frugifer autem est interpretatio huius
20 nominis Eufrates quare significat tropologiam. Magnus enim est fructus in illis in quibus consistit tropologia scilicet in morum sinceritate. Dicitur enim tropologia a tropos, quod est conversio, et logos, quod est sermo. Inde tropologia id est sermo conversus ad nostram eruditionem. Tribus omissis agit Magister de sola historia.+
25 *Premittit autem epistolam, quam dirigit archiepiscopo Remensi quondam Senonensi*, +in qua materiam prelibat, causam operis suscepti assignat, ordinem et modum etiam declarat+. *Historie vero dicit se principaliter insistere, licet quedam incidentia ethnicorum id est gentilium ut historiam Troianorum et huiusmodi frequentius interponat, ubi comparat se Magister rivulo qui, licet

diverticula que secus alveum invenit repleat, cursum tamen solitum non 30
dimittat.* +Hec epistola est prologus ante rem; demum ponit proemium in re,
in quo Sacram Scripturam dividendo ad illam speciem de qua intendit
descendit+.

*Sic ergo incipit: IMPERATORIE MAIESTATIS. In hoc prohemio quandam
similitudinem assignat inter aliquem mundanum imperatorem et summum 35
Deum, quorum uterque tres habet mansiones et ab eis diversa divinorum
vocabula sortiuntur.* +Nota quod de cenaculo Domini ponit hoc exemplum:
ambulavimus in domo Domini cum consensu. Sed cum in hoc exemplo non ponatur
nomen cenaculi sed nomen domus, non videtur exemplum circumquaque
conveniens. Melius ergo ut nobis videtur pro exemplo cenaculi quod pro Sacra 40
Scriptura ponitur diceret: *in loco pascue ibi me collocavit.* Pascua enim Sacram
significat Scripturam.+ +CENACULI TRES SUNT PARTES. Videtur quod quattuor
essent ponende ad hoc, ut propria esset similitudo inter cenaculum et
Scripturam. Scripture enim sunt superius in quattuor partes assignate.
Asserimus quod dici potest una pars cenaculi aliam continere, ita et una pars 45
Sacre Scripture aliam, ut allegoria anagogen.+ *ANNALIS HISTORIA. Que narrat
gesta unius anni vel plurium usque ad decem; unde hystoria Troianorum dici
potest annalis.* *KALENDARIA. Que narrat gesta unius mensis vel plurium infra
annum ut hystoria Iudith.* *EPHIMERA. Unius diei vel plurium infra mensem,
sicut a quodam pisce qui tantum per unum diem vel paucos durat.* 50
*ALLEGORIA...PER FACTUM ALIUD +FACTUM+ FIGURAT. Non est hec sufficiens
assignatio allegorie. Sumitur enim quandoque a persona, a loco, a tempore, a
re, a negotio, ut per mortem Golie significatur destructio diaboli, a numero, ut
per quinarium, qui infaustus est numerus, significantur quinque sensus.*
*Quattuor premisse species Sacre Scripture circa unum notari possunt: 55
Ierusalem quantum ad hystoriam civitas terrestris, allegorice est ecclesia
militans, anagogice ecclesia triumphans, tropologice anima fidelis.* ~~AB IPSIUS
FUNDAMENTI PRINCIPIO id est a libro Genesis, qui est principium historie~~.
+PRINCIPIUM LOQUENDI. Proposuerat enim forsitan componere allegorias.
Quod tamen non invenimus fecisse Magistrum.+ 60
  +Historia scolastica.+

*IN PRINCIPIO ERAT VERBUM. Convenienter notantur in hoc PRINCIPIO duo
Cherubyn sese respicere id est Vetus et Novum Testamentum. Vetus enim
Testamentum sic inchoat Moyses: *In principio creavit Deus celum et terram.*
Iohannes vero Evangelium suum, quod hic sumimus quasi pro initio Novi 65
Testamenti, sic: *In principio erat Verbum.* Hec duo Testamentorum initia
coniungit Magister dicens: *IN PRINCIPIO ERAT VERBUM ET VERBUM ERAT IN*

PRINCIPIO, IN QUO VERBO ET PER QUOD *CREAVIT* MUNDUM, *IN PRINCIPIO* itaque id est in Filio *CREAVIT DEUS* MUNDUM, et hoc resume, *IN PRINCIPIO* TEMPORIS.

70 Dicitur autem Deus creare in Filio vel per Filium, quia Filius est eiusdem essentie cum Patre et eorum operatio est indivisa. Sumitur ergo hoc nomen principio semel positum equivoce in initio Geneseos, scilicet pro Filio Dei et pro temporis initio.* *CREAVIT* MUNDUM. Sive pro empireo celo mundum accipias sive mundum appelles sensilem, qui sensilis dicitur ad differentiam empirei celi,

75 quod propter suam subtilitatem nullo sensu percipitur, seu etiam mundum appelles sublunarem regionem, que est pars sensilis mundi. Convenienter et vere dicitur *CREAVIT*. Creari enim est ex nichilo fieri. Si mundum accipias pro homine, qui microcosmos dicitur a Grecis, id est minor mundus, non dicitur proprie *CREAVIT* MUNDUM, id est hominem, nisi verbum creandi sumas pro

80 verbo plasmandi. Immo fecit hominem ex materia preiacenti iam creata. Inter opinionem Platonis et Aristotelis hec erat convenientia, quod uterque voluit tria esse ab eterno. Hec erat differentia, quod Plato dixit Deum esse operatum in ylem per ydeas, id est formas. Aristoteles vero dixit mundum esse formatum et ydeis distinctum ab eterno sicut modo est. Licet ergo dicat Magister Pla-

85 tonem dixisse duo fuisse ab eterno, scilicet Deum et mundum, per mundum tamen duo intelligimus scilicet materiam et formam.* ~~PAN eo quod omnia contineret, sicut ait philosophus>, sed mentitus est QUIA ETC…OMNIS CREATURA quia convenientiam habet cum omni. Et vide quod creare dupliciter dicitur, altero improprie. SUPERIORES a luna sursum.~~ *INANE. Est vacuitas que remaneret

90 me recedente in loco quem ego repleo intellecto quod nichil subintraret, nec aër scilicet nec aliud.* +ATOMI. Corpora sunt vix perceptibilia aliquo sensu. PROPHETAVIT. Est enim prophetia de preterito sicut de futuro.+ *SOLUS DEUS EST ETERNUS sed forsitan quedam fuerunt ab eterno que non sunt eterna ut enuntiabilia. Require aliunde differentiam inter perpetuum, sempiternum,

95 temporale sive perhenne, et eternum.* *QUOD SIMUL FACTUM EST. Simul creavit Deus celum et terram, alioquin contrarie essent iste due auctoritates: *initio tu Domine terram fundasti et opera manuum tuarum sunt celi*, et quod hic dicitur, *in principio creavit Deus celum et terram*.* *QUANDAM DISPOSITIONEM. Que notatur in sequenti capitulo ubi dicit: *divisit lucem ac tenebras*.*

100 ~~Capitulum sive distinctio, TERRA AUTEM, cui premittitur rubrica hee~~: De primaria mundi confusione.

TERRA AUTEM. Nota tria vocabula quibus appellat primariam mundi materiam: terra, aqua, abyssus. Quare vero eam indifferenter his nominibus appellat ipse in fine capituli manifestat. Abyssus dicitur ab a et byssus; byssus est

105 species lini candidissimi. Unde adhuc dicitur omnis locus abyssus qui sine

claritate est. Philosophi vero etiam aliis nominibus predictam materiam appellant: silvam, ylem, chaos, que vel proprie vel translative bene eam significant.* *INUTILIS quantum ad illum statum. INFRUCTUOSA tunc non habens fructum, sicut dicitur planta inutilis et infructuosa dum est tenella.* *VACUA ORNATU SUO id est ornatu quem erat habitura. Erat autem materia illa 110 quasi mustum in quo purus liquor superenatat, turbulenta subsident. Unde quidam: "levis ignis in altum, terra gravis pessum, mediotenus humor et aër."* *QUOD VERO DICTUM EST *TENEBRE ERANT*, dogmatizaverunt quidam tenebras esse eternas. Erant enim tenebre, cum fieret mundus. Asserimus illos deceptos fuisse. Non enim habetur: "tenebre fuerunt cum fieret mundus" – hoc enim 115 esset <falsum> – sed *TENEBRE ERANT*, quod quidem verum est. Oritur hic questio utrum tenebre sint aliquid. Quidam dicunt quod non. Huiusmodi enim nomina, tenebre, nuditas, nichil ponunt; immo privant potius, sicut hec nomina: carentia, absentia. Pro qua opinione facere videtur quod dicit Magister: "tenebre nichil aliud erant quam lucis absentia." Talia ergo nomina 120 significant aliquid sed nichil copulant nec appellant, sicut hoc nomen falsum, cum dicitur aliquid est falsum. Significat enim falsitatem sed nichil copulat. Significat etiam veritatem id est dat intelligi more nominis relativi. Si enim aliquid est falsum, oportet quod aliquid est verum, cuius respectu dicitur aliquid falsum esse. Similiter cum dicitur "homo est malus," hoc nomen malus nichil 125 predicat ibi vel copulat. Significat tamen id est dat intelligi bonam naturam quam privat malus. Idem dicunt de his nominibus, tenebre, nuditas, scilicet quod hoc nomen nichil copulat vel appellat. Dat tamen lucem intelligi. Unde hec argumentatio probabilis est: locus est tenebrosus, ergo lux fuit futura. Nobis autem videtur quod non potest dici de hoc nomine tenebre quod dicitur de his 130 nominibus, malus, falsum, que sunt adiectiva, quia hoc nomen tenebre substantivum est. Et cum non sit nomen figmenti ut chimera, aliquid debet appellare. Dicimus ergo quod tenebre sunt aliqua, alioquin nichil esset dictu: *TENEBRE ERANT*. Et quod Dominus *DIVISIT LUCEM AC TENEBRAS* – et etiam aliter non posset relatio fieri ad hoc nomen tenebre, nisi aliquid supponeret – nostram 135 opinionem confirmat.* *QUOD IN CATALOGO id est enumeratione creaturarum dicitur: *Benedicite, lux et tenebre, Domino.** ~~MATERIAM DOMUS ligna scilicet et lapides strata coram se in area. QUID DE QUO scilicet columpnam, basem vel epistilium. DUCTILEM tamquam ceram mollem in manu artifices. PRO SUPER-FEREBATUR quod est in littera nostra. SIRA LINGUA que in plerisque consona est~~ 140 ~~Hebreo.~~ +Quod autem dicit Magister quod tenebre nichil quam lucis absentia, intellige de tenebris que fuerant primo die ante lucem creatam; nichil enim erant. Postea vero sunt tenebre create a Deo quando lux est creata; illas dicimus

esse aliquas.+ +QUIDAM IRRIDENT DEUM VETERIS TESTAMENTI quod creasset prius
145 tenebras quam lucem. Irrideant heretici. Nos dicimus hoc ad litteram verum
esse et mystice bene convenit. Dominus enim in tenebrosis id est peccatoribus
facit fulgere lucem gratiarum.+ *FOVEBAT Hoc verbo notatur duplex sedulitas
scilicet producendi fetus et custodiendi, que etiam videbantur esse in Deo per
effectum.* ~~MALE quia Spiritum Sanctum nil aliud intellexit esse quam~~
150 ~~<animam> mundi. Descenderat enim in Egyptum ut *legeret annales*~~
~~Egyptiorum, inter quos repperit hoc opus Moysi et *quoddam* apposuit libris~~
~~suis.~~
~~Capitulum.~~ *De opere prime diei*.
DIXIT *AUTEM* DEUS +FIAT LUX+ ~~Rubrica: De opere prime diei~~. Quamvis
155 ~~tamen~~ precedentia fuerint opus prime diei, id est spacii viginti quattuor
horarum que pro primo die sumuntur, creatio *tamen* lucis proprie dicitur
opus prime diei secundum qualitatem scilicet diei illuminate per *ipsam* lucem
creatam, *id est nubem lucidam, et sic in illo spatio quod computatur pro primo
die prius erant *tenebre* quam *lux*.* +DIXIT AUTEM DEUS FIAT LUX id est verbum
160 mentale sive mentis conceptum, qui est ipsius Filius. GENUIT IN QUO et per
quem operatus est lucem et omnia. Nota quod quando aliquis profert verbum,
potest dici gignere verbum quod in mente concipit, sed Spiritus, qui non
loquitur nec instrumenta loquendi habet, quomodo gignit verbum? Asserimus
quod a<nimam> vel illum spiritum gignere verbum est ipsum cogitare vel
165 habere aliquid mente conceptum ab eterno. Hoc modo dicitur Deus genuisse
Verbum, id est habuisse mentis conceptum ab eterno, in quo et per quem omnia
creavit. Illud enim verbum mentale est Filius Dei.+ *TAM FACILE supple *fecit* UT
QUIS VERBO diceret, et sic ostenditur facilitas creandi.* +VIDERI FECIT angelis,
qui iam erant creati.+ *UT NUMQUAM SIMUL Hoc potius refer ad qualitatem
170 quam ad locorum distantiam.* +*APPELLAVIT DIEM* A DIAN GRECO id est previdit
esse appellandam.+ *FACTUM EST VESPERE* Prius fuit factum vespere quam mane.
Erat enim ordo talis: nubes illa lucida revoluta est ab oriente in occidentem, et
sic FACTUM EST VESPERE. Eadem revoluta est per inferius emisperium ad orientem, FACTUM EST MANE, et sic DIES UNUS.* +Ex quo patet quod mane secunde
175 diei est pars diei precedentis. Unde hec argumentatio non valet: est mane huius
diei, ergo pars est huius diei. Instantia: hec est tua mater, ergo est tua mulier.
Non. Licet enim sit mulier alterius, tamen est mulier alterius mater. Ita et mane
alterius diei est mane alterius pars.+
~~Capitulum.~~ *~~SECUNDA DIE~~.* ~~Et~~ de opere secunde diei.
180 *SECUNDA DIE* +DISPOSUIT...REPLETUM SANCTIS ANGELIS Sed quid potest
repleri rebus simplicibus? Tenetur ergo improprie repletum. Habundantiam

tamen vult notare. SANCTIS Non quod essent tunc confirmati, sed SANCTIS id est caritatem habentibus.+ IN MEDIO AQUARUM superiorum ~~scilicet~~, +que sunt super ipsum+, et inferiorum, +que sunt sub ipso. Quare sint aque sub firmamento vel super firmamentum non solvit Magister sed Deo solvendum remittit+. +NE 185
IGNE SOLVI POSSENT Hoc est intelligendum de aquis que sunt sub firmamento, que possunt dissolvi igne supposito, qui calet et urit, nisi ita essent congelate. Superiores enim aque ita sunt congelate, quod non possunt dissolvi igne, nec etiam ignis ethereus ad illas potest pervenire. Ignis vero superior nec urit nec dissolvit. Unde Plato de illo inquit: "est mulcebris, non peremptorius."+ 190
*QUOD AUTEM DICTUM EST, *FIAT* ETC., nota: fit aliquid mentaliter, fit materialiter, fit essentialiter, quod notatur per *FIAT, FECIT, FACTUM EST.** ~~QUIDAM~~
~~QUARTUM ETC. Et hanc, inquit, opinionem audivi a quibusdam, et vidi scriptam~~
~~et etiam pictam in Trecensi Ecclesia, ubi ad celum empireum in quadam vitrea~~
~~baiulis nubibus fertur Christus. Et illud saphirium est et angelis repletum, supra~~ 195
~~quod est sperula admodum rubicunda.~~ *ET CUM HUIUS DIEI BONUM Innuit Magister querendum quare non benedixit Dominus operi secunde diei sicut et prime operi. Ipsemet solvit tripliciter. Ultimam solutionem potius approbamus, scilicet quod ideo non benedixit, quia quoddam opus inchoaverat secundo die, quod non eodem consumavit. Immo in tercio die complevit videlicet aquarum 200
dispositionem vel collectionem, que iam create fuerant. Reservavit ergo Dominus benedictionem suam operi consummato.* ~~ANGELUS FACTUS EST DIABOLUS a~~
~~se ipso, et solet, inquit, extra esse glosula: id est Sathael, Lucifer: *Satan*, adver-~~
~~sarius; *Hel*, deus, et invenitur hoc nomen in epistola Clementis tantum.~~
~~CANTARE CONSUEVERUNT Et hoc, inquit, maxime persequabatur Magister~~ 205
~~G<uillelmus>, eo quod de dominica cantandum est per totam ebdomadam.~~
+Solet in quibusdam codicibus in hac distinctione inveniri quedam notula sic incipiens: "quidam querunt etc."+
   TERCIA DIE Agitur in hoc capitulo de distinctione elementorum scilicet terre et aëris remotis aquis vaporabilibus et locatis VAPORABILES id est tenues et 210
subtiles sicut vapor aque et vini quasi fumus tenuis et rarus. IN UNUM LOCUM id est occeanum vel UNUM LOCUM id est in viscera terre, que accipit pro uno loco. SPATIUM AËRIS…VAPORABILES SOLIDATE MODICUM…LOCUM sicut videri potest in panno humectato, quem si igni appropies totam domum obnubilabit aqua inde vaporanti quasi fumo. subsedit per cavationem in quibusdam locis. 215
PROPRIE HUMUS DICTA EST ab humore. SOLUM a solidate, quod gallice dicitur soil, et dicitur de terra humida quod non habet soil. Rationes aliorum nominum patent in littera. COMPLETO OPERE AQUARUM quod etiam ad secundum diem pertinebat, in quo create sunt aque. ET ADDIDIT ALIUD pertinens ad tercium

220 diem, et tunc benedixit simul toti operi sicut habetur ex premissis. SED IN MAR-
TIO FACTUM DOGMATIZAT ECCLESIA quod quidem verum est, sed arbores non
fecit Deus in forma plantarum tenellarum; immo fecit eas tunc ferentes fructus suos. Unde quidam decepti dixerunt mundum creatum esse in autumpno.
Sed tunc erant magne arbores principia plantarum, sicut modo plante sunt prin-
225 cipia magnarum arborum. Et ne mireris. Dominus enim magister est et dominus nature. NOTA CUM PRIMO in hoc capitulo invenis differentiam inter hec
nomina: SEMEN, SEMENTIS, SEMENTIVUM. In libro Fastorum sementinum est
dum est in ipso semine ut granum sementis dum est in calamo, et sementiva est
nulla reperta dies. NEC VOS MOVEAT Hic innuit dispositionem aëris quam
230 notavimus a principio huius capituli. Hec predicta sufficiant de creatione et dispositione quas operatus est Dominus in primo die, secundo, et tercio.

B.1: The prefaces and opening chapters of Comestor's *Historia evangelica*.

Capitulum I. Incipit historia de conceptione precursoris Christi.
FUIT AUTEM IN DIEBUS HERODIS REGIS IUDEE fluxis annis regni eius undetriginta [id est xxviiii, et est una dictio] SACERDOS NOMINE ZACHARIAS DE VICE
ABIA ET UXOR EIUS AARONITA NOMINE ELISABETH. David enim ampliare volens
cultum Dei viginti quattuor instituit summos sacerdotes, quorum unus tan-   5
tum maior erat. Qui princeps sacerdotum dicebatur. Statuit autem sedecim
viros de Eleazar et octo de Ithamar, et SECUNDUM SORTES dedit unicuique ebdomadam VICIS SUE, [ne forte inter eos esset contentio de septimanis, quia una
erat melior altera, id est lucrosior]. Habuit autem Abias octavam ebdomadam,
de cuius genere ZACHARIAS. Cum in die propitiacionis INCENSUM PONERET,   10
PREDIXIT EI ANGELUS NASCITURUM SIBI FILIUM DE UXORE. QUI CONSIDERANS
STERILITATEM UXORIS SUE ET UTRIUSQUE SENECTUTEM NON CREDIDIT, ET OB
HOC OBMUTUIT USQUE AD DIEM PARTUS. NOMEN QUOQUE PUERI ET MAGNIFI-
CENTIAM CUM ABSTINENTIA EI INDICAVIT. CONCEPIT AUTEM ELISABETH ET
OCCULTABAT SE MENSIBUS QUINQUE.   15

Capitulum II. De conceptione Salvatoris.
MENSE AUTEM SEXTO MISSUS EST ANGELUS GABRIEL IN NAZARETH AD
MARIAM DESPONSATAM IOSEPH. CUMQUE EA SALUTATA DIXISSET EAM PARITURAM
IESUM FILIUM ALTISSIMI QUESISSETQUE QUOMODO HOC FIERET, cum se non cog-
nituram virum in animo vovisset, nisi aliter Deus disponeret, ADDIDIT ANGELUS   20
NON DE VIRO SED OPERE SPIRITUS SANCTI CONCEPTURAM, ET ETIAM CONCEPISSE
COGNATAM SUAM ELISABETH SIBI INDICAVIT. Permixte enim erant tribus sacer-
dotalis et regia, nam et Aaron uxorem habuit de Iuda Helisabeth sororem Naa-
son, et Ioiada pontifex Iocabet filiam regis Ioram. ET AIT MARIA: FIAT MIHI
SECUNDUM VERBUM TUUM, et statim conceptus est Christus de virgine plenus   25
homo in anima et carne, ita tamen quod liniamenta corporis et membrorum
visibus discerni non possent. Creditur autem conceptus octavo Kalendas
Apriles, et revolutis triginta tribus annis eadem die mortuus est. [Unde Iudei

transgressi sunt illud: *non coques hedum in lacte matris sue*, id est non occides Chris-
30 tum in die conceptionis sue.]

Capitulum III. De ortu precursoris.

EXURGENS AUTEM MARIA…ABIIT IN CIVITATEM IUDA. Iuda nomen est regni, non tribus. Ierusalem enim erat in tribu Beniamin, per quam forte transivit ad oppidum in quo dicunt tunc Zacharias habitasse quarto miliario a Ierusalem. Et
35 ibi natum Iohannem, et legitur in libro Iustorum quod beata Virgo primo eum levavit a terra. ET CUM SALUTASSET ELISABETH *EXULTAVIT INFANS IN UTERO EIUS.* ET CUM MATREM DOMINI SUI ET BEATAM PROPHETARET *ELISABETH,* EDIDIT DOMINO MARIA CANTICUM DICENS: *MAGNIFICAT ANIMA MEA DOMINUM ETC.* *MANSIT AUTEM MARIA* IBI *TRIBUS MENSIBUS* MINISTRANS COGNATE SUE DONEC
40 PARERET, ET TUNC REDIIT *IN DOMUM SUAM.*

OCTAVO AUTEM *DIE* CUM CIRCUMCIDERETUR PUER, ET VOCARENT *EUM NOMINE PATRIS* SUI ZACHARIE, AIT *MATER: IOHANNES EST NOMEN EIUS.* ID IPSUM SCRIPSIT ET PATER SUMPTO PUGILLARI. Est autem pugillaris tabella que pugno potest includi, vel calamus scriptoris. ET *APERTUM EST OS* ZACHARIE, ET
45 PROPHETANS CANTICUM FECIT DOMINO: *BENEDICTUS DOMINUS DEUS ISRAEL ETC.* [Hec duo cantica non cantantur in ecclesia eo ordine quo sunt edita. Prius enim cantatur, quod secundo est editum. Quia enim in cantico Zacarie legitur, *et erexit cornu salutis nobis*, quod est factum in resurrectione Domini, quasi loquitur ad puerum dum fuit in aurora solis, ideo canitur in Laudibus.[1] Et quia legitur
50 in cantico Virginis, *respexit humilitatem ancille sue*, Ecclesie scilicet et ipsius Marie, quod quidem factum est in sexta etate, et agit de incarnatione ibi: *suscepit Israel puerum suum*, et ideo canitur ad Vesperas in sexto scilicet officio diurno. Tercium canticum Simeonis, quod sequitur, canitur in septimo officio, id est Comple-torio, quia orat se dimitti in pace, quod fit in septima quiescentium. Et quia hec
55 evangelica cantica sunt, ideo stando cantamus ea.][2] *PUER AUTEM CRESCEBAT ET CONFORTABATUR SPIRITU. ET ERAT IN* DESERTIS LOCIS *USQVE AD DIEM OSTENSIO-NIS AD ISRAEL.*

REVERTENS AUTEM MARIA NAZARETH *INVENTA EST* A SPONSO *IN UTERO HABENS DE SPIRITU SANCTO.* QUI NOLENS *EAM TRADUCERE* IN CONIUGEM,
60 *OCCULTE VOLUIT EAM DIMITTERE. IN SOMNIS* AUTEM ADMONITUS EST AB ANGELO, UT ACCIPERET EAM IN *CONIUGEM.* Et ne suspicaretur adulterium, CONCEPTUM PUERUM *DE SPIRITU SANCTO* INDICAVIT. ET UT *IESUM* VOCARET PRECEPIT, QUIA *SALVUM* FACERET *POPULUM SUUM A PECCATIS EORUM.* Ex hoc cognovit Ioseph Deum nasciturum, qui solus peccata dimittit, ET ACCIPIENS SPONSAM IN
65 UXOREM, CUM VIRGINE VIRGO PERMANSIT. Habuit autem Virgo virum, ne

gravida infamaretur, et ut viri solatio ministerioque frueretur,[3] et ut Diabolo occultaretur Dei partus.

1{Laudes matutine in memoriam Dominice resurrectionis fiunt. Inde est quod iubilus ille, qui in fine antiphonarum cantatur et ardens desiderium future resurrectionis notat. In aliquibus ecclesiis tacetur in matutinis laudibus. Habita 70 enim resurrectione nil amplius expectamus.}

2 [[Dum evangelium audimus, tria observamus: stamus spe future beatitudinis, que nobis eo promittitur; disco operta capita habemus, quia nuda et aperta sunt mysteria evangelii; tacemus, quia nichil amplius quam eo quod evangelio nobis promittitur expectamus.]] 75

3 [[Ad representandum ministerium Ioseph in quibusdam ecclesiis quam provecte persone ministrant in natum Domini.]]

Capitulum IV. De descriptione orbis.

IN DIEBUS ILLIS EXIIT EDICTUM A CAESARE AUGUSTO UT DESCRIBERETUR UNIVERSUS ORBIS. Volens Caesar scire numerum regionum in orbe que Romane 80 suberant ditioni, numerum civitatum in qualibet regione, numerum quoque capitum in qualibet civitate, preceperat ut de suburbanis oppidis et vicis et pagis ad suam confluerent homines civitatem, et maxime ubicumque habitarent ad civitatem convenirent unde trahebant originem, et quisque denarium argenteum − pretii nummorum decem usualium, unde et denarius dicebatur − pre- 85 sidi provincie tradens, se subditum Romano imperio profiteretur. Nam et nummus[2] imaginem preferebat Cesaris et superscriptionem nominis, et quia numerus eorum qui censicapites[1] ferebantur certo determinabantur numero et redigebatur in scriptis, ideo professio huiusmodi descriptio est vocata.

HEC DESCRIPTIO PRIMA FACTA EST A PRESIDE SYRIE CIRINO. PRIMA dicta est 90 quantum ad Cirinum Syrie presidem. Quia enim Iudea in umbilico terre habitabilis esse zone dicitur, provisum est ut in ea inchoaretur, et deinde per circumstantes nationes alii presides prosequerentur. Vel forte PRIMA universalis, quia alie precesserant particulares. Vel forte *PRIMA* capitum in civitate fiebat a preside, secunda civitatum in regione a legato Cesaris, tercia regionum in orbe 95 coram Cesare. Hic primum Iudea facta est stipendiaria Romanis. Hec descriptio fieri quot [id est singulis] annis videtur, quia in Evangelio legitur: *magister vester non solvit hoc anno tributum.*

ASCENDIT AUTEM ET IOSEPH A NAZARETH IN BETHLEEM, EO QUOD ESSET DE DOMO ET FAMILIA DAVID, UT PROFITERETUR CUM MARIA UXORE SUA PREGNANTE. 100 Si mulieres profitebantur, iungendum est sic: *UT PROFITERETUR CUM MARIA.* Si soli viri, sic est ordo: *ASCENDIT IOSEPH CUM MARIA.*

1 [[Sunt qui dicunt censi capite esse unam dictionem tercie declinationis et ablativi casus, et tunc sic exponitur quia numerus eorum qui ferebantur id est 105 referebantur censi capite id est numeratione capitis. Alii item dicunt qualis sit una dictio prime declinationis.]]

2 [[Ab isto nummo dicta fuit era que scribitur in tabula Dionysii et in kalendariis ecclesie. Era singulorum annorum est constituta a Cesare Augusto, quando primum exegit ac Romanum orbem descripsit. Dicta est era ex eo quod 110 omnis orbis ei professus est rei publice.]]

Capitulum V. De ortu Salvatoris.

FACTUM EST AUTEM CUM ESSENT IBI PEPERIT VIRGO *PRIMOGENITUM FILIUM SUUM*, non post quem alius sed ante quem nullus, *ET PANNIS INVOLUTUM RECLINAVIT EUM IN PRESEPIO, QUIA NON ERAT EI ALIUS LOCUS IN DIVERSORIO.* [Dici-115 tur quia fenum in quo Iesus iacuit delatum est Rome ab Helena et est in Ecclesia Sancte Marie Maioris. Infra Basilicam non longe a presepio quiescit Ieronimus; Paula quoque et Eustochium in Bethleem quiescunt.] Difficile erat pauperibus pro frequentia multorum qui ob id ipsum convenerant vacuas invenire domos, et in communi transitu qui erat inter duas domos operimen-120 tum habens, quod diversorium dicitur, se receperunt. Sub quo cives vel ad colloquendum vel ad convisendum in diebus ocii vel pro aëris intemperie divertebant. Forte ibi Ioseph presepium fecerat et bovi et asino quos secum duxerat, in quo repositus est Iesus. Ad quod quidam referunt illud Isaie: *cognovit bos possessorem suum et asinus presepe domini sui*, et illud Abaccuch: *in medio duorum ani-125 malium cognosceris*. Et in picturis ecclesiarum, que sunt quasi libri laicorum, hoc representatur nobis.

Capitulum VI. De natu domini.

Natus est autem Salvator anno regni Augusti Cesaris quadragesimo secundo. Annos enim duodecim qui a morte Iulii fluxerant usque ad Actium 130 bellum regno Augusti communeramus. Anno vero regni Herodis trigesimo universo orbe paccato natus est Dominus, [Olympiadis[1] centesime octogesime tertie anno tertio, ab urbe condita septingentesimo quinquagesimo secundo]. Natus est autem nocte dominice diei, [quia si tabulam compoti retro percurras, invenies eius anni concurrentem quinarium regularem ianuarii 135 ternarium quibus iunctis et sublatis septem unum remanet. Itaque kalendis ianuarii in Dominica invenies, quod occurrit] [ab hoc, quia kalende Aprilis fuerunt sexta feria post mortem Iesu. In anno eodem sequens dies nativitatis eius fuit in dominica et idem fuit in anno conceptionis et nativitatis.][2] Nam eadem die qua *dixit fiat lux et facta est lux*, visitavit nos oriens ex alto. Inchoata est 140 vero secundum quosdam sexta etas a nativitate Christi, ut secundum Apostolum qui ait: *cum venerit plenitudo temporis etc.*, secundum alios a die qua baptizatus est propter vim regenerativam datam aquis, secundum alios a passione, quia tunc aperta est porta et inchoata est septima etas quiescentium. Fluxerant quidem ab Adam anni quinque milia centum nonaginta sex, ab Abraham bis mille duodecim [secundum septuaginta, secundum Hebreos vero longe 145 pauciores.]

1 [[Olympus fuit mons iuxta Elidom civitatem ubi quattuor annis transpositis ludos exercebant, et ideo aliquando quarto aliquando quinto anno leguntur facti.]]

2 [[Rome templum pacis corruit, fons olei erupit. Cesar preceperat, ne quis 150 eum dominum vocaret. Dum quadam die Cesar ovans urbem ingrederetur hora tertia instar arcus celestis orbem sol ambire visus est.]]

Capitulum VII. De canticu angelorum et circumcisione Domini.

ET PASTORES ERANT UNO MILIARIO A BETHLEEM *IN REGIONE EADEM CUSTO-DIENTES VIGILIAS SUPER GREGEM SUUM.* Mos fuit antiquioribus in utroque sol- 155 sticio vigilias noctis custodire ob solis venerationem, qui forte et apud Iudeos ex usu cohabitantium inoleverat. *ET ECCE ANGELUS[1] DOMINI STETIS IUXTA ILLOS* ANNUNCIANS EIS SALVATOREM NATUM IN BETHLEEM. ET *IN SIGNUM POSITUM* PUERUM *IN PRESEPIO[2]* NUNTIAVIT. ET *FACTA EST CUM ANGELO MULTITUDO* ANGELORUM *DICENTIUM: GLORIA IN EXCELSIS DEO ET IN TERRA PAX HOMINIBUS* 160 *BONE VOLUNTATIS*, quia per Christum glorificatus est Pater. Et facta est pax inter Deum et hominem, inter angelum et hominem, inter Iudeum et gentilem. [In gestis pontificum legitur quod ea que sequuntur evangelica verba Thelesphorus Papa adiecit.] Pro hac multitudine angelorum vel pro grege pastorum volunt quidam locum istum in Michea prophetice dictum turrim Gregis ibi: *et tu* 165 *turris Gregis nebulosa.* Cum iam tamen primo contraxerat hoc nomen locus idem, quia Iacob gregem ibi pavit, cum Rachel parturiret. *ET TRANSEUNTES PASTORES* *USQUE BETHLEEM INVENERUNT VERBUM QUOD FACTUM* ERAT AD EOS. *ET QUI* AUDIEBANT EOS MIRABANTUR SUPER HIS QUE DICEBANTUR *A PASTORIBUS AD* EOS. *MARIA AUTEM CONSERVABAT OMNIA VERBA HEC CONFERENS IN CORDE SUO,* de 170 qua natus est Iesus, ut putabatur filius Ioseph. Christi enim generatio sic erat: prima quidem hominis creatio vel condicio de terra; secunda de latere viri; tercio de viro et femina; quarta sic erat, ut sine viro hic nasceretur homo de femina. Unde et adpropriata circumlocutione pro nomine Christus filius hominis dictus est. Prima et secunda generatio ruerunt; in tercia de ruina generamur; in 175 quarta de ruina resuscitamur. OCTAVO DIE CIRCUMCIDERUNT PUERUM ET DECLARAVERUNT *NOMEN EIUS* IESUM[3], QUOD IMPOSITUM ERAT EI *AB ANGELO, PRIUSQUAM CONCIPERETUR.*

1 [[Eadem die angelus est missus suspensus Christus et in cruce est Petrus
180 ereptus, Jacobus sub Herode peremptus, Melchizedek offert (*sic*) rex pacis, Isaac
imponitur aris.]]

2 [[Aliud est divortium id est separatio, aliud diverticulum scilicet vie
compendium, aliud diversorium scilicet a situ inter duos muros.]]

3 [[Dicitur quod prepucium Domini delatum est ab angelo Karolo Magno
185 in templo Domini et translatum ab eo Aquas Grani, et post a Karolo calvo positum in Ecclesia Salvatoris apud Carosium.]]

Capitulum VIII. De muneribus et de oblatione magorum.

Tercia decima vero die ECCE MAGI VENERUNT ab oriente HIEROSOLIMAM,
DICENTES: UBI EST QUI NATUS EST REX IUDEORUM? VIDIMUS ENIM STELLAM EIUS
190 IN ORIENTE ET VENIMUS ADORARE EUM. Successores fuerunt isti doctrine Bal-
aam, qui stellam noverunt eius vaticinio; et a magnitudine scientie magi nun-
cupati. Quos enim Greci philosophos, Perse magos appellant. Venerunt enim de
finibus Persarum et Chaldeorum, ubi fluvius est Sabaa, a quo et Sabea regio
dicitur. Quidam tamen non eos primo Magos dictos putant, sed postquam
195 dolum Herodis per aliam viam revertentes fefellerunt. Chrisostomus dicit stellam multo ante tempore quam Christus nasceretur apparuisse eis et ita multo
tempore de longinquo venerunt. Potuit tamen fieri in tredecim diebus super
dromedarios longa terrarum spacia transmearent.

AUDIENS MAGOS HERODES REX TURBATUS EST ET OMNIS IEROSOLIMA CUM
200 ILLO. Timuit rex, ne aliquis de semine Hircani vel Aristoboli natus esset reg-
naturus se tanquam alienigena destituto. Turbatur autem civitas novitate mira-
culi perculsa. CUMQUE DILIGENTER DIDICISSET REX ORTUM STELLE A MAGIS, UT
PER EAM NATALEM PUERI COGNOSCERET, ETIAM A SACERDOTIBUS ET SCRIBIS
SCISCITABATUR UBI CHRISTUS NASCERETUR. QUI IUXTA MICHEAM IN BETHELEEM
205 EPHRATA NASCITURUM DIXERUNT. Bethleem prius dicta est Ephrata ab uxore
Caleph, que ibi sepulta est. Quam quidam suspicantur filiam fuisse Hur et
Marie sororis Moysis. Postea vero, post famosam sterilitatem pro qua Elim-
elech cum domo sua adiit Moabitas, cum reddita fuisset ei incredibilis ubertas,
dicta est Bethleem, quod sonat domus panis. DIXIT AUTEM REX MAGIS, UT
210 INVENTUM PUERUM SIBI INDICARENT, UT VENIENS ADORARET EUM. Iam enim
animum direxerat ad perdendum puerum. QUOS EGREDIENTES DE IERUSALEM
STELLA ANTECEDEBAT USQUE DUM VENIENS STARET SUPER DOMUM UBI ERAT
PUER. [Dicit Fulgentius stellam tunc creatam notabilem et discretam a ceteris et
in splendore, quam lux diurna non impedit, et in loco, quia neque in firma-
215 mento cum stellis minoribus erat, nec in ethere cum planetis, sed in aëre vicinas terre tenebat vias, et in motu, quia prius immobilis super Iudeam Magis

dedit signum veniendi in Iudeam, quia ex deliberatione sua Ierusalem tamquam caput Iudee adierunt. Quibus egressis tunc primum motu notabili precessit eos. Que peracto officio mox esse desiit, revertens in preiacentem materiam unde sumpta fuerat. Tamen quidam dicunt Bedam voluisse quod in puteum Beth- 220 leemitanum ceciderit et post in diebus Paule et Eustochii quasdam virgines Deo dicatas eam miraculose vidisse. Quod quia fabulosum estimaverunt fratres, cum quibus monasticam vitam ducebat, eum a communione sua quandoque separaverunt.]

B.2: The prefaces and opening chapters of the first version, namely the classroom lectures, of Stephen Langton's course on the *Historia evangelica.*

Capitulum. *FUIT IN DIEBUS ETC.* Sic incipit Lucas evangelium suum, et incipit hic Historia evangelica secundum distinctiones huius voluminis. Alii distinguunt aliter, ibi scilicet MORTUO SYMONE ETC. UNDETRIGINTA una dictio, id est viginti novem. AARONITA de tribu Aaron. DAVID ENIM Responsio est ad
5 hoc quod dixerat de vice Abia. DE ELYAZAR primogenito Aaron. YTHAMAR post genitus, quorum iam defunctorum familie supererant. *SECUNDUM* SORTES, ne litigarent de melioribus vel minus bonis ebdomadis. Prestat enim quandoque una septimana in redditibus altaris. OCTAVAM et in mense Septembri. STERILI-TATEM…ET…SENECTUTEM que duo sunt repugnantia partui. MAGNIFICENTIAM
10 cum ait: *hic erit magnus coram Domino.* CUM ABSTINENTIA ubi ait: *vinum et siceram non bibet. OCCULTABAT SE* pre verecundia partus.

Capitulum. *MENSE AUTEM ETC.* QUESISSETQUE Beata Virgo scilicet CUM SE NON COGNITURAM Sic enim exponunt sancti: *quoniam virum non cognosco* id est me non cognituram propositum habeo. DE OPERE SPIRITUS SANCTI cum ait:
15 *Spiritus Sanctus superveniet in te etc.* COGNATAM SUAM de regio semine ex parte matris. NAM ET AARON de cuius filiabus erat hec Elizabeth mater Iohannis. OCTAVO KALENDAS et sic representat Ecclesia sollempnizans eadem die de conceptione sive annunciatione Beate Virginis.

Capitulum. *EXURGENS MARIA ETC.*, ut assisteret cognate parienti, sed cum
20 extra Ierusalem habitaret Zacharias, ut plures alii sacerdotum – in ebdomadibus vero suis singuli habitabant Ierusalem – ipsa per Ierusalem eo transivit. INFANS scilicet Baptista MATREM DOMINI SUI…PROPHETARET dicens: *unde hoc mihi ut veniat mater Domini mei ad me?* ET BEATAM ut *et beata que credidisti etc.* ET TUNC post partum cognate *IOHANNES EST* Non ait erit quasi dicens iam habet nomen.
25 *PUER ENIM* super hoc ponit Magister glosam extrinsecam ubi reddit causam de preposteratione horum canticorum. *USQUE IN DIEM OSTENSIONIS SUE* quando factum est verbum Domini ad eum per Spiritum Sanctum, ut exiret desertum et predicans baptizaret. *IN UTERO HABENS* – ibi pausa – id est gravida, postea supple quod erat *DE SPIRITU SANCTO.* Si enim diceres Ioseph hoc totum nosse,

non hesitaret unde gravida esset. UT VOCARET IESUM id est salvatorem. Sother 30
enim grece, Iesus hebraice. Salvator latine idem sonat ut Christus grece,
hebraice messias, unctus latine. DEUM NASCITURUM ex ea.

    Capitulum. *IN DIEBUS ETC…DESCRIBERETUR* id est in scriptum redigeretur
quot regiones in Imperio Romano, quot civitates in singulis regionibus, quot
capita hominum in civitatibus singulis, ita ut omnes de appendiciis cuiusque 35
civitatis pro civibus illius civitatis numerarentur. PREFEREBAT in sculptura FERE-
BANTUR id est tenebantur CENSICAPITE una dictio, cuius nominativus censicaput id est tali censu capitis. *HEC DESCRIPTIO PRIMA* hoc de Evangelio DEINDE
PER CIRCUMSTANTES sicut fit lapide in aquam proiecto. PARTICULARES ut sub
Pompeio et tempore David, qui populum numeravit. STIPENDIARIA non dico 40
tributaria, quia tributum summam pecunie notat a communi datam, a quibusdam plus, a quibusdam minus. Stipendia singulorum dona intelliguntur hic et
omnium paria. QUOT ANNIS per singulos annos. *HOC ANNO* ac si dicerent de aliis
annis: nil querimus sed de hoc. SI MULIERES PROFITEBANTUR….SI SOLI hoc est
quod, inquit, non credo, tamen dubium est. 45

    Capitulum. *FACTUM EST ETC.* NON POST QUEM ALIUS ut mentitus est
Eliodius hereticus dicens Beatam Virginem et peperisse fratres Christo de
Ioseph. Christum tamen de Virgine natum non negabat. Cum ergo hoc nomen
primogenitum quasi duplicem habebat difinitionem scilicet ante quem nullus
et post quem alius. Hic tamen in prima accipitur, sicut finalem sillabam post 50
quam nulla in eadem dictione et ante quam alia, tamen Priscianus dicit plus
finalem sillabam et o principalem vocalem in mons non quod eam sequatur alia
in eadem sillaba. ALIUS LOCUS istud alius glosa est. Hic leges glosam extrinsecam: DICITUR QUIA ETC. – QUIESCUNT non longe a presepio. FORTE IBI Responsum: videbatur enim pocius ibi esse sedilia quam presepia. LIBRI LAICORUM quod 55
legunt in pariete quod nos in codice.

    Capitulum. NATUS EST ETC. quod sic, inquit, pronunciatur eadem die in
capitulo nostro. Anno regni Augusti quadragesimo secundo natus est Dominus Iesus in Bethleem Iude. ANNOS DUODECIM quibus corregnavit Antonio.
QUIA SI TABULAM Probat auctoritas Bede quod dominica die natus sit Christus. 60
Legitur enim in scripturis suis hec dixisse. SI TABULAM COMPOTI ETC. Dionysii
scilicet HUIUS ANNI in quo natus est Christus. QUIBUS IUNCTIS scilicet quinario
et ternario. Compotistarum, inquit, est hec considerare, et quantum ad presentem locum attinet. Sciendum est numerum concurrencium usque ad septenarium progredi nec ultra. Habet autem quilibet annus suum concurrentem ut 65
primum secundum et sic usque ad septimum, et quilibet mensis suum regularem habet usque ad ternarium. Si vis ergo perpendere quota feria intrat men-

sis, iunge concurrentem eiusdem anni et regularem illius mensis de quo queris.
Et si excrevit summa in septenarium vel infra, tota feria intrabit mensis scilicet
70 sexta vel septima etc. Si vero summa illa superexcrescat septenario, abice septenarium et tota feria intrabit mensis quotus numerus supererit, ut si unitas supersit, ut tunc fuit, prima feria intrabit mensis id est die dominica. Et hec est glosa
extrinseca ab eo loco: QUIA SI TABULAM ETC. NAM EADEM DIE Hoc de littera quod
de dominica dicitur, qua Deus creavit post celum empireum et angelos et mate-
75 riam omnium corporum simul et statim eadem die creavit lucem id est nubem
quandam lucidam et hec omnia dicuntur opus prime diei. Item alia glosa, que
est: AB HOC ETC. Idem probat quod premissa scilicet Christum natum in
dominica die. Octavo siquidem kalendas Aprilis conceptus est et octavo kalendas Ianuarii natus. Hoc irrefragibiliter tenet Ecclesia, in utroque illorum dierum
80 sollempnizans: in altero de conceptione seu annunciatione Beate Virginis, que
duo eadem die facta sunt, et de Christi nativitate in altero, sed iterum constat
quod eadem die mortuus est qua conceptus iuxta expositionem illius prophetie:
ne coquas edum in lacte matris, id est ne interficias Christum in die conceptionis sue,
quod transgressi sunt sed in anno illo quo mortuus est, scilicet in sexta feria.
85 Fuerunt kalende Aprilis sexta feria et kalende Ianuarii in prima, et eodem modo
fuit in anno illo quo conceptus est et natus. Ergo sexta feria conceptus et in
prima natus et sic in dominica. Item ponit extra Magister quedam signa
dominice nativitatis que in eadem nocte qua natus est contigerunt.

Capitulum. ET PASTORES ETC. Duo, inquit, miliaria leugam faciunt. IN
90 UTROQUE SOLSTICIO estivali circa festum Beati Iohannis et yemali circa nativitatem Domini. EX USU COHABITANTIUM quia vicini gentibus erant. IN SIGNUM
Unde Lucas: *et hoc vobis signum*. ET TU TURRIS in Michea. HOC NOMEN scilicet turris Gregis. VERBUM INVENERUNT id est rem verbo angeli significatam. CHRISTI
ENIM quasi putabatur filius eius, sed non erat ab aliquo temporaliter generatus.
95 CHRISTI ENIM GENERATIO SIC ERAT Et statim exponit quomodo. DECLAR-
AVERUNT ubi dico imposuerunt.

Capitulum. TERTIA DECIMA DIE a nativitate Domini secundum Hieronimum, quamvis secundum Crisostomum ante tunc per annum inceperunt, sed
Hieronimum sequimur. Et fuerunt, inquit, dicti Magi in scientia non ab arte
100 magica, vel secundum alios Magi dicti sunt, hoc est delusores, postquam
deluserunt Herodem, quod non credimus. VIDIMUS STELLAM EIUS IN ORIENTE
Sic ordina nos existentes in oriente id est in orientali mundi parte VIDIMUS ETC.
scilicet in Iudea. EIUS VATICINIO Etiam signum audierunt, quod tale fuit: *orietur*
stella ex Iacob et exurget in Ierusalem, qui regat populum suum, et sic habetur in
105 Numerorum. ET OMNIS IEROSOLIMA CUM ILLO sed aliter aliud determinat.

HELIMELECH cuius uxor Noemi, que mortuo viro et duobus filiis apud Moab audita volunt reverti in Iudeam. Et sequebantur eam due nurus eius vidue, quas de Moab duxerant filii Noemi, sed cum ipse moneret eas ut remanerent inter contribules suos altera redeunte sola Ruth secuta est eam. Quam postea duxit Booth contribulis defuncti. DIXIT AUTEM REX in dolo SUPRA DOMUM id est 110 diversorium QUAM LUX DIURNA NON IMPEDIVIT sicut stella facit PRIUS IMMO-BILIS dum venirent IERUSALEM ADIERUNT putantes se ibi invenire illum UNDE SUMPTA FUERAT ut columba in qua Spiritus Sanctus apparuit quandoque per aliud tempus.

B.3: The prefaces and opening chapters of the second version, namely the first revision (accomplished before 1176), of Stephen Langton's course on the *Historia evangelica*.

~~Capitulum~~. *FUIT IN DIEBUS ETC.* Sic incipit Lucas evangelium suum, et incipit hic Historia evangelica secundum distinctiones huius voluminis. Alii *aliter incipiunt*, ibi scilicet MORTUO SYMONE ETC. <UNDETRIGINTA> una dictio +est+, id est viginti novem. AARONITA de tribu Aaron. DAVID ENIM Respon-
5 sio est ad hoc quod dixerat de vice Abia. +VIGINTI QUATTVOR INSTITUIT, ut quisque illorum viginti quattuor ebdomadam suam facerent et secundum proiectionem sortium. ABIAS HABUIT OCTAVAM, a quo descendit iste Zacarias+. DE ELEAZAR primogenito Aaron. UTAMAR post genitus, quorum iam defunctorum familie supererant. *SECUNDUM* SORTES, ne *contentio fieret* de melioribus
10 vel minus bonis ebdomadis. Prestat enim quandoque una septimana in redditibus altaris. OCTAVAM et in mense Septembri. STERILITATEM ET SENECTUTEM que duo sunt repugnantia partui. MAGNIFICENTIAM cum ait: *hic erit magnus coram Domino*. CUM ABSTINENTIA ubi ait: *vinum et siceram non bibet*. OCCULTABAT SE pre verecundia partus, +ne forte diceretur quod modo inciperet lascivire et talibus
15 operam dare+.

~~Capitulum~~. *MENSE AUTEM ETC.....+AD MARIAM COGNATAM illius ELIZABETH DESPONSATAM nondum traductam+. QUESISSETQUE Beata Virgo ~~scilicet CVM~~ SE NON COGNITURAM Sic enim exponunt sancti: *quoniam virum non cognosco* id est *propositum habeo me non cognituram*. ~~DE~~ OPERE SPIRITUS SANCTI cum ait:
20 *Spiritus Sanctus superveniet in te etc.* COGNATAM SUAM de regio semine ex parte matris. NAM ET AARON de cuius filiabus erat hec Elizabeth mater Iohannis. +*FIAT MIHI SECUNDUM VERBUM TUUM* ET STATIM ad concessionem ipsius Virginis+. OCTAVO KALENDAS +APRILES+ et *hoc* representat Ecclesia sollempnizans eadem die de conceptione sive annunciatione *Salvatoris*.

25 ~~Capitulum~~. *EXURGENS ~~MARIA~~ ETC.* +Audivit Virgo quod cognata sua conceperat et surgens venit ad eam+, *ut parienti assisteret*, sed cum extra Iherusalem habitaret Zacharias, ut plures alii sacerdotum – in ebdomadibus vero suis singuli habitabant Iherusalem – ipsa per Iherusalem eo transivit. *INFANS* scilicet Baptista MATREM DOMINI SUI...PROPHETARET dicens: *unde hoc*

mihi ut veniat ~~mater Domini mei ad me~~*?* ET BEATAM ut *et beata que credidisti etc.* ET   30
TUNC post partum +scilicet+ cognate *IOHANNES EST* Non *dixit* erit +sed est,
quia tum predictum fuerat ab angelo+ quasi dicens iam habet nomen. ~~PUER
ENIM super hoc ponit Magister glosam extrinsecam ubi reddit causam de preposteratione horum canticorum.~~ *USQUE IN DIEM* OSTENSIONIS SUE quando factum est verbum Domini ad eum per Spiritum Sanctum, ut exiret [in] deser-   35
tum et predicans baptizaret. *IN UTERO HABENS* – ibi pausa – id est gravida, postea
supple quod erat *DE SPIRITU SANCTO.* Si enim diceres Ioseph hoc totum nosse,
non hesitaret unde gravida esset. UT VOCARET *IESUM* id est Salvatorem. Sother
enim grece, Iesus hebraice. Salvator latine idem sonat ut Christus grece,
hebraice messias, unctus latine. DEUM NASCITURUM ex ea.   40

    ~~Capitulum.~~ *IN DIEBUS* +*ILLIS EXIIT*+ *ETC…DESCRIBERETUR* ~~id est~~ in *scrip-
tis* redigeretur quot regiones in Imperio Romano, quot civitates in regionibus
singulis, quot capita hominum in civitatibus singulis, ita ut omnes de appendiciis cuiusque civitatis pro civibus illius civitatis numerarentur. PREFEREBAT in
sculptura FEREBANTUR id est tenebantur CENSICAPITE una dictio +est+, cuius   45
nominativus censicaput id est tali censu capitis. +Dicebatur enim denarius ille
censicaput, quia unusquisque quando reddebat presidi provincie ponebat illum
super caput suum et proprio ore profitebatur se esse subditum Romano Imperio, et inde dicebatur professio id est proprii oris fassio, et hoc fiebat coram
omni populo+. *HEC DESCRIPTIO PRIMA* hoc de Evangelio DEINDE PER CIRCUM-   50
STANTES sicut fit lapide in aquam proiecto. PARTICULARES ut sub Pompeio et
tempore David *quo* populum numeravit, +et forte alii suas fecerunt descrip-
tiones+. STIPENDIARIA non dico tributaria, +nec vos turbet quod supradictum
est scilicet quod Pompeius fecit tributariam Iudeam et hic dicitur quod facta
est stipendiaria. Aliud est enim hoc et aliud illud+. Tributum +enim+ summam   55
pecunie notat a communi datam, a quibusdam plus, *ab aliis* minus, +sicut
centum vel mille talenta+. Stipendia singulorum dona intelliguntur hic et
omnium paria. +Denarii enim qui in tali descriptione colligebantur militibus
dabantur pro stipendiis+. QUOT ANNIS *id est singulis annis*. *HOC ANNO* ac si
dicerent de aliis annis: nil querimus sed de hoc. SI MULIERES PROFITEBANTUR   60
cum viris, quod dubium est.

    ~~Capitulum.~~ *FACTUM EST ETC.* +Ascendit Ioseph ut supradictum est in Beth-
leem cum Maria pregnante+ NON POST QUEM ALIUS ut mentitus est *Eludius*
hereticus dicens Beatam Virginem et peperisse fratres Christo de Ioseph. Christum tamen de Virgine natum non negabat. ~~Cum ergo hoc nomen primogeni-   65
tum quasi duplicem habebat difinitionem scilicet ante quem nullus et post quem
alius. Hic tamen in prima accipitur, sicut finalem sillabam post quam nulla in~~

~~eadem dictione et ante quam alia, tamen Priscianus dicit plus finalem sillabam~~
~~et o principalem vocalem in mons non quod eam sequatur alia in eadem sillaba.~~
70 *LOCUS ALIUS* istud alius glosa est. ~~Hic leges glosam extrinsecam: DICITUR~~
~~QUIA ETC.~~ QUIESCUNT non longe a presepio. FORTE IBI Responsum: videbatur
enim pocius ibi esse sedilia quam presepia. +ET BOVI ad vendendum vel aliud
faciendum ASINO asinum forte duxerat super quem venerat Beata Virgo. Unde
et quando fugit in Egyptum super asinam legitur sedisse.+ LIBRI LAICORUM +ut
75 in eis instruantur laici, sicut nos in libris+ quod +qui+ legunt in pariete quod nos
in codice.

~~Capitulum.~~ *NATUS EST ETC.* quod sic, inquit +Magister+, pronunciatur
eadem die in capitulo nostro. Anno regni Augusti +Cesaris+ quadragesimo
secundo natus est Dominus Iesus in Bethleem Iude. ANNOS DUODECIM quibus
80 conregnavit Antonio. QUIA SI TABULAM Probat +autem+ *auctoritate* Bede
quod dominica die natus sit Christus. Legitur enim in scripturis suis hec dixisse.
SI TABULAM COMPOTI Dionysii scilicet *EIUS* ANNI in quo natus est Christus.
QUIBUS IUNCTIS scilicet quinario et ternario. Compotistarum, ~~inquit~~, est hec
considerare, et quantum ad presentem locum *continet*. Sciendum est
85 numerum concurrencium usque ad septenarium progredi nec ultra. Habet
autem quilibet annus suum concurrentem ut primum secundum et sic usque
ad septimum, et quilibet mensis suum regularem habet ~~usque ad ternarium~~. Si
vis ergo perpendere quota feria intrat mensis, iunge concurrentem eiusdem anni
et regularem illius mensis de quo queris. Et si *excreverit* summa in septenar-
90 ium vel infra, tota feria intrabit mensis scilicet *septima vel sexta* ~~etc~~. Si vero
summa illa superexcrescat septenario, abice septenarium et tota feria intrabit
mensis quotus numerus supererit, ut si unitas supersit, ut tunc fuit, prima feria
intrabit mensis id est die dominica. ~~Et hec est glosa extrinseca ab eo loco: QUIA~~
~~SI TABULAM ETC.~~ NAM EADEM DIE ~~Hoc de littera quod de dominica dicitur~~ qua
95 Deus creavit post celum empireum et angelos et materiam omnium corporum
simul et statim eadem die creavit lucem id est nubem quandam lucidam et hec
omnia dicuntur opus prime diei. Item alia ~~glosa, que est: AB HOC ETC.~~ +proba-
tio, sed hic continuatur: IN DOMINICA INVENIES.+ AB HOC Idem probat quod
premissa scilicet Christum natum in dominica die. Octavo siquidem kalendas
100 Aprilis conceptus est et octavo kalendas Ianuarii natus. Hoc irrefragibiliter tenet
Ecclesia, in utroque illorum dierum sollempnizans: in altero de conceptione
seu annunciatione Beate Virginis, que duo eadem die facta sunt, et de Christi
nativitate in altero, sed iterum constat quod eadem die mortuus est qua conceptus iuxta expositionem illius prophetie: *ne coquas *hedum* in lacte matris*, id est
105 ne interficias Christum in die conceptionis sue, *quam* transgressi sunt sed in

anno illo quo mortuus est, scilicet ~~in~~ sexta feria. Fuerunt kalende Aprilis sexta feria et *kalendis* Ianuarii sexta feria et eodem fuit modo in anno illo quo conceptus est et natus. Ergo sexta feria conceptus et in prima natus et sic in dominica. Item ponit extra Magister quedam signa dominice nativitatis que in eadem nocte qua natus est contigerunt +ut hec.+ +ROME TEMPLUM PACIS ETC. 110 Romani tempore Augusti Cesaris, quia pax fuit continua fere per duodecim annos, templum pacis edificaverunt, quia pulcerrimum erat et mirabile in oculis hominum. Qui consulantes Apollinem quantum duraret, receperunt responsum: quousque virgo pareret. Hoc audientes dixerunt: ergo in eternum stabit, quia impossibile eis videbatur secundum cursum solitum nature quod virgo 115 pareret. Unde in foribus illius templi titulum scripserunt: templum pacis eternum. Nocte vero qua Beata Virgo peperit totum ita destructum est, quod non remansit ibi lapis super lapidem. Et eadem nocte qua natus est Dominus FONS OLEI ERUPIT et fluxit usque in Tiberim, sed quantum duraverit nescio.+

~~Capitulum.~~ *ET PASTORES ETC.* +UNO MILIARIO+ Duo ~~inquit~~ miliaria leugam 120 faciunt. +ANTIQUIORIBUS scilicet gentilibus.+ IN UTROQUE SOLSTICIO estivali circa *festivitatem* Beati Iohannis et hiemali circa nativitatem Domini. EX USU COHABITANTIUM quia vicini gentibus erant. *IN SIGNUM* Unde Lucas: *et hoc vobis* +in+ *signum.* +*GLORIA IN EXCELSIS ET IN TERRA PAX HOMINIBUS BONE VOLUNTATIS* Hucusque dixerunt angeli, sed quod prosequimur ad finem − "laudamus te, 125 benedicimus etc." − additum est a Beato Hylario Pictaviensis episcopo.+ *ET TU TURRIS* in Michea. HOC NOMEN scilicet turris Gregis. *INVENERUNT VERBUM* id est rem verbo angeli significatam. +*CONFERENS* ea cum prophetiis. Videbat enim iam quasdam prophetias adimpleri.+ CHRISTI ENIM +GENERATIO SIC ERAT+ Quasi +dicens+ putabatur filius *Ioseph*, sed non erat ab aliquo temporaliter 130 generatus. ~~CHRISTI ENIM GENERATIO SIC ERAT Et statim exponit quomodo.~~+Ioseph enim fuit pater eius putativus, sed SIC ERAT de sola virgine SINE VIRO quod consequenter+ exponit +DE VIRO ET FEMINA, sicut cotidie videmus.+ +FILIUS HOMINIS unius id est virginis. PRIMA ET SECUNDA sed Adam et Eva.+ +ET+ DECLARAVERUNT *non* dico *immo posuerunt*. 135

B.4: The prefaces and opening chapters of the third version, namely the second revision (accomplished before 1193), of Stephen Langton's course on the *Historia evangelica*.

FUIT IN DIEBUS ETC. Sic incipit Lucas evangelium suum, et hic incipit Historia evangelica secundum distinctiones huius voluminis. Alii *altius* incipiunt, ibi scilicet MORTUO SIMONE ETC. +Et notandum quod quicquid dictum est a fine libri Machabeorum usque ad hunc locum scriptum est de Iosepho et Egesipo historiographo, et non continetur in Veteri Testamento, sed ideo interseruit Magister ut Vetus Testamentum congrue continuaretur Novo+. UNDE-TRIGINTA una dictio est: ~~id est~~ viginti novem. AARONITA de tribu Aaron. DAVID ENIM Responsio ~~est~~ ad hoc quod dixerat de vice *sua*. VIGINTI QUATTUOR INSTI-TUIT, ut quisque illorum viginti quattuor ebdomadam suam *faceret* et secundum proiectionem sortium. ABIAS HABUIT OCTAVAM, a quo descendit iste Zacharias. DE ELEAZAR primogenito ~~Aaron~~. YTHAMAR post genitus, quorum iam defunctorum familie supererant. *SECUNDUM* SORTES, ne contentio fieret de melioribus vel minus bonis ebdomadibus. Prestat enim quandoque una septimana in redditibus altaris. OCTAVAM ~~et~~ in mense Septembri. STERILITATEM ET SENECTUTEM que duo sunt repugnantia partui. MAGNIFICENTIAM cum ait: *hic erit magnus coram Domino* CUM ABSTINENTIA ~~ubi ait~~: *vinum et siceram non bibet.* *OCCULTABAT SE* pre verecundia partus, ne forte diceretur quod modo inciperet lascivire et talibus operam dare.

MENSE AUTEM +SEXTO+ ETC....AD MARIAM cognatam illius Elizabeth *DESPONSATAM* nondum traductam QUESISSETQUE Beata Virgo SE ~~NON~~ COGNI-TURAM Sic enim exponunt sancti: *quia* *virum non cognosco* id est propositum habeo me non cognituram. *OPERE SPIRITUS SANCTI* cum ait: *Spiritus Sanctus* ~~superveniet in te~~ etc. COGNATAM SUAM de regio semine ex parte matris NAM ET AARON de cuius filiabus erat ~~hec~~ Elizabeth mater Iohannis *FIAT MIHI SECUNDUM VERBUM TUUM* ET STATIM ad concessionem ipsius Virginis OCTAVO KALENDAS APRILES et hoc representat Ecclesia sollempnizans ~~eadem die~~ de conceptione sive annunciatione Salvatoris.

Capitulum. *EXURGENS* ETC. Audivit +Beata+ Virgo quod cognata sua conceperat et surgens venit ad eam, ut parienti assisteret, sed cum extra Ierusalem

habitaret Zacharias, ut plures alii sacerdotum – in ebdomadibus vero suis sin- 30
guli habitabant +in+ Ierusalem – ipsa per Ierusalem eo transivit. INFANS scilicet
Baptista MATREM DOMINI SUI...PROPHETARET dicens: *unde hoc mihi ut veniat ad*
me mater Domini mei etc. ET BEATAM ut *et beata que credidisti etc.* ET TUNC *scilicet
post partum* cognate IOHANNES EST Non dixit erit sed est, quia *iam* predictum fuerat ab angelo quasi dicens iam habet nomen. OSTENSIONIS SUE quando 35
factum est verbum Domini ad eum per Spiritum Sanctum, ut exiret in desertum et predicans baptizaret. IN UTERO HABENS – ibi pausa – id est gravida, postea
supple quod *deerat* DE SPIRITU SANCTO Si enim diceres Ioseph hoc totum
nosse, non hesitaret unde gravida esset. UT VOCARET IESUM id est Salvatorem.
Sother enim graece, Iesus hebraice, Salvator latine idem *sonant* ut Christus 40
grece, hebraice messias, latine *inunctus*. DEUM NASCITURUM ex ea. +UT MARIA
VIRI Inde est quod maiores in quibusdam ecclesiis sicut in ecclesia Parisiensi
ministrant altari in vigilia natalis Domini scilicet in ferendo candelabra turibula
et in omnibus aliis in quibus Parisii solent ministrare aliis diebus+.

    Capitulum. IN DIEBUS ILLIS EXIIT ETC...DESCRIBERETUR in scriptis redi- 45
geretur quot regiones in Imperio Romano, quot civitates in singulis regionibus, quot capita hominum in singulis civitatibus, ita ut omnes de appendiciis
cuiusque civitatis pro civibus illius civitatis numerarentur. PREFEREBAT in sculptura FEREBANTUR *et* tenebantur. CENSICAPITE una dictio est, cuius nominativus censicaput id est tali censu capitis. Dicebatur enim denarius ille censica- 50
put, quia unusquisque quando reddebat presidi provincie ponebat illum super
caput suum et proprio ore profitebatur se esse subditum Romano Imperio, et
inde dicebatur professio id est proprii oris fassio, et hoc fiebat coram omni populo. HEC DESCRIPTIO PRIMA hoc de Evangelio DEINDE PER CIRCUMSTANTES sicut
fit lapide in aquam proiecto. PARTICULARES ut sub Pompeio et tempore David 55
quo populum numeravit, et forte alii suas fecerunt descriptiones. STIPENDIARIA
Non dico tributaria, *quia hoc fecit Pompeius*. Tributum enim summam pecunie notat a communi datam, a quibusdam plus, a quibusdam minus, sicut centum vel mille talenta. Stipendia singulorum dona intelleguntur et omnium
paria. Denarii enim qui in tali descriptione colligebantur militibus dabantur 60
pro stipendiis, +qui pro orbe defendendo pugnabant+. QUOT ANNIS id est singulis annis, HOC ANNO ac si dicerent de aliis annis: nil querimus sed de hoc. SI
MULIERES PROFITEBANTUR cum viris, quod dubium est.

    Capitulum. FACTUM EST ETC. Ascendit Ioseph ut supradictum est in Beth-
leem cum Maria pregnante NON POST QUEM ALIUS ut mentitus est *Eliudius* 65
hereticus dicens Beatam Virginem et peperisse fratres Christo de Ioseph. Christum tamen *natum de Virgine* non negabat. LOCUS ALIUS istud alius glosa est.

QUIESCUNT non longe a presepio. FORTE IBI Responsum: Videbatur enim *ibi pocius esse* sedilia quam presepia. ET BOVI *vel ad vendendum vel ad aliud
70 faciendum* ASINO asinum forte duxerat, super quem venerat Beata Virgo. Unde et quando fugit in Egyptum super asinam legitur sedisse. LIBRI LAICORUM ut in eis instruantur laici, ~~sicut nos in libris quod qui legunt in pariete quod nos in codice~~.

Capitulum. *NATUS EST ETC.* quod sic, inquit Magister, pronunciatur eadem
75 die in capitulo nostro. Anno regni Augusti Cesaris quadragesimo secundo natus est Dominus Iesus in Bethleem Iude. ANNOS *VIGINTI DUO* quibus conregnavit Antonio. QUIA SI TABULAM +COMPOTI+ Probat ~~autem~~ auctoritate Bede quòd dominica die natus sit Christus. Legitur enim in scripturis suis hec dixisse. ~~si~~ TABULAM COMPOTI Dionysii scilicet EIUS ANNI in quo natus est Christus. QUIBUS
80 IUNCTIS scilicet quinario et ternario. Compotistarum est hec considerare, *sed* quantum ad presentem locum *attinet*. Sciendum est numerum concurrentium usque ad septenarium progredi nec ultra. Habet autem quilibet annus suum concurrentem ut primum +vel+ secundum ~~et sic~~ usque ad septimum, et quilibet mensis suum regularem ~~habet~~. Si vis ergo perpendere quota feria intrat
85 mensis, iunge concurrentem eiusdem anni et regularem illius mensis de quo queris. Et si excreverit summa in septenarium vel infra, tota feria intrabit mensis scilicet septima vel sexta. Si vero summa illa superexcrescat septenario, abice septenarium et tota feria intrabit mensis quotus numerus supererit, ut si unitas supersit, ut tunc fuit, *in* feria intrabit mensis id est die dominica. NAM EADEM
90 DIE qua Deus creavit *celum empireum post* et angelos et materiam omnium corporum simul et statim eadem die creavit lucem id est nubem quandam lucidam et hec omnia dicuntur opus prime diei. Item alia probatio sed hic continuatur: IN DOMINICA INVENIES. AD HOC Idem probat quod premissa scilicet Christum natum in dominica die. Octavo *kalendas siquidem* Aprilis conceptus est
95 et octavo kalendas Ianuarii natus. Hoc irrefragabiliter tenet Ecclesia, in utroque illorum dierum sollempnizans: in altero de conceptione seu annunciatione Beate Virginis, que duo eadem die facta sunt, et de Christi nativitate in altero, sed iterum constat quod eadem die mortuus est *quo* conceptus iuxta *opinionem* illius prophetie: *ne coquas hedum in lacte matris*, id est ne interficias Chris-
100 tum in die conceptionis sue, *quod* transgressi sunt +Iudei+ sed in anno illo quo mortuus est, scilicet sexta feria. Fuerunt +octavo+ *kalendas* Aprilis sexta feria et +octovo+ *kalendas* Ianuarii sexta feria et eodem modo fuit in anno illo quo conceptus est et natus. Ergo +in+ sexta feria conceptus et in prima natus et sic in dominica. +Et nota quod quotiens est festum annunciationis sexta feria,
105 sequens dies nativitatis est in dominica.+ Item ponit ~~extra~~ Magister quedam

signa dominice nativitatis que in eadem nocte qua natus est contigerunt ut hec. ROME TEMPLUM PACIS ETC. Romani tempore Augusti Cesaris, quia pax fuit continua fere per duodecim annos, templum pacis edificaverunt, *quod* pulcherrimum erat et mirabile in oculis hominum. Qui consulentes Apollinem quantum duraret, acceperunt responsum: quousque virgo pareret. Hoc audientes 110 dixerunt: ergo in eternum *durabit*, quia impossibile videbatur eis +scilicet+ secundum cursum solitum nature quod virgo pareret. Unde in foribus illius templi titulum scripserunt: templum pacis eternum. Nocte vero qua Beata Virgo peperit totum destructum est, ita quod non remansit lapis super lapidem. Et eadem nocte qua natus est Dominus FONS OLEI ERUPIT et fluxit usque 115 in Tyberim, sed quantum duraverit nescio.

ET PASTORES ETC. UNO MILIARIO Duo miliaria leugam faciunt. ANTIQUIORIBUS scilicet gentilibus. IN UTROQUE SOLSTICIO estivali circa *festum* Beati Iohannis et hyemali circa *natale* Domini. EX USU COHABITANTIUM quia vicini gentibus erant. IN SIGNUM Unde Lucas: *et hoc vobis in signum*. GLORIA IN 120 EXCELSIS ~~ET IN TERRA PAX HOMINIBUS BONE VOLUNTATIS~~ +ETC.+ Hucusque dixerunt angeli, sed quod prosequimur usque ad finem +scilicet+ – "laudamus te, benedicimus etc." – additum est a Beato Hylario Pictaviensis episcopo. ET TU TURRIS +Hoc+ in Michea. HOC NOMEN scilicet turris Gregis. INVENERUNT *VERBIS* id est rem verbo ~~angeli~~ significatam. CONFERENS ea cum prophetiis. 125 Videbat enim iam quasdam prophetias adimpleri. CHRISTI ~~ENIM~~ GENERATIO ~~SIC ERAT~~ Quasi dicens putabatur filius Ioseph, sed non erat ab aliquo temporaliter generatus. Ioseph enim fuit pater eius putativus, sed SIC ERAT +id est+ de sola virgine SINE VIRO quod consequenter exponit DE VIRO ET FEMINA sicut cotidie videmus. FILIUS HOMINIS unius id est virginis PRIMA ~~ET~~ SECUNDA *scilicet* Adam 130 et Eva. ET DECLARAVERUNT non dico *imposuerunt*. +Et nota quod dicitur preputium esse apud Carosium, sed non est credendum, cum auctoritas habeat quod de veritate nostre humane in resurrectione nil peribit. Unde credimus quod in resurrectione Domini rediit preputium ad locum suum et omnes circumcisi preputiati resurgent. Aliter multum periret de veritate humane 135 nostre.+

Bibliography

Manuscripts

Avranches, Bibliothèque municipale, MS 36
Durham, Durham Cathedral A.III.26
Heidelberg, Universitätsibliothek Salem, IX 62
London, British Library, Royal 4 D.VII
Magdeburg, Bibliothek des Domgymnasium, MS 238
Naples, Biblioteca Nazionale, MS VII.C.14
Oxford, Bodleian MS, Laud. misc. 291
Paris, Bibliothèque de l'Arsenal, MS 177
Paris, Bibliothèque nationale de France, lat. 14414
Paris, Bibliothèque nationale de France, lat. 14417
Paris, Bibliothèque nationale de France, lat. 16943
Tarragona, Biblioteca Publica, MS 130
Troyes, Bibilothèque municipale, MS 290
Troyes, Bibilothèque municipale, MS 1024
Uppsala, University Library, C 134
Victoria, State Library Victoria, MS 206
Vienna, Bibliothek des Dominikanerklosters, MS B 42
Vienna, Östereichische Nationalbibliothek, MS 363

Primary Sources

Andrew of St. Victor. *Expositio hystorica in Librum Regum*. Ed. Frans van Liere. CCCM 53A. Turnhout: Brepols, 1996.
—. *Expositio in Ezechielem*. Ed. Michael Alan Signer. CCCM 53E. Turnhout: Brepols, 1991.
—. *Expositio super Danielem*. Ed. Mark Zier. CCCM 53F. Turnhout: Brepols, 1990.
—. *Expositio super Heptateuchum*. Ed. Charles Lohr and Rainer Berndt. CCCM 53. Turnhout: Brepols, 1986.

—. *Expositiones historicae in libros Salomonis*. Ed. Rainer Berndt. CCCM 53B. Turnhout: Brepols, 1991.

—. *Super duodecim prophetas*. Ed. Frans van Liere and Mark Zier. CCCM 53G. Turnhout: Brepols, 2007.

Anthony, of Padua, Saint. S. *Antonii Patavini Sermones dominicales et festivi*. Ed. Beniamino Costa, Leonardo Frasson, Giovanni M., with Paulo Marangon. 3 vols. Padua: Centro studi antoniani, 1979.

Augustine, Saint. *De civitate Dei*. CCSL 48. Turnhout: Brepols, 1955.

—. *De Genesi ad litteram libri duodecim*. Ed. Joseph Zycha. CSEL 28.1. Vienna: F. Tempsky, 1894.

—. *De Genesi contra Manichaeos*. PL 34.

—. *Quaestiones in Heptateuchum*. Ed. Lucas Verheijen. CCSL 33: 1–377. Turnhout: Brepols, 1958.

Béda, Noël. *Scholastica declaratio sententiae et ritus ecclesiae de unica Magdalena contra magistrorum Jacobi Fabri et Judoci Clichtovei contheologici scripta*. Paris, 1519.

Bede, the Venerable. *Libri quattuor in principium Genesis*. Ed. C.W. Jones. CCSL 118A. Turnhout: Brepols, 1967.

Bible. *Biblia latina cum glossa ordinaria: Facsimile Reprint of the Editio Princeps* (Adolph Rusch of Strassburg, 1480–1481). Introduction by Karlfried Froehlich and Margaret T. Gibson. 4 vols. Turnhout: Brepols, 1992.

—. *Biblia Sacra iuxta latinam vulgatam versionem*. 3rd rev. ed. Ed. Boniface Fischer. Stuttgart: Deutsche Bibelgesellschaft, 1983.

—. *Biblia Sacra iuxta latinam vulgatam versionem ad codicum fidem cura et studio monachorum Abbatiae Pontificiae S. Hieronymi in Urbe OSB Edita*. 17 vols. Rome: Typis polyglottis Vaticanis, 1926–1987.

—. *Vetus latina: Die Reste der Altlateinischen Bibel*. Ed. Boniface Fischer. Freiburg im Breisgau: Herder, 1951–1954.

Chartularium Uniuersitatis parisiensis. Ed. Heinrich Denifle and Émile Chatelain. 4 vols. Paris, 1889–1897.

Clichtove, Josse. *De Maria Magdalena et triduo Christi disceptatio*. Paris, 1517.

—. *De tribus et unica Magdalena*. Paris, 1519.

Constitutiones antiquae ordinis Fratrum Praedicatorum. Ed. A.H. Thomas. In *De oudste constituties van der Dominicanen: Voorgescheidenis, tekst, bronnen, onstaan en ontwikkeling (1215–1237)*, 304–369. Bibliothèque de la Revue d'histoire ecclésiastique 42. Leuven: Bureel van de R.H.E., 1965.

"The Constitution of the Dominican Order, 1216 to 1360." Based on London, British Library, Add. MS 23935. Ed. G.R. Galbraith. *Publications of the University of Manchester: Historical Series* 44 (1925): 203–253.

Dante. *Paradiso*. Trans. Charles S. Singleton. 2 vols. Bollingen Series 80. Princeton: Princeton University Press, 1975.

Gregory the Great. *Moralia in Iob.* Ed. M. Adrien. CCSL 143, 143A, 143B. Turnhout: Brepols, 1979–1985.

Haimo of Auxerre. *Commentarius in Genesim.* PL 131: 51–134.

Hangest, Jérome de. *A difesa dell'Università* (De Academiis in Lutherum, 1532). Introd. and trans. R. Quinto. La filosofia e il suo passato 27. Padova: CLEUP, 2009.

Hugh of St. Victor. *Adnotationes elucidatorie in Pentateuchon.* PL 175: 29–86.

——. *De sacramentis Christianae fidei.* PL 176: 173A–618B.

——. *De sacramentis Christianae fidei.* Ed. Rainer Berndt. Corpus Victorinum: Textus historici 1. Münster: Aschendorff, 2008.

——. *On the Sacraments of the Christian Faith.* Trans. Roy Deferrari. Cambridge, MA: The Mediaeval Academy of America, 1951.

——. *De scripturis et scriptoribus sacris.* PL 175: 9–28.

——. *Didascalicon de studio legendi.* Ed. Charles Buttimer. Washington, DC: Catholic University Press, 1939.

——. *Didascalicon de studio legendi.* Ed. and trans. into German by Thilo Offergeld. Fontes Christiani 27. Freiburg im Breisgau: Herder, 1997.

——. *The Didascalicon of Hugh of St. Victor: A Medieval Guide to the Arts.* Trans. Jerome Taylor. New York: Columbia University Press, 1961.

Jerome, Saint. *Quaestiones hebraicae in Genesim.* Ed. Paul de LaGarde. CCSL 72: 1–56. Turnhout: Brepols, 1959.

——. *St. Jerome's Hebrew Questions on Genesis.* Trans. with an introduction and commentary by C.T.R. Hayward. Oxford Early Christian Studies. Oxford: Clarendon Press, 1995.

Josephus. *Antiquitates Judaicae: The Latin Josephus; Genesis.* Ed. Franz Blatt. Aarhus: Universitetsvorlaget, 1958.

Langton, Stephen. *Commentary on the Book of Chronicles.* Ed. Avrom Saltmann. Ramat-Gan: Bar-Ilan University Press, 1978.

——. *Quaestiones theologiae,* Liber I. Ed. Riccardo Quinto and Magdalena Bieniak. Auctores Britannici Medii Aevi. Oxford: Oxford University Press for The British Academy, 2014.

——. *Selected Sermons of Stephen Langton.* Ed. Phyllis Barzillay Roberts. Toronto Medieval Latin Texts 10. Toronto: Pontifical Institute of Mediaeval Studies, 1980.

Opera de vita regulari. Ed. Joachim Joseph Berthier. 2 vols. Rome: Typis A. Befani, 1888–1889.

Otto of St. Blaise. *Continuatio Sanblasiana* [continuation of Otto of Freising's *Chronicon*]. Ed. Roger Wilmans. MGH, Scriptores in folio 20: 302–337. Hannover: Hahn, 1868.

Peter the Chanter. *Verbum Abbreviatum.* PL 205: 23–370.

——. *An Edition of the Long Version of Peter the Chanter's Verbum Abbreviatum: Petri Cantoris Parisiensis Verbum adbreviatum; Textus conflatus.* Ed. Monique Boutry. CCCM 196. Turnhout: Brepols, 2004.

Peter Comestor. *De sacramentis*, ed. Raymond-M. Martin, as appendix to *Maître Simon et son groupe De sacramentis*, ed. Heinrich Weisweiler. Louvain: Spicilegium Sacrum Lovaniense, 1937.

—. *Scolastica historia Liber Genesis*. Ed. Agneta Sylwan. CCCM 191. Turnhout: Brepols, 2005.

Peter Lombard. *Sententiae in IV libris distinctae*. Ed. Ignatius Brady. 3rd rev. ed. 2 vols. Grottaferrata: Collegii S. Bonaventurae ad Claras Aquas, 1971–1981.

Peter Lombard. *The Sentences, Book 4: On the Doctrine of Signs*. Trans. Guilio Silano. Mediaeval Sources in Translation 48. Toronto: Pontifical Institute of Mediaeval Studies, 2010.

Pseudo-Methodius. *Sermo de novissimus temporibus*. In *Sibyllinische Texte und Forschungen: Pseudo-Methodius, Adso und die Tiburtinische Sibylle*, ed. Ernst Sackur, 60–96. Halle: Max Niemeyer, 1898.

Remigius of Auxerre. *Commentarius in Genesim*. PL 131: 51B–134C.

—.*Expositio super Genesim*. Ed. Burton Van Name Edwards. CCCM 136. Turnhout: Brepols 1999.

Robert of Auxerre. *Chronicon*. Ed. O. Holder-Egger. MGH, Scriptores in folio 26. Hannover: Hahn, 1882.

Robert Kilwardby. *Quaestiones in librum secundum Sententiarum*. Ed. Gerhard Liebold. Veröffentlichungen der Kommission für die Herausgabe Ungedruckter Texte aus der Mittelalterlichen Geisteswelt 16. Munich: Verlag der Bayerischen Akademie der Wissenschaften, 1992.

Rupert of Deutz. *De sancta Trinitate et opus eius*. Ed. Rh. Haacke. CCCM 21–24. Turnhout: Brepols, 1971–1972.

Statuta Antiqua Universitatis Oxoniensis. Ed. Strickland Gibson. Oxford: Clarendon Press, 1931.

Wireker, Nigel. *Nigellus de Longchamp dit Wireker: Tractatus contra curiales et officiales clericos*. Ed. André Boutemy. Paris: Presses universitaires de France, 1959.

Secondary Sources

Andrée, Alexander. "Anselm of Laon Unveiled: The *Glosae svper Iohannem* and the Origins of the *Glossa Ordinaria* on the Bible." *Mediaeval Studies* 73 (2011): 217–260.

—. "Laon Revisited: Master Anselm and the Creation of a Theological School in the Twelfth Century." *The Journal of Medieval Latin* 22 (2012): 257–281.

Balduinus, P[ater], ab Amsterdam. "*Historia Scholastica* Petri Comestoris in *Sermonibus* S. Antonii Patavani." *Collectanea Franciscana* 24 (1954): 83–109.

Baldwin, John. *Masters, Princes, and Merchants: The Social Views of Peter the Chanter and His Circle*. 2 vols. Princeton: Princeton University Press, 1970.

Bataillon, Louis-Jacques. "Les douze prophètes enseignés et prêchés par Étienne

Langton." In *Étienne Langton (1228): Prédicateur, bibliste et théologien*, ed. Louis-Jacques Bataillon, Nicole Bériou, Gilbert Dahan, and Riccardo Quinto, 427–448. Turnhout: Brepols, 2010.

Berndt, Rainier. *André de Saint-Victor: Exégète et Théologien*. Bibliotheca Victorina 2. Paris and Turnhout: Brepols, 1991.

——. "Pierre le Mangeur et André de Saint-Victor: Contribution à l'étude de leurs sources." *Recherches de théologie ancienne et médiévale* 61 (1994): 88–114.

Bogaert, P.-M. "La Bible française au moyen âge, des premières traductions aux débuts de l'imprimerie." In *Les Bibles en français: Histoire illustrée, du moyen âge à nos jours*, ed. P.-M. Bogaert, 13–46. Turnhout: Brepols, 1991.

Brady, Ignatius. "Peter Manducator and the Oral Teachings of Peter Lombard." *Antonianum* 41 (1966): 454–90.

——. "The Three Editions of the 'Liber Sententiarum' of Master Peter Lombard (1882–1977)." *Archivum Franciscanum Historicum* 70 (1977): 400–411.

Buc, Phillippe. *L'Ambiguïté du livre: Prince, pouvoir, et people dans les commentaries de la Bible au moyen âge*. Paris: Beauchesne, 1994.

Châtillon, Jean. "La Bible dans les Écoles du XIIe siècle." In *Le Moyen Age et la Bible*, ed. Pierre Riché and Guy Lobrichon, 163–197. Bible de tous les temps 4. Paris: Éditions Beauchesne, 1984.

Chenu, Marie-Dominique. *Introduction à l'étude de saint Thomas d'Aquin*. 2nd ed. Montreal: Institut d'études médiévales; Paris: Vrin, 1954.

——. *La théologie au douzième siècle*. 2nd ed. Paris: Vrin, 1966.

Clark, Mark J. "The Biblical *Gloss*, the Search for Peter Lombard's Glossed Bible, and the School of Paris." *Mediaeval Studies* 76 (2014): 57–113.

——. "The Commentaries of Stephen Langton on the *Historia Scholastica* of Peter Comestor." In *Étienne Langton:Prédicateur, bibliste, théologien*, ed. Louis-Jacques Bataillon, Nicole Bériou, Gilbert Dahan, and Riccardo Quinto, 373–393. Turnhout: Brepols, 2010.

——. "The Commentaries on Peter Comestor's *Historia scholastica* of Stephen Langton, Pseudo-Langton, and Hugh of St. Cher." *Sacris erudiri* 44 (2005): 301–446.

——. "Le cours d'Étienne Langton sur *l'Histoire scolastique* de Pierre le Mangeur: Le fruit d'une tradition unifiée." In *Pierre le Mangeur ou Pierre de Troyes, maître du XIIe siècle*, éd. Gilbert Dahan, 243–266. Bibliothèque d'histoire culturelle du moyen âge 12. Turnhout, Brepols, 2013.

——. "Glossing Genesis 1.2 in the Twelfth Century, or How Andrew of St. Victor and Peter Comestor Dealt with the Intersection of *nova* et *vetera* in the Biblical *Glossa ordinaria*." *Sacris erudiri* 46 (2007): 241–286.

——. "How to Edit the *Historia scholastica* of Peter Comestor." *Revue Bénédictine* 116 (2006): 83–91.

——. "Peter Comestor and Peter Lombard: Brothers in Deed." *Traditio* 60 (2005): 85–142.

—. "Peter Comestor and Stephen Langton: Master and Student, and Co-Makers of the *Historia scholastica.*" *Medioevo* 35 (2010): 123–149.

—. "Stephen Langton and Hugh of St. Cher on Peter Comestor's *Historia scholastica*: The Lombard's *Sentences* and the Problem of Sources Used by Comestor and His Commentators." *Recherches de Théologie et Philosophie médiévales* 74 (2007): 63–117.

Colish, Marcia. *Peter Lombard.* 2 vols. Brill's Studies in Intellectual History 41. Leiden: Brill, 1994.

—. "The Pseudo-Peter of Poitiers Gloss." In *Mediaeval Commentaries on the Sentences of Peter Lombard*, vol. 2, ed. Philipp W. Rosemann, 1–34. Leiden: Brill, 2010.

—. "Scholastic Theology at Paris around 1200." In *Crossing Boundaries at the Medieval Universities*, ed. Spencer E. Young, 29–50. Education and Society in the Middle Ages and Renaissance 36. Leiden: Brill, 2010.

Dahan, Gilbert. *L'Exégèse chrétienne de la Bible en occident médiéval, XIIe–XIVe siècle.* Patrimoines Christianisme. Paris: Cerf, 1999.

—. "Une leçon biblique au XIIe siècle: Le commentaire de Pierre le Mangeur sur Matthieu 26, 26–29." In *Ancienne Loi, Nouvelle Loi: Recherches interdisciplinaires sur les textes classique*, ed. Jean-Pierre Bordier, 19–38. Littérature et revelation au Moyen Âge 3. [Nanterre]: Université Paris Ouest Nanterre La Défense, 2009.

Daly, Saralyn R. "Peter Comestor: Master of Histories." *Speculum* 32 (1957): 62–73.

De Ghellinck, Joseph. *L'essor de la littérature latine au XIIe siècle.* 2 vols. Museum Lessianum, Section historique 4–5. Paris: Desclée de Brouwer, 1946.

—. *Le mouvement théologique du XIIe siècle.* 2nd rev. ed. Museum Lessianum, Section historique 10. Bruges: De Tempel, 1948.

De Hamel, C.F.R. *Glossed Books of the Bible and the Origins of the Paris Book Trade.* Woodbridge, England: D.S. Brewer, 1984.

De Lubac, Henri. *Exégèse médiévale: Les quatre sens de l'écriture*, 2 parts, each in 2 vols. Paris: Aubier, 1961–1964.

Denifle, Heinrich. "Die Constitutionen des Predigerordens in der Redaction Raimunds von Peñafort." *Archiv für Literatur und Kirchengeschichte des Mittelalters* 5 (1889): 530–564.

Edwards, Burton Van Name. "In Search of the Authentic Commentary on Genesis by Remigius of Auxerre." In *L'École carolingienne d'Auxerre de Murethach à Rémi*, ed. Dominique Iogna-Prat, Colette Jeudy, and Guy Lobrichon, 399–412. Paris: Beauchesne, 1991.

Étienne Langton: Prédicateur, bibliste, théologien. Ed. Louis-Jacques Bataillon, Nicole Bériou, Gilbert Dahan, and Riccardo Quinto. Turnhout: Brepols, 2010.

Franklin, Alfred. *Les anciennes bibliothèques de Paris.* Paris: Imprimerie impériale, 1867.

Gibson, Margaret. "The Place of the *Glossa Ordinaria* in Medieval Exegesis." In *Ad litteram: Authoritative Texts and Their Medieval Readers*, ed. Mark D. Jordan and Kent Emery, Jr., 5–27. Notre Dame: University of Notre Dame Press, 1992.

—. "The Twelfth-Century Glossed Bible." In *Papers Presented to the Tenth International*

Conference on Patristic Studies Held in Oxford 1187, ed. Elizabeth A. Livingstone, 232–244. Studia Patristica 23. Leuven: Peeters, 1989.

Glorieux, Palémon. *Répertoire des maîtres en théologie de Paris au XIIIe siècle*. 2 vols. Études de Philosophie Médiévale 17–18. Paris: Vrin, 1933–1934.

Glunz, Hans. *History of the Vulgate in England from Alcuin to Roger Bacon*. Cambridge: Cambridge University Press, 1933.

Goering, Joseph. *William de Montibus (c. 1140–1213): The Schools and the Literature of Pastoral Care*. Studies and Texts 108. Toronto: Pontifical Institute of Mediaeval Studies, 1992.

Goy, Rudolf. *Die Überlieferung des Werke Hugos von St. Viktor*. Stuttgart: Hiersemann, 1976.

Grabmann, Martin. *Die Geschichte der scholastischen Methode*. 2 vols. Freiburg in Breisgau: Herder, 1911.

Haastrup, Niels. "Zur frühen Pariser Bibel–auf Grund Skandinavischer Handschriften." *Classica et Mediaevalia* 24 (1963): 242–269.

—. "Zur frühen Pariser Bibel II." *Classica et Mediaevalia* 26 (1965): 394–401.

Halphen, Louis. "Les entrevues des rois Louis VII et Henry II durant l'exil de Thomas Becket en France." In *Mélanges d'histoire offerts à M. Charles Bémont*. Paris: F. Alcan, 1913.

Harkins, Franklin T. "Following with Unequal Step: Andrew of St. Victor, the *Glossa ordinaria*, and Compilatory Exegesis in the Twelfth Century." In *Transforming Relations: Essays on Jews and Christians throughout History in Honor of Michael A. Signer*, ed. Franklin T. Harkins, 150–178. Notre Dame: University of Notre Dame Press, 2010.

—. *Reading and the Work of Restoration: History and Scripture in the Theology of Hugh of St. Victor*. Studies and Texts 167. Toronto: Pontifical Institute of Mediaeval Studies, 2009.

Hugues de Saint-Cher († 1263), bibliste et théologien. Ed. Louis-Jacques Bataillon, Gilbert Dahan, and Pierre-Marie Gy. Bibliothèque d'histoire culturelle du Moyen Âge 1. Turnhout: Brepols, 2004,

Interpretation of Scripture: Theory; A Selection of Works of Hugh, Andrew, Richard, and Godfrey of St. Victor, and of Robert of Melun. Ed. and trans. Franklin T. Harkins and Frans von Liere. Victorine Texts in Translation 3. Turnhout: Brepols, 2012.

Kaeppeli, Thomas. *Scriptores ordinis praedicatorum medii aevi*. 4 vols. Rome: S. Sabinae, 1975–1993.

Karp, Sandra Rae. "Peter Comestor's *Historia scholastica*: A Study in the Development of Literal Scriptural Exegesis." Ph.D. diss., Tulane University, 1978; Microfilm, Ann Arbor, 1982.

Lacombe, George. "Studies on the Commentaries of Cardinal Stephen Langton, Part I." *Archives d'histoire et littéraire du môyen age* 5 (1930): 5–151.

—, and Beryl Smalley. "The Lombard's Commentary on Isaias and other Fragments." *The New Scholasticism* 5 (1931): 123–161.

Landgraf, Artur. *Dogmengeschichte der Frühscholastik.* 4 vols. Regensburg: Friedrich Pustet, 1952–1956.

—. *Introduction à l'histoire de la littérature théologique de la scolastique naissante.* Rev. Albert M. Landry. Trans. from the German, *Einführung in die Geschichte der theologischen Literatur der Frühscholastik* (Regensburg, 1948), by Louis-B. Geiger. Montreal: Institut d'études médiévales, 1973.

—. "Recherches sur les écrits de Pierre le Mangeur." *Recherches de théologie ancienne et médiévale* 3 (1931): 292–306.

—. "Recherches sur les écrits de Pierre le Mangeur: Le traité *De Sacramentis.*" *Recherches de théologie ancienne et médiévale* 3 (1931): 341–372.

Le Goff, Jacques. *La Naissance du Purgatoire.* Paris: Gallimard, 1981.

Lehtinen, Anja Inkeri. "The Apopeciae of the Manuscripts of Hugh of St. Cher's Works." *Medioevo* 25 (1999–2000): 1–167.

Lerner, Robert E. "Poverty, Preaching, and Eschatology in the Revelation Commentaries of Hugh of St. Cher." In *The Bible in the Medieval World: Essays in Memory of Beryl Smalley,* ed. Katherine Walsh and Diana Wood, 157–189. Oxford: Blackwell, 1985.

Light, Laura. "Versions et révisions du texte biblique." In *Le Moyen Age et la Bible,* ed. Pierre Riché and Guy Lobrichon, 55–93. Bible de tous les Temps 4. Paris: Éditions Beauchesne, 1984.

Little, A.G. and F. Pelster. *Oxford Theology and Theologians, c. A.D. 1282–1302.* Oxford: Clarendon Press, 1934.

Lobrichon, Guy. "Une nouveauté: Les gloses de la Bible." In *Le Moyen Age et la Bible,* ed. Pierre Riché and Guy Lobrichon, 95–114. Bible de tous les Temps 4. Paris: Éditions Beauchesne, 1984.

Loewe, Raphael. "The Medieval History of the Latin Bible." In *The West from the Fathers to the Reformation,* vol. 2 of *The Cambridge History of the Bible,* ed. G.W.H. Lampe, 102–154. Cambridge: Cambridge University Press, 1969.

Longère, Jean. *Oeuvres oratoires des maîtres parisiens au XIIe siècle: Étude historique et doctrinale,* 2 vols. Paris: Études Augustiniennes, 1975.

—. "Pierre Le Mangeur" (1986). In *Dictionnaire de spiritualité: ascétique et mystique, doctrine et histoire,* 12: 1614–1626. 17 vols. in 21. Paris: Beauchesne, 1932–1995.

Luscombe, David. "Peter Comestor." In *The Bible in the Medieval World: Essays in Honor of Beryl Smalley,* ed. Katherine Walsh and Diana Wood, 109–129. Oxford: Basil Blackwell, 1985.

—. "Peter Comestor and Biblical Chronology." *Irish Theological Quarterly* 80 (2015): 135–148.

Marsden, Richard. *The Text of the Old Testament in Anglo-Saxon England.* Cambridge Studies in Anglo-Saxon England 15. Cambridge: Cambridge University Press, 1995.

Martin, Raymond-M. "Notes sur l'oeuvre littéraire de Pierre le Mangeur." *Recherches de théologie ancienne et médiévale* 3 (1931): 54–66.

Moore, Philip S. *The Works of Peter of Poitiers: Master in Theology and Chancellor of Paris (1193–1205).* Notre Dame: University of Notre Dame Press, 1936.

Moore, W.L. "The Role of the Fathers in the Three Marys Controversy." In *'Auctoritas Patrum': Zur Rezeption der Kirchenväter im 15. und 16. Jahrhundert,* ed. L. Grane, A. Schindler, and M. Wriedt, 129–141. Mainz: Verlag Philipp von Zabern, 1993.

Morey, James H. "Peter Comestor, Biblical Paraphrase, and the Medieval Popular Bible." *Speculum* 68 (1993): 6–35.

Mulchahey, Michèle. *"First the Bow is Bent in Study…: Dominican Education before 1350."* Studies and Texts 132. Toronto: Pontifical Institute of Mediaeval Studies, 1998.

Pierre le Mangeur ou Pierre de Troyes, maître du XIIe siècle. Ed. Gilbert Dahan. Bibliothèque d'histoire culturelle du moyen âge 12. Turnhout: Brepols, 2013.

Poirel, Dominique. *Hugues de Saint-Victor.* Paris: Cerf, 1998.

Post, Gaines. "Alexander III, the 'Licentia Docendi' and the Rise of the University." In *Haskins Anniversary Essays in Mediaeval History,* ed. Charles H. Taylor and John L. La Monte, 255–277. Cambridge: Harvard University Press, 1929.

Powicke, F.M. "Bibliographical Note on Recent Work upon Stephen Langton." *The English Historical Review* 48, no. 192 (1933): 554–557.

—. *Stephen Langton: Being the Ford Lectures Delivered in the University of Oxford in Hilary Term 1927.* London: Merlin Press, 1928.

Pozt McGerr, R. "Guyart Desmoulins, the Vernacular Master of Histories, and the Bible Historiale." *Viator* 14 (1983): 211–244.

Quinto, Riccardo. "La constitution du texte des *Quaestiones theologiae* d'Étienne Langton." In *Étienne Langton (1228): Prédicateur, bibliste et théologien,* ed. Louis-Jacques Bataillon, Nicole Bériou, Gilbert Dahan, and Riccardo Quinto, 525–562. Turnhout: Brepols, 2010.

—. "Divine Goodness, Divine Omnipotence and the Existence of Evil: A Discussion of Augustine's *Enchiridion,* 24–26, from Anselm of Laon to Stephen Langton." *Przegląd Tomistyczny* 17 (2011): 1–23.

—. *Doctor Nominatissimus: Stefano Langton († 1228) e la tradizione delle sue opere.* Beiträge zur Geschichte der Philosophie und Theologie des Mittelalters, Neue Folge 39. Münster: Aschendorff, 1994.

—. "Hugh of St. Cher's Use of Stephen Langton." In *Medieval Analyses in Language and Cognition,* ed. Sten Ebbesen and Russell L. Friedman, 281–300. Copenhagen: The Royal Danish Academy of Sciences and Letters, 1999.

—. "The Influence of Stephen Langton on the Idea of the Preacher in Humbert of Romans' De Eruditione Predicatorum and Hugh of St.-Cher's Postille on the Scriptures." In *Christ Among the Medieval Dominicans: Representations of Christ in the Texts and Images of the Order of Preachers,* ed. Kent Emery, Jr. and J. Wawrikow, 49–91. Notre Dame: University of Notre Dame Press, 1998.

—. "Peter the Chanter and the 'Miscellanea del Codice del Tesoro' (Etymology as a way for constructing a Sermon)." In *Constructing the Medieval Sermon*, ed. R. Andersson, 33–81. Sermo 6. Brepols: Turnhout, 2007.

—. "Stefano Langton e i quattro sensi della Scrittura." *Medioevo* 15 (1989): 67–109.

—. "Stephano Langton e la teologia dei maestri secolari di Parigi tra XII e XIII secolo." *Archa Verbi: Yearbook for the Study of Medieval Theology* 5 (2008): 122–142.

—. "Stephen Langton." In *Mediaeval Commentaries on the Sentences of Peter Lombard*, vol. 2, ed. Philipp W. Rosemann, 36–76. Leiden: Brill, 2010.

—. "La teleologia dei maestri di Parigi e la prima scuola domenicana." In *L'Origine dell'Ordine dei Predicatori e l'Università di Bologna = Divus Thomas* 44 (2006): 81–104.

Roberts, Phyllis Barzillay. *Stephanus de Lingua-Tonante: Studies in the Sermons of Stephen Langton*. Studies and Texts 16. Toronto: Pontifical Institute of Medieval Studies, 1968.

Roest, Bert. *A History of Franciscan Education (ca. 1210–ca. 1517)*. Leiden: Brill, 2000.

Rorem, Paul. *Hugh of St. Victor*. Great Medieval Thinkers. Oxford: Oxford University Press, 2009.

Rosemann, Philipp W. *Peter Lombard*. New York: Oxford University Press, 2004.

—. *The Story of a Great Medieval Book: Peter Lombard's "Sentences."* Toronto: University of Toronto Press, 2007.

Saccenti, Riccardo. "The *Materia super libros Sententiarum* attributed to Peter Comestor: Study of the Text and Critical Edition." *Bulletin de philosophie médiévale* (2011): 155–215.

Schreckenberg, Heinz. *Die Flavius-Josephus-Tradition in Antike und Mittelalter*. Arbeiten zür Literatur und Geschichte des hellenistischen Judentums 5. Leiden: Brill, 1972.

Signer, Michael A. "The *Glossa Ordinaria* and the Transmission of Medieval Anti-Judaism." In *A Distinct Voice: Medieval Studies in Honor of Leonard E. Boyle O.P.*, ed. Jacqueline Brown and William P. Stoneman, 591–605. Notre Dame: University of Notre Dame Press, 1998.

Smalley, Beryl. "Andrew of St. Victor, Abbot of Wigmore: A Twelfth-century Hebraist." *Recherches de théologie ancienne et médiévale* 10 (1938): 358–373.

—. "The Bible in the Medieval Schools." In *The West from the Fathers to the Reformation*, vol. 2 of *The Cambridge History of the Bible*, ed. G.W.H. Lampe, 197–219. Cambridge: Cambridge University Press, 1969.

—. "Gilbertus Universalis, Bishop of London (1128–34) and the Problem of the 'Glossa ordinaria' I." *Recherches de théologie ancienne et médiévale* 7 (1935): 235–263.

—. "Gilbertus Universalis, Bishop of London (1128–34) and the Problem of the 'Glossa ordinaria' II." *Recherches de théologie ancienne et médiévale* 8 (1936): 24–60.

—. "Glossa Ordinaria." In *Theologische Realenzyklopädie*, ed. Gerhard Müller et al., 13: 452–457. 36 vols. Berlin: Walter de Gruyter, 1976–2004.

—. "La *Glossa ordinaria*: Quelques prédécesseurs d'Anselme de Laon." *Recherches de théologie ancienne et médiévale* 8 (1937): 24–60.

—. *The Gospels in the Schools, c. 1100–c. 1280.* London and Ronceverte: The Hambledon Press, 1985.

—. "Peter Comestor on the Gospels and his Sources." *Recherches de théologie ancienne et médiévale* 46 (1979): 84–129.

—. "The School of Andrew of St. Victor." *Recherches de théologie ancienne et médiévale* 11 (1939): 146–151.

—. "Some Gospel Commentaries of the Early Twelfth Century." *Recherches de théologie ancienne et médiévale* 45 (1978): 147–180.

—. *The Study of the Bible in the Middle Ages.* 1941. 3rd rev. ed. Oxford: Basil Blackwell, 1984.

—, and Alys L. Gregory. "Studies on the Commentaries of Cardinal Stephen Langton, Part 2." *Archives d'histoire doctrinale et littéraire du Moyen Âge* 5 (1930): 152–266.

—, and George Lacombe. "The Lombard's Commentary on Isaias and other Fragments." *The New Scholasticism* 5 (1931): 123–161.

Smith, Lesley. *The "Glossa ordinaria": The Making of a Medieval Bible Commentary.* Leiden: Brill, 2009.

Spatz, Nancy K. "Approaches and Attitudes to a New Theological Textbook: The *Sentences* of Peter Lombard." In *The Intellectual Climate of the Early University: Essays in Honor of Otto Gründler*, ed. Nancy van Deusen, 27–52. Kalamazoo: Medieval Institute Publications, Western Michigan University, 1997.

—. "Evidence of Inception Ceremonies in the Twelfth-Century Schools of Paris." *History of Universities* 13 (1994): 3–19.

Stegmüller, Friedrich. *Repertorium Biblicum Medii Aevi.* 11 vols. Madrid: Instituto Francisco Súarez, 1950–1980.

Stirneman, Patricia. "Où ont été fabriqués les livres de la Glose ordinaire dans la première moitié du XIIe siècle?" In *Le XIIe siècle: Mutations et renouveau en France dans la première moitié du XIIe siècle*, ed. Françoise Gasparri, 257–301. Cahiers du Léopard d'Or 3. Paris: Le Léopard d'Or, 1994.

Sylwan, Agneta. "Petrus Comestor, *Historia Scholastica*: Une nouvelle edition." *Sacris erudiri* 39 (2000): 345–382.

Valente, Luisa. "*Phantasia contrarietatis*": *Contradizzioni scritturali, discorso teologico e arti del linguaggio nel De tropis loquendi di Pietro Cantore (†1197).* Testi e studi per il "Corpus philosophorum Medii Aevi"13; Fonti per la storia della logica 2. Florence: Leo S. Olschki, 1997.

Van den Berghe, F. *De invloed van Petrus Comestor op de Schriftuurverklaring van Jan van Ruusbroec.* Mededelingen van de Koninklijke Vlaamse Academie voor Wetenschappen, Letteren en Schone Kunsten van België; Klasse der Letteren 11.10. Brussels: Paleis der Academiën, 1949.

Van Engen, John H. *Rupert of Deutz.* Berkeley: University of California Press, 1983.

Van Liere, Frans. "Andrew of St. Victor and the Gloss on Samuel and Kings." In *Media Latinitas: A Collection of Essays to Mark the Occasion of the Retirement of L.J. Engels*, ed.

R.I.A. Nip, H. Van Dijk, E.M.C. Van Houts, C.H. Kneepkens, and G.A.A. Korte-kaas, 249–253. Instrumenta Patristica 28. Turnhout: Brepols, 1996.

Verger, Jacques. "L'Exégèse de l'Université." In *Le Moyen Âge et la Bible*, ed. Pierre Riché and Guy Lobrichon, 199–230. Bible de tous les Temps 4. Paris: Éditions Beauchesne, 1984.

Wielockx, R. "Autour de la Glossa ordinaria." *Recherches de théologie ancienne et médiévale* 49 (1982): 222–228.

Zier, Mark. "The *Expositio super Danielem* of Andrew of St. Victor." Ph.D. diss., University of Toronto, 1983.

—. "The Manuscript Tradition of the *Glossa ordinaria* for Daniel and Hints at a Method for a Critical Edition." *Scriptorium* 47 (1993): 3–25.

Zinn, Grover. "'Historia fundamentum est': The Role of History in the Contemplative Life according to Hugh of St. Victor." In *Contemporary Reflections on the Medieval Christian Tradition: Essays in Honor of Ray C. Petry*, ed. George H. Shriver, 135–158. Durham, NC: Duke University Press, 1974.

Index of Scriptural Citations

General Index